Dedication

To my wife, Hedy, and my daughters, Lillian, Anne, and Vivian. And, in memory of my parents, Kang and Trez-yu.

— *Dan Chang*

To my wife, Michiko, and daughter, Tomomi. And, to my parents, Howard and Barbara.

— *Dan Harkey*

Client/Server
Data Access
2
with
Java and XML

Dan Chang • Dan Harkey

WILEY COMPUTER PUBLISHING

JOHN WILEY & SONS, INC.

New York   Chichester   Weinheim   Brisbane   Singapore   Toronto

Publisher: Robert Ipsen
Editor: Theresa Hudson
Managing Editor: Angela Murphy
Text Design & Composition: Dan Chang and Dan Harkey
Cover Art: Vivian Chang
Graphic Art: David Pacheco

Designations used by companies to distinguish their products are often claimed as trademarks. In all instances where John Wiley & Sons, Inc. is aware of a claim, the product names appear in initial capital or all capital letters. Readers, however, should contact the appropriate companies for more complete information regarding trademarks and registration.

This text is printed on acid-free paper. ∞

This publication is designed to provide accurate and authoritative information in regard to the subject matter covered. It is sold with the understanding that the publisher is not engaged in rendering legal, accounting, or other professional service. If legal advice or other expert assistance is required, the services of a competent professional person should be sought.

The authors and publisher of this book have used their best efforts in preparing this book. The authors and publisher make no warranty of any kind, expressed or implied, with regard to the documentation contained in this book. The authors and publisher shall not be liable in any event for incidental or consequential damages in connection with, or arising out of the use of, the information in this book.

The product descriptions are based on the best information available at the time of publication. Product prices are subject to change without notice.

Some illustrations incorporate clip art from Corel Systems Corporation's Corel Draw 5.0 clip art library.

All the views expressed in this book are solely the authors' and should not be attributed to IBM or any other IBM employee. The two authors contributed equally to the production of this book.

Library of Congress Cataloging-in-Publication Data:

Chang, Dan
    Client/server Data Access with Java and XML / Dan Chang and Dan Harkey.
        p.   cm.
    "Wiley Computer Publishing."
    Includes index.
    ISBN 0-471-24577 -1 (pbk. /CD-ROM: alk. paper)
    1. Client/server computing. 2. Java (Computer program language)
    3. Database searching.   I. Harkey, Dan   II. Title
    QA76.9.C55C45   1998   98-4731
    005.2'762--dc21

Printed in the United States of America
10 9 8 7 6 5 4 3 2 1

Foreword

This book fulfills an important need. I'll explain this by telling you its story. It all started about two years ago when Dan Harkey and I were going over the curriculum for our *Client/Server with Distributed Objects* Master's degree program. We had four core courses: 1) Introduction to Client/Server Middleware, 2) Advanced Java Programming, 3) Distributed Objects and CORBA, and 4) Client/Server Component Design. We complemented these courses with a very popular CORBA/Java Lab. Today, we have over 200 graduate students in the program.

The meeting I was having with Dan Harkey was to decide on the next course we would add to this curriculum. Based on our own observations (and on constant student feedback), it seemed we desperately needed a course that covered SQL data access as well as object persistence. So on the back of an envelope, we created a wish list of what such a course would cover. Here's what we came up with:

- SQL, SQL3 object extensions, and object/relational mappers
- Java Persistence—including JDBC, SQLJ, and JavaBeans Serialization
- Object Databases—including the ODBMS standard
- ORB-based persistence—including CORBA persistence and OLE DB
- Web data access standards (like XML)

As you can see from this list, persistence is a very vast and bleeding-edge topic. A quick search of the curricula of major universities indicated that none had such an all-inclusive data course. Yet, it's absolutely vital for computer scientists. So the million dollar question was: Who could teach such a course?

Dan and I knew it would be mission impossible for us to teach. So we asked ourselves: Who are the most qualified computer scientists in the whole world who could teach such a course. We came up with a very short list—three to be exact. Dan Chang of IBM's STL Database Technology Institute was at the top of our short list.

So let me introduce Dan Chang. Dan is an SQL expert who is also the co-author of two CORBA standards. In addition, he is a Java expert who also loves to code. He was involved with mobile Java data objects when he worked on the Aglets project. Dan is also very well plugged-in; he seems to know about every leading-edge development in the database industry. So Dan was the perfect fit. Now we had to find a way to bring him on board.

To make a long story short, we approached Dan and asked him to teach the persistence course and integrate it with the CORBA/Java lab. He agreed on the condition that one of us would help him teach the course and develop its lab. Dan

Harkey volunteered for the job. The two Dans have jointly taught the course for the last four semesters. It has become a hit with our students. I personally find it a great joy to sit in; it gives me a chance to catch up on the latest and greatest in object persistence.

However, our students always seem to want more. In this case, they were spoiled by the fact that Dan Harkey and I use our books to teach the other courses in the program. The persistence course didn't have a book—just copious notes that the two Dans would hand out or post on the Web site.

We (the students and I) were able to successfully convince the Dans to write this book. So here you have it in your hands. It's the persistence Bible for the Object Web. This book tells you about the latest and greatest data-related technologies for the Web. Reading it is the next best thing to attending the Dans' classes. Happy reading.

— Robert Orfali

Preface

Java is hot enough to burn Bill Gates.

> — *Business Week*
> *November 10, 1997*

Reinventing the Web: XML and DHTML will bring order to the chaos.

> — *Byte Magazine*
> *March, 1998*

According to the commentary made by Ira Sager and Robert D. Hof in the *Business Week* quoted above, Java is taking hold in the computer industry, and it is one of those fundamental shifts that may be unstoppable. The only questions, according to them, are: How fast will it spread and who's smart enough to come out on top? A key reason for Java's eminence is its ability to integrate legacy systems with new Internet applications. That is, Java is being used to develop the so-called middleware software, which makes these legacy applications or databases accessible from the Internet.

The cover article by Scott Mace, Udo Flohr, Rich Dobson, and Tony Graham in the *BYTE* magazine quoted above, on the other hand, discussed the current illness of the Web and its potential cure through *eXtensible Markup Language (XML)*. They call to arms and urge the immediate migration from HTML to XML because the future of the Web depends on it. A key reason for XML's prominence is that it provides a standard format for describing and exchanging data over the Web. Therefore, XML is indispensable whenever two or more heterogeneous Web applications or data sources need to interact with each other; this is often the case in electronic commerce.

Java? XML? Internet data access? Web data interchange? These are the topics of this book. They are new. They are hot. They are important. And they are rapidly evolving.

Client/Server Data Access Going Internet

You probably still remember the 1996 Centennial Olympic Games in Atlanta: the closing ceremony with Muhammud Ali on the podium, the courage and triumph of Keri Strug, the last hurrah of Carl Lewis, and the bomb scare. However, from the point of view of *client/server data access*, the most significant and memorable event happened shortly before the games started. It was the opening of the *Official Olympic Web site (http://www.olympic.org/)*, which marked the first time that client/server data access had gone Internet in a big, global way. The Web site provided millions of fans information on the games, schedules, and competition results. This was repeated at the 1998 Winter Olympic Games in Nagano, Japan (*http://www.nagano.olympic.org/*). Both Web sites were hosted and run by IBM. Among the client/server data access technologies used in building the Web sites were **Net.Data** and **DB2**, which we will cover in this book.

Web and Java: The Universal Reach

It is probably safe to say that your working day involves using the Web browser for one reason or another. You most likely keep a hot list of URLs that you frequently visit. This list could consist of sites on intranets, extranets, or the Internet. As far as you are concerned, the location and distance of each site are unimportant. All that matters is knowing the correct URL. And, you are free to traverse the intranets, extranets, or Internet: within the firewall, across firewalls, or through the firewall. As you do so, if you pay attention, you will see messages like *"Connect: host ... contacted. Waiting for reply ..."* and *"Document: Done."* on the footer of the browser. From time to time, you may also see the message *"Starting Java ..."* in between the other messages. None of these would surprise you. In fact, if you don't pay attention, which you are more likely to do, you won't even "see" the messages. One estimate has it that, by the 1998, 70 million people will be using a Web browser in their daily life and were just like you, not "seeing" the messages. So the Web and Java are everywhere. We can no longer talk about client/server data access without also talking about the Web and Java.

What This Book Covers

This book is a comprehensive in-depth guide to client/server data access technologies using Java and XML. It is also a gentle introduction to its basics: Web, Java, and database systems. The only thing we do not cover is the Java language. We assume that you already know it. (If you don't, please see the references on Java listed in the back of this book.) We also assume that you have some familiarity with the JDK (Java Development Kit) 1.1 or later, particularly what is contained in the *java.lang* package. Other than these, we will cover everything else you need to know about client/server data access with Java and XML.

This book consists of an Introduction, six Parts that build on each other, and a Conclusion:

■ **Introduction** gives an overview of *client/server data access* and this book. We discuss how the *Web* has affected client/server data access and the significance of *Java*. We then give an overview of the evolution of *database systems*, and the rapidly developing technologies of *Java and Web data access*. The usefulness of data access is isolated and limited unless you can exchange the data among applications. This leads us to *XML*, which is quickly becoming the *lingua franca* of the Web and which will revolutionize Web data interchange, presentation, and search. We finish by taking a glance at the big picture: data access and interchange as critical components in an integrated *Java and Web application architecture*. Throughout, we point to key *emerging technologies* that will shape the future of client/server data access.

■ **Part 1** includes four chapters that review the *foundation of client/server data access*. It covers the basics of the *Web* (HTTP and HTML), the fundamentals of *Java* (execution model, reflection, threads, events, and archive), *relational databases* (relational data model and SQL-92), and *object-oriented databases* (ODMG 2.0 and OQL). The fifth chapter defines the **ArcWorld** sample database, which is used in all examples throughout this book.

■ **Part 2** includes three chapters that discuss *Java data access*, which can be used with or independent of the Web. It covers *JDBC* (a SQL call-level API), *SQLJ* (embedding SQL in Java), and the *ODMG Java binding* (for accessing object-oriented databases). The fourth chapter contains *programming examples* that illustrate and contrast the use of each of these in data access.

■ **Part 3** consists of three chapters that deal with *Web data access*, which enables client/server data access to be universally available. It covers some of the major techniques that can be used to generate *dynamic Web pages* based on live data: *Web gateway tools, Java applets, Java servlets*, and *dynamic HTML*.

■ **Part 4** consists of three chapters that discuss *Java client/server computing* and the mechanisms you can use to exercise explicit control over the client/server computing piece in data access, either for application-specific reasons or for performance reasons. It covers *Java object serialization* (for passing Java objects by value across client/server), *Java RMI* (for pure Java distributed-object applications), and *Java ORBs* (for CORBA-compliant distributed-object applications).

■ **Part 5** consists of three chapters that deal with *Web data interchange:* the key ingredients you can use to exchange data over the Web among applications and with people. It covers *XML* (including X-Link and X-Pointer), *Document Object Model* (core and XML), and *XMI* (XML Metadata Interchange).

■ **Part 6** consists of two chapters that discuss *Java component architectures*, in which data access is just one element, though the most important element from our perspective. It covers *JavaBeans* (the client component model) and *Enterprise JavaBeans* (the server component model).

■ The **Conclusion** discusses *emerging technologies* that will shape the future of client/server data access. They include WebDAV (for distributed authoring), *Jini* (a new programming model for Java client/server computing), *object-relational databases* (and SQL3), *JDBC 2.0*, *SQLJ Part 1 & Part 2* (Java stored procedures, Java user-defined functions, and Java objects), *DASL* (for distributed searching and locating), *JavaMail* (for asynchronous distributed computing), *XSL* (for displaying XML documents), and finally *Java and Web component architectures* that will put the most important pieces discussed in this book into a coherent whole and deliver a new, integrated platform for developing client/server, data-intensive applications for the Web (the Internet, intranets, and extranets).

How To Read This Book

It is probably difficult, if not impossible, to ask your boss for a paid, two-week sabbatical to sit on a beach and read this book, so it is best that you plan for a few (say, six) long weekends to go to various beautiful parks (ideally, Yosemite) to read this book in parts. Doing it leisurely, one part at a time, will allow you to enjoy the surrounding natural beauty while reading; you will avoid intellectual exhaustion.

It is highly recommended that you bring along a partner. It will be great if your partner will also be reading this book. The resulting intellectual interchange can be insightful and refreshing. It is OK, though, if your partner reads something else. In any case, please remember to bring along tons of *Iced Java* and plenty of *Web Straws*. They will help quench your thirst, and that of your partner.

You can read this book in various ways. It helps if you start with the Introduction, which gives you a broad overview and perspective. Then, depending on your background, you should read Part 1 or certain chapters in it. From there on, if your interest is mainly on Java data access, you can read Part 2, Part 4, Part 6, and the Conclusion (the Java portions of it). On the other hand, if your interest is mainly on Web data access, you can read Part 3, Part 5, and the Conclusion (the Web portions of it). But we think you should and will be interested in both Java and Web data access. In which case, you can take your pick of Part 2 to Part 6 in the order that you like. But don't forget about the Conclusion.

In any case, we think you will find this book a lot of fun, the surrounding natural beauty enchanting, and your partner loving and understanding.

Who Is This Book For?

This book is for anyone involved with client/server data access: programmers, designers, architects, planners, and managers. It is particularly important for the following readers:

- Java programmers who need to understand client/server data access, particularly on the Web.

- Web programmers who need to understand client/server data access, particularly using Java.

- MIS programmers who are evaluating Java and Web technologies for client/server data access.

- Client/server architects and designers who need up-to-date and in-depth knowledge about data access over the Web using Java.

Sooner or later, everyone involved in the information industry will have to know about Java and XML, and the prominent and critical roles they will play in building the new infrastructure for electronic commerce and information retrieval. So, even if you are a planner or manager, you will find that reading this book is time well spent. You can either skip over or quickly glance at the programming examples and API descriptions.

A Few Words about Notations and APIs

The following notations are used throughout this book:

- Square brackets ("[" and "]") are used to denote optional items. The exception is when they are used to denote arrays.
- Vertical bar ("|") is used to denote alternatives.
- Angle Brackets ("<" and ">") are used to denote substitutable items. The exception is when they are used for XML tags.
- Java class names and package names are written in **bold**. A class name is always prefixed with its package name unless the package is **java.lang** or the context in which the class name is used makes it clear what the package is.
- Java method and variable names are written in *italic*.
- Database names are written in **bold**.
- Table names are written in **bold**.
- Column names are written in *italic*.

Java interfaces and classes are presented in a manner similar to that generated by the *javadoc* tool:

- For each interface or class, the order of presentation is: class constants/variables, class methods, constructors, variables, and methods.
- Modifiers and exceptions are not listed for ease of presentation.

In general, exception classes are not provided, again for ease of presentation. This in no way implies a lack of importance of exception classes (or their declarations in methods). As you know, exception declaration and handling are of critical importance in Java programming.

Software and Book Web Site

The software used to produce the programming examples in this book includes:

- **Operating systems**—Windows NT 4.0, Windows 95

- **Web browsers**—Internet Explorer 4.0, Netscape Communicator 4.05

- **Web servers**—Internet Information Server 3.0, Netscape Enterprise Server 3.5

- **Java** (including JDBC, Java object serialization, and RMI)—Java Development Kit 1.1.6

- **Relational databases**—DB2 Universal Database Version 5, SQL Server 6.5

- **Object-oriented databases/ODMG Java binding** (Chapters 5, 6, 9, 10)—POET 5.0

- **SQLJ** (Chapters 8, 10)—Reference Implementation 0.7.1.1

- **Dynamic Web pages** (Chapter 11)—Net.Data 2.0

- **Servlets** (Chapter 12)—Java Web Server 1.0.2

- **Dynamic HTML** (Chapter 13)—Internet Explorer 4.0 Author's Toolkit

- **Java ORBs** (Chapter 16)—VisiBroker for Java 3.2

- **XML/DOM/SAX** (Chapters 17, 18)—XML for Java 1.0

- **JavaBeans** (Chapter 20)—JavaSoft Beans Development Kit 1.0

- **Enterprise JavaBeans** (Chapter 21)—WebLogic Tengah 3.1

Our Web site is at **http://www.javaxml.engr.sjsu.edu.** The products and architectures described in this book are evolving rapidly, so plan to visit our Web site often for updates on the latest product information, sample programs, and answers to your questions.

Acknowledgments

Many people have helped us with this book. We would like to say thanks to:

- Bob Orfali for nudging us to work together on this book and for writing the foreword.

- Deans Don Kirk and Nabil Ibrahim of San Jose State University for providing us with a world-class Java/Web/CORBA lab and for letting us set up a graduate course around this book.

- Jo Cheng, Don Haderle, and Ken Ausich for their ongoing support and for providing a challenging and exciting professional environment with ready access to the best technologies on client/server data access and related areas.

- The technical people in different companies who helped us, in various ways, to understand the broad topics covered in this book.

- Our graduate students. Your enthusiasm and inquisitiveness were "bar none."

- Vivian Chang for creating the beautiful book cover and other artwork in this book.

- Dave Pacheco for making the wonderful technical illustrations in this book.

- Our tireless copy editor, Larry Mackin.

- Our proof reader, Shelley Flannery.

- The people at Wiley—especially Terri Hudson.

Contents

concepts

concepts

concepts

code

concepts

concepts

Chapter 8. Introduction to SQLJ 143

concepts

Chapter 9. Java Binding for OODB 173

Contents

Objects. 176
Java ODL. 176
   Attributes 176
   Operations 176
Java OML. 176
   Attributes 176
   Operations 177
   Object Life Cycle 177
   Collection Interfaces 177
   Transactions 178
   Database Operations 179
Java OQL 180
POET 5.0. 181
   Extents, Keys, and Names. 181
   An Example 182
Conclusion 184

Chapter 10. Sample Data Access Applications. 187

JDBC 188
   Database Administration. 189
   Data Access. 196
SQLJ. 202
   Data Access. 202
Java Binding for OODB 208
   Database Administration. 208
   Data Access. 214

Part 3. Web Data Access 221

Chapter 11. Dynamic Web Pages. 223

code

product

concepts

concepts

xxiii

concepts

Chapter 1

Introduction to Client/Server Data Access

concepts

Client/server data access deals with the subject of accessing, from a client computer, data that resides on a server computer across a computer network, as shown in Figure 1-1. (By *access* we mean not just query or retrieval, but also insertion, update, and deletion.) The client computer tends to be a desktop computer, but it can also be a laptop computer, a workstation, a network computer, or even a network device. The server computer can range from mainframes, to minicomputers, to workstations, to desktop computers. The computer network is likely to be a local area network, a wide area network, or a mixture of the two.

Data normally resides in a database, but it can also reside in a file system or other storage systems. Most of the data is *structured* or *semistructured*, but the more interesting data include text, graphics, image, audio, or video as part of its content.

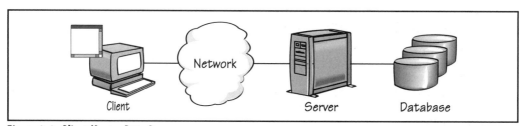

Figure 1-1. Client/Server Data Access.

The nature of the data can range from public information, to airline schedule and seating information, to confidential information, to top-secret information that affects corporate security or national security. The world cannot function without this data, so it is not too far-fetched to say *"Client/server data access makes the world go around."*

THE IMPACT OF THE WEB

Before the birth of the Web, the field of client/server data access was an obscure one. It had the following characteristics:

- **Myriad of platforms and technologies**. Client/server data access by nature involved four different types of platforms and associated technologies: client, network, server, and database. It was (and still is) not uncommon to find a company's information infrastructure involve three types of clients, two types of networks, four types of servers, and three types of databases. This would amount to a multiple of seventy-two different combinations of technologies to consider when developing client/server data access applications.

- **Limited number of end users**. The myriad of platforms and technologies meant that client/server data access applications tended to be one of a kind with little commonality between them. The end users required special training to use them, and their number was limited. Some typical examples of such end users included airline reservation clerks and bank tellers.

- **Restricted scope of access**. The myriad of platforms and technologies also meant that client/server data access applications could only run on the selected platforms. Their scope was restricted. The largest ones belonged to multi-national corporations, such as IBM.

- **Small group of expert developers**. The myriad of platforms and technologies further meant that only a small group of expert developers knew how to develop client/server data access applications. Even for these developers, their expertise tended to be limited to specific technologies and platforms.

The Web, however, *has fundamentally changed the landscape of client/server data access*. With the Web, client/server data access has gained:

- **A universal infrastructure**. The Web has reduced the myriad of platforms and technologies to a single user interface (HTML), a single client platform (the Web browser), a single network protocol (HTTP), and a single server platform (the Web server). The major variation left is the backend database. This is very powerful because it provides a single, universal infrastructure for developing client/server data access applications, as shown in Figure 1-2.

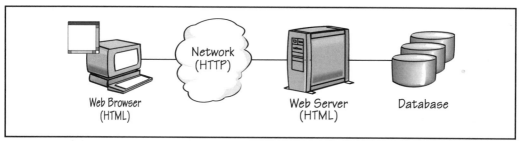

Figure 1-2. Web-based Client/Server Data Access.

■ *Tens of millions of end users*. The Web browser, with its easy-to-use and easy-to-understand hyperlinked document (HTML) metaphor, has gained millions of end users. One estimate has set the number of Web users by 1978 at 70 million. These users include all age groups, and most of them have no special training. Any of them can be a potential user of Web-based data access applications.

■ *A global scope of access*. Thanks to URLs and HTTP, a Web user can (almost) instantly reach anywhere in the world where there is a Web server running. Therefore, Web-based data access applications no longer have geographical boundaries. The issue, for an application provider, becomes how to make your Web server and data access applications known to the public or intended users.

■ *Hundreds of thousands of potential developers*. The simplicity of HTML/HTTP and the availability of easy-to-use Web-based tools mean that hundreds of thousands of people can now build Web-based data access applications. All they need is some additional working knowledge of databases and Web data access. They need to deal with only a single, universal infrastructure that is globally accessible to millions of end users, which gives them great incentives to learn the skill, practice the trade, and make a fortune.

Client/server data access, therefore, is no longer obscure. It has come to the forefront and received broad attention. *Client/server data access will be the centerpiece and cornerstone of information retrieval, digital library, electronic commerce, and essentially anything that runs on the Web and that has something to do with data.*

THE SIGNIFICANCE OF JAVA

The Web provides a single, universal infrastructure for developing client/server data access applications. However, it is lacking major features and components to be a complete platform. For example, it is static and stateless. It provides only simple

GUI functionality, and it has no support for common data types such as integer or real number.

In the early days, if you wanted to overcome any of the above limitations, you would have to use CGI (on the Web server) or plug-ins (on the Web client), and do a lot of programming in Perl (on the Web server) or C (on the Web server or client). These solutions were tailor made and platform dependent. They tainted the Web and made it much less universal.

Java, fortunately, provides a single, universal means for solving these problems. Java is dynamic (class loading and linking); it can maintain state (Java objects); it supports a more sophisticated GUI (Swing and AWT); and it supports all major data types and even user-defined data types. In addition, Java is portable (bytecode and Java virtual machine) and runs on all platforms, like the Web.

Java is more than just a programming language. It is quickly becoming a complete computing platform. The existence of the following facilities (or class libraries) has made client/server data access that much easier: *reflection*; *security*; *database access* (JDBC, SQLJ, and ODMG Java Binding); *Web integration* (applets and servlets); *networking enablement* (URL and streams); *distributed object computing* (object serialization, RMI, and Java ORBs); *component architecture* (JavaBeans and Enterprise JavaBeans).

Java, therefore, *is a perfect match for the Web. It provides a universal programming language and computing platform for Web-based client/server data access applications*, as shown in Figure 1-3.

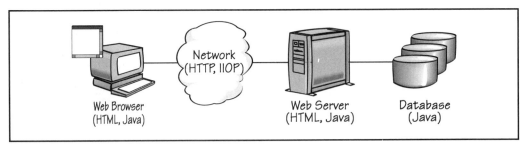

Figure 1-3. Java and Web-based Client/Server Data Access.

THE EVOLUTION OF DATABASE SYSTEMS

The Web and Java made client/server data access easier by allowing us to concern ourselves with a single programming language, a single computing platform, and a single underlying infrastructure. This frees us from many peripheral tasks and allows us to concentrate on the essential tasks of client/server data access—for example, getting the relevant data, delivering it in a form ready for presentation, representing it in a form suitable for interchange or application usage, encapsulating it with behavior to enhance usability, etc.

Among these tasks, getting the relevant data efficiently and effectively poses the single most significant challenge for client/server data access. How well this can be done depends to a large degree on the underlying *database systems* that are used to store and manage the data. These systems can also heavily impact other tasks. For example, they tend to dictate what form their data can be delivered or represented.

Central to any database system is the *data model* on which it is based. The data model prescribes how data can be represented and what operations are available for accessing and manipulating the data, both from an external (or user) point of view. In theory, the data model, being external, allows complete freedom of implementation and full opportunity for performance optimization. In practice, the data model, though external, tends to drive implementation and allows only limited opportunity for optimization. Therefore, a data model is more than just being external and all data models are not equal.

The most dominant database systems in use today are *relational database systems*. The fact that relational databases have become so popular has a lot to do with the *relational data model*. The relational data model is simple and easy to understand. It provides a high degree of data independence, and it has a theoretical foundation in set theory and first-order logic. The other major reason for its popularity is *SQL (Structured Query Language)*, the relational database language that allows you to define and manipulate data, as well as control its access, in a relational database. All relational database vendors support SQL, with only minor deviations and extensions.

With the advent of object-oriented languages, *object-oriented database systems* have gained some popularity. These systems were developed basically to add *persistence* to objects that are used in an object-oriented programming language. Their focus is on the transparent integration of database capability with a specific programming language. A second focus is on providing fast navigational access of persistent objects in that programming language. To query the persistent objects, you can use *OQL (Object Query Language)*, which is like SQL but has extensions for path expressions (for navigational access) and method invocation.

Relational database systems were designed for on-line transaction processing and ad hoc queries. They do an excellent job on these. However, they have run into major problems when used to support new types of applications. Among the problems are: limited support of predefined data types, lack of support for user-defined data types, "impedance mismatch" when accessed from an object-oriented programming language, and slow navigational access. Object-oriented database systems, on the other hand, were designed to provide object persistence in an object-oriented programming language. They do an excellent job for that specific programming language. However, they tend to lose their benefit when accessed from a different programming language, even object-oriented. Also, they have poor support for ad hoc queries, both in terms of ease-of-use and performance.

A major new trend is the development of the so-called *object-relational database systems*. These systems are based on relational database systems, but they have extensions to support object-oriented features. The intent is to preserve what is good about relational database systems (for example, on-line transaction processing, ad hoc queries, reliability, scalability, and security) and to overcome their current shortcomings (such as limited support of predefined data types, lack of support for user-defined data types, "impedance mismatch" when accessed from an object-oriented programming language, and slow navigational access) by adopting what is good about object-oriented database systems. Concurrent with this trend is the development of *SQL3*, the new object-relational database language.

Whether it is the relational database system, object-oriented database system, or object-relational database system, the design is focused on managing *structured* data or objects. Most of the world's data, however, is not structured or is *semistructured* (for example, in HTML format). With the rapid growth of the Web, this semistructured data is exploding and growing in importance. HTML documents are not easy to manage and search because they tend not to be well-formed and they are designed mainly for presentation. However, *XML (eXtensible Markup Language) documents* do not have these problems. They are always well-formed, and they are independent of presentation. XML has the potential to revolutionize the Web (for data interchange, for data presentation, for search, and so on). If so, *XML repositories and database systems will become the next Holy Grail of the database industry,* and *XQL (XML Query Language) will become as well known as SQL and OQL.*

DATA ACCESS MADE EASIER IN JAVA

Data access using a programming language was required, ever since the birth of database systems (mainly relational database systems), to build database applications in that programming language. The earliest approach was *Embedded SQL*. Embedded SQL is embedding SQL statements in a programming language. The programming language is called the host language, and an embedded program is a mixture of the host language and SQL. Embedded SQL can contain either static SQL statements or dynamic SQL statements. Static SQL statements are processed at program compile time, whereas dynamic SQL statements are processed at program run time.

Later, *call-level interfaces*, such as *ODBC (Open Database Connectivity)*, were developed to overcome some of the major limitations of *Embedded SQL*, particularly in a client/server environment. Embedded SQL requires a pre-compiler and involves a two-step process when developing code. The pre-compiler, in general, is database system-specific and produces non-portable code. The code involves the use of global data, which is troublesome in a client/server environment. Call-level interfaces do not have these limitations. Database applications developed using call-level interfaces can be ported in binary to any database systems that support compliant drivers. Call-level interfaces, however, deal only with dynamic SQL statements.

Java, being a new and object-oriented language with some distinct features, such as dynamicity and automatic memory management, provided a golden opportunity to do data access "right," or at least easier. Java allows the use of objects to represent database "objects" or concepts, such as driver manager, driver, connection, statement, result set, and cursor. These concepts existed in ODBC. However, ODBC was based on procedural languages, so it had to use more obscure constructs (such as handles) to represent these database "objects." In Java, you can access and manipulate these database objects directly using either call-level interfaces (*JDBC*) or embedded SQL (*SQLJ Part 0*).

Java is an object-oriented language so it also provided a unique opportunity for accessing object-oriented databases, in the form of a *Java binding* to object-oriented databases. As the name suggests, the focus of Java binding is quite different from that of Java access. In the case of Java access (JDBC or SQLJ), the focus is on retrieving and manipulating in Java the data stored in relational databases. Such focus is *data-centric*. In the case of Java binding, on the other hand, the focus is on making Java objects transparently persistent. The focus is programming *objects-centric*.

As relational database systems move to object-relational database systems, Java provides further opportunities to make data access easier and more transparent. These systems are reflected in the new features to be provided in *JDBC 2.0* and *SQLJ Part 1 & Part 2*, in the form of direct support for Java objects and user-defined data types in databases, for example.

JAVA AND WEB DATA ACCESS: THE UNIVERSAL REACH

Java data access (JDBC, SQLJ, and Java binding to OODB) is localized within a single machine or within a local area network (if the underlying database system is distributed). To attain universal reach, it must be integrated with the Web.

The Web started with just static HTML pages, but it soon adopted dynamic HTML page generation capabilities using live data (data retrieved at run time from various data sources, in particular relational databases). The earliest approaches used CGI programming, which was cumbersome and custom made. The development of *Web gateway tools* eliminated most of the grunt work. They also provided additional functionality, such as maintaining a pool of live connections to data sources to improve performance. Web gateway tools are server oriented, which means most of their processing (particularly data access) takes place at the Web server. (As mentioned in the Preface, **Net.Data**, a Web gateway tool, was used in hosting both the Atlanta and Nagano Olympics sites.)

With or without Web gateway tools, the simplest way to integrate Java data access with the Web is to use Java applets or Java servlets for data access. Java applets allow data access to take place at the Web client, while Java servlets allow data access to take place at the Web server. Using Java applets is simpler and allows you to develop a more sophisticated GUI using the Java AWT or Swing components. However, Java applets which do data access require a fatter client and may have performance problems due to downloading the applets and JDBC drivers and due to network traffic when querying and retrieving data. Using Java servlets needs only a thin client, is more scalable (data access can be encapsulated from the client), and tends to perform better (particularly for large result sets). However, Java servlets can display result data only in standard HTML format.

For more sophisticated applications, you can use Java applets with server Java applications. In this case, Java applets are used for client GUIs, and server Java applications are used for data access. In addition, RMI is used for communication between Java applets and server Java applications. RMI allows Java objects to be passed by value through Java object serialization. In theory, this can reduce network traffic because you can pass a large result set in a single network transmission. However, the current implementation of Java object serialization has a lot of overhead.

An alternative to RMI is to use a Java ORB. Java ORBs are more cumbersome to use but they use IIOP as the protocol and can work with non-Java systems. RMI in the future will also use IIOP as the protocol; therefore, it will work with non-Java systems as well.

XML: THE LINGUA FRANCA OF THE WEB

If the result of data access can only be used for direct presentation to an end user, its usefulness is limited. In many cases, the result needs to be used by an application. In many other cases, the result needs to be combined or merged with other results, possibly retrieved from different types of data sources, before presentation to an end user or usage by an application.

Data interchange between applications can be looked at both from syntactic (format) and semantic (meaning) perspectives. Syntactically, data interchange requires that the applications agree on a common format for the data (for example, data types, structures, and relationships). Semantically, data interchange requires that the applications additionally agree on a common meaning for the data (the data vocabularies).

Before the existence of XML, data interchange on a global scale was difficult. For example, there was no commonly accepted format for data. Therefore, even though there are some data vocabularies within certain industries, they are expressed in their own format and are not interchangeable with each other.

XML will revolutionize data interchange on the Web. It defines a standard format for describing and exchanging data on the Web. With its recent adoption by W3C, many industries are working to convert their existing data vocabularies to the XML format or to develop new data vocabularies in the XML format.

XML separates structure from presentation. Therefore, the same data represented in XML can be presented (for example displayed, printed, and stored) in various forms. With the expected adoption by W3C of a standard stylesheet language for XML, *it will also revolutionize data presentation on the Web*.

XML will further revolutionize search and authoring on the Web. So far Web search can only be based on keywords because, even though HTML pages have some structure, the structure is display oriented. By separating structure from presentation, XML structure (for example, a book containing sections) has meaning and can be used to provide a more meaningful search. If appropriate XML vocabularies are available, the search can even be semantically based.

JAVA AND WEB APPLICATION ARCHITECTURE

So what is the big picture for client/server data access? We said that the Web provides a universal infrastructure, Java provides a universal programming language and computing platform, and XML provides a universal data interchange format. Putting these together, a *universal Java and Web application architecture* for building client/server, data-intensive applications will look like Figure 1-4.

In the figure, we have used JavaBeans instead of just Java to emphasize the critical importance of Java components in the architecture. Using JavaBeans on the client allows you to take advantage of the many benefits of client components: plug and play, customization using tools, event-based programming, and reuse. Using (Enterprise) JavaBeans on the server, on the other hand, allows you to exploit the many benefits of server components: transparent access, state management, transaction management, and security management.

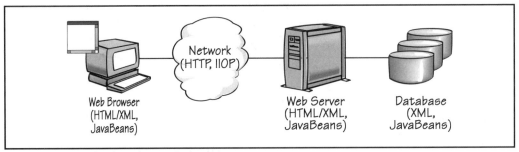

Figure 1-4. Java and Web Application Architecture.

CONCLUSION

Now that you have a good overview and understanding of the landscape of client/server data access and its future directions, the rest of the book will help you gain the expertise needed to become a master of it (and of all the acronyms mentioned in this chapter):

- **Part 1** reviews the *foundation of client/server data access*. It covers the basics of the *Web* (HTTP and HTML), the fundamentals of *Java* (execution model, reflection, threads, events, and archive), *relational databases* (relational data model and SQL-92), and *object-oriented databases* (ODMG 2.0 and OQL).

- **Part 2** discusses *Java data access*—including *JDBC* (a SQL call-level API), *SQLJ* (embedding SQL in Java), and the *ODMG Java binding* (for accessing object-oriented databases).

- **Part 3** deals with *Web data access* and the major techniques that you can use to generate *dynamic Web pages* based on live data: *Web gateway tools, Java applets, Java servlets*, and *dynamic HTML*.

- **Part 4** discusses *Java client/server computing*, including *Java object serialization* (for passing Java objects by value across client/server), *RMI* (for pure Java distributed-object applications), and *Java ORBs* (for CORBA-compliant distributed-object applications).

- **Part 5** deals with *Web data interchange* and covers *XML* (including XLink and XPointer), *Document Object Model* (core and XML), and *XMI (XML for Metadata Interchange)*.

- **Part 6** discusses *Java component architectures*, including *JavaBeans* (the client component model) and *Enterprise JavaBeans* (the server component model).

■ The **Conclusion** discusses *emerging technologies* that will shape the future of client/server data access—including WebDAV (for distributed authoring), *Jini* (a new programming model for Java client/server computing), *object-relational databases* (and SQL3), *JDBC 2.0, SQLJ Part 1 & Part 2* (Java stored procedures, Java user-defined functions, and Java objects), *DASL* (for distributed searching and locating), *JavaMail* (for asynchronous distributed computing), *XSL* (for displaying XML documents), and finally *Java and Web component architectures* that promise to deliver a new, integrated platform for developing client/server, data-intensive applications for the Web.

Part 1
Foundation of
Client/Server Data Access

An Introduction to Part 1

The Web and Java have revolutionized client/server data access by making it universally available at the global scale. In Part 1, we will review the foundation of client/server data access before we start exploring Java and Web data access:

- Web
- Java
- Relational database and SQL
- Object-oriented database and ODMG 2.0

We will also define the **ArcWorld** sample database that we will use in all examples throughout this book.

We cover the following:

- *Chapter 2* discusses the basics of the Web, which has become the universal infrastructure for client/server data access. The Web provides a universal naming scheme (URL), a universal network protocol (HTTP), and a universal user interface (HTML). We review the essence of each in this chapter.

- *Chapter 3* reviews the fundamentals of Java, which is becoming the universal programming language and computing platform for client/server data access. We review in this chapter Java data types and the Java API. We identify those parts of the Java API that are of critical importance to client/server data access and that will be covered in various chapters throughout this book.

- *Chapter 4* introduces the basics of relational database: the relation data model and SQL. Relational databases are becoming ever more popular, available on all kinds of platforms and used to manage all sorts of data. Here, we go over the key concepts and major types of SQL statements that are needed for this book.

- *Chapter 5* introduces the basics of object-oriented database: the object data model and ODMG 2.0. If you are mainly interested in making programming objects persistent, object-oriented databases have the advantage over relational databases because they are easier to use and perform better. Here we present the essence of the ODMG 2.0 specification.

- *Chapter 6* defines the **ArcWorld** sample database that we will use as illustration throughout this book. **ArcWorld** is presented here both as a relational database and as an object-oriented database. This chapter starts our programming examples in this book.

So Part 1 is an overview of the cornerstones of Internet-era client/server data access: the Web, Java, relational database, and object-oriented database. It should give you a good preparation for Part 2 and beyond.

Chapter 2

Web Basics

concepts

Before we can start exploring Java and Web data access, we need to do some preparation work. In this chapter, we will begin by reviewing the basics of the fundamental infrastructure for client/server data access: the *Web* (see Figure 2-1). The Web provides the universal client (the Web browser), the universal network transport (HTTP), the universal server (the Web server), and the universal user interface (HTML documents) for client/server data access.

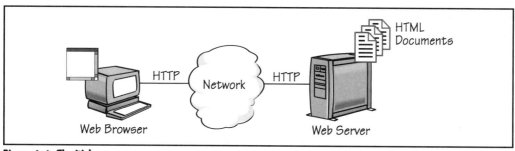

Figure 2-1. The Web.

As we have mentioned in the Introduction, prior to the birth of the Web, client/server data access was restricted to mainly local area networks. There were a myriad of platforms and technologies, a limited number of end users, and a small number of expert developers. But the Web has changed all that. In the post-Web era, client/server data access is typified by global reaches. There is a single universal infrastructure, tens of millions of potential end users, and hundreds of thousands of potential developers. It is an entirely new ball game, where the three most important words are: *universal, universal,* and *universal.*

WEB—THE UNIVERSAL DATA ACCESS INFRASTRUCTURE

Three mechanisms have contributed to making the Web the universal data access infrastructure on a global scale:

- **URL** provides a *universal naming scheme* to give access to any resource on the Web.

- **HTTP** provides a *universal network protocol* to enable the exchange of named resources over the Web.

- **HTML** provides a *universal user interface* for easy presentation of and navigation among resources.

We will give detailed explanations of each in this chapter.

URL

Every resource on the Web has an address that may be encoded by a *Uniform Resource Locator* (URL). A URL typically consists of three parts:

- The name of the *protocol* to be used to transport the resource over the Web
- The name of the *machine* hosting the resource
- The name of the *resource* itself, given as a *path*

A URL has the following format:

```
protocol://host-name[:port-number]/path
```

The *protocol* is typically, for example, *http* or *ftp* and the format and interpretation of *path* depend on the specific protocol used. URLs in general are case-sensitive, with the exception of host name.

If you need to refer to a certain part within a resource, you can use a *fragment URL* that ends with "#" followed by a part identifier. An example is:

```
http://www.w3.org/TR/REC-html32.html#section_2
```

This URL points to *section_2* of the HTML 3.2 specification.

Instead of the full URL, where appropriate, you can also use a *relative URL* that does not contain any protocol or host information. Relative URLs contain relative path components (".." means the parent location). A full URL is then derived from a relative URL by attaching a "base" part to the relative URL. The base part is a URL that comes from one of the following sources (in increasing precedence):

■ HTTP transfer protocol header information
■ Metadata information in an HTML document
■ Explicit base path information in an HTML document

If no base information is available, the base URL designates the location of the current resource.

Given a base URL and a relative URL, the full URL is derived as follows:

■ If the base URL ends with a slash, by appending the relative URL to the base URL
■ If the base URL does not end with a slash, by appending the relative URL to the parent of the base URL

For example, if the base URL is the one shown previously and the relative URL is "REC-html40", then the derived URL is:

> http://www.w3.org/TR/REC-html40

This points to the HTML 4.0 specification.

HTTP

The *Hypertext Transfer Protocol (HTTP)* is an application-level protocol for distributed, collaborative, hypermedia information systems. It is a generic, stateless, object-oriented protocol. The Internet Engineering Task Force (IETF) is responsible for its definition. The current version is *HTTP/1.1*.

HTTP has been in use on the Web since 1990. The first version, referred to as HTTP/0.9, was a simple protocol for raw data transfer. HTTP/1.0 improved the protocol by allowing messages to be in the format of *MIME (Multipurpose Internet Mail Extensions)*-like messages, containing meta-information about the data being transferred. HTTP/1.1 considers the effects of hierarchical proxies, caching, the need for persistent connections, and virtual hosts. In addition, it includes more stringent requirements to ensure reliable implementation of its features.

A key feature of HTTP is the typing and negotiation of *data representation*, which allows systems to be built independent of the data being transferred. A second one is the open-ended set of *methods* that can be used to indicate the purpose of a request. This allows systems to be built with diverse functionality.

The HTTP protocol is a *request/response protocol*. A client sends a *request* to the server in the form of:

- A request method
- URI (Uniform Resource Identifier)—a combination of URL and URN (Uniform Resource Name)
- Protocol version
- A MIME-like message containing request modifiers, client information, and possibly body content

The server responds with a *response* in the form of:

- Protocol version
- A success or error code
- A MIME-like message containing server information, entity meta-information, and possibly entity-body content

An *entity* is the information transferred as the payload of a request or response. It consists of meta-information in the form of *entity-header* fields and optional content in the form of an *entity-body*.

We will take a closer look at these in the following sections.

HTTP Messages

HTTP messages consist of *requests* from client to server and *responses* from server to client. Both types of message consist of:

- A start line
- One or more header fields
- An empty line indicating the end of the header fields
- An optional message body

HTTP header fields include *general header, request header, response header*, and *entity header* fields. Each header field consists of a name followed by a colon (:) and the field value. Field names are always case insensitive.

The message body of an HTTP message is used to carry the entity body associated with a request or response. For request messages, the presence of a message body in a message depends on the request method. For response messages, whether or not a message body is included with a message depends on both the request method and the response status code.

General Headers

General-header fields apply to both request and response messages. They apply only to the message being transmitted and do not apply to the entity being transferred. General headers are listed in Table 2-1.

Table 2-1. HTTP General Headers.

Header	Description
Cache-Control	Specifies request/response caching directives.
Connection	Specifies options that are desired for a particular connection.
Date	Contains the date and time at which the message was originated.
Pragma	Specifies implementation-specific directives.
Transfer-Encoding	Indicates what (if any) type of transformation has been applied to the message.
Upgrade	Lists what additional communication protocols a client supports and would like to use.
Via	Used by gateways and proxies to indicate the intermediate protocols and recipients.

Entity Headers

Entity-header fields define optional meta-information about the entity body or, if no body is present, about the resource identified by the URI. Entity headers are listed in Table 2-2.

Table 2-2. HTTP Entity Headers.

Header	Description
Allow	Lists methods supported by the resource.
Content-Base	Specifies the base URL.
Content-Encoding	Indicates what additional content codings have been applied to the entity body.

Table 2-2. HTTP Entity Headers. (Continued)

Header	Description
Content-Language	Specifies the natural language(s) of the intended audience for the entity body.
Content-Length	Indicates the size of the message body.
Content-Location	Supplies the resource location for the entity.
Content-MD5	Contains an MD5 digest of the entity body.
Content-Range	Sent with a partial entity body to specify where the partial body should be inserted in the full entity body.
Content-Type	Indicates the media type of the entity body.
ETag	Defines the entity tag for the entity.
Expires	Specifies the date and time after which the response should be considered stale.
Last-Modified	Contains the date and time at which the origin server believes the resource was last modified.

HTTP Requests

An HTTP request consists of:

- A request line
- A general header
- A request header
- An entity header
- An empty line
- A message body

Among these, only the request line is required, which consists of the method to be applied to the resource, the URI of the resource, and the protocol version in use. Request headers are listed in Table 2-3, and HTTP methods are listed in Table 2-4.

Table 2-3. HTTP Request Headers.

Header	Description
Accept	Specifies media types that are acceptable for the response.
Accept-Charset	Indicates what character sets are acceptable for the response.

Table 2-3. HTTP Request Headers. (Continued)

Header	Description
Accept-Encoding	Specifies content codings that are acceptable for the response.
Accept-Language	Specifies natural languages that are preferred for the response.
Authorization	Consists of credentials containing authentication information of the user agent. (A user agent is a browser, editor, or other end-user tool.)
Expect	Indicates what specific server behaviors are required by the client.
From	Contains an Internet e-mail address for the user.
Host	Specifies the Internet host and port number of the resource.
If-Modified-Since	Contains the date and time to be used by the GET method.
If-Match	Contains the condition to be used by a method.
If-None-Match	Contains the condition to be used by a method.
If-Range	Contains the information to be used by the GET method.
If-Unmodified-Since	Contains the date and time to be used by a method.
Max-Forwards	Specifies the maximum number of proxies or gateways that can forward the request to the next inbound server.
Proxy-Authorization	Allows the client to identify itself to a proxy that requires authentication.
Range	Specifies a byte range in the entity body.
Referer	Specifies the URI of the resource.
User-Agent	Contains information about the user agent originating the request.

Table 2-4. HTTP Methods.

Method	Description
POST	Requests that the server accept the enclosed entity.
GET	Retrieves whatever information identified by the URI.
HEAD	Retrieves only header information identified by the URI.
PUT	Requests that the server store the enclosed entity.
DELETE	Requests that the origin server delete the resource identified by the URI.
OPTIONS	Requests for information about the communication options available.
TRACE	Invokes a remote, application-layer loop-back of the request message.

Here is an example of an HTTP request message using the GET method:

```
GET /path/file.html    HTTP/1.1
Accept: text/html
Accept: audio/x
User-Agent: Navigator
```

HTTP Responses

An HTTP response consists of:

- A status line
- A general header
- A response header
- An entity header
- An empty line
- A message body

Among these only the status-line is required, which consists of the protocol version in use followed by a numeric status code and its associated textual phrase. Response headers are listed in Table 2-5.

Table 2-5. HTTP Response Headers.

Header	Description
Accept-Ranges	Indicates acceptance of range requests.
Age	Contains an estimate of the amount of time since the response was generated at the origin server.
Location	Indicates the proxy setting.
Proxy-Authenticate	Indicates the authentication scheme and parameters applicable to the proxy.
Public	Lists the set of methods supported by the server.
Retry-After	Indicates how long the service is expected to be unavailable to the client.
Server	Contains information about the software used by the origin server to handle the request.
Set-Proxy	Carries information to redirect a client to use a different proxy.
Vary	Signals that the response entity was selected using server-driven negotiation.

Table 2-5. HTTP Response Headers. (Continued)

Header	Description
Warning	Carries additional information about the status of the response.
WWW-Authenticate	Indicates the authentication scheme and parameters applicable to the URI.

Here is an example of an HTTP response message:

```
HTTP/1.1 200 OK
Server: IIS
Content_type: text/html

<HTML>
   .
   .
</HTML>
```

HTML

The *HyperText Markup Language (HTML)* is an application of the *Standard Generalized Markup Language (SGML)*, which is a language for defining markup languages. HTML is being defined by the W3C Consortium, and the current recommended practice is *HTML 4.0*. HTML files are usually given the extension ".*html*" or ".*htm*".

HTML defines *elements* that represent structure, presentation, and interactivity of hypertext documents. An *element* consists of three parts: a start tag, content, and an end tag. An element's start tag is written <*element-name*> and its end tag is written with a slash before its name: </*element-name*>. Some HTML elements are not required to have end tags (for example, <P> for paragraphs); other HTML elements have no content (for example, <BR> for line breaks). Element names are always case insensitive. By convention, they are written in uppercase letters.

Elements may have properties, called *attributes*, to which you can assign values. Any number of attribute value pairs, separated by spaces, may appear in an element's start tag. Here is an example:

```
<H1 align="right">
```

The *align* attribute is set for the *H1* (Heading 1) element. Attribute values must be delimited by either double quotation marks (") or single quotation marks ('). They are generally case insensitive. Attribute names are always case insensitive. By convention, they are written in lowercase letters.

An HTML document generally consists of a descriptive header section and a body, which contains the document's content. The following elements are used to define its global structure:

- *HTML*. An HTML document should be enclosed by the *HTML* element.

- *HEAD*. The *HEAD* element contains information about the document, such as its title (defined by the *TITLE* element), keywords (defined by the *META* element) that may be useful to search engines, and other data that is not part of the document content. These include the *BASE* element that defines the base URL.

- *BODY*. The *BODY* element contains the document's content.

The body of an HTML document may contain:

- **Headings**. There are six levels of headings in HTML: *H1, H2, H3, H4, H5,* and *H6; H1* is the most significant, and *H6* is the least.

- **Text**. You can use various elements to structure the text. Among these, the *P* element defines a paragraph, the *BR* element breaks the current line of text, and the *PRE* element defines preformatted text.

- **Lists**. These include unordered (*UL*) and ordered (*OL*) lists. Both types of lists consist of sequences of list items defined by the *LI* element. In addition, there are definition lists (*DL*), whose list items are made up of two parts: a title (*DT*) and a description (*DD*).

- **Tables**. The HTML table model allows you to organize data in tabular structures. Tables are important for presenting the results of data access; we will discuss the HTML table model later.

- **Links**. You can create links between HTML documents. (They are one of the key reasons why the Web has been so successful because they allow you to browse from document to document.) You can use the *A* element to define an anchor (using the *name* attribute), a link (using the *href* attribute), or both. (An anchor is a named section in an HTML document.) Here is an example:

```
<A href="http://www.w3.org/">W3C Web Site</A>
```

- **Inclusions**. There are various mechanisms that allow you to include a resource in an HTML document. The *IMG* element lets you embed an image. The *APPLET* element allows you to embed an applet. Applets are important for accessing data from the client; we will discuss the *APPLET* element later.

In the following sections, we will discuss in detail some major HTML constructs that are important for Web-based client/server data access, for example:

- **Forms** to enable user input
- **Tables** to represent results of data access
- **Scripts** to verify user input
- **Applets** to access data from the client and/or to present results of data access
- **Objects**—a new element replacing applet (and others) in HTML 4.0

We will show how they are used in Part 3, "Web Data Access."

Forms

An HTML form is a section of an HTML document that contains special elements called *controls*, which accept and respond to user inputs. They may be, for example, checkboxes or radio buttons. Users generally "complete" forms by providing the required inputs and then submitting them for processing.

The *FORM* element acts as a container for controls. It specifies:

- The layout of the form (given by its content or controls).
- The program that will handle the submitted form (defined by the *action* attribute).
- The HTTP method that will be used to send user data to the form handler (defined by the *method* attribute). The two possible methods are *post*, which includes user data in the body of the form, and *get*, which appends user data to the URL.

Among the various control elements that you can use to enable user input, the *INPUT* element is the most widely used. It has the following key attributes:

- *type*—the type of input control
- *name*—the name of the control
- *value*—the initial value of the control
- *size*—the initial width of the control display area

Some of the major types of input controls include:

- *text*—a single-line text box.
- *password*—same as the text box, but the input text is rendered hidden.
- *checkbox*—an on/off switch. Its value is submitted only when the switch is on. Several checkbox buttons within the same form may bear the same name.

- **radio**—an on/off switch. Its value is submitted only when the switch is on. Several radio buttons within the same form may bear the same name. However, only one of these buttons may be "on" at any one time.
- **submit**—a submit button. When this button is activated by the user, the form is submitted for processing.
- **image**—a graphical *submit* button.
- **reset**—a reset button. When this button is activated by the user, all of the form's controls have their values reset to the initial values.

The following is an example of a simple form for adding user information to a database (see Figure 2-2):

```
<FORM action="../program/addUser" method="post">
    <P> Please enter the following information: <BR>
    First name: <INPUT type="text" name="firstName"> <BR>
    Last name: <INPUT type="text" name="lastName"> <BR>
    e-mail: <INPUT type="text" name="eMail"> <BR>
    <INPUT type="radio" name="sex" value="Male"> Male
    <INPUT type="radio" name="sex" value="Female"> Female <BR>
    <INPUT type="submit" value="Submit"> <INPUT type="reset">
</FORM>
```

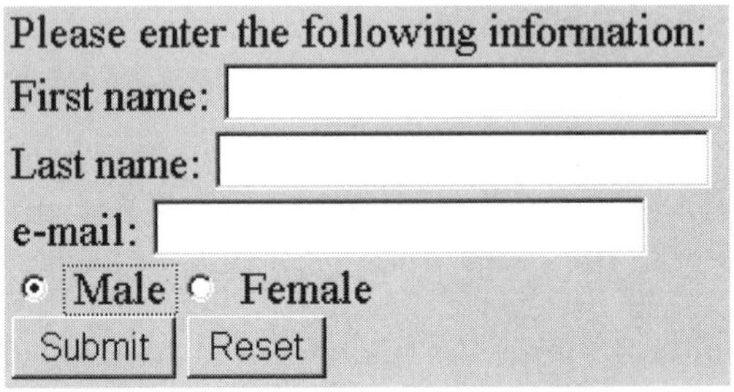

Figure 2-2. A Sample HTML Form.

Tables

The HTML table model allows you to organize data in tabular structures. In this model, rows and columns may be grouped together. An HTML table has the following structure:

- An optional caption.

- One or more groups of rows. Each row group consists of an optional head section, an optional foot section, and a list of rows.
- One or more groups of columns.
- Each row consists of one or more cells. Each cell may contain either header information or data. A cell may span more than one row or column.

The *Table* element is a container of all other elements that include:

- *CAPTION*. This describes the nature of the table.

- *TR*. The *TR* element acts as a container for a row of cells.

- *TH* and *TD*. The *TH* element defines header information, while the *TD* element defines data. Each can span more than one row or column, as defined by the *rowspan* and *colspan* attributes.

- *THEAD*, *TFOOT*, and *TBODY*. These define the head, foot, and body of a row group.

- *COLGROUP* and *COL*. These define column groups.

Here is an example of a simple table showing the average height and weight of males and females (see Figure 2-3):

```
<TABLE border="border">
    <CAPTION> Average height and weight </CAPTION>
    <TR> <TH rowspan="2"> <TH colspan="2">Average
        <TH rowspan="2">Number of<BR>students
    <TR> <TH>height <TH>weight
    <TR> <TH>Male <TD>6.1 <TD>210 <TD>3000
    <TR> <TH>Female <TD>5.6 <TD>140 <TD>2500
</TABLE>
```

Average height and weight			
	Average		Number of students
	height	weight	
Male	6.1	210	3000
Female	5.6	140	2500

Figure 2-3. A Sample HTML Table.

Scripts

A client-side script is a program that may accompany an HTML document or be embedded in it. The program executes on the client's machine when the document is downloaded, or at a later time when a link is activated. Scripts provide a means to extend HTML documents in highly active and interactive ways. For example, scripts may accompany a form to process user input data to ensure that they are within predetermined ranges of values. The support for scripts in HTML is independent of the scripting language used.

The *SCRIPT* element places a script within an HTML document. The following attributes define its type and location:

- *type*—specifies the scripting language
- *src*—specifies the location of an external script

If the *src* attribute is not set, the script may be defined within the content of the *SCRIPT* element.

Here is an example of a script:

```
<SCRIPT type="text/javascript" src="../program/jscalc">
</SCRIPT>
```

Applets

Applets are another, but much more powerful, way to make an HTML document active and interactive. (In fact, this was how applets became the "killer" application for Java. Applets turned static HTML pages into active ones with animation.) In addition, applets allow you to access data from the client and/or to present the results of data access. (We will discuss this in Part 3, "Web Data Access.")

The *APPLET* element allows you to embed an applet in an HTML document. Its major attributes include:

- *codebase*—the base URL for the applet
- *code*—the relative URL for the applet's class file
- *name*—useful for applets on the same page to communicate with each other
- *width*—the initial width of the applet display area
- *height*—the initial height of the applet display area

You can use the *PARAM* element to supply initial values to the applet. It specifies a name/value pair through the *name* and *value* attributes. You can include any number of *PARAM* elements.

An example is given in the following:

```
<APPLET code="Rectangle.class" width="250" height="125">
    <PARAM name="color" value="blue">
</APPLET>
```

Objects

The *OBJECT* element allows you to include all types of resource in a document. Its major attributes include:

- *codebase*—the base URL for the object
- *classid*—the relative URL of a rendering mechanism
- *codetype*—the media type expected by the rendering mechanism
- *data*—the location of the data (if any) to be rendered
- *type*—the media type for the data
- *name*—useful for objects on the same page to communicate with each other
- *width*—the initial width of the object display area
- *height*—the initial height of the object display area

As a result, among others, the *APPLET* element is now deprecated. The following shows how the *Applet* example given earlier may be written with *Object*:

```
<OBJECT codetype="application/octet-stream"
        classid="java:Rectangle.class"
        width="250" height="125">
    <PARAM name="color" value="blue">
</OBJECT>
```

CONCLUSION

We have completed the first piece of preparation work for exploring Java and Web data access: understanding the basics of the Web (URL, HTTP, and HTML) as the universal data access infrastructure. If you need to know the complete and exact syntax and semantics of HTTP or HTML, please refer to the reference specifications listed in the back of this book. If you want to see discussions and examples of their use in client/server data access, please go to Part 3, "Web Data Access."

Among the three mechanisms that have made the Web what it is, *URL* is here to stay as the universal naming scheme. There have been some challenges to *HTML* as the universal user interface, mainly from *Java* and *XML (eXtensible Markup Language)*. However, it is most likely that they will complement HTML and not replace it. (We will discuss Java in the next chapter and XML in Chapter 17, "Introduction to XML.") The strongest challenge to *HTTP* as the universal network protocol has been from *IIOP (Internet Inter-ORB Protocol)*. But even here it still looks as if IIOP will complement HTTP and not replace it. (We will discuss IIOP in Chapter 16, "Introduction to Java ORBs.")

Chapter 3

Java
Primer

concepts

We will continue with our preparation work in this chapter. We will review some salient features of the computing platform for client/server data access: *Java* (see Figure 3-1). Without Java, the Web, though providing a universal infrastructure, is not sufficient and not very useful for client/server data access. Without Java, the Web is static and stateless, and it does not provide a direct mechanism for accessing data. With Java, the Web comes alive, can maintain state, and provides a rich set of mechanisms for accessing data.

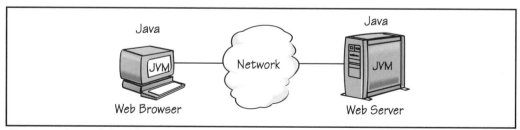

Figure 3-1. Java and the Web.

As we have mentioned in the Preface, we assume that you already know the Java language and have some familiarity with JDK 1.1 or later. Therefore, in this chapter, we will take a random walk in Java land. We will first discuss why Java is rapidly becoming the universal data access language and platform. We will then take a bird's-eye view of the Java API so that you will get a good feeling of what it is, where it is going, and what part of it is covered in this book. We will finish by doing a bit of Java tasting. The purpose here is "filling the gaps," so to speak. Starting with Part 2, we will comprehensively discuss many major Java topics that are directly related to client/server data access. However, there are some topics that are smaller in scope and indirectly related to client/server data access. Their understanding, nevertheless, is required or helpful for later discussions. These will be covered in the Java tasting section.

JAVA—THE UNIVERSAL DATA ACCESS LANGUAGE AND PLATFORM

There has been some debate (and positioning) going on between Microsoft and Sun Microsystems as to whether Java is just another programming language or really a computing platform. From the point of view of client/server data access, the importance of Java is that it is both a *programming language* and a *computing platform*. It started out as a programming language, but it is rapidly evolving into a comprehensive, distributed computing platform.

From the programming language perspective, Java is important to client/server data access because of the following characteristics: *object-orientation, portability, safety,* and *dynamicity.* Java's object orientation makes it easy to represent key data access concepts as objects (for example, **Connection** in JDBC and **Database** in ODMG Java Binding, which we will discuss in later chapters) and to exploit the emerging distributed object computing paradigm for data access. Java's architectural neutrality and bytecode representation make it possible to *"write once, and run anywhere."* This is important to client/server data access, which invariably involves a myriad of platforms and technologies (as discussed in Chapter 1, "Introduction to Client/Server Data Access"). Java's safety features include the lack of pointers and automatic memory management, which make it acceptable to download code from the server to run in a client. This (the so-called *mobile code* computing paradigm) is made possible by Java's dynamic and remote loading/linking capability. Both safety and dynamicity are critical in enabling data access from universal (or anonymous) clients to centralized servers.

As a computing platform, Java is still in the early development stage. However, the existence of the following facilities (or class libraries) has already made client/server data access that much easier: *reflection; security; database access* (JDBC, SQLJ, and ODMG Java Binding); *Web integration* (applets and servlets); *networking enablement* (URL and streams); *distributed object computing* (Object Serialization, RMI, and Java IDL); and *component architecture* (JavaBeans and Enterprise JavaBeans). (We will discuss all of these in detail in the rest of this book.) Nevertheless, just having good or excellent facilities is not sufficient. If these facilities are not widely available, they will not do any good for client/server data access on the global scale. Fortunately, the situation is quite the opposite for Java. The Java Virtual Machine is included in every Web browser and every Web server, and it is installed on most, if not all, database servers. Therefore, we very much have a universal, uniform computing platform (*Java*) sitting on top of a universal infrastructure (the *Web*), and it's ready for developing, deploying, and running client/server data access applications on the global scale.

No wonder Java is rapidly becoming the *universal data access language and platform*. Soon, the most important words for client/server data access will be: *Java* (on the Web client), *Java* (on the Web server), *Java* (on the application server), and *Java* (on the database server).

In the following sections, we will first take a look at Java data types and the Java platform. We will then give an overview of the Java API and do some Java tasting.

Java Data Types

Java data types are of critical importance when we discuss data access, because they determine what kind of data in Java we can retrieve from and store into a database. For object-oriented databases, all data types defined in the Java language can be stored into and retrieved from a database (see Chapter 9, "Java Binding for OODB"). For relational databases, however, currently only a subset of the data types defined in the Java language and certain additionally defined data types can be retrieved from and stored into a database (see Chapter 7, "JDBC in a Nutshell" and Chapter 8, "Introduction to SQLJ"). These data types are listed in Table 3-1.

Table 3-1. Java Data Types for Relational Database Access.

Java Data Type	Description	Wrapper Object
byte	8-bit signed	Byte
short	16-bit signed	Short
int	32-bit signed	Integer
long	64-bit signed	Long
float	32-bit IEEE 754	Float
double	32-bit IEEE 754	Double
java.math.BigDecimal		
String		
boolean	true, false	Boolean

Table 3-1. Java Data Types for Relational Database Access. (Continued)

Java Data Type	Description	Wrapper Object
byte[]		
java.sql.Date		
java.sql.Time		
java.sql.Timestamp		

The following are data types specifically defined for the purpose of relational database access (**BigDecimal** can also be used for more general purposes and is included as part of the **java.math** package, not the **java.sql** package):

- **java.math.BigDecimal** represents arbitrary-precision signed decimal numbers. It consists of an arbitrary-precision integer value and a non-negative integer scale, which represents the number of decimal digits to the right of the decimal point. The class definition provides operations for basic arithmetic, scale manipulation, comparison, format conversion, and hashing.

- **java.sql.Date** represents the SQL DATE value. It is a thin wrapper around **java.util.Date**. It adds formatting and parsing operations to support the JDBC escape syntax for date values.

- **java.sql.Time** represents the SQL TIME value. It is a thin wrapper around **java.util.Date**. It adds formatting and parsing operations to support the JDBC escape syntax for time values.

- **java.sql.Timestamp** represents the SQL TIMESTAMP value. It is a thin wrapper around **java.util.Date**. It adds the ability to hold the SQL TIMESTAMP nano value; it also provides formatting and parsing operations to support the JDBC escape syntax for timestamp values.

The Java Platform

The *Java Platform* sits on top of existing operating systems. A program written in the Java language compiles to a binary file that can run wherever the Java Platform is present, and on any underlying operating system. The Java Platform has two basic parts:

- Java Virtual Machine
- Java Application Programming Interface (Java API)

The *Java Virtual Machine* is key to the independence of the underlying operating system. It defines a machine-independent format for binary files called the *class (.class) format*. This format includes instructions for a virtual computer in the form of bytecodes. The *bytecodes* are a high-level representation of the program such that, if needed, optimization and machine-code generation can be done at that level via a *JIT (Just-In-Time) compiler*.

We will discuss the Java API in the next section. Before that, we should point out that the Java Platform enables developers to create two different kinds of programs:

■ *Applets*. These are programs that require a Web browser to run. As discussed in Chapter 2, "Web Basics," the <applet> tag is embedded in a Web page and identifies the applet to be run. When that page is accessed by a user, the applet is automatically downloaded from the server and runs on the client machine. Because applets are downloaded, they tend to be designed small and modular to avoid large download times and to accommodate thin clients. They also tend to have security restrictions regarding, for example, file access and network connection.

■ *Applications*. These are programs that do not require a Web browser to run. They have no built-in downloading mechanism. When an application is invoked, it runs. Therefore, applications are just like programs written in other languages. They can be small or big, and they tend to not have any security restrictions.

THE JAVA API

The *Java API* forms a standard, comprehensive interface to applets and applications, independent of the underlying operating systems. The Java API is the essential framework for application development. It consists of the following APIs:

■ *Java Basic API*. These APIs provide the basic *applet*, *AWT* (Abstract Window Toolkit), *I/O* (or streams, including *object serialization*), *language* (including *reflection*), *math*, *network*, and *utility* (including *data structures* and *events*) services. (We will discuss the essence of some of these in the section on Java tasting. We will discuss the **Java Applet API** in Chapter 12, "Java Applets and Servlets" and the **Java Streams and Object Serialization API** in Chapter 14, "Java Streams and Object Serialization.")

■ *Java Enterprise API*. These APIs support connectivity to enterprise databases and legacy applications. They allow corporate developers to build distributed client/server applets and applications in Java that run on any operating system. Java Enterprise APIs currently encompass the following:

◆ *JDBC* is a standard SQL database access interface, providing uniform access to a wide range of relational databases. (We will discuss this in Chapter 7, "JDBC in a Nutshell.")

◆ *Java RMI* is remote method invocation between peers or between client and server, when programs at both ends of the invocation are written in Java. (We will discuss this in Chapter 15, "Java RMI Overview.")

◆ *Java IDL* provides seamless interoperability and connectivity with CORBA (Common Object Request Broker Architecture), the open industry standard for distributed, heterogeneous computing. (We will discuss this in Chapter 16, "Introduction to Java ORBs.")

◆ *Java Naming and Directory Interface (JNDI)* is a standard interface to multiple naming and directory services in the enterprise, enabling seamless connectivity to heterogeneous enterprise naming and directory services. (We will discuss this in Chapter 21, "Enterprise JavaBeans.")

■ *JavaBeans API*. This API specifies a portable, platform-independent API for software components. Users will be able to compose applications using Java-Bean components in builder tools. (We will discuss this in Chapter 20, "Java-Beans.")

■ *Java Security API*. This API is a framework for developers to easily include security functionality in their applets and applications. This functionality includes crytography with digital signatures, encryption, and authentication.

■ *Java Foundation Classes (JFC) API*. These APIs let you build graphical user interfaces for Java programs. In addition to the existing AWT, they include:

◆ *Swing Set* refers to a group of lightweight components, building on those in the AWT, which range from simple buttons and to full-featured text areas to tree views and tabbed folders.

◆ *Accessibility API* provides a clean interface for assistive technologies, such as screen readers and speech recognition systems, that exposes state and property information about JFC and AWT components.

■ *Java Server API*. These APIs refer to:

◆ *Java Servlet API* enables the creation of Java servlets and allows developers to incorporate servlets into their Web applications. (We will discuss this in Chapter 12, "Java Applets and Servlets.")

◆ *Java Server API* provides uniform and consistent access to the Web server and administrative system resources required for developers to quickly develop Java Web servers.

■ *Java Commerce API*. This API will bring secure purchasing and financial management to the Web. *Java Wallet* is the initial component, which specifies a client-side framework for credit cards, debit cards, and electronic cash transactions.

■ *Java Media and Communication API*. These APIs support the integration of audio and video clips, animated presentations, 2D fonts, graphics, images, 3D models, and telephony. They include the following:

    ◆ *Java 2D API* is a set of classes for advanced 2D graphics and imaging, encompassing line art, text, and images in a single comprehensive model.

    ◆ *Java 3D API* is a set of classes for writing 3D graphics applications and 3D applets. It provides high-level constructs for creating, manipulating, and rendering 3D geometry. Developers can describe very large *virtual worlds* using these constructs.

    ◆ *Java Media Framework API* specifies a unified architecture, messaging protocol, and programming interface for media players, media capture, and conferencing.

    ◆ *Java Sound API* is an interface for developing a very high-quality 32-channel audio rendering and MIDI-controlled sound synthesis engine.

    ◆ *Java Speech API* defines a cross-platform interface to support command and control recognizers, dictation systems, and speech synthesizers.

    ◆ *Java Telephony API* is a portable interface for Java-based computer-telephony applications; it is intended for a broad audience, ranging from call center application developers to Web page designers.

■ *Java Management API*. This API provides a rich set of extensible objects and methods for the development of seamless system, network, and service management solutions for heterogeneous networks.

■ *PersonalJava API*. This API is designed for network-connected personal consumer devices for home, office, and mobile use, including hand-held computers, set-top boxes, game consoles, and smart phones.

■ *EmbeddedJava API*. This API is designed for high-volume embedded devices, such as mobile phones, pagers, process control instrumentation, office peripherals, network routers, and network switches.

The Java Core API

The Java API is classified into the following two categories:

■ *Core.* Core APIs belong to the minimal set of APIs that form the standard Java Platform. They are available on the Java Platform, regardless of the underlying operating system. The Core API grows with each release of JDK. (*PersonalJava* and *EmbeddedJava* are exceptions, which means they do not conform to the standard Java Platform.)

■ *Standard Extension.* These APIs are outside the Core API.

The *Java Core API* includes the following subset of the Java API:

■ Java Basic API
■ Java Enterprise API, except JNDI
■ JavaBeans API
■ Java Security API
■ Swing Set
■ Java 2D

All other Java APIs are standard extensions.

JAVA TASTING

As promised, we are going to do a little tasting of Java in the following sections. We will go over a number of topics that are smaller in scope and indirectly related to client/server data access. Their understanding, nevertheless, is required or helpful for later chapters. The Java classes and interfaces referred to in the discussion are described in the next section on Java tasting API.

The Java Execution Model

A Java Virtual Machine starts execution by invoking the *main()* method of some specified class, say **Demo**, passing it a single argument as an array of strings. Before the execution can take place, the following prerequisites must be met:

1. *Loading the class*. A binary representation (in the class format) of the **Demo** class must be loaded by a *class loader* that implements the **ClassLoader** interface. This involves constructing a **Class** object to represent the **Demo** class.

2. *Linking the class*. Linking involves *verification, preparation,* and *resolution. Verification* checks that the loaded representation of the **Demo** class is well-formed, with a proper symbol table. It also checks that the code that implements the **Demo** class obeys the semantic requirements of Java and the Java Virtual Machine. *Preparation* involves allocation of static storage and internal data structures used by the Java Virtual Machine. *Resolution* is the process of checking symbolic references from the **Demo** class to other classes and interfaces. It does this check by loading the classes and interfaces to determine if the references are correct. Different forms of resolution may be

used. In the "static" form of resolution, all symbolic references are resolved recursively at the time of initial linkage. In the "laziest" form of resolution, a symbolic reference is resolved only when it is actively used.

3. ***Initializing the class***. Initialization consists of the execution of any *class variable initializers* and *static initializers* of the **Demo** class in textual order. But before this can happen, its direct superclass must be initialized, and its direct superclass, recursively, until the **Object** class has been initialized. This may involve loading, verification, preparation, and resolution of the superclass, and its superclass, recursively.

When the **Demo** class is no longer needed, it will automatically be *unloaded*. A class may not be unloaded while any *instance* of it is still reachable. It also may not be unloaded while the **Class** object that represents it is still reachable. If a class declares a class method *classFinalize()*, then this method will be invoked before the class is unloaded.

A Java Virtual Machine terminates all its activity and *exits* when one of two events happens (we will discuss Java threads shortly):

- All the threads that are not daemon threads terminate.
- Some threads invoke the *exit()* method of **Runtime** class or **System** class, and the operation is legal.

Java Reflection

The Java Reflection API provides a type-safe and secure API that supports *introspection* about the classes and objects in the current Java Virtual Machine. If permitted by security policy, the API can be used to:

- Discover information about the *fields*, *methods*, and *constructors* of loaded classes
- Construct new class instances and new arrays
- Access and modify fields of objects and classes
- Access and modify elements of arrays
- Invoke methods on objects and classes

The API accommodates either applications (for example, JavaBeans and Enterprise JavaBeans) that need access to the *public members* of a target object based on its class, or applications (for example, Java Object Serialization) that need access to all *declared members* of a given class.

The major components of the Java Reflection API include the following classes:

■ **Class** provides for the construction of new instances of **Field**, **Method**, and **Constructor** classes, which correspond to underlying public or declared members of the class.

■ **Field, Method,** and **Constructor** provide reflective information about the underlying member as well as a type-safe means to use the reflected member to operate on Java objects. These classes implement the **Member** interface and are final classes. Only the Java Virtual Machine may create instances of these classes.

   ◆ **Field**—the underlying field may be a class (static) variable or an instance variable.
   ◆ **Method**—the underlying method may be an abstract method, a class (static) method, or an instance method.

■ **Array** provides methods to dynamically construct and access Java arrays. This class is a final class and thus uninstantiable.

■ **Modifier** helps decode Java language modifier information (for example, public and static) about classes and their members. This class is uninstantiable.

Security Model

The Java security manager controls access to the Java Reflection API on a class-by-class basis. There are two levels of checks:

■ The methods of the **Class** class that give reflective access to a member or a set of members of a class are the only source for instances of **Field**, **Method**, and **Constructor.** These methods first delegate security checking to the system security manager.

■ Once the system security manager grants reflective access to a member, any code may use the reflected member to operate on Java objects (to get or set field values, to invoke methods, or to create and initialize new objects). However, standard Java language access controls will occur for *protected*, default access (*package*), and *private* classes and members.

Introspection in Java is easier, safer, and more natural than in other programming languages and platforms (for example, COM or CORBA). We will see its use when we discuss JavaBeans (see Chapter 20, "JavaBeans").

Java Threads

A *concurrent program* consists of multiple tasks that behave as if they are all executing at the same time. Concurrency can be used, among other things, to provide high availability of services and to exploit available computing power (for example, parallelism) to improve performance. Java supports concurrent programming through built-in language constructs, class library, and run-time support (scheduler, monitor, and locking primitives).

In Java, the tasks of a concurrent program are implemented using *threads*. A thread is a single sequential flow of control within a program. Threads may share access to memory with other threads, and have means of coordinating their activities with those of other threads.

Thread Creation

The Java thread framework requires that the principal methods executed in threads be called *run()* and that their classes implement the **Runnable** interface. There are two ways you can do this. You can subclass from the **Thread** class, which implements **Runnable**, and override its *run()* method, or you can implement directly the **Runnable** interface and the *run()* method.

By default, every thread is created as a member of a **ThreadGroup**. Newly created threads are added to the **ThreadGroup** of the thread which creates the new thread. A thread group enforces security policies by dynamically restricting access to thread operations, such as stopping a thread from execution. It may also place a ceiling on the maximum priority that any member thread can possess. The thread groups form a *tree* in which every thread group except the initial one has a parent. Members of a thread group and its ancestor groups can invoke operations that affect the behavior of all members.

A thread can be marked as a *daemon thread*, which represents service providers or background activities that never exit. As mentioned before, a Java Virtual Machine terminates all its activity and *exits* when all the threads that are not daemon threads terminate.

Thread Life Cycle

During its life cycle, a thread may exist in one of the following states (see Figure 3-2):

- *New*. The thread is created but not yet running.

- **Runnable.** The thread is started but may not yet be running. The *start()* method causes a thread to call its *run()* method.
- **Blocked.** The thread is blocked. It may return to the *runnable* state if the blocking condition is removed.
- **Dead.** The thread has been terminated, which means the *stop()* method has been called.

A thread is *alive* if it is in the *runnable* or *blocked* state.

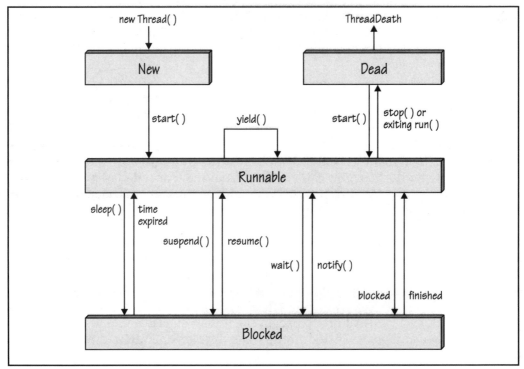

Figure 3-2. The Java Thread Life Cycle.

Thread Priorities

In general, because of the limitation on CPU availability, each runnable thread must take turns executing. When they are not running, runnable threads are held in *priority-based scheduling* queues managed by the Java Virtual Machine. By default, each new thread has the same priority as the thread that created it. However, thread priorities can be changed by calling the *setPriority()* method.

If there are multiple runnable threads at any given time, the Java Virtual Machine picks the one with the highest priority to run. If there is more than one thread with the highest priority, it picks an arbitrary one. A running lower-priority thread is *preempted* if there is a higher-priority thread that needs to run.

Synchronization

One of the challenges of multi-threaded programming is synchronization—coordinating the activities of multiple threads so that they do not interfere with each other. The mechanism provided in Java to serialize access to objects is the *synchronized method* or the *synchronized statement*. Every Java object has an associated *monitor*, which is implicitly obtained by a thread when a synchronized method is called or when a synchronized statement is executed. (A *monitor* is a set of code in which only one thread at a time may be executing.) A synchronized method is just like any other method, except that it uses the *synchronized* keyword as a modifier. A synchronized statement is similar, except that the object for which the monitor is obtained is specified as a parameter followed by a block of code.

Any synchronized method or statement is executed in its entirety (unless explicitly suspended via the *wait()* method) before the object is allowed to execute any other synchronized method called from any other thread. Declaring a method as *synchronized*, however, is not sufficient to guarantee exclusive access: any other method that is *not* declared as *synchronized* may run concurrently with it.

If an object's monitor cannot be obtained on entry to a synchronized method or statement because another thread owns it, the current thread is blocked until the monitor is released. *Deadlock* may occur if two (or more) threads are waiting for the monitors owned by each other. Java does nothing to protect you from deadlock.

Waiting and Notification

To coordinate their activities, threads may need to signal each other when certain events occur. This is done with the *wait()*, *notify()*, and *notifyAll()* methods. When a thread calls *wait()*, it must own a monitor on the object. The thread is then added to an internal wait queue, and the monitor is released. A thread in an object's wait queue is blocked until the *notify()* or *notifyAll()* method is called by another thread. When the *notify()* method is called, an arbitrary thread in the wait queue is chosen and unblocked. When the *notifyAll()* method is called, all threads in the wait queue are chosen and unblocked.

Concurrent (multi-threaded) programming in Java is easier and more natural than in other programming languages. We will see examples of its use when we discuss applets and servlets (see Chapter 12, "Java Applets and Servlets").

Java Events

The Java event model was designed for use in *AWT* (Abstract Window Toolkit) and JavaBeans (see Chapter 20, "JavaBeans"), though it can be used for general event-driven programming. It provides a mechanism for propagating *state change notifications* between a *source* object and one or more target *listener* objects.

The event model provides a generic, extensible event mechanism that:

- Provides for the definition and application of an extensible set of *event types* and *propagation methods.*
- Enables the discovery of the events that a source object's class may *generate.*
- Enables the discovery of the events that a listener object's class may *observe.*
- Provides an *event registration mechanism* that permits the dynamic manipulation of the relationships between *event sources* and *event listeners.*
- Promotes *high-performance propagation of events* between sources and listeners.

The key components of the event model include (see Figures 3-3 and 3-4):

- *Event notifications*. These are propagated from sources to listeners by *method invocation*s on the target listener objects.

- *Event listeners*. Each distinct type of event notification is defined as a distinct *event notification method*. These methods are grouped in **EventListener** interfaces that extend **java.util.EventListener.** Event listener classes identify themselves as interested in observing a certain set of events by implementing the corresponding set of **EventListener** interfaces.

- *Event objects*. The *state* associated with an event notification is encapsulated in an event object that extends **java.util.EventObject** and that is passed as the sole argument to the event notification method.

- *Event sources*. They identify themselves as the source for generating particular events by defining *registration methods* that conform to a specific *design pattern* and accept references to objects with particular **EventListener** interfaces.

- *Event adapters*. In circumstances where event listeners cannot directly implement a particular interface, or when some addition behavior is required, an *event adapter* may be interposed between an event source and one or more event listeners to establish the relationship or to augment the behavior.

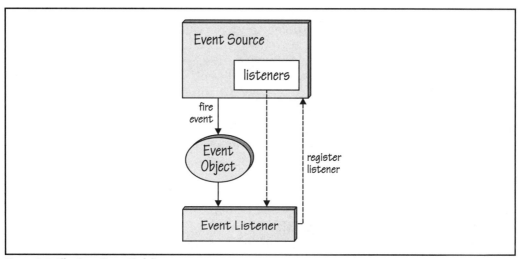

Figure 3-3. The Java Event Model.

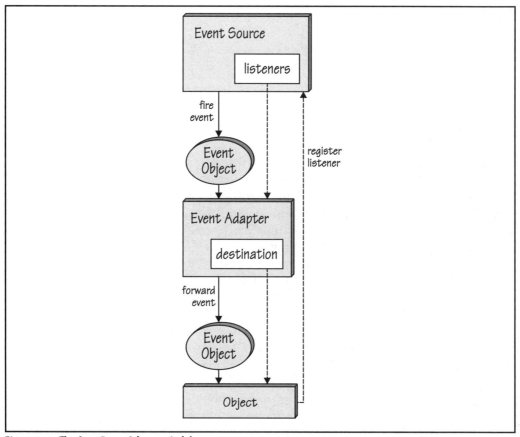

Figure 3-4. The Java Event Adapter Model.

The Java event model is very versatile. We will see examples of its use in AWT with applets (see Chapter 12, "Java Applets and Servlets") and in JavaBeans (see Chapter 20, "JavaBeans") later.

Java Archive

JAR (Java Archive) is a platform-independent *file format* that aggregates many files into one. Multiple Java applets, Beans, or enterprise Beans and their requisite components (.class files, images, sounds, and so on) can be bundled in a *JAR file* and treated as a single unit for download or other purposes. The JAR format supports:

■ *Compression* which reduces the file size
■ *Digital signatures* on individual entries to authenticate their origin

JAR Files

A JAR file consists of an *archive file*, a *manifest file*, and potentially *signature files*. The manifest file has the pathname:

```
META-INF/MANIFEST.MF
```

The signature files have pathname:

```
META-INF/<name>.SF
```

The archive file can be of any format that supports hierarchical paths. In most cases, information contained within the manifest file or signature files is represented as "name: value" pairs. Groups of name-value pairs are known as a "section." Sections are separated from each other by empty lines.

The *manifest file* consists of a list of files present within the archive. Not all files in the archive need to be listed in the manifest file, but all files to be signed must be listed. The following headers are required:

```
Name: <path</<name>.class
Digest-Algorithms: (list of algorithms)
(algorithm)-Digest: (base-64 representation of digest)
```

The following is an example manifest file:

```
Manifest-Version: 1.0
```

```
Name: common/class1.class
Digest-Algorithms: MD5
MD5-Digest: (base64 representation of MD5 digest)


Name: http://woodview.ibm.com/common/class2.class
Digest-Algorithms: MD5, SHA
MD5-Digest: (base64 representation of MD5 digest)
SHA-Digest: (base64 representation of SHA digest)
```

Each signer is represented by a *signature file*. Signature files consist of sections that are essentially lists of names; all must be present in the manifest file. A digest is also present, but this is a digest of the entry in the manifest file. The following is an example signature file for the above manifest file:

```
Signature-Version: 1.0


Name: common/class1.class
Digest-Algorithms: MD5
MD5-Digest: (base64 representation of MD5 digest)


Name: http://woodview.ibm.com/common/class2.class
Digest-Algorithms: MD5
MD5-Digest: (base64 representation of MD5 digest)
```

To validate a file, a digest value in the signature file is compared against a digest calculated against the corresponding entry in the manifest file. Then, a digest value in the manifest file is compared against a digest calculated against the actual data referenced in the "Name:" header.

JAR files are used to package (among other things) SQLJ applications, JavaBeans, and Enterprise JavaBeans. We will see examples later (in Chapter 8, "Introduction to SQLJ," Chapter 20, "JavaBeans," and Chapter 21, "Enterprise JavaBeans").

JAVA TASTING API

Here are some of the classes and interfaces referred to in the Java tasting section:

- **Object, Class,** and **ClassLoader** are applicable in general and contained in the **java.lang** package.
- **Member, Field, Method, Constructor, Array,** and **Modifier** are applicable to Java reflection and contained in the **java.lang.reflect** package.
- **Runnable, Thread,** and **ThreadGroup** are applicable to Java threads and contained in the **java.lang** package.

- **EventListener,** and **EventObject** are applicable to Java events and contained in the **java.util** package.

Object Class

The **Object** class is the root of the Java class hierarchy, which means it is the superclass of all Java classes.

Constructors

- **Object**() constructs a new object.

Methods

- **getClass**() returns the run-time **Class** object of this object.

- **clone**() creates a copy of this object and returns the newly created **Object**. This method will only clone an object whose class implements the **Cloneable** interface.

- **equals**(Object obj) compares two objects for equality; returns true (boolean) if they are.

- **hashCode**() returns a hash code value (int) for this object.

- **toString**() returns a "textual" representation (**String**) of this object.

- **finalize**() called by the garbage collector before garbage collecting this object.

The following methods are related to *Java threads*:

- **notify**() wakes up a single thread that is waiting on this object's monitor. This method should only be called by a thread that is the owner of this object's monitor.

- **notifyAll**() wakes up all threads that are waiting on this object's monitor. This method should only be called by a thread that is the owner of this object's monitor.

- **wait**() waits to be notified by another thread of a change in this object. The current thread must own this object's monitor. It releases the ownership and waits until it is notified and until it can re-obtain ownership of the monitor.

- **wait**(long timeout) waits to be notified by another thread of a change in this object. The current thread must own this object's monitor. It releases the ownership and waits until it is notified or the timeout period (in milliseconds) has elapsed, and until it can re-obtain ownership of the monitor.

- **wait**(long timeout, int nanos) waits to be notified by another thread of a change in this object. The current thread must own this object's monitor. It releases the ownership and waits until it is notified or the timeout period (in milliseconds plus nanoseconds) has elapsed, and until it can re-obtain ownership of the monitor.

Class Class

The **Class** class is a final class and implements the **java.io.Serializable** interface. Instances of the **Class** class (the **Class** objects) represent *classes, interfaces, arrays,* or *primitive types* (in the form of nine "wrapper" classes: **Byte, Short, Integer, Long, Float, Double, Boolean, Character,** and **Void**) in a running Java application. **Class** objects are automatically constructed by the Java Virtual Machine as classes are loaded and by calls to the *defineClass* method in the class loader.

Class Methods

- **forName**(String className) returns the **Class** object associated with the class with the given name. This method attempts to locate, load, link, and initialize the class, as needed.

Methods

- **getName**() returns the fully qualified name (**String**) of the type (class, interface, array, or primitive) represented by this **Class** object.

- **getClassLoader**() returns the **ClassLoader** for this class.

- **getSigners**() returns the signers (**Object**[ ]) of this class.

- **getResource**(String name) returns a resource (as a **java.net.URL**) with the specified name.

- **getResourceAsStream**(String name) returns a resource (as an **java.io.Input-Stream**) with the specified name.

■ **toString**() returns a **String** that is either "class" or "interface" followed by a space and then the fully qualified name of this class or interface.

The following methods are related to *Java reflection*:

■ **newInstance**() creates a new instance of this class and returns the newly created **Object**.

■ **isInstance**(Object obj) returns true (boolean) if the specified object is non-null and can be cast to the type represented by this **Class** object.

■ **isAssignableFrom**(Class cls) returns true (boolean) if this class or interface is either the same as, or is a superclass or superinterface of, the class or interface represented by the specified **Class** object.

■ **isInterface**() returns true (boolean) if this **Class** object represents an interface type.

■ **isArray**() returns true (boolean) if this **Class** object represents an array type.

■ **isPrimitive**() returns true (boolean) if this **Class** object represents a primitive Java type.

■ **getSuperclass**() returns the **Class** object representing the superclass of this class.

■ **getInterfaces**() returns an array of **Class** objects (**Class**[]) representing the interfaces which are implemented by this class or interface.

■ **getComponentType**() returns the **Class** object representing the component type of the array if this **Class** object represents an array type.

■ **getModifiers**() returns the modifiers (int) for this class or interface encoded in an integer.

■ **getDeclaringClass**() returns the **Class** object representing the class of which this class or interface is a member.

■ **getClasses**() returns an array of **Class** objects (**Class**[]) representing all the public classes and interfaces that are members of this class.

■ **getFields**() returns an array of **Field** objects (**Field**[]) reflecting all the public fields of this class or interface.

- **getMethods**() returns an array of **Method** objects (**Method**[ ]) reflecting all the public methods of this class or interface.

- **getConstructors**() returns an array of **Constructor** objects (**Constructor**[ ]) reflecting all the public constructors of this class.

- **getField**(String name) returns a **Field** object reflecting the specified public member field of this class or interface.

- **getMethod**(String name, Class[ ] parameterTypes) returns a **Method** object reflecting the specified public member method of this class or interface.

- **getConstructor**(Class[ ] parameterTypes) returns a **Constructor** object reflecting the specified public constructor of this class.

- **getDeclaredClasses**() returns an array of **Class** objects (**Class**[ ]) representing all the classes and interfaces declared as members of this class.

- **getDeclaredFields**() returns an array of **Field** objects (**Field**[ ]) reflecting all the fields declared by this class or interface.

- **getDeclaredMethods**() returns an array of **Method** objects (**Method**[ ]) reflecting all the methods declared by this class or interface.

- **getDeclaredConstructors**() returns an array of **Constructor** objects (**Constructor**[ ]) reflecting all the constructors declared by this class.

- **getDeclaredField**(String name) returns a **Field** object reflecting the specified declared member field of this class or interface.

- **getDeclaredMethod**(String name, Class[ ] parameterTypes) returns a **Method** object reflecting the specified declared member method of this class or interface.

- **getDeclaredConstructor**(Class[ ] parameterTypes) returns a **Constructor** object reflecting the specified declared constructor of this class.

ClassLoader Class

The **ClassLoader** class is an abstract class. Applications implement subclasses of **ClassLoader** to extend the manner in which the Java Virtual Machine dynamically loads classes. Normally, the Java Virtual Machine loads classes from the local file system in a platform-dependent manner, without the use of a class loader. However, some classes may not originate from a file; instead they may originate from a network, or they could be constructed by an application. In these cases, a class loader is required.

Class Methods

■ **getSystemResource**(String name) returns a system resource (as a **java.net.URL**) with the specified name.

■ **getSystemResourceAsStream**(String name) returns a system resource (as a **java.io.InputStream**) with the specified name.

Constructors

■ **ClassLoader**() constructs a new class loader and initializes it.

Methods

■ **loadClass**(String name) requests the class loader to load and resolve (by calling the *resolveClass()* method) a class with the specified name. Returns the **Class** object representing the class.

■ **loadClass**(String name, boolean resolve) requests the class loader to load and, if the *resolve* flag is true, resolve (by calling the *resolveClass()* method) a class with the specified name. Returns the **Class** object representing the class.

■ **defineClass**(String name, byte[] data, int offset, int length) converts an array of bytes to an instance of the **Class** class with the specified name. Returns the **Class** object representing the class. Before it can be used, it must be resolved.

■ **resolveClass**(Class c) resolves the specified **Class** object so that an instance of the class can be created or one of its methods can be called.

■ **findSystemClass**(String name) finds the system class with the specified name and loads it if needed. Returns the **Class** object representing the class.

■ **findLoadedClass**(String name) finds the class with the specified name and returns the **Class** object representing the class.

■ **setSigners**(Class cl, Object[] signers) sets the signers of the specified class. This method is called after defining a class by signature-aware, class-loading code.

■ **getResource**(String name) returns a resource (as a **java.net.URL**) with the specified name.

■ **getResourceAsStream**(String name) returns a resource (as a **java.io.Input-Stream**) with the specified name.

Member Interface

The **Member** interface reflects identifying information about a single field, method, or constructor.

Class Constants

■ **PUBLIC** (int) identifies the set of all public members of a class or interface.

■ **DECLARED** (int) identifies the set of all declared members of a class or interface.

Methods

■ **getDeclaringClass**() returns the **Class** object representing the class or interface that declares this member.

■ **getName**() returns the name (**String**) of this member.

■ **getModifiers**() returns the modifiers (int) of this member.

Field Class

The **Field** class is a final class; it implements the **Member** interface. It provides information about, and dynamic access to, a single field of a class or interface. The reflected field may be a class (static) field or an instance field.

Methods

■ **getDeclaringClass**() returns the **Class** object representing the class or interface that declares this field.

■ **getName**() returns the name (**String**) of this field.

- **getModifiers**() returns the modifiers (int) of this field.

- **getType**() returns a **Class** object identifying the declared type for this field.

- **equals**(Object obj) compares two fields for equality. Returns true (boolean) if they are.

- **hashCode**() returns a hash code value (int) for this field.

- **toString**() returns a **String** describing this field.

The following methods provide dynamic access:

- **get**(Object obj) returns the value (**Object**) of this field on the specified object.

- **getBoolean**(Object obj) returns the value of this field as a boolean on the specified object.

- **getByte**(Object obj) returns the value of this field as a byte on the specified object.

- **getChar**(Object obj) returns the value of this field as a char on the specified object.

- **getShort**(Object obj) returns the value of this field as a short on the specified object.

- **getInt**(Object obj) returns the value of this field as an int on the specified object.

- **getLong**(Object obj) returns the value of this field as a long on the specified object.

- **getFloat**(Object obj) returns the value of this field as a float on the specified object.

- **getDouble**(Object obj) returns the value of this field as a double on the specified object.

- **set**(Object obj, Object value) sets this field on the specified object to the specified value.

- **setBoolean**(Object obj, boolean value) sets the value of this field as a boolean on the specified object.

- **setByte**(Object obj, byte value) sets the value of this field as a byte on the specified object.

- **setChar**(Object obj, char value) sets the value of this field as a char on the specified object.

- **setShort**(Object obj, short value) sets the value of this field as a short on the specified object.

- **setInt**(Object obj, int value) sets the value of this field as an int on the specified object.

- **setLong**(Object obj, long value) sets the value of this field as a long on the specified object.

- **setFloat**(Object obj, float value) sets the value of this field as a float on the specified object.

- **setDouble**(Object obj, double value) sets the value of this field as a double on the specified object.

Method Class

The **Method** class is a final class; it implements the **Member** interface. It provides information about, and dynamic access to, a single method of a class or interface. The reflected method may be a class (static) method or an instance method (including an abstract method).

Methods

- **getDeclaringClass**() returns the **Class** object representing the class or interface that declares this method.

- **getName**() returns the name (**String**) of this method.

- **getModifiers**() returns the modifiers (int) of this method.

- **getReturnType**() returns a **Class** object identifying the formal return type of this method.

- **getParameterTypes**() returns an array of **Class** objects (**Class**[]) identifying the formal parameter types, in declaration order, of this method.

- **getExceptionTypes**() returns an array of **Class** objects (**Class**[ ]) identifying the checked exceptions thrown by this method.

- **equals**(Object obj) compares two methods for equality. Returns true (boolean) if they are.

- **hashCode**() returns a hash code value (int) for this method.

- **toString**() returns a **String** describing this method.

The following method provides dynamic access:

- **invoke**(Object obj, Object[ ] args) invokes this method on the specified object with the specified parameters and returns the result as an **Object**.

Constructor Class

The **Constructor** class is a final class and implements the **Member** interface. It provides information about, and dynamic access to, a single constructor for a class.

Methods

- **getDeclaringClass**() returns the **Class** object representing the class that declares this constructor.

- **getName**() returns the name (**String**) of this constructor.

- **getModifiers**() returns the modifiers (int) of this constructor.

- **getParameterTypes**() returns an array of **Class** objects (**Class**[ ]) identifying the formal parameter types, in declaration order, of this constructor.

- **getExceptionTypes**() returns an array of **Class** objects (**Class**[ ]) identifying the checked exceptions thrown by this constructor.

- **equals**(Object obj) compares two constructors for equality. Returns true (boolean) if they are.

- **hashCode**() returns a hash code value (int) for this constructor.

- **toString**() returns a **String** describing this constructor.

The following method provides dynamic access:

- **newInstance**(Object[ ] initargs) uses this constructor to create and initialize a new instance of the constructor's declaring class with the specified initialization parameters. Returns the newly created **Object.**

Array Class

The **Array** class is a final class and is uninstantiable. It provides class methods to dynamically create and access Java arrays.

Class Methods

- **newInstance**(Class componentType, int length) creates and returns a new array (**Object**) with the specified component type and length.

- **newInstance**(Class componentType, int[ ] dimensions) creates and returns a new array (**Object**) with the specified component type and dimensions.

- **getLength**(Object array) returns the length (int) of the specified array object.

- **get**(Object array, int index) returns the value (**Object**) of the indexed component in the specified array object.

- **getBoolean**(Object array, int index) returns the value of the indexed component as a boolean in the specified array object.

- **getByte**(Object array, int index) returns the value of the indexed component as a byte in the specified array object.

- **getChar**(Object array, int index) returns the value of the indexed component as a char in the specified array object.

- **getShort**(Object array, int index) returns the value of the indexed component as a short in the specified array object.

- **getInt**(Object array, int index) returns the value of the indexed component as an int in the specified array object.

- **getLong**(Object array, int index) returns the value of the indexed component as a long in the specified array object.

- **getFloat**(Object array, int index) returns the value of the indexed component as a float in the specified array object.

- **getDouble**(Object array, int index) returns the value of the indexed component as a double in the specified array object.

- **set**(Object array, int index, Object value) sets the value of the indexed component of the specified array object to the specified value.

- **setBoolean**(Object array, int index, boolean value) sets the value of the indexed component as a boolean in the specified array object.

- **setByte**(Object array, int index, byte value) sets the value of the indexed component as a byte in the specified array object.

- **setChar**(Object array, int index, char value) sets the value of the indexed component as a char in the specified array object.

- **setShort**(Object array, int index, short value) sets the value of the indexed component as a short in the specified array object.

- **setInt**(Object array, int index, int value) sets the value of the indexed component as an int in the specified array object.

- **setLong**(Object array, int index, long value) sets the value of the indexed component as a long in the specified array object.

- **setFloat**(Object array, int index, float value) sets the value of the indexed component as a float in the specified array object.

- **setDouble**(Object array, int index, double value) sets the value of the indexed component as a double in the specified array object.

Modifier Class

The **Modifier** class provides class methods and constants to decode class and member access modifiers.

Class Constants

- **ABSTRACT** (int)

- **FINAL** (int)

- **INTERFACE** (int)

- **NATIVE** (int)

- **PRIVATE** (int)

- **PROTECTED** (int)

- **PUBLIC** (int)

- **STATIC** (int)

- **SYNCHRONIZED** (int)

- **TRANSIENT** (int)

- **VOLATILE** (int)

Class Methods

- **isAbstract**(int mod) returns true (boolean) if the specified integer includes the *abstract* modifier.

- **isFinal**(int mod) returns true (boolean) if the specified integer includes the *final* modifier.

- **isInterface**(int mod) returns true (boolean) if the specified integer includes the *interface* modifier.

- **isNative**(int mod) returns true (boolean) if the specified integer includes the *native* modifier.

- **isPrivate**(int mod) returns true (boolean) if the specified integer includes the *private* modifier.

- **isProtected**(int mod) returns true (boolean) if the specified integer includes the *protected* modifier.

- **isPublic**(int mod) returns true (boolean) if the specified integer includes the *public* modifier.

- **isStatic**(int mod) returns true (boolean) if the specified integer includes the *static* modifier.

- **isSynchronized**(int mod) returns true (boolean) if the specified integer includes the *synchronized* modifier.

- **isTransient**(int mod) returns true (boolean) if the specified integer includes the *transient* modifier.

- **isVolatile**(int mod) returns true (boolean) if the specified integer includes the *volatile* modifier.

- **toString**(int mod) returns a **String** describing the specified modifier.

Constructors

- **Modifier**()

Runnable Interface

The **Runnable** interface should be implemented by any class whose instances are intended to be executed by a thread.

Methods

- **run**()—when an object implementing the Runnable interface is used to create a thread, starting the thread causes this method of the object to be called in that thread.

Thread Class

The **Thread** class implements the **Runnable** interface. One way to create a new thread of execution in Java is to declare a class to be a subclass of **Thread**. You can then create and start an instance of the subclass with its own thread of execution. This subclass should override the *run()* method.

Class Constants

- **MIN_PRIORITY** (int) identifies the minimum priority that a thread can have.

- **NORM_PRIORITY** (int) identifies the default priority that is assigned to a thread.

- **MAX_PRIORITY** (int) identifies the maximum priority that a thread can have.

Class Methods

■ **currentThread**() returns the currently executing **Thread** object.

■ **yield**() causes the currently executing thread to temporarily pause and then allows other threads to execute.

■ **sleep**(long mills) causes the currently executing thread to sleep (temporarily pause) for the specified number of milliseconds.

■ **sleep**(long mills, int nanos) causes the currently executing thread to sleep (temporarily pause) for the specified number of milliseconds plus the specified number of nanoseconds.

■ **interrupted**() returns true (boolean) if the current thread has been interrupted.

■ **activeCount**() returns the current number (int) of active threads in this thread group.

■ **enumerate**(Thread[ ] tarray) copies into the specified array every active thread in this thread group and its subgroups. Returns the number (int) of threads copied.

■ **dumpStack**() prints a stack trace of the current thread.

Constructors

■ **Thread**() constructs a new **Thread** object.

■ **Thread**(Runnable target) constructs a new **Thread** object so that it has target as its run object.

■ **Thread**(String name) constructs a new **Thread** object with the specified name.

■ **Thread**(ThreadGroup group, Runnable target) constructs a new **Thread** object so that it has target as its run object and belongs to the specified thread group.

■ **Thread**(ThreadGroup group, String name) constructs a new **Thread** object so that it has the specified name and belongs to the specified thread group.

■ **Thread**(Runnable target, String name) constructs a new **Thread** object so that it has target as its run object and has the specified name.

■ **Thread**(ThreadGroup group, Runnable target, String name) constructs a new **Thread** object so that it has target as its run object, has the specified name, and belongs to the specified thread group.

Methods

■ **start**() causes this thread to begin execution; the Java Virtual Machine calls the *run()* method of this thread. The result is that two threads are running concurrently.

■ **run**()—if this thread was constructed using a separate **Runnable** object, then that object's *run()* method is called; otherwise, this method does nothing and returns. Subclasses of **Thread** should override this method.

■ **interrupt**() interrupts this thread.

■ **suspend**() suspends this thread.

■ **resume**() resumes this thread.

■ **join**() waits for this thread to die.

■ **join**(long milis) waits at most the specified milliseconds for this thread to die.

■ **join**(long milis, int nanos) waits at most the specified milliseconds plus the specified nanoseconds for this thread to die.

■ **stop**() forces this thread to stop executing.

■ **stop**(Throwable o) forces this thread to stop executing and to throw the specified **Throwable** object.

■ **destroy**() destroys this thread without any cleanup.

The following are accessor methods:

■ **checkAccess**() determines if the currently running thread has permission to modify this thread.

■ **countStackFrame**() counts and returns the number (int) of stack frames in this thread, which must be suspended.

■ **isAlive**() returns true (boolean) if this thread is alive.

- **isInterrupted**() returns true (boolean) if this thread has been interrupted.

- **isDaemon**() returns true (boolean) if this thread is a daemon thread.

- **setDaemon**(boolean on) marks this thread as a daemon thread if the specified flag is true.

- **getName**() returns this thread's name (**String**).

- **setName**(String name) sets the name of this thread to the specified name.

- **getPriority**() returns this thread's priority (int).

- **setPriority**(int newPriority) sets the priority of this thread to the specified value within the bound of the maximum permitted priority of the thread's thread group.

- **getThreadGroup**() returns this thread's **ThreadGroup**.

- **toString**() returns a **String** representing this thread, including the thread's name, priority, and thread group.

ThreadGroup Class

A thread group represents a set of threads. It can include other thread groups. The thread groups form a tree in which every thread group except the initial one has a parent.

Constructors

- **ThreadGroup**(String name) constructs a new thread group with the specified name. The parent of this new thread group is the thread group of the currently running thread.

- **ThreadGroup**(ThreadGroup parent, String name) constructs a new thread group with the specified name and the specified parent thread group.

Methods

- **suspend**() suspends all threads in this thread group.

- **resume**() resumes all threads in this thread group.

- **stop**() stops all threads in this thread group.

- **destroy**() destroys this thread group and all of its subgroups. This thread group must be empty.

- **allowThreadSuspension**(boolean b) is used by the Java Virtual Machine to control low memory implicit suspension. Returns a boolean.

- **uncaughtException**() is called by the Java Virtual Machine when a thread in this thread group stops because of an uncaught exception.

The following are accessor methods:

- **activeCount**() returns an estimate of the number of active threads in this thread group.

- **activeGroupCount**() returns an estimate of the number of active thread groups in this thread group.

- **checkAccess**() determines if the currently running thread has permission to modify this thread group.

- **enumerate**(Thread[] list) copies into the specified array every active thread in this thread group and its subgroups. Returns the number (int) of threads copied.

- **enumerate**(Thread[] list, boolean recurse) copies into the specified array every active thread in this thread group and its subgroups (if the specified flag is true). Returns the number (int) of threads copied.

- **enumerate**(ThreadGroup[] list) copies into the specified array every active subgroup in this thread group and its subgroups. Returns the number (int) of threads copied.

- **enumerate**(ThreadGroup[] list, boolean recurse) copies into the specified array every active subgroup in this thread group and its subgroups (if the specified flag is true). Returns the number (int) of threads copied.

- **isDaemon**() returns true (boolean) if this thread group is a daemon thread group.

- **setDaemaon**(boolean on) marks this thread group as a daemon thread group if the specified flag is true.

- **isDestroyed**() returns true (boolean) if this thread group has been destroyed.

- **getName**() returns the name (**String**) of this thread group.

- **getParent**() returns the parent (**ThreadGroup**) of this thread group.

- **parentOf**(ThreadGroup g) returns true (boolean) if this thread group is the specified thread group or one of its ancestor thread groups.

- **getMaxPriority**() returns the maximum priority (int) of this thread group.

- **setMaxPriority**(int pri) sets the maximum priority of this thread group.

- **list**() prints information about this thread group.

- **toString**() returns a **String** representing this thread group.

EventListener Interface

The **EventListener** interface is a tagging interface that all event listeners must extend.

EventObject Class

The **EventObject** class implements the **Serializable** interface. It represents the event generated by an event source and passed to an event listener.

Constructors

- **EventObject**(Object source) constructs a new event object with the specified source.

Fields

- **source** (Object) identifies the source of this event.

Methods

- **getSource**() returns the source of this event.

- **toString**() returns a **String** representing this event.

CONCLUSION

We are now done with our second piece of preparation work. In this chapter, we have reviewed some salient features of Java as the universal data access platform: Java data types, the Java platform, and the Java API. We have also done a little Java tasting: going over the Java execution model, Java reflection, Java threads, Java events, and Java archive. With these and with what we are going to cover in the rest of this book, you should be quite ready to explore Java data access, at least from the Java perspective. (We still have some preparation work on database systems that we need to do in the next two chapters.)

Note that we did not and will not discuss Java GUI (AWT and JFC) because of time and space limitations. We assume you already know AWT and JFC or you are willing to learn about them on your own when needed. In some of the programming examples throughout this book, we will use them when necessary.

Chapter 4

Relational
Databases
and SQL

concepts

We will continue our preparation work in the next two chapters, but we will switch our focus to the server, to where the data is. First, we will take a look at databases, where data is stored, and see how it can be structured. We will then look at database languages and find out how data can be defined, manipulated, and controlled in a database. In this chapter, we will go over the relational databases, which are the most popular type of databases in existence, and SQL, the *lingua franca* for data access. In the next chapter, we will go over the object-oriented databases, which are an emerging technology and have the advantage of providing seamless data access from some object-oriented languages, and ODMG 2.0, their standard.

We will use the **ArcWorld** sample database for illustration throughout this book, starting with this chapter. **ArcWorld** is a database (a virtual world) containing architectural treasures found across the three continents of North America, Europe, and Asia, specifically in the three magnificent cities of Washington, Paris, and Beijing. As an extra benefit of exploring the mystical world of Java and Web data access, you will have a chance to (virtually) visit some of the most famous buildings along the way. We will give a full description of **ArcWorld** in Chapter 6, "The ArcWorld Sample Database."

THE RELATIONAL DATA MODEL

The fact that relational databases have become so popular has a lot to do with the *relational data model*. (This model is the basis from which relational databases are architected and designed.) First, the relational data model is a simple, easy to understand data model. *Tables*, *columns*, and *rows* are concepts easy for people to grasp. Second, it provides a high degree of *data independence*. The tabular format is what the users see. The underlying data organization can be quite different and can be optimized for data access. Third, it has a *theoretical foundation* in set theory and first-order logic. This helps ensure that when new features are added, the relational data model remains coherent.

Relations

The basic constructs in the relational data model are *relations*, or *tables*. A relation is a set of elements called *tuples*, or *rows*. The number of tuples in a relation (or the number of rows in a table) is the *cardinality* of the relation.

The *attributes* of a relation corresponds to the *columns* of a table. These are what the relation is about: a relation relates its attributes together. The *degree* of a relation refers to the number of attributes in the relation (or the number of columns in a table).

As an example, let us look at the **Building** table in Table 4-1, which is extracted from the **ArcWorld** database. This table has four columns (a degree of 4): **name, type, city**, and **yearBuilt**. It has four rows (a cardinality of 4) with information on the Lincoln Memorial, the National Gallery, The Capitol, and the Washington Monument, four famous buildings in Washington.

Table 4-1. The Building Table.

name	type	city	yearBuilt
Lincoln Memorial	Memorial	Washington	1922
National Gallery	Museum	Washington	1941
The Capitol	Government	Washington	1793
Washington Monument	Monument	Washington	1884

Domains

The *domains* of a relation are the sets of values from which attributes draw their values to form tuples of the relation (or from which columns draw their values to form rows of the table). As examples, in Table 4-1, the domain for the **type** column is all types of buildings that we consider to be architectural treasures in **ArcWorld**. The domain for the **city** column is Washington, Paris, and Beijing, because these are the three cities we include in **ArcWorld**.

Domains are not fully supported by most commercial relational database products. Instead, they support a weaker form of *basic data types* (such as integer) together with *constraints* (such as > −300) to restrict the set of data values permitted in a column.

Normalization

Tables in relational databases are simple; they are of *first normal form*. Each *field* (a field is a single entry in a column, basically an intersection of a column and a row in a table) must be a single value taken from the domain on which that column is defined. Values from multiple domains cannot appear in a single field, and multiple values cannot appear in the same domain.

There are other normal forms, each with increasing restrictions. For example, for *second normal form* tables, any column must be dependent on the entire key; no partial key dependencies are allowed. For *third normal form* tables, no column may be dependent on any column that is not part of the key; no non-key dependencies are allowed. We will discuss keys later.

Integrity Constraints

Earlier, we mentioned the use of constraints to restrict the set of data values permitted in a column. This constraint on data values ensures what is called *domain integrity*. As an example, in Table 4-1, the **yearBuilt** column has a constraint of > -300 to go with the data type of integer, because the most famous buildings in Washington, Paris, and Beijing are known to be built after 300 b.c.

There are two other major uses of constraints: to ensure *entity integrity* and *referential integrity*, which we will discuss next.

Entity Integrity

The relational data model is *value-based*; that is, each row of a table is represented by and only by its column values. Therefore, to be uniquely identifiable, each row must be distinguishable from every other row by one or more of its column values. The corresponding column or columns form the *key* of the table. There may be more than one key in the table. In this case, one of the keys is selected as the *primary key* of the table. Values of the primary key are then used to distinguish one row from the other. For example, in Table 4-1, the **name** column is the primary key of the **Building** table, and every building is uniquely identifiable by its name. (Please be aware that for most commercial relational database products, the use of keys is a user option. Therefore, redundant rows can be introduced in tables without keys. Such tables are *multisets* and not sets; strictly speaking they are not part of the relational data model.)

To deal with missing information, relational databases generally allow users to specify the use of *default values* or *null* (which indicates unknown or inapplicability) for column values. However, they are not permitted in any part of a primary key. This constraint ensures what is called *entity integrity*. Without such a constraint, the primary keys of two rows that involve default values or null may be indistinguishable from each other. We don't want this to happen, because neither of the rows will be uniquely identifiable.

Referential Integrity

The relational data model is value based, so it doesn't provide a direct mechanism for a row to reference (or link to) another row, whether they belong to the same table or not. Many times when modeling the real world, it is necessary to link one row to another. The relational data model provides an indirect mechanism for linking rows together through the use of *foreign keys*. A foreign key references a previously defined primary key and is defined by using the same domain(s).

As an example, let us first look at the **City** table in Table 4-2, which is also extracted from the **ArcWorld** database. The table has two columns: **name** and **country**. It has three rows with information on Beijing, Paris, and Washington, the three cities in **ArcWorld**. The **name** column is the primary key of this table because it uniquely identifies each city. (While this may not be so in the real world—obviously, there are cities with the same name—it is true in **ArcWorld**.)

If we now go back and look at the **Building** table in Table 4-1, it should be apparent that in the **city** column, there is actually a foreign key because it refers to the primary key of the **City** table.

Table 4-2. The City Table.

name	country
Beijing	China
Paris	France
Washington	USA

To ensure that there are no dangling references (for example, foreign keys referencing primary keys that do not exist), the value entered for a foreign key must be one already existing as a primary key somewhere else or null. This constraint ensures what is called *referential integrity.* Now what happens if the primary key gets updated or its row gets deleted? The foreign key will be dangling. To prevent this from happening, additional constraints are required. The *update rule* constraint disallows such updates from happening. The *delete rule* constraint lets a user choose among the following: disallowing deletion from happening, setting the foreign key to null, or deleting the row containing the foreign key (which then may have a cascading effect on other dependent rows by causing one deletion after another).

Relational Algebra

The relational data model has three parts. The first part deals with data structure (relational data objects such as relations and domains). The second part deals with data integrity, or relational integrity constraints. We have discussed these two so far. The third and final part of the relational data model deals with data manipulation, or relational data operations. This part is called *relational algebra* and, as the name implies, is more mathematical than the other two parts.

The relational algebra consists of eight operations in two groups:

1. The relation operations called *restriction, projection, join,* and *division*

2. The set operations called *union, intersection, difference,* and (Cartesian) *product*

The output from each of these operations when applied to a relation (or table) is another relation (or table). This is the so-called *relational closure* property. It is an important property; it ensures that an output from one operation can become input for another operation. This allows us to write nested expressions, and it has important consequences for relational database implementations.

The following are brief definitions of these operations, which are illustrated in Figure 4-1. Later, when we discuss SQL, you will see many of these operations in action, either explicitly or implicitly, within SQL statements.

- **Restriction** extracts entire rows from a table. It can extract just those rows that satisfy a certain condition or all rows in the table.

- **Projection** extracts entire columns from a table. It can extract certain specified columns or all columns in the table.

- **Product** returns a table from two tables. Its rows are formed by taking each row from the first (outer) table and concatenating it with every row of the second (inner) table.

- **Join (or Natural Join)** returns a table from two tables. The two tables must contain the so-called "join columns" that share a common domain. Its rows are formed by taking rows from the first (outer) table and concatenating it with rows of the second (inner) table—if and only if—a certain condition holds for the values of the join columns. The join column appears only once in the resulting table.

- **Division** returns a unary table from two tables, one binary and one unary. One of the columns of the binary table, the so-called "common column," must share a common domain with the column of the unary table. Its rows are formed by taking all values from the other column that match (in the common column) all values in the unary table.

- **Union** returns a table from two tables. The two tables must have the same number of columns that further must be defined on the same domains. Its rows consist of all rows appearing in either or both of the two tables.

- **Intersection** returns a table from two tables. The two tables must have the same number of columns that further must be defined on the same domains. Its rows consist of all rows appearing in both of the two tables.

- **Difference** returns a table from two tables. The two tables must have the same number of columns that further must be defined on the same domains. Its rows consist of all rows appearing in the first, and not the second, table.

SQL

Now that we have a good understanding of the relational data model, from which relational databases are architected and designed, we will look at relational database

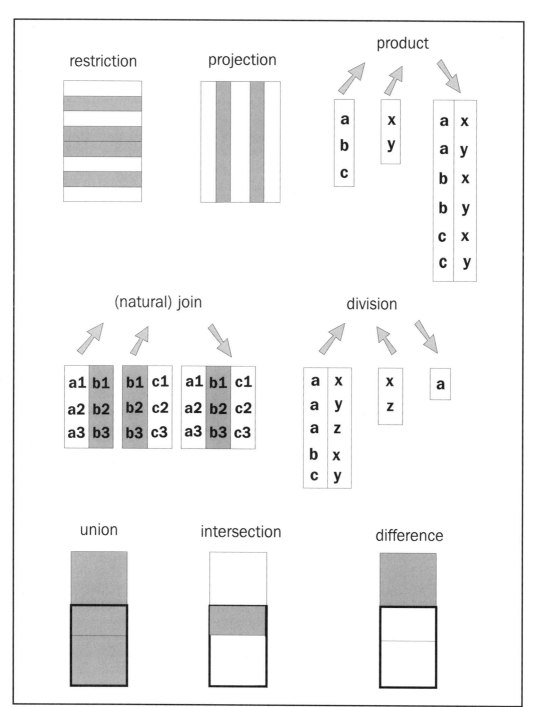

Figure 4-1. Relational Algebra Operations.

languages and see how data can be defined, manipulated, and controlled in a relational database. Fortunately for us, all relational database languages are based on *SQL*, and they differ from each other mainly in features and minor details. (These differences exist because SQL has been undergoing standardization by ANSI and ISO and because all major relational database vendors are supportive of the SQL standardization effort.) Therefore, we need to focus on only a single language: SQL.

The SQL standard has gone through a number of revisions since 1986, when it was first published: SQL-86, SQL-89, and SQL-92. *SQL-92*, particularly *Entry Level*, is now being provided by most relational database products, and we will discuss this next. (It is not surprising, therefore, that both the JDBC Specification and the OMG Object Query Service Specification require compliance to SQL-92 Entry Level.) The current draft being worked on by ANSI and ISO is called *SQL3*, which we will discuss when we talk about future trends in Chapter 22, "Conclusion: Emerging Technologies."

SQL Data Types

SQL is a full database programming language; it covers data definition, data manipulation (including query), and data control. Before we go over these, let us first look at SQL data types. These are extremely important because they define what types of data can be stored and manipulated in relational databases.

Table 4-3 lists the SQL data types that are considered in the JDBC Specification. (Because our major interest is Java data access and because both JDBC and SQLJ deal with SQL data types considered in the JDBC specification, we restrict our consideration to these as well. They differ from the full SQL data types only in minor ways.) It also indicates where any of the data types is not applicable or is provided differently in **DB2 UDB** and **SQL Server**, the two relational database products we use for developing our programming examples.

SQL data types consist of the following major categories: integers (TINYINT, SMALLINT, INTEGER, and BIGINT), floating-point numbers (REAL, FLOAT, and DOUBLE), fixed-point numbers (DECIMAL and NUMERIC), character strings (CHAR, VARCHAR, and LONGVARCHAR), boolean (BIT), binary strings (BINARY, VARBINARY, and LONGVARBINARY), and date/time data (DATE, TIME, and TIMES-TAMP).

Table 4-3. SQL Data Types.

SQL Data Type	Notes	DB2 UDB	SQL Server
TINYINT	8-bit	n/a	
SMALLINT	16-bit		
INTEGER	32-bit		
BIGINT	64-bit	n/a	n/a
REAL	32-bit, 7 digits of mantissa	n/a	
FLOAT	64-bit, 15 digits of mantissa		FLOAT(N)
DOUBLE	64-bit, 15 digits of mantissa		n/a
DECIMAL(P,S)			
NUMERIC(P,S)			
CHAR(N)	N <= 254 (typical)		
VARCHAR(N)	N <= 32K (typical)		
LONGVARCHAR	Megabytes	(also) CLOB, DBCLOB	n/a
BIT		n/a	
BINARY(N)		n/a	
VARBINARY(N)	N <= 32K (typical)	n/a	
LONGVARBINARY	Megabytes	BLOB	n/a
DATE	year, month, day		DATETIME
TIME	hour, minute, second		DATETIME
TIMESTAMP	year, month, day, hour, minute, second, microsecond		

Data Definition Statements

The *data definition statements* of SQL allow you to create, alter, and destroy database objects such as tables, views, and indexes. *Tables*, as can be expected, contain all data stored in a database. *Views* are "virtual" tables that are derived from the real tables. *Indexes* help the *relational database system* (or the *relational database management system)* access the rows in a table quickly, provide an ordering on the rows, and optionally enforce the uniqueness of the rows.

The relational database system automatically maintains a set of tables, called *catalog tables* or *system tables*, which contain schema definitions of all objects in the database. Data definition statements cause automatic updates to these tables.

CREATE TABLE Statement

Tables are the basic objects used to store data in a database. Therefore, the CREATE TABLE statement is the most fundamental data definition statement in SQL. It allows you to create a table with a specified name and the names and data types of its columns. Optionally, you can specify that one or more columns constitute the primary key, certain columns do not accept null values, and the constraints on data values for specific columns.

As an example, the following is a CREATE TABLE statement that might be used to create the **Building** table in the **ArcWorld** sample database. (Please note that names of database objects and keywords in SQL are case insensitive. By convention, we will use *mixed-case letters* to represent names of database objects in SQL statements. We will use *uppercase letters* to represent SQL keywords and data types.)

```
CREATE TABLE Building
  (name CHAR(32) NOT NULL PRIMARY KEY,
   type CHAR(32),
   city CHAR(32),
   yearBuilt INTEGER CHECK (yearBuilt > -300),
   FOREIGN KEY (city) REFERENCES City)
```

You can see that the **name** column is a PRIMARY KEY and is NOT NULL. The **city** column is a FOREIGN KEY. (For this statement to work, the **City** table, which the foreign key column REFERENCES, must have been created previously, using a CREATE TABLE statement.) The **yearBuilt** column has a CHECK constraint, as discussed earlier.

ALTER TABLE Statement

Once a table is created, you can use the ALTER TABLE statement to add columns or constraints and to delete keys and constraints. When a new column is added, any existing rows in the table receive a default value for the column.

The following is an example of using the ALTER TABLE statement to add an **address** column to the **Building** table:

```
ALTER TABLE Building
   ADD COLUMN address VARCHAR(255)
```

CREATE VIEW Statement

One of the most useful features of relational databases are *views*, which is a feature object-oriented databases have failed to provide so far. Views are "virtual" tables that are derived in some way from the real tables. You can use views to present a user with a single logical view of information that is spread across multiple tables. You can also use them as a security mechanism to hide sensitive information from certain users.

For example, in the case of **ArcWorld**, let's assume some users are interested only in museums and not other types of buildings. To serve these users in a more friendly and efficient manner, we might define a **Museum** view using the following CREATE VIEW statement:

```
CREATE VIEW Museum AS
   SELECT *
   FROM Building
   WHERE type = 'Museum'
```

You can see that a view is exactly a query, but defined with a name. (We are a little out of order here by talking about queries and using the SELECT statement without first defining it. We will correct the situation shortly, when we discuss data manipulation statements.) Optionally, you can name its columns by listing the names after the view name. A view can be derived from real tables, from other views, or from some combination of real tables and views.

CREATE INDEX Statement

Indexes are aids that help the relational database system access the rows in a table quickly, provide an ordering on the rows, and optionally enforce the uniqueness of the rows. An index can be created using one or more columns of the table. The relational database system automatically creates a unique index for each primary key.

For instance, we might want to create an index on the **Building** table using the **type** column because users tend to ask about buildings of a certain type. The CREATE INDEX statement would look like:

```
CREATE INDEX t1 ON Building(type DESC)
```

The keyword DESC denotes descending order. (The keyword ASC denotes ascending order, which is the default.)

DROP Statements

You can use a DROP statement to delete from the database any database objects that are created using a CREATE statement. (You may recall that you can use the ALTER TABLE statement to drop keys and constraints from a table.) When you drop an object such as a table, view, or index, it may affect other objects which are dependent on the object being dropped. In this case, the relational database system may repair the dependent object, drop the dependent object (for example, dropping a table automatically drops all views and indexes defined on that table), or disallow you from dropping the object.

The following are examples of DROP statements:

```
DROP TABLE Building
DROP VIEW Museum
DROP INDEX t1
```

Data Manipulation Statements

The *data manipulation statements* of SQL allow you to select (or retrieve) data stored in one or more tables, and to insert, update, or delete rows from a table. SQL is *set-oriented*; it always references tables, and it always produces results in tabular form. SQL is also *relational complete*; it expresses the equivalent of the basic set of relational algebra operations without using iterative operations. This will become clear when we finish discussing data manipulation statements.

INSERT Statement

Once a table is created, the INSERT statement lets you add data (or rows) to the table. The basic form of the INSERT statement is:

```
INSERT INTO table
  [(column 1, column 2, ...)]
  VALUES (value 1, value 2, ...) [, (value 1, value 2, ...) ...]
```

If you insert values for all columns then you can omit the column names. Otherwise, column names must be included, and values for columns not included are assigned the default values (if specified during the table creation) or a null value. (Please note that primary keys cannot have default values and cannot be null, so their values must be provided.)

The following is an example of the INSERT statement that you might use to populate the **Building** table:

```
INSERT INTO Building
  (name, type, city)
  VALUES ('Lincoln Memorial', 'Memorial', 'Washington'),
         ('National Gallery', 'Museum', 'Washington'),
         ('The Capitol', 'Government', 'Washington'),
         ('Washing Monument', 'Monument', 'Washington')
```

The **city** column is a foreign key. As a result, for the previous statement to work, you must first populate the **City** table with something like this (remember referential integrity?):

```
INSERT INTO City
  (name, country)
  VALUES ('Washington', 'USA')
```

SELECT Statement

The SELECT statement is the most frequently used data manipulation statement in SQL, and the most frequently used SQL statement of all. It is the richest in terms of options and variations, it can be the most complicated to understand, and it is likely to be the most costly to execute. Therefore, people tend to associate SQL with the SELECT statement and relational database implementers spend a lot of time optimizing the execution of the SELECT statement.

The basic form of the SELECT statement is:

```
SELECT [DISTINCT] columns
  FROM tables
  [WHERE predicates]
  [ORDER BY columns]
```

Earlier, we used the following example when creating the **Museum** view (where the wild card * is used to indicate all columns):

```
SELECT *
  FROM Building
  WHERE type = 'Museum'
```

If you want to retrieve all Memorial buildings, list their name, city, and country, and order them by cities, you can do this by using the following SELECT statement:

```
SELECT Building.name, city, country
  FROM Building, City
  WHERE type = 'Memorial' AND city = City.name
  ORDER BY city
```

UPDATE Statement

To update data in a table, you can use the UPDATE statement, which has the following basic form:

```
UPDATE table
  SET column = value [, column = value ...]
  [WHERE predicates]
```

(When you do so, please remember that the update rule is in effect.)

For example, you might use the following UPDATE statement to add values to the **yearBuilt** column in the **Building** table:

```
UPDATE Building
  SET yearbuilt = 1922
  WHERE name = 'Lincoln Memorial'
```

DELETE Statement

Normally, you don't need to remove data (or delete rows) from a table. However, in case you need to do so, you can use the DELETE statement, which has the following basic form:

```
DELETE FROM table
  [WHERE predicates]
```

(When you do so, please remember that the delete rule is in effect.)

The following example shows how you can easily delete The Capitol (from the virtual **ArcWorld** anyway) if you get tired of all the politics going on there:

```
DELETE FROM Building
  WHERE name = 'The Capitol'
```

More on Views

Now that we have finished discussing data manipulation statements, let's go back and look at views again and tie up a couple of loose ends. You may recall that a view is exactly a query, but defined with a name. As such, some views are *read-only*, while others are *updatable*. Read-only views can only be queried in a SELECT statement, but updatable views can also be involved in INSERT, UPDATE, and DELETE statements. In general, a view is updatable if each of its rows can be uniquely mapped to a row in a real table. This uniqueness makes it possible for the relational database system to map insertion, update, and deletion operations on the view to the same operation on the underlying table.

If a view is updatable, you can update its existing rows or insert new rows. When you do so, you may want to ensure that the affected rows remain or are valid rows of the view. This can be done by creating the view with the CHECK OPTION. If a view is created as such, each row that is updated or inserted using the view must satisfy the view definition.

Data Control Statements

Most databases are used to maintain shared data. When data is shared among multiple users, *data security* and *data consistency* must be ensured. Relational database systems provide a set of very comprehensive facilities and mechanisms to control data security and to ensure data consistency. These are reflected in the SQL *data control statements*. (By the way, this is another major area where object-oriented database systems have not been able to compete so far.)

Privileges

Data security can be controlled by granting or revoking *privileges* (or access rights) on various database objects to the user. The *GRANT statement* is used to grant privileges, which has the following basic form:

```
GRANT privileges
   ON objects
   TO users
```

Any of the privileges that have been granted can later be revoked using the *REVOKE statement*:

```
REVOKE privileges
   ON objects
   FROM users
```

Some of the typical privileges that can be granted or revoked on tables include:

- **select**—rows can be retrieved
- **insert**—rows can be inserted
- **update**—rows can be updated
- **delete**—rows can be deleted

Transaction

When more than one user can have access to the same data, they potentially can step on each other's toes. For example, this can happen if one user is updating rows in a table when another is simultaneously retrieving the same rows from the same table. To ensure *data consistency*, which means that each user sees a consistent state of data, the concept of a *transaction* is used.

A *transaction*, or the so-called *ACID transaction*, has the following properties:

- **Atomicity**—either all operations within a transaction are performed or none takes place
- **Consistency**—each transaction's work represents a consistent transformation of the database's state
- **Isolation**—concurrent transactions do not affect each other
- **Durability**—all updates of a transaction are preserved, even in case of system or media failures

Among these, isolation can severely limit concurrency. For example, to ensure total isolation, two transactions may have to be executed serially. SQL defines four levels of isolation, from the least severe to the most severe:

- **Read Uncommitted**—dirty read, nonrepeatable read, and phantom are possible
- **Read Committed**—nonrepeatable read and phantom are possible
- **Repeatable Read**—phantom is possible
- **Serializable**—none of the three phenomena are possible

The *dirty read* phenomenon means that a transaction can see changes made by other concurrent transactions, even before they commit. The *nonrepeatable read* phenomenon means that a transaction may read a row once and, if it tries to read the same row again, the row might have been changed or deleted by another concurrent transaction. Finally, the *phantom* phenomenon means that a set of rows a transaction reads once might be a different set of rows if it tries to read them again.

You can use the COMMIT and ROLLBACK statements to commit and rollback a transaction, respectively:

```
COMMIT
ROLLBACK
```

Once you commit a transaction, all updates of the transaction become permanent. If you rollback a transaction, all updates of the transaction are discarded.

Connection

Before you can execute any of the SQL statements we have discussed (and almost all other SQL statements that we don't have time to discuss), you must first establish a *connection* to the database using the CONNECT statement, which has the following basic form:

```
CONNECT TO database
```

Later, when you are done with executing the SQL statements that are of interest to you and when you have committed or rolled back your work, you can terminate the connection using the DISCONNECT statement:

```
DISCONNECT database
```

CONCLUSION

So we are done with another piece of preparation work. Hopefully you now have a good grasp of the basics of relational databases and SQL. From here on, everything we covered in this chapter will be used and taken for granted. Many of the examples we used in this chapter are taken from the definitions of the **ArcWorld** sample database. You will find the complete definitions in Chapter 6, "The ArcWorld Sample Database."

In case you want to know the exact syntax and semantics of various SQL statements, please consult the books by Melton and Simon (SQL-92) and by Chamberlin (DB2). If you are looking for in-depth discussions of the relational data model and related topics, please read the book by Date. These references can be found at the end of this book.

The technology of relational databases is evolving at a very fast pace. A major trend is its evolution toward becoming the so-called *object-relational database*. This comes about for three main reasons: the need to provide *non-traditional data types* (particularly multimedia data types), the need to allow users to define *new data types* (to represent business objects, for example), and, not the least, the challenge posed by *object-oriented databases*. We will introduce object-oriented databases in the next chapter, and we will discuss object-relational databases and SQL3 in Chapter 22, "Conclusion: Emerging Technologies."

Chapter 5

Object-Oriented Databases and ODMG 2.0

concepts

Object-oriented database systems (or *object-oriented database management systems*) were developed to add *persistence* to objects that are used in an object-oriented programming language (OOPL) such as Smalltalk or C++. Consequently, they are frequently referred to as *persistent programming language systems*. Their focus is on the transparent integration of database capability with the programming language (see Figure 5-1). Specifically, they:

■ Extend the programming language with *transparently persistent data, associative queries, concurrency control, transactions,* and other database capabilities

■ Make *database objects* appear as programming language objects

As discussed in the previous chapter, relational database systems all have a common relational data model, SQL, as a standard database language, and similar database server architectures. Therefore, it is common to find relational database applications that are portable across various relational database products, particularly if they conform to SQL-92 Entry Level. The situation is very different for object-oriented database systems. It is difficult, if not impossible, to find any object-oriented database application that is portable across more than one object-oriented database product. This is due to the following major design and architectural differences among object-oriented database systems:

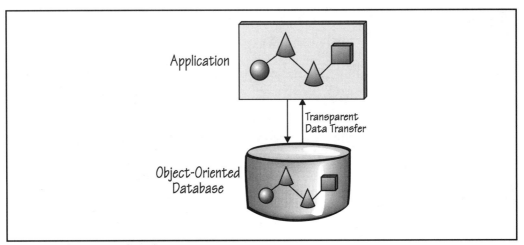

Application

Transparent
Data Transfer

Object-Oriented
Database

Figure 5-1. Object-Oriented Databases

■ ***Persistent class vs. persistent instance.*** With the *persistent class* approach, all instances of a persistent class are, by definition, persistent, and all instances of a non-persistent class are, again by definition, transient. With the *persistent instance* approach, any instance of any class can be declared and made persistent. (Therefore, persistence is orthogonal to or independent of class in this case.) This difference affects the programming model.

■ ***Programming language differences.*** *Smalltalk* is different from *C++*, which is different from *Java*, which is different from *OO Cobol*, and so on. In fact, in the case of C++, a complier from one vendor is different from another. These language differences make it very difficult to port an application from one language to another.

■ ***Page server vs. object server.*** In the *page server* approach, the server is "dumb"; all intelligence resides on the client, and the client is "fat." In the *object server* approach, the server is "smart" and the client can be "thin." This difference affects, among other things, whether you can execute methods only on the client or also on the server.

ODMG 2.0

The *ODMG (Object Database Management Group)* was formed by major object-oriented database vendors in 1991 to develop and promote standards for object-oriented databases. The primary goal of the group is to alleviate the previously mentioned problem and to present a set of standards, thus allowing an object-oriented database customer to write applications that ensure:

- **Portability** of data schema, query language, and programming language bindings

- **Interoperability** between object-oriented database products

The current version of the standard is *ODMG 2.0*. It consists of the following major components:

- **Object Model.** This defines the common data model, which is based on the OMG Object Model. It includes a new meta-object model.

- **Object Specification Languages.** This consists of the *Object Definition Language (ODL)*, which is a database schema definition language and is based on the OMG Interface Definition Language (IDL), and the *Object Interchange Format (OIF)*, which can be used to exchange objects between databases.

- **Object Query Language (OQL).** This is a declarative language for querying and updating database objects; it is based on SQL.

- **OOPL Language Binding.** These include *Java*, *C++*, and *Smalltalk* language bindings. Each language binding consists of an ODL, an *OML (object manipulation language)*, and an OQL binding. Unlike SQL, ODMG does not define a common OML. Instead, the data manipulation languages are tailored to specific programming languages.

A typical use of an object-oriented database system that conforms to ODMG 2.0 is shown in Figure 5-2. The programmer writes declarations for the application schema in ODL or its language binding (labeled OOPL ODL), plus a source program for the application in a programming language (labeled OOPL). The declarations and application source are then compiled and linked with the system runtime (labeled OODBS Runtime) to produce the running application, which accesses the database at run time.

In the following sections we will discuss in more detail the Object Model, ODL, and OQL. (We will discuss the Object Model and ODL together and use ODL for illustration of the Object Model.) We will discuss the Java binding in Chapter 9, "Java Binding for OODB," as part of our discussion on Java data access. We will not discuss the meta-object model, OIF, or other language bindings further. If you are interested in any of these, please refer to the book by Cattell, et al. listed in the back of this book.

THE OBJECT MODEL AND ODL

The Object Model defines the constructs that are supported by an object-oriented database system. Its essential features include the following:

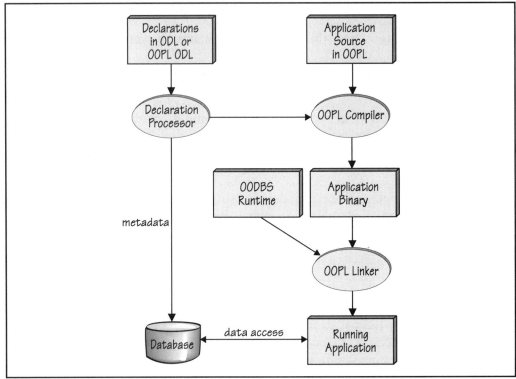

Figure 5-2. Using an Object-Oriented Database System.

■ The basic modeling constructs are *objects* and *literals*. Each object has a unique identifier.

■ Objects and literals are categorized by their *types*. All instances of a given type have a common range of *state* and a common *behavior*.

■ The *state* of an object is characterized by the values of its *properties*. These properties can be *attributes* of the object or *relationships* between the object and other objects. The state of a literal is characterized by its value.

■ The *behavior* of an object is defined by the set of *operations* that can be executed on the object. A literal has no behavior.

■ A *database* stores and manages objects, allowing them to be shared by multiple users and applications. A database is defined by a *schema*, specified in ODL.

Types

A *type* has a specification and one or more implementations. The *specification* defines the external characteristics of the type. These include the properties that can be accessed, the operations that can be invoked on its instances, and any exceptions that can be raised by its operations. The *implementation* defines the internal aspects of the type: the implementation of its properties, operations, and other internal details (such as the creation and initialization of its instances).

There are three kinds of type specifications: interface definition, class definition, and literal type definition; the first two are for *object types*. An *interface definition* defines only the abstract behavior of an object type. A *class definition* defines the abstract behavior and abstract state of an object type. A *literal type definition*, on the other hand, defines the abstract state of a *literal type*. Interfaces are types that cannot be directly instantiated. Classes and literal types, on the other hand, are types that are directly instantiable. The following are examples of each:

```
interface Employee {...};

class Person {...};

struct Complex {float real; float imaginary};
```

Please note that the Object Model supports the following built-in literal types:

- *long, short, unsigned long, unsigned short*
- *float, double*
- *char, string* (fixed or variable length)
- *boolean*
- *octet*
- *enum*
- *array, sequence*
- *struct, union*

The implementation of a specification is to be carried out using a programming language and the corresponding *language binding*. An implementation of an object type consists of a *representation* and a set of *methods*. The representation consists of data structures derived from the type's properties through language binding. For each property, an *instance variable* is defined. The methods consist of ones derived from the type's operations. For each operation, a method is defined. There can also be methods that have no direct counterpart to the operations. Each language binding also defines a *mapping for literal types*. We will discuss Java language binding in Chapter 9, "Java Binding for OODB," and examples of Java implementation in Chapter 10, "Sample Data Access Applications."

Inheritance

There are two kinds of inheritance supported for object types in the Object Model: *inheritance of behavior* (the *is-a* relationship) and *inheritance of behavior and state* (the *EXTENDS* relationship). The is-a relationship is a multiple inheritance relationship between interfaces or between classes and interfaces. The following are examples:

```
interface Professor : Employee {...};

interface Associate_Professor : Professor {...};

class Salaried_Employee : Employee {...};
```

The EXTENDS relationship is a single inheritance relationship between two classes. The following is an example:

```
class Church extends Building {...};
```

Extents and Keys

The *extent* of an object type is the set of all instances of that type within a particular database. Unlike relational database systems that automatically maintain an extent for every defined table, a user can specify whether the object-oriented database system should automatically maintain the extent of each type. The following are examples of such specifications:

```
class Building (extent buildings) {...}

class Church (extent churches) {...}
```

The *key* of an object type is the property or set of properties whose value or values can uniquely identify the individual instances of that type. A *simple key* consists of a single property; a *compound key* consists of a set of properties. The scope of uniqueness is the extent of the type; therefore, a type must have an extent to have a key. The following is an example of a type with a simple key:

```
class Building
(    extent buildings
     key name)
{
     attribute string<32> name;
     ...
};
```

This definition includes an attribute, which we will discuss next.

Properties

Two kinds of properties are supported for object types in the Object Model: *attribute* and *relationship*. An attribute is a characteristic of a single type. A relationship is defined between two types.

Attributes

The attribute definitions specify the *abstract state* of a type. For example, the **Building** class in the **ArcWorld** database (see Chapter 6, "The ArcWorld Sample Database") contains the following attribute definitions:

```
class Building
(   extent buildings
    key name)
{
    attribute string<32>      name;
    attribute string<32>      type;
    attribute string<256>     address;
    attribute City            city;
    attribute long            yearBuilt;
    attribute Architect       architect;
    attribute string<32>      style;
    attribute sequence<char>  description;
    attribute sequence<octec> picture;
};
```

A particular instance of **Building** would have a specific value for each of the attributes. An attribute's value is either a literal or an object identifier. (In the previous example, all attributes except *city* and *architect* have values that are literals. **City** and **Architect** are classes defined in the ArcWorld database. We will discuss object identifiers and literals later.)

Relationships

The Object Model supports only *binary relationships*, which are relationships between two object types. A relationship is defined implicitly by declaration of *traversal paths* that provide logical connections between the objects participating in the relationship. Traversal paths are declared in pairs, one for each direction of traversal. Here is an example:

```
interface Professor {
    ...
    relationship set<Course> teaches
      inverse Course::is_taught_by;
    ...
};

interface Course {
    ...
    relationship Professor is_taught_by
      inverse Professor::teaches;
    ...
};
```

The object-oriented database system is responsible for maintaining *referential integrity* of relationships. This means that if an object that participates in a relationship is deleted, then any transversal path to that object must also be deleted. For example, if a particular **Course** instance is deleted, then both its reference to a **Professor** instance in the *is_taught_by* traversal path and the reference in the corresponding **Professor** instance's *teaches* traversal path to the **Course** instance are deleted.

Operations

Behavior is specified in the Object Model as a set of *operation signatures*. Each signature defines the name of the operation, the name and type of each of its *arguments* (which can be *in*, *out*, or *inout*), the type of the return value, and the names of any *exceptions* that the operation can raise. *Operation dispatching* is based on the *classical object model*. An example of an operation definition is shown in the following:

```
class Person {
    attribute Date birth_date;
    ...

    short age();
    ...
};
```

In this example, **Date** is a built-in structured object type.

The Object Model supports dynamically nested exception handlers. Exceptions are themselves objects. A root type *Exception* is provided. We will see examples of exception definitions in the following sections.

Objects

Objects are instances of classes and are created by invoking creation operations on *factory objects* that implement *factory interfaces* such as:

```
interface ObjectFactory {
    Object new()
};
```

All objects implement the following interface, which is implicitly inherited by all classes:

```
interface Object {
    enum Lock_Type(read, write, upgrade);
    exception LockNotGranted{};

    boolean same_as(in Object obj);
    Object copy();
    void delete();

    void lock(in Lock_Type mode) raises(LockNotGranted);
    boolean try_lock(in Lock_Type mode);
};
```

Objects, once created, are explicitly deleted from the database using the *delete()* operation.

The lifetime of an object is specified at the time the object is created. Two lifetimes are supported: *transient* or *persistent*. An object whose lifetime is *transient* is allocated memory that is managed by the programming language runtime system. An object whose lifetime is *persistent* is allocated memory and storage managed by the object-oriented database system. (Persistent objects are also referred to as *database objects*.) An important aspect of object lifetimes is that they are independent of types. That is, *object persistence is orthogonal to or independent of object type*.

Object Identifiers and Names

All database objects have *identifiers* that are unique within a database and which remain the same throughout each object's entire lifetime. Object identifiers are generated by the object-oriented database system and are not visible to a user. Literals do not have identifiers.

A database object may be given one or more *names* that are meaningful and visible to a user. These names are unique within a database and can be used as entry points into the database.

Therefore, there are three ways to locate an object in a database:

- If the object has a name, use the name to locate the object. The name is independent of the object's state.
- If the object has a key, use the key value to locate the object. The key depends on the object's class, and the key value is part of the object's state.
- If the object has neither a name nor a key, locate the object by navigating from an object that has a name or a key and that references the object directly or indirectly.

There actually is another way to locate an object in a database, which is to use OQL. We will discuss this later.

Atomic Objects

An atomic object type is *user-defined*. There are no built-in atomic object types provided in the Object Model.

Collection Objects

Collection objects consist of elements; each element can be an atomic object, another collection object, or a literal. However, all the elements of the collection must be of the same type. The collection types supported by the Object Model include:

- Set
- Bag
- List
- Array
- Dictionary

Each of these inherits the following **Collection** interface:

```
interface Collection {
    exception InvalidCollectionType{};
    exception ElementNotFond(any element;};

    unsigned long cardinality();
    boolean is_empty();
```

```
        boolean is_ordered();
        boolean allows_duplicates();

        boolean contains_element(in any element);
        void insert_element(in any element);
        void remove_element(in any element) raises(ElementNotFond);

        Iterator create_iterator(in boolean stable);
        BidirectionalIterator create_bidirectional_iterator(
          in boolean stable) raises(InvalidCollectionType);
    };
```

An iterator can be created to traverse a collection. There are two kinds of iterators: an **Iterator** that supports forward-only transversal on all collections, or a **BidirectionalIterator** which supports bidirectional traversal on ordered collections, as follows:

```
    interface Iterator {
        exception NoMoreElemnets{};
        exception InvalidCollectionType{};

        boolean is_stable();

        boolean at_end();
        void reset();

        void next_position() raises(NoMoreElements);

        any get_element() raises(NoMoreElements);
        void replace_element(in any element) raises(NoMoreElements);
    };

    interface BidirectionalIterator : Iterator {
        boolean at_beginning();
        void previous_position() raises(NoMoreElements);
    };
```

A stable iterator is one for which modifications made to a collection during iteration will not affect traversal. Also, when an iterator is first created, it is positioned to the first element in the iteration.

Structured Objects

The Object Model supports the following *structured object* types:

- Date
- Time
- Timestamp
- Interval

These have definitions similar to those in SQL.

Literals

The Object Model supports the following four types of literals:

- **Atomic literals**—including *long, short, unsigned long, unsigned short, float, double, boolean, octet, char, string,* and *enum.*
- **Collection literals**—including *set, bag, list, array,* and *dictionary.*
- **Structured literals**—including *date, time, timestamp, interval,* and *struct.*
- **Null literals**—for every literal type, another literal type exists, which supports a null value (for example, nullable_float).

Transactions

The Object Model supports *ACID transactions* on persistent objects, which means it guarantees *atomicity, consistency, isolation,* and *durability* (as discussed in the previous chapter) of operations on persistent objects. Transient objects are not subject to transaction semantics.

Two interfaces are defined to support transaction activity within an object-oriented database system: **TransactionFactory** and **Transaction**. The TransactionFactory interface supports the creation of transactions:

```
interface TransactionFactory {
    Transaction new();
    Transaction current();
};
```

Once a **Transaction** object is created, it can be manipulated through the following interface:

```
interface Transaction {
    exception TransactionInProgress{};
    exception TransactionNotInProgress{};

    void begin() raises(TransactionInProgress);
```

```
        void commit() raises(TransactionNotInProgress);
        void abort() raises(TransactionNotInProgress);
        void checkpoint() raises(TransactionNotInProgress);

        void join();
        void leave();

        boolean is_open();
    };
```

An explicit *begin()* operation is required to open a transaction. The *commit()* operation causes all persistent objects created or modified during a transaction to be written to the database and all locks held to be released. It further causes the transaction to complete and become closed. The *abort()* operation also causes a transaction to complete and become closed. However, the database is returned to the state it was in before the beginning of the transaction. The *checkpoint()* operation is equivalent to a *commit()* operation followed by a *begin()* operation, except that locks are not released.

If the object-oriented database system allows multiple active **Transaction** objects to exist, the *join()* and *leave()* operations allow the current thread to alternate between them.

Database Operations

An object-oriented database system may manage one or more logical databases. Each database is represented by an instance of the **Database** type, which can be created using a factory that implements the following interface:

```
    interface DatabaseFactory {
        Database new()
    };
```

Once a **Database** object is created, it can be manipulated through the following interface:

```
    interface Database {
        void open(in string database_name);
        void close();

        void bind(in any obj, in string name);
        Object unbind(in string name);
        Object lookup(in string name);
```

```
    Module schema();
};
```

The *open()* operation must be invoked before any access can be made to the database. The *close()* operation must be invoked when all access to the database has been completed. The *bind()*, *unbind()*, and *lookup()* operations allow you to associate names with objects in the database and to use the names to look up the objects. (The **Module** interface is part of the meta-object model.)

OQL

OQL provides *declarative access* to objects stored and managed by an object-oriented database system. It is based on *SQL-92* and adds the following *object-oriented extensions*:

- Object identity
- *C*omplex objects
- Path expressions
- Operation invocation
- Polymorphism and late binding

A major difference between OQL and SQL is that OQL does not provide explicit *insert()*, *update()*, and *delete()* operations, instead, it depends on such operations defined on objects for that purpose. Also, OQL is a *functional language* where operators can freely be composed, as long as the operands respect the type system.

Query

OQL allows querying denotable entities (objects or literals) starting from their names, which provide entry points to a database. Here is an example:

```
SELECT x.type
   FROM buildings x
   WHERE x.name = "Washington Monument"
```

You do not always have to use a SELECT-FROM-WHERE clause. For example:

```
buildings
```

retrieves the set of all buildings.

Depending on how it is formulated, a query may return:

- *A collection of objects.* For example:
       SELECT x FROM buildings x WHERE x.type = "Monument"
  returns a collection of **Building** objects whose type is "Monument".

- **An object.** For example:
       ELEMENT (SELECT x FROM buildings x WHERE x.name = "The Capitol")
  returns the **Building** object which is "The Capitol".

- *A collection of literals.* For example:
       SELECT x.address FROM buildings x WHERE x.type = "Monument"
  returns a collection of strings giving the addresses of buildings whose type is "Monument".

- *A literal.* For example:
       ELEMENT (SELECT x.address FROM buildings x
          WHERE x.name = "The Capitol")
  returns a string which is the address of "The Capitol".

Path Expressions

OQL lets you *navigate* from one object to another using the *dot* (.) notation. This allows you not only to go inside complex objects, but also to follow relationships. For example, assume we have the previous **Building** class and the following **City** class (also taken from the **ArcWorld** database):

```
class City
...
{
    attribute string<32>      name;
    attribute Country         country;
    attribute sequence<octet> arch_map;
};
```

If we have a building *b* and we want to know the name of the city where the building is located, we can do so using the following path expression:

```
b.city.name
```

On the other hand, if we want to know the name of the country where the building is located, we can use the following path expression:

```
b.city.country.name
```

This assumes the **Country** class is defined as:

```
class Country
...
{
    attribute string<32>     name;
    attribute sequence<octet> city_map;
};
```

The path expression, therefore, can be used to any depth as long as there is no ambiguity.

Operation Invocation

OQL also allows you to invoke an operation with or without parameters wherever the result type of the operation matches the expected type in the query. If the operation has no parameters, the notation for invoking an operation is exactly the same as that for accessing an attribute or traversing a relationship. For example, assume we have the following definition of the **Person** class:

```
class Person
(   extent persons)
{
    attribute Date birth_date;
    ...
    relationship set<Person> children
      inverse Person::parents;
    relationship set<Preson> parents
      inverse Person::children;
    ...
    short age();
    boolean lives_in(in string city);
    ...
};
```

We can now find the ages of all the oldest children of all persons who live in Paris by:

```
SELECT max(SELECT c.age FROM p.children c)
   FROM persons p
   WHERE p.lives_in("Paris")
```

OQL allows for *polymorphism* and uses the *late-binding* mechanism when invoking operations. As an example, we assume that we have the following three classes:

```
class ProjectMember
(   extend projectMembers)
{
    ...
    string activities();
    ...
};

class ProjectLeader extends ProjectMember {
    ...
    string activities();
    ...
};

class TestLeader extends ProjectMember {
    ...
    string activities();
    ...
};
```

We can use the following query to find out about the activities of all project members:

```
SELECT m.activities
   FROM projectMembers m
```

Depending on the current m, the appropriate operation is invoked. If m is a **ProjectLeader**, OQL invokes the *activities()* operation defined for the ProjectLeader class; if m is a **TestLeader**, OQL invokes the *activities()* operation defined for the **TestLeader** class.

CONCLUSION

We are now done with the final piece of preparation work. You should have a good understanding of the basics of object-oriented databases and ODMG 2.0. In case you want to know the exact syntax and semantics of ODL or OQL, please consult the book by Cattell, et al. listed at the end of this book. Many of the examples we used in this chapter are taken from the definitions of the **ArcWorld** sample database. You will find the complete definitions in Chapter 6, "The ArcWorld Sample Database."

Object-oriented database products have existed for over ten years. They have remained a niche market. One major problem is that, as discussed in the beginning of this chapter, it is very difficult, if not impossible, to write object-oriented database applications that are portable across more than one object-oriented database product. The intent of ODMG was to solve this problem. However, the ODMG standard has existed since 1993 (first with *ODMG-93*, and now *ODMG 2.0*), but the compliance from major object-oriented database vendors has been scarce. The new *Java binding* may change this picture, given the popularity of Java, but only time will tell.

Object-oriented databases are very different from relational databases in one important aspect: *They cannot be used without a programming language.* Therefore, language binding is of central importance. We will discuss the Java binding in Chapter 9, "Java Binding for OODB," and its sample applications in Chapter 10, "Sample Data Access Applications." Other than these chapters, we will not discuss object-oriented databases further. We will instead concentrate on the use of relational databases, which are the mainstream, in our examples. Nevertheless, you will find that the key focus of object-oriented databases—*the transparent integration of database capability with the programming language*—has been utilized in many places for accessing relational databases.

Chapter 6

The ArcWorld Sample Database

code

In this chapter we will define the **ArcWorld** sample database that we will use as illustration throughout this book. **ArcWorld** is presented here both as a relational database and as an object-oriented database. As a relational database, it has been implemented using **DB2 UDB 5.0** and **SQL Server 6.5**. As an object-oriented database, the Java binding (see Chapter 10, "Sample Data Access Applications") has been implemented using **POET 5.0**, which is the first object-oriented database system that conforms to the ODMG Java binding. (However, since the ODL compiler in POET 5.0 does not support ODMG 2.0, the ODL statements listed in this chapter have not been verified.)

THE ARCWORLD RELATIONAL DATABASE

The **ArcWorld** relational database consists of five tables: **Country, City, Architect, Building**, and **Church**. The following are the SQL DDL statements that you can use to create these tables:

```
CREATE TABLE Country ( name        CHAR(32) NOT NULL PRIMARY KEY,
                       cityMap      IMAGE)

CREATE TABLE City ( name           CHAR(32) NOT NULL PRIMARY KEY,
```

```
                    country          CHAR(32),
                    archMap          IMAGE,
                    FOREIGN KEY (country) REFERENCES Country)

CREATE TABLE Architect ( name          CHAR(32) NOT NULL PRIMARY KEY,
                    nationality CHAR(32),
                    picture     IMAGE)

CREATE TABLE Building ( name          CHAR(32) NOT NULL PRIMARY KEY,
                    type        CHAR(32),
                    address     VARCHAR(256),
                    city        CHAR(32),
                    yearBuilt   INTEGER
                                CHECK (yearBuilt > -300),
                    architect   CHAR(32),
                    style       CHAR(32),
                    description TEXT,
                    picture     IMAGE,
                    FOREIGN KEY (city)
                            REFERENCES City,
                    FOREIGN KEY (architect)
                            REFERENCES Architect)

CREATE TABLE Church ( name          CHAR(32) NOT NULL PRIMARY KEY,
                    type        CHAR(32),
                    address     VARCHAR(255),
                    city        CHAR(32),
                    yearBuilt   INTEGER
                                CHECK (yearBuilt > -300),
                    architect   CHAR(32),
                    style       CHAR(32),
                    description TEXT,
                    picture     IMAGE,
                    denomination CHAR(32),
                    pastor      CHAR(32),
                    FOREIGN KEY (city) REFERENCES City,
                    FOREIGN KEY (architect) REFERENCES Architect)
```

Because of the interdependencies among the above tables, you must create them in the proper order (e.g., in the order shown).

This database demonstrates the use of some of the salient features of relational databases that were discussed in Chapter 4, "Relational Databases and SQL":

■ Primary keys and entity integrity (not null)

- Referential integrity
- Domain integrity (check constraint)

It also uses a couple of advanced data types that will not be discussed until Chapter 22, "Conclusion: Emerging Technologies":

- IMAGE
- TEXT

We include them here for completeness. Also please note that these data types are created for **DB2 UDB** using the following statements:

```
CREATE DISTINCT TYPE IMAGE AS BLOB(32K)
CREATE DISTINCT TYPE TEXT AS CLOB(32K)
```

THE ARCWORLD OBJECT-ORIENTED DATABASE

The **ArcWorld** object-oriented database consists of five classes: **Country, City, Architect, Building**, and **Church**. The following are the ODMG ODL statements that can be used to create these classes:

```
class Country
(   extent countries
    key    name)
{
    attribute string<32>      name;
    attribute sequence<octet> city_map;
};

class City
(   extent cities
    key    name)
{
    attribute string<32>      name;
    attribute Country         country;
    attribute sequence<octet> arch_map;
};

class Architect
(   extent architects
    key    name)
{
    attribute string<32>      name;
    attribute string<32>      nationality;
```

```
        attribute sequence<octec> picture;
};

class Building
(   extent buildings
    key     name)
{
    attribute string<32>        name;
    attribute string<32>        type;
    attribute string<256>       address;
    attribute City              city;
    attribute long              yearBuilt;
    attribute Architect         architect;
    attribute string<32>        style;
    attribute sequence<char>    description;
    attribute sequence<octec>   picture;
};

class Church extends Building
(   extent churches
    key     name)
{   attribute string<32> denomination;
    attribute string<32> pastor;
};
```

This database demonstrates the use of some of the salient features of object-oriented databases that were discussed in Chapter 5, "Object-Oriented Databases and ODMG 2.0":

■ Extents
■ Primary keys
■ Object references (identifiers)

However, it also shows that object-oriented databases (or ODMG 2.0) fail to provide:

■ Entity integrity (not null)
■ Referential integrity (unless binary relationships are used in place of object references)
■ Domain integrity (check constraint)

These must then be provided in application logic.

Part 2
Java Data Access

An Introduction to Part 2

We are now ready to start exploring Java and Web data access. In Part 2, we will begin with Java data access, which can be used with or independent of the Web. The facilities to be discussed here are critical in making Java the universal data access language and platform. We will go over the fundamentals of Java data access, including:

- JDBC
- SQLJ
- Java binding for object-oriented databases

We will then go over some programming examples to illustrate and contrast the use of each of these.

Here is what we will be covering in Part 2:

- *Chapter 7* gives an overview of JDBC, the popular Java call-level interface to SQL databases, which is becoming a de facto standard. The JDBC API is part of the Java Core API, and all kinds of JDBC drivers are available on many platforms for accessing various types of databases. So using JDBC is almost as convenient as using Java. JDBC is the cornerstone of Java data access. Here, we go over the essentials of JDBC.

- *Chapter 8* introduces SQLJ, the newly proposed standard for embedding SQL in Java. SQLJ complements JDBC. JDBC is dynamic, whereas SQLJ is static. JDBC is more flexible to use, but SQLJ provides compile-time schema and type checking, and it may perform better.

- *Chapter 9* discusses Java binding for object-oriented databases. First, we introduce ODMG's Java binding, the new standard that was recently published. We then go over **POET** to see how one particular system works.

- *Chapter 10* continues our programming examples in this book. Here, we go over some basic database administration and data access applications, and then show how they are done in JDBC, SQLJ, and **POET**, respectively. This is the only place in this book where you will find programming examples for SQLJ and object-oriented databases. For simplicity and consistency, we will only use JDBC in the remaining programming examples where Java data access is used.

Part 2 is a must, particularly Chapter 7, and should be fun. You will learn how to access data in Java, and you will also get a good feel for some of the basic trade-offs involved in data access in general: dynamic approach vs. static approach, query vs. navigation, and relational databases vs. object-oriented databases.

Chapter 7

JDBC
in a
Nutshell

concepts

The introduction of the JDBC API as part of the Java core API and the JDBC-ODBC Bridge Driver as part of JDK 1.1 is one of the most significant events in Java data access. Before JDBC, it was difficult to access SQL databases from Java. (Here, we refer to *SQL databases* instead of relational databases, because JDBC depends only on SQL for database access and the underlying databases can be anything that provides SQL access.) No SQL database system provided direct Java support, so developers had to write Java native methods to access SQL databases through their C API (mostly the ODBC API). This process is tedious, error prone, and best left to experts. Among other things, it involves mapping and conversion between data types in Java (an object-oriented language with no pointers), C (a procedural language with pointers), and SQL (a set-oriented language). Also, the resulting implementation is not binary-portable and may not be source-portable to other platforms.

JDBC was not a completely new invention. Most of its concepts were derived from ODBC: driver manager, driver, connection, statement, result set, and cursor. However, ODBC was based on procedural languages (C and COBOL) and had to use more obscure constructs (handles such as the connection handle, and function calls associated with the handle such as *disconnect()*) to represent database objects and their operations. JDBC, on the other hand, is based on Java and can use objects to directly and naturally represent database objects and their operations (such as the **Connection** object and its *close()* method).

JDBC also was neither the first attempt to provide an object-oriented API for accessing databases nor the first one trying to "standardize" such an API. The OMG, through its Persistent Object Service (POS) specification, had tried to do both earlier. However, POS was based on IDL (which defines only interfaces) and not on a real programming language. It tried to address both object persistence and object access to databases, and tried to cover object-oriented databases, relational databases, and file systems. As a result, it took the least-common-denominator approach and failed to do well in many key areas. (The OMG is in the process of revising POS.) Conversely, JDBC is very focused. It is specifically designed for Java, it addresses only database access, and it deals only with SQL databases. As a result, JDBC can be your best choice for (dynamic) Java access to SQL databases.

We must also attribute JDBC's success to other major factors. These include: Java's momentum, JavaSoft's effort to get major SQL database vendors involved in specifying JDBC, and JavaSoft's focus on getting an implementation (the JDBC-ODBC Bridge Driver) out at the same time the specification was finalized. All of these factors contribute to making the development of JDBC one of the best examples on how to quickly develop a successful de facto standard from scratch.

In the following sections, we will first give an overview of JDBC: its design goals, architecture, and usage scenarios. We will then go over SQL/Java mapping, both from SQL to Java and from Java to SQL. Finally, we will delve into the details of the JDBC API.

JDBC OVERVIEW

JDBC is part of the Java core and is a key component in making Java suitable for use in developing enterprise applications, because these applications invariably involve access to corporate databases. *Object data access* by nature deals with two potentially very different domains: object-oriented programming languages on the one hand, and database systems on the other. Each programming language has its own data model, type system, syntax, and semantics; each database system also has its own data model, type system, syntax, and semantics. Therefore, the designer of an object data access API faces a number of major and difficult design choices:

■ *To focus on object persistence or object access to databases*. Focusing on object persistence means that you should start with the data model and type system of the programming language(s) and concentrate on preserving these (for example, inheritance) when making object state persistent. A major design goal would be to make the transition between transient state and persistent state seamless. Focusing on database access, on the other hand, means that you would start with the data model and type system of the database system(s) and concentrate on preserving these (for example, table) when retrieving data from databases. A major design goal would be to make data retrieval (query) and manipulation easy. *JDBC's focus is on database access.*

■ ***To focus on a single programming language or more than one programming language***. If you could focus on a single programming language, then you would directly utilize its specific syntax and semantics. A major design goal would be to fully exploit all major language constructs (for example, operator overloading in C++) to make things "natural" to the language programmer. On the other hand, if you must consider more than one language, then you must do things in a "language-neutral" way (for example, using the OMG IDL) and then rely on language mappings to take care of language specificities. A major design goal would be to enable programmers to reuse concepts and constructs when moving from one language to another. *JDBC's focus is on a single programming language, Java.*

■ ***To focus on a single database system or more than one database system***. Focusing on a single database system allows you to fully support its specific data model and type system. A major design goal would be to make all database functionality (for example, multimedia extenders in **DB2 UDB**) available to the programmer. Focusing on more than one database system, on the other hand, means that you must consider only concepts and constructs that apply to all database systems under consideration and rely on schema mappings to take care of database system specificities. *JDBC's focus is on a single type of database systems, SQL databases, and JDBC relies on the drivers to take care of schema mappings for individual database systems.*

JDBC Design Goals

Now that we know what JDBC's overall design focuses are, let us look at some of its specific design goals. These are important, because they help us understand where JDBC's strength and weakness are and keep things in proper perspective.

■ *A call-level, dynamic SQL API.* JDBC is the Java equivalent of ODBC and X/Open CLI. It is intended to be a common low-level API that supports basic SQL functionality. Higher-level APIs—for example, one that provides direct mapping of tables to Java classes—are expected to be built on top of JDBC. (Please note that the current versions of JDBC provide less functionality than ODBC or X/Open CLI.)

■ *Implementable on top of common SQL level APIs.* JDBC was designed to be readily implementable on top of ODBC and X/Open CLI. This ensured that JDBC drivers, particularly JDBC-ODBC bridge drivers, could be quickly developed in the marketplace.

- *SQL conformance.* JDBC was designed to work with SQL. It can accommodate any SQL dialect as long as there is a JDBC driver that can handle it. However, to ensure the portability of JDBC applications across multiple JDBC drivers, *a JDBC-compliant driver must support SQL-92 Entry Level.*

- *Strong, static typing.* JDBC assumes that, under most circumstances, a programmer has the type information about his application at development time. Therefore, its API was designed with as much type information as possible expressed statically. This is consistent with the design philosophy of other Java core class libraries. Dynamic typing (i.e., obtaining and processing type information at run time), however, is supported.

- *Simple API for common cases.* JDBC was designed with the 80-20 rule in mind: It is intended to be a simple API to use for 80% of the cases. For the other 20% of the cases, you may have to accomplish your tasks in more than one step. In order of decreasing degree of ease of use, JDBC can be used for:

  1. SQL (SELECT, INSERT, UPDATE, DELETE) statements without parameters and SELECT statements returning a single result set of simple types

  2. SQL statements with IN, INOUT, or OUT parameters and SELECT statements returning multiple result sets with maybe large objects (for example, LONG-VARs)

  3. Metadata access, which includes obtaining metadata information about result sets or databases

The JDBC Architecture

The JDBC architecture is shown in Figure 7-1. You can see that it consists of two layers of APIs: the DriverManager API and the Driver API. The DriverManager API is what a JDBC user sees and uses; the Driver API is what a JDBC (driver) implementor sees and implements. The DriverManager API consists mostly of interfaces and abstract classes; the Driver API consists of concrete classes that implement these interfaces and abstract classes. We will go over these later when we discuss the JDBC API.

JDBC Driver Types

The JDBC drivers depicted in Figure 7-1 can be classified into the following four types; each type has particular implementation characteristics that affect its portability and usage:

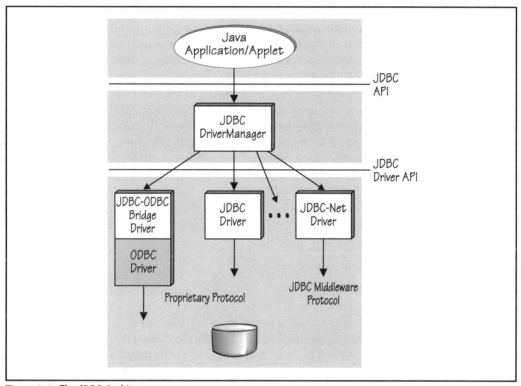

Figure 7-1. The JDBC Architecture.

- *Type 1— JDBC-ODBC bridge driver.* Type 1 drivers do not access databases directly; they depend on the (backend) ODBC drivers for actual access to databases. They are implemented using Java native methods written in C, which call the ODBC API. As a result, Type 1 drivers are not binary portable to other platforms. Also, they are not callable from Java applets because of Web browsers' security constraints. Therefore, Type 1 drivers are suitable for use by Java applications, and not by Java applets. An example of Type 1 drivers is *JavaSoft's JDBC-ODBC Bridge Driver.*

- *Type 2—Native-API, partly-Java driver.* Type 2 drivers are implemented using Java native methods written in C, which call a database-system native API. As a result, Type 2 drivers are not binary portable to other platforms. Also, they are not callable from Java applets because of security constraints on Web browsers. Therefore, Type 2 drivers are suitable for use by Java applications, and not by Java applets. An example of Type 2 drivers is *IBM's DB2 JDBC Application Driver.*

- *Type 3—Net-protocol, all-Java driver.* Type 3 drivers are implemented using pure Java methods, which use a database-system independent, network protocol for client/server communication. Type 3 drivers are binary portable to other platforms, callable from Java applets, and work in a client/server environment. Therefore, Type 3 drivers are suitable for use by Java applets. An example of Type 3 drivers is *Visigenic's VisiChannel.* (If the network protocol used is supported by Web servers—for example, HTTP—then Type 3 drivers can be used for Internet access. Otherwise, they can only be used for intranet access.)

- ***Type 4—Native-protocol, all-Java driver.*** Type 4 drivers are implemented using pure Java methods, which use a database-system native, network protocol for client/server communication. Type 4 drivers are binary portable to other platforms, callable from Java applets, and work in a client/server environment. Therefore, Type 4 drivers are suitable for use by Java applets. An example of Type 4 drivers is *IBM's DB2 JDBC Applet Driver.* (The network protocol used is unlikely to be supported by Web servers, so Type 4 drivers in general can only be used for intranet access.)

JDBC Products

The Java interfaces and classes that constitute the JDBC DriverManager API are part of the JDK. They form the **java.sql** package. Also included in the JDK is a (Type 1) JDBC-ODBC Bridge driver, which is contained in the **sun.jdbc.odbc** package. Therefore, if you are interested in writing Java applications that access SQL databases through ODBC drivers (either used locally or used on an application server as part of a 3-tier architecture), you have everything you need in the JDK.

If you are interested in writing Java applets that access SQL databases, or if you are not satisfied going through ODBC drivers (for example, for performance reasons), then you will need other types of JDBC drivers. Many different types of JDBC drivers are available on the market. These are provided either by database system vendors or by data access middleware vendors. The former ones tend to make additional database-system specific functionality (for example, very large objects) available for your access; the latter ones tend to allow you to access multiple types of databases at the same time. You can find a list of available JDBC drivers in the *JDBC Database Access API* reference in the back of the book.

JDBC Usage Scenarios

You can use JDBC in an almost endless group of scenarios. Because the JDBC DriverManager API is part of the JDK and therefore is available wherever Java is, JDBC essentially can be used in any scenario where Java can be used and where there is an appropriate JDBC driver. You will see many examples of JDBC usage in this book. Here, we will briefly describe four common usage scenarios.

In the first usage scenario (Figure 7-2), a Java application runs on the client and uses JDBC to access either local or remote databases. The application has no security restrictions; it can access local files, make connections to any host, and use local information for identification of databases. In this scenario, you can use a JDBC application driver (Type 1 or Type 2); this driver resides on the client. In most cases, the driver will access the databases through a client application enabler provided by the database system. You will see examples of this in Chapter 10, "Sample Data Access Applications."

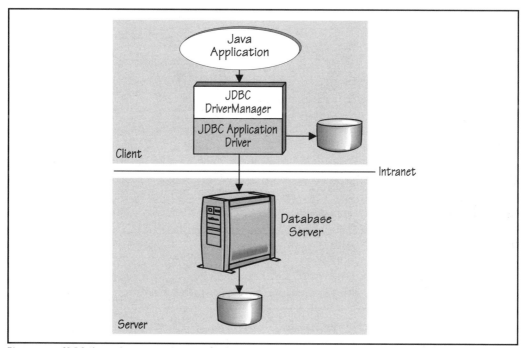

Figure 7-2. JDBC Usage Scenario—Java Application.

In the second scenario (Figure 7-3), a Java applet is downloaded from a Web server to the client and the applet uses JDBC to access remote databases. The applet has to abide by the security restrictions posed by the Web browser; it cannot access local files, it can only make connections to the originating host, and it cannot access local information for identification of databases. Therefore, a JDBC applet driver (Type 3 or Type 4) must be used; this driver can be automatically downloaded from the Web server. In most cases, the driver will access the remote databases by communicating with the JDBC applet server provided by the database system. This scenario is the so-called *JDBC 2-Tier* scenario. You will see examples of this in Chapter 12, "Java Applets and Servlets."

The third usage scenario also involves a Java applet. In this scenario (see Figure 7-4), a Java applet is downloaded from a Web server to the client, but it does

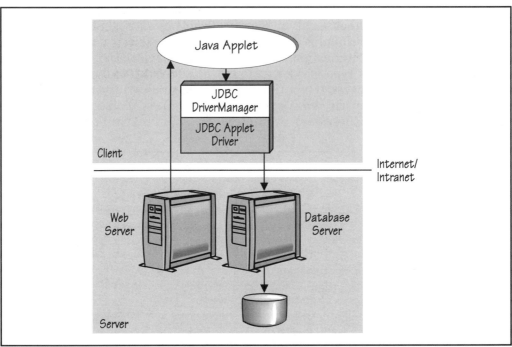

Figure 7-3. JDBC Usage Scenario—Java Applet (I).

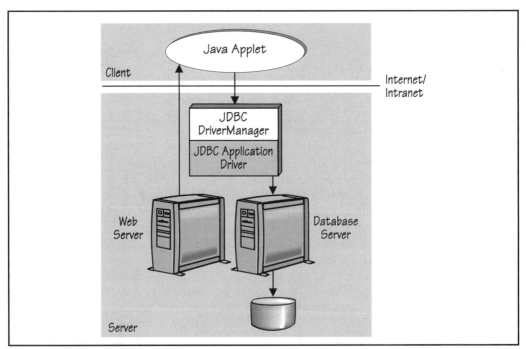

Figure 7-4. JDBC Usage Scenario—Java Applet (II).

not directly use JDBC to access remote databases. Instead, for performance or other reasons, it uses a client/server middleware (such as Java RMI or a Java ORB) to indirectly access remote databases through JDBC. As described earlier, the applet has to abide by the security restrictions posed by the Web browser. However, the server piece of the client/server middleware has no such restrictions. Therefore, a JDBC application driver (Type 1 or Type 2) can be used, which resides on the originating host. This scenario is the so-called *JDBC 2-Tier Plus* scenario. You will see examples of this in Part 4, "Java Client/Server Computing."

The last scenario is the so-called *JDBC 3-Tier* scenario. In this scenario (Figure 7-5), JDBC runs on the application server, where it is accessed by Java business objects. Therefore, at least as far as JDBC is concerned, this scenario is just a special case of the first scenario; here, Java business objects play the role of Java applications. You will see examples of this in Part 6, "Java Component Architectures."

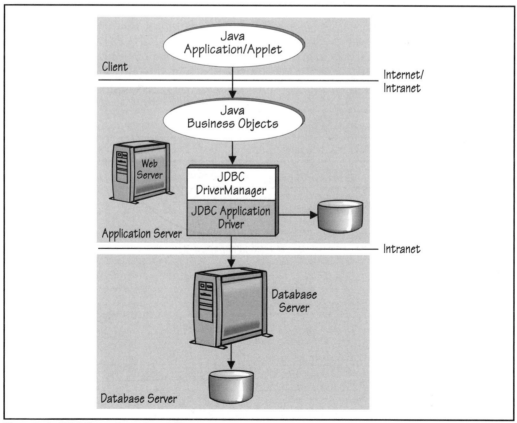

Figure 7-5. JDBC Usage Scenario—3-Tier.

SQL/JAVA DATA TYPE MAPPING

Now that we have a good overview of JDBC—its design goals, architecture, and usage scenarios—we are ready to delve into the JDBC API. Before we do that, we will take a short break and have a quick look at SQL/Java data type mapping. This is very important because it is used either explicitly or implicitly in the JDBC API. (If you need additional motivation, you should be pleased to know that SQLJ, which we will discuss in the next chapter, uses the same standard as SQL/Java data type mapping.)

SQL to Java Mapping

The standard SQL to Java data type mapping is shown in Table 7-1. (You may want to review the definitions of SQL data types and Java data types in Chapter 4, "Relational Databases and SQL," and Chapter 3, "Java Primer," respectively, if you have forgotten what they are.) This is the default mapping that JDBC uses when retrieving data from SQL databases into Java. Note that for TINYINT and SMALLINT, the matching Java object types probably should be Byte and Short, respectively. Integer is used in the JDBC specification probably to ensure upward compatibility of applications which used earlier versions of JDK when Byte and Short were not available.

Table 7-1. Standard SQL to Java Data Type Mapping.

SQL Data Type	Java Data Type
TINYINT	byte or Integer
SMALLINT	short or Integer
INTEGER	int or Integer
BIGINT	long or Long
REAL	float or Float
FLOAT	double or Double
DOUBLE	double or Double
DECIMAL(P,S)	java.math.BigDecimal
NUMERIC(P,S)	java.math.BigDecimal
CHAR(N)	String
VARCHAR(N)	String

Table 7-1. Standard SQL to Java Data Type Mapping. (Continued)

SQL Data Type	Java Data Type
LONGVARCHAR	String
BIT	boolean or Boolean
BINARY(N)	byte[]
VARBINARY(N)	byte[]
LONGVARBINARY	byte[]
DATE	java.sql.Date
TIME	java.sql.Time
TIMESTAMP	java.sql.Timestamp

Java to SQL Mapping

The standard Java to SQL data type mapping is shown in Table 7-2. This is the default mapping that JDBC uses when inserting or updating data from Java to SQL databases. (Byte and Short, two Java object types, probably should have been included in the JDBC specification.)

Table 7-2. Standard Java to SQL Data Type Mapping.

Java Data Type	SQL Data Type
byte	TINYINT
short	SMALLINT
int or Integer	INTEGER
long or Long	BIGINT
float or Float	REAL
double or Double	DOUBLE
java.math.BigDecimal	NUMERIC(P,S)
String	VARCHAR(N) or LONGVARCHAR
boolean or Boolean	BIT
byte[]	VARBINARY(N) or LONGVARBINARY

Table 7-2. Standard Java to SQL Data Type Mapping. (Continued)

Java Data Type	SQL Data Type
java.sql.Date	DATE
java.sql.Time	TIME
java.sql.Timestamp	TIMESTAMP

THE JDBC API

The JDBC API is contained in the **java.sql** package. It consists of eight interfaces, six classes, and three exceptions. The most commonly used interfaces and classes are shown in Figure 7-6, where we also show the following method calls and their sequencing when making a simple SQL query:

1. **DriverManager.***getConnection*(url) returns a **Connection** object that repre-sents the connection established to a database identified by the *url* string.

2. **Connection.***createStatement()* returns a **Statement** object that can be used to execute simple SQL statements (without parameters).

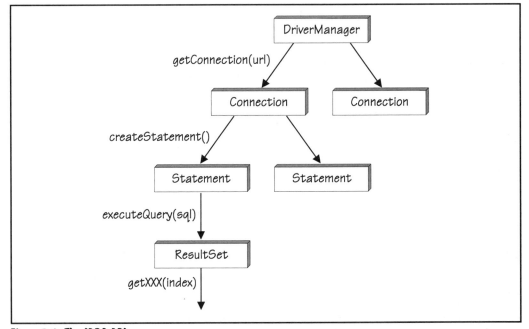

Figure 7-6. The JDBC API.

3. **Statement.***executeQuery*(sql) executes the *sql* string that is a SQL SELECT statement and returns a **ResultSet** object that represents the result of the query.

4. **ResultSet.***getXXX*(index) retrieves the field data from the current row for the column represented by *index*. XXX is the desired data type (for example, Int).

We have omitted some detail, a few steps, and a lot of explanation in this list, and in the figure. However, we hope you get the idea of how simple it is to execute a SQL query using JDBC. In the following sections we will fill in the missing details, steps, and explanation so that you will have a good understanding of JDBC by the time you finish reading this chapter.

DriverManager Class

The **DriverManager** class manages JDBC drivers and provides a uniform interface for establishing connections to databases. It delegates the actual work to a chosen driver.

■ *Choosing a driver.* The **DriverManager** uses the database URL to choose a driver. (We will discuss the database URL later when we go over the **Connection** class.) It will use the first driver it finds that can successfully connect to the URL. The driver must be trusted or loaded from the same class loader as the current applet or application.

■ *Loading a driver.* There are two ways a **Driver** class can be loaded:

◆ By explicitly calling **Class.***forName*(driverClassName). This is the recommended way because it is more reliable.

◆ By adding the **Driver** class name to the **java.lang.System** property *jdbc.drivers*. This is automatic (loaded by the **DriverManager**), but it requires a preset environment that is persistent.

■ *Registering a driver.* A newly loaded **Driver** class must create an instance of itself and register it by calling **DriverManager.***registerDriver()*.

Class Methods

■ **getConnection**(String url, java.util.Properties info) establishes a connection to the database represented by the given *url* and returns a **Connection** object.

- **getConnection**(String url, String user, String password) establishes a connection to the database represented by the given *url* and returns a **Connection** object.

- **getConnection**(String url) establishes a connection to the database represented by the given *url* and returns a **Connection** object.

- **getLoginTimeout**() returns the maximum time in seconds (int) that all drivers can wait when attempting to log in to a database.

- **setLoginTimeout**(int seconds) sets the maximum time in seconds that all drivers can wait when attempting to log in to a database.

- **getLogStream**() returns the current log stream (**java.io.PrintStream**) that is used by the **DriverManager** and all drivers.

- **setLogStream**(java.io.PrintStream out) sets the current log stream that is used by the **DriverManager** and all drivers.

- **println**(String message) prints the given *message* to the current log stream.

The following class methods relate to *drivers*:

- **registerDriver**(Driver driver) registers the specified *driver*. This method should be called by a newly loaded **Driver** class.

- **deregisterDriver**(Driver driver) drops the specified *driver* from the list of registered drivers.

- **getDriver**(String url) returns a **Driver** object that understands the given *url*.

- **getDrivers**() returns an **Enumeration** containing all currently loaded **Driver** objects.

Driver Interface

JDBC allows for multiple database drivers. Each driver must supply a class that implements the **Driver** interface. As discussed previously, the **DriverManager** will try to load as many drivers as it can find and then, whenever a connection request is made, it will ask each driver in turn to try to establish a connection to the database URL. When a **Driver** class is first loaded, it must create an instance of itself and register with the **DriverManager**.

Methods

■ **acceptURL**(String url) returns true (boolean) if this driver understands the given *url*.

■ **connect**(String url, java.util.Properties info) establishes a connection to the database represented by the given *url* and returns a **Connection** object.

■ **getPropertyInfo**(String url, java.util.Properties info) returns a **DriverProperty-Info** object that can be used to discover and supply information on connections.

■ **getMajorVersion**() returns this driver's major version number (int).

■ **getMinorVersion**() returns this driver's minor version number (int).

■ **jdbcCompliant**() returns true (boolean) if this driver passes the JDBC compliance tests.

Connection Interface

A **Connection** object represents a connection (or session) established with a database. A connection includes the SQL statements that are executed and the results that are returned over that connection. A single application can open one or more connections with a single database. It can also open multiple connections with many different databases.

■ ***Opening a connection.*** We have already discussed how to open a connection. You simply call **DriverManager.***getConnection()* and pass in the database URL and, as required, other parameters. The **DriverManager** in turn will choose a driver and call **Driver.***connect()* to establish the connection.

■ ***Database URL***. A JDBC URL provides a mechanism to uniquely identify a database. It has the following format:

jdbc:<subprotocol>:<subname>

A JDBC driver needs to understand only the subprotocol. The syntax and content of the subname can vary, depending on the subprotocol. The following is an example of an URL using the DB2 subprotocol:

*jdbc:db2:*sample

A special case is the ODBC subprotocol. It has been reserved for URLs that specify ODBC data sources and has the following syntax for the URL:

jdbc:odbc:<data-source-name>[;<attribute-name>=<attribute-value>]*

JavaSoft (*jdbc@wombat.eng.sun.com*) is acting as an informal registry for JDBC subprotocol names.

- ***SQL Statements***. There are three types of SQL statements that can be executed over a given connection (we will go over these in detail in the next section):

    ◆ **Statement**: SQL statements with no parameters

    ◆ **PreparedStatement**: Pre-compiled SQL statements with IN parameters

    ◆ **CallableStatement**: SQL stored procedures with IN, OUT, and INOUT parameters

- ***Transactions***. A new **Connection** is in *auto-commit* mode by default, which means that all its SQL statements will be executed and committed as individual transactions. You can override this by calling **Connection**.*setAutoCommit*(false). If auto-commit mode has been disabled, a transaction will not terminate until **Connection**.*commit()* or **Connection**.*rollback()* is called explicitly. When a transaction is terminated, every **Statement**, **PreparedStatement**, **CallableStatement**, and **ResultSet** associated with the **Connection** is closed.

    You can set the *transaction isolation level* by calling **Connection**.*setTransactionIsolation()*. There are five different levels you can set (as described in Chapter 4, "Relational Databases and SQL"):

    - NONE
    - READ_UNCOMMITTED
    - READ_COMMITTED
    - REPEATABLE_READ
    - SERIALIZABLE

Class Constants

- **TRANSACTION_NONE** (int): Transactions are not supported.

- **TRANSACTION_READ_UNCOMMITTED** (int): Dirty reads, non-repeatable reads, and phantom reads can occur.

- **TRANSACTION_READ_COMMITTED** (int): Dirty reads are prevented; non-repeatable reads and phantom reads can occur.

- **TRANSACTION_REPEATABLE_READ** (int): Dirty reads and non-repeatable reads are prevented; phantom reads can occur.

- **TRANSACTION_SERIALIZABLE** (int): Dirty reads, non-repeatable reads, and phantom reads are prevented.

Methods

- **createStatement**() creates and returns a **Statement** object, which can be used to execute SQL statements without parameters.

- **prepareStatement**(String sql) creates and returns a **PreparedStatement** object, which contains the pre-compiled SQL statement for the given *sql* string.

- **prepareCall**(String sql) creates and returns a **CallableStatement** object, which contains the SQL stored procedure call specified by the *sql* string.

- **nativeSQL**(String sql) returns the native form (**String**) of the SQL statement specified by the *sql* string.

The following methods relate to *transactions*:

- **getAutoCommit**() returns the current auto-commit state (boolean).

- **setAutoCommit**(boolean autoCommit) sets the auto-commit state. If the **Connection** is in auto-commit mode, then all its SQL statements will be executed and committed as individual transactions.

- **commit**() commits the current transaction. This method should only be used when auto-commit has been disabled.

- **rollback**() rolls back the current transaction. This method should only be used when auto-commit has been disabled.

- **getTransactionIsolation**() returns the current transaction isolation level (int) of this connection.

- **setTransactionIsolation**(int level) sets the current transaction isolation level of this transaction.

The following are additional methods:

- **close**() closes this connection and releases its JDBC resources. (A connection is automatically closed when its corresponding **Connection** object is garbage collected.)

- **isClosed**() returns true (boolean) if this connection is closed.

- **getMetaData**() returns a **DatabaseMetaData** object, which contains information about the database to which this connection is connected.

- **getCatalog**() returns the current catalog name (**String**) of this connection.

- **setCatalog**(String catalog) sets the current catalog name of this connection to the given one.

- **isReadOnly**() returns true (boolean) if this connection is in read-only mode.

- **setReadOnly**(boolean readOnly) sets the read-only mode of this connection.

- **getWarnings**() returns a **SQLWarning** object that contains the warning report.

- **clearWarnings**() clears the warning report.

Statement, PreparedStatement, and CallableStatement

As mentioned before, JDBC provides three types of **Statement** objects that can be used to execute SQL statements:

- **Statement**: SQL statements with no parameters. It can be created by calling **Connection**.*createStatement()*.

- **PreparedStatement**: Pre-compiled SQL statements with IN parameters. It can be created by calling **Connection**.*prepareStatement()*. The IN parameters can be set by using various *set* methods.

- **CallableStatement**: SQL stored procedures with IN,OUT, and INOUT parameters. It can be created by calling **Connection**.*prepareCall()*. The IN and INOUT parameters can be set by using various *set* methods. The INOUT and OUT parameters must be registered before use, and their values can be obtained by using various *get* methods.

Statement Interface

A **Statement** object can be used to execute SQL statements with no parameters. You can choose one of three different methods to execute the statement, depending on the nature of the statement (this also applies to **PreparedStatement** and **CallableStatement** because they are subtypes of **Statement**):

■ *executeQuery()* for SQL SELECT statements returning a single **ResultSet** object.

■ *executeUpdate()* for SQL INSERT, UPDATE, DELETE, or DDL statements. It returns the number of rows updated.

■ *execute()* for SQL statements that may return more than one result set, more than one update count, or a combination of result sets and update counts. You need to use a combination of *getResultSet()*, *getUpdateCount()*, and *getMore-Results()* to process the results. (We will give an example how to do this later.)

All of these methods close the current result set if there is one open.

SQL Escape Syntax

Details

JDBC allows you to execute SQL statements that use SQL escape syntax. The escape syntax signals to the JDBC driver that the code within it should be treated differently. The driver will then translate it into code that the particular database understands. This makes escape syntax database-system independent.

An escape clause is demarcated by curly brackets and a keyword:
```
{keyword ... parameters ...}
```
The keyword indicates what kind of escape clause it is. The various kinds of escape clauses supported in JDBC include:

■ *call* or *? = call* for stored procedures, for example:
```
{call procedureName[(?, ?, ...)]}
```
    or
```
{? = call procedureName[(?, ?, ...)]}
```

■ *d, t,* and *ts* for date and time literals, for example:
```
{d 'yyyy-mm-dd'}
```

- *escape* for *LIKE* escape characters, for example:

  ```
  {escape '\'}
  ```

- *fn* for scalar functions, for example:

  ```
  {fn concat("Iced", "Java")}
  ```

- *oj* for outer joins, for example:

  ```
  {oj outer-join}
  ```
  where outer-join is an outer join expression

Methods

- **executeQuery**(String sql) executes a SQL SELECT statement and returns a single **ResultSet.**

- **executeUpdate**(String sql) executes a SQL INSERT, UPDATE, DELETE, or DDL statement and returns the count (int) of rows updated.

The following methods relate to *execute()*:

- **execute**(String sql) executes a SQL statement that may return one or more result sets, one or more update counts, or a combination of result sets and update counts. It returns true (boolean) if the next result is a result set.

- **getResultSet**() returns the current result set as a **ResultSet** object. It returns null if the result is an update count or if there are no more results. It should only be called once per result.

- **getUpdateCount**() returns the current update count (int). It returns −1 if the result is a result set or if there are no more results. It should only be called once per result.

- **getMoreResults**() moves to this statement's next result. It returns true if the result is a result set. There are no more results when (!*getMoreResults()* && (*getUpdateCount()* == -1).

The following methods relate to *results*:

- **setCursorName**(String name) sets the cursor name that is associated with the result set. The name can be used in positioned updates and positioned deletes.

- **getMaxFieldSize**() returns the maximum amount (int) of data in bytes that can be returned for any field; it only applies to columns of the following types: BINARY, VARBINARY, LONGVARBINARY, CHAR, VARCHAR, and LONGVAR-CHAR.

- **setMaxFieldSize**(int max) sets the maximum amount of data in bytes that can be returned for any field; it only applies to columns of the following types: BINARY, VARBINARY, LONGVARBINARY, CHAR, VARCHAR, and LONGVAR-CHAR.

- **getMaxRows**() returns the maximum number (int) of rows that a result set can contain.

- **setMaxRows**(int max) sets the maximum number of rows that a result set can contain.

The following are additional methods:

- **close**() closes this statement and releases its JDBC resources. (A statement is automatically closed when its associated **Statement** object is garbage collected.)

- **cancel**() can be used by one thread to cancel a statement that is being executed by another thread.

- **getQueryTimeout**() returns the number (int) of seconds the driver will wait for this statement to execute.

- **setQueryTimeout**(int seconds) sets the number of seconds the driver will wait for this statement to execute.

- **setEscapeProcessing**(boolean enable) sets escape processing on or off. If escape processing is on, a JDBC driver will do escape substitution before sending the SQL to the database.

- **getWarnings**() returns a **SQLWarning** object that contains the warning report.

- **clearWarnings**() clears the warning report.

Using the execute() Method

Details

The *execute()* method may return one or more result sets, one or more update counts, or a combination of result sets and update counts. How can you be sure that you have accessed all the result sets and update counts? The following code demonstrates one way to do that (stmt is a **Statement** object):

```
    stmt.execute(queryString);

while (true) {
    int rowCount = stmt.getUpdateCount();

    if (rowCount > 0) {      // update
        System.out.println("Rows changed = " + rowCount);
        stmt.getMoreResults();
        continue;
    }

    if (rowCount = 0) {      // DDL or 0 update
        System.out.println("No rows updated or DDL");
        stmt.getMoreResults();
        continue;
    }

    // rowCount = -1: result set or no more results
    ResultSet rs = stmt.getResultSet();
    if (rs != null) {      // result set
        ...
        while (rs.next()) {      // process result
            ...
        }
        stmt.getMoreResults();
        continue;
    }

    break;      // no more results
}
```

PreparedStatement Interface

A **PreparedStatement** object can be used to pre-compile and execute SQL statements with IN parameters.

■ *Creation.* The SQL statement may contain IN parameter markers like the ones in this example:

```
PreparedStatement pstmt = con.prepareStatement(
    "UPDATE Building SET type = ? WHERE name = ?");
```

- *IN parameters.* The IN parameters must be set before execution using the following *set* methods:

    ◆ *setXXX()* for predefined datatypes. It uses the standard Java to SQL data type mapping to map a Java data type to a SQL data type.

    ◆ *setObject()* for Java objects. If the target SQL data type is specified, it will perform data conversion. If the target SQL data type is not specified, it will use the standard Java to SQL data type mapping to map a Java object type to a SQL data type.

    ◆ *setAsciiStream()*, *setBinaryStream()*, *setUnicodeStream()* for setting large amounts of data incrementally.

- *Null values.* The SQL NULL value can be set by passing a Java null value for a Java object or by using the following method:

    ◆ *setNull()*

The **PreparedStatement** interface extends the **Statement** interface.

Methods

- **executeQuery**() executes the prepared SQL SELECT statement and returns a **ResultSet** object.

- **executeUpdate**() executes the prepared SQL INSERT, UPDATE, DELETE, or DDL statement and returns the count (int) of rows updated.

- **execute**() executes the prepared SQL statement, which may return more than one result set, more than one update count, or a combination of more than one result set and update counts.

The following methods can be used to *set IN parameters of predefined data types*:

- **setByte**(int parameterIndex, byte x)

- **setShort**(int parameterIndex, short x)

- **setInt**(int parameterIndex, int x)

- **setLong**(int parameterIndex, long x)

- **setFloat**(int parameterIndex, float x)

- **setDouble**(int parameterIndex, double x)

- **setBigDecimal**(int parameterIndex, BigDecimal x)

- **setString**(int parameterIndex, String x)

- **setBoolean**(int parameterIndex, boolean x)

- **setBytes**(int parameterIndex, byte[] x)

- **setDate**(int parameterIndex, Date x)

- **setTime**(int parameterIndex, Time x)

- **setTimestamp**(int parameterIndex, Timestamp x)

The following methods can be used to *set IN parameters which are Java objects*:

- **setObject**(int parameterIndex, Object x, int targetSqlType, int scale)

- **setObject**(int parameterIndex, Object x, int targetSqlType)

- **setObject**(int parameterIndex, Object x)

The following methods can be used to *set large IN parameters incrementally*:

- **setAsciiStream**(int parameterIndex, java.io.InputStream x, int length)

- **setBinaryStream**(int parameterIndex, java.io.nputStream x, int length)

- **setUnicodeStream**(int parameterIndex, java.io.InputStream x, int length)

The following are additional methods related to IN parameters:

- **setNull**(int parameterIndex, int sqlType) sets a parameter to SQL NULL.

- **clearParameters**() clears all IN parameters.

CallableStatement Interface

A **CallableStatement** object can be used to execute SQL stored procedures with IN, OUT, and INOUT parameters.

- *Stored procedures.* SQL stored procedures can be called in a standard way by using the SQL cape syntax discussed earlier:

    ```
    {call procedure_name[(?, ?. ...)]}
    ```

    or

    ```
    {? = call procedure_name[(?, ?. ...)]}
    ```

- *Creation.* The SQL stored procedure call may contain IN, OUT, or INOUT parameter markers like the ones in this example:

    ```
    CallableStatement cstmt = con.prepareCall(
      "{call getTestData(?, ?)}"
    ```

- *OUT parameters.* Each OUT parameter must be registered before the stored procedure can be executed:

    - *registerOutParameter()* registers an OUT parameter with a specified SQL data type.

    After execution, all results must be retrieved before retrieving the OUT parameters using the following:

    - *getXXX()* returns predefined data types. The correct method to use is the Java data type, which conforms to the standard SQL to Java data type mapping.

    - *getObject()* returns Java objects.

    The **CallableStatement** class does not provide a mechanism for retrieving large amounts of data incrementally.

- *INOUT parameters.* Each INOUT parameter must be registered and set before the **CallableStatement** can be executed:

    - *registerOutParameter()*

    - *setXXX(), setObject()*

After execution, the INOUT parameters can be retrieved using:

- ◆ *getXXX()*, *getObject()*

- ■ *NULL values*. The value returned to an OUT parameter may be SQL NULL. When this happens, the value returned by a *getXXX()* method will be *null, 0,* or *false*, depending on the Java data type. You can test if a value of *0* or *false* was originally SQL NULL by calling:

- ◆ *wasNull()*

The **CallableStatement** interface extends the **PreparedStatement** interface.

Methods

- ■ **registerOutParameter**(int parameterIndex, int sqlType, int scale) registers an OUT parameter. Each OUT parameter must be registered before this stored procedure can be executed.

- ■ **registerOutParameter**(int parameterIndex, int sqlType) registers an OUT parameter. Each OUT parameter must be registered before this stored procedure can be executed.

The following methods can be used to *retrieve OUT parameters of predefined data types*:

- ■ **getByte**(int parameterIndex) returns a byte.

- ■ **getShort**(int parameterIndex) returns a short.

- ■ **getInt**(int parameterIndex) returns an int.

- ■ **getLong**(int parameterIndex) returns a long.

- ■ **getFloat**(int parameterIndex) returns a float.

- ■ **getDouble**(int parameterIndex) returns a double.

- ■ **getBigDecimal**(int parameterIndex) returns a **BigDecimal**.

- ■ **getString**(int parameterIndex) returns a **String**.

- ■ **getBoolean**(int parameterIndex) returns a boolean.

- **getBytes**(int parameterIndex) returns a byte[ ].

- **getDate**(int parameterIndex) returns a **Date**.

- **getTime**(int parameterIndex) returns a **Time**.

- **getTimestamp**(int parameterIndex) returns a **Timestamp**.

The following are additional methods related to *OUT parameters*:

- **getObject**(int parameterIndex) returns a Java object.

- **wasNull**() returns true (boolean) if the last value read was SQL NULL.

ResultSet Interface

A **ResultSet** object contains a set or multiset of rows of data returned from a SQL query, executed using a **Statement**, **PreparedStatement**, or **CallableStatement** object.

- *Cursor.* Each result set maintains a cursor that points to its current row of data. Initially, the cursor is positioned before the first row. The cursor can be moved to point to the next row by calling:

    ◆ *next()*

    The cursor has a name, which can be used in positioned updates or positioned deletes.

- *Result values*. The value of a field of the current row can be retrieved by index or by name:

    ◆ *getXXX()* for predefined datatypes. You should use the Java data type that conforms to the standard SQL to Java data type mapping. You can use other Java data types as long as they are compatible. (Please see the *Java Database Access API* reference at the back of the book for the specification of compatible Java data types for each SQL data type.)

    ◆ *getObject()* for Java objects. It uses the standard SQL to Java data type mapping to map a SQL data type to a Java object type.

    ◆ *getAsciiStream()*, *getBinaryStream()*, *getUnicodeStream()* for retrieving large amounts of data incrementally.

- *Null values*. The value returned from a SQL query may be SQL NULL. When this happens, the value returned by a *getXXX()* method will be *null, 0, or false*, depending on the Java data type. You can test if a value of *0* or *false* was originally SQL NULL by calling:

  - *wasNull()*

Methods

- **next()** moves the cursor to the next row. Returns true (boolean) if the new current row is valid.

The following methods can be used to *retrieve result data of predefined data types*:

- **getByte**(int columnIndex) returns a byte.

- **getByte**(int columnName) returns a byte.

- **getShort**(int columnIndex) returns a short.

- **getShort**(int columnName) returns a short.

- **getInt**(int columnIndex) returns an int.

- **getInt**(int columnName) returns an int.

- **getLong**(int columnIndex) returns a long.

- **getLong**(int columnName) returns a long.

- **getFloat**(int columnIndex) returns a float.

- **getFloat**(int columnName) returns a float.

- **getDouble**(int columnIndex) returns a double.

- **getDouble**(int columnName) returns a double.

- **getBigDecimal**(int columnIndex) returns a **BigDecimal**.

- **getBigDecimal**(int columnName) returns a **BigDecimal**.

- **getString**(int columnIndex) returns a **String**.

- **getString**(int columnName) returns a **String**.

- **getBoolean**(int columnIndex) returns a boolean.

- **getBoolean**(int columnName) returns a boolean.

- **getBytes**(int columnIndex) returns a byte[ ].

- **getBytes**(int columnName) returns a byte[ ].

- **getDate**(int columnIndex) returns a **Date**.

- **getDate**(int columnName) returns a **Date**.

- **getTime**(int columnIndex) returns a **Time**.

- **getTime**(int columnName) returns a **Time**.

- **getTimestamp**(int columnIndex) returns a **Timestamp**.

- **getTimestamp**(int columnName) returns a **Timestamp**.

The following methods can be used to *retrieve result data that are Java objects*:

- **getObject**(int columnIndex) returns a Java object.

- **getObject**(int columnName) returns a Java object.

The following methods can be used to *retrieve large result data incrementally*:

- **getAsciiStream**(int columnIndex) returns an InputStream

- **getAsciiStream**(int columnName) returns an InputStream

- **getBinaryStream**(int columnIndex) returns an InputStream

- **getBinaryStream**(int columnName) returns an InputStream

- **getUnicodeStream**(int columnIndex) returns an InputStream

- **getUnicodeStream**(int columnName) returns an InputStream

The following are additional methods:

- **close**() closes this result set and releases its JDBC resources. (The result set is automatically closed when its corresponding **ResultSet** object is garbage collected.)

- **wasNull**() returns true (boolean) if the last value read was SQL NULL.

- **findColumn**(String columnName) returns the column index (int) corresponding to the given column name.

- **getCursorName**() returns the cursor name (**String**), which can be used in positioned updates or positioned deletes.

- **getMetaData**() returns a **ResultSetMetaData** object that contains information about this result set.

- **getWarnings**() returns a **SQLWarning** object that contains the warning report.

- **clearWarnings**() clears the warning report.

ResultSetMetaData Interface

A **ResultSetMetaData** object contains information on the types and properties of the columns of a result set.

Class Constants

- **columnNoNulls** (int)

- **columnNullable** (int)

- **columnNullableUnknown** (int)

Methods

- **getColumnCount**() returns the number (int) of columns in the result set.

The following methods can be used to obtain *column name and other information*:

- **getColumnLabel**(int column) returns the column title (**String**) for use in printout or display.

- **getColumnName**(int column) returns the column name (**String**).

- **getColumnType**(int column) returns the column's SQL data type (int).

- **getColumnTypeName**(int column) returns the column's SQL data type name (**String**).

- **getPrecision**(int column) returns the column's number (int) of decimal digits.

- **getScale**(int column) returns the column's number (int) of digits to the right of the decimal point.

- **getColumnDisplaySize**(int column) returns the column's normal max width (int) in chars.

The following methods can be used to obtain *catalog information*:

- **getCatalogName**(int column) returns the column's table catalog name (**String**).

- **getSchemaName**(int column) returns the column's table schema name (**String**).

- **getTableName**(int column) returns the column's table name (**String**).

The following methods can be used to test *column properties*:

- **isAutoIncrement**(int column) returns true (boolean) if the column is automatically numbered, and thus read-only.

- **isCaseSensitive**(int column) returns a boolean.

- **isCurrency**(int column) returns a boolean.

- **isNullable**(int column) returns a boolean.

- **isReadOnly**(int column) returns a boolean.

- **isSearchable**(int column) returns a boolean. Searchable means the column can be used in a WHERE clause.

- **isSigned**(int column) returns a boolean.

- **isWritable**(in column) returns a boolean.

- **isDefinitelyWritable**(int column) returns a boolean.

DatabaseMetaData Interface

A **DatabaseMetaData** object contains information about the database as a whole. The **DatabaseMetaData** interface has over 40 class constants and over 130 methods. The following list contains only a few of the most commonly used methods.

Methods

- **getURL**() returns the database URL **(String)**.

- **getUserName**() returns the user name **(String)**.

- **getDatabaseProductName**() returns the database product name **(String)**.

- **getDatabaseProductVersion**() returns the database product version **(String)**.

- **getDriverName**() returns the name **(String)** of the JDBC driver.

- **getMaxConnections**() returns the maximum number (int) of active connections allowed.

The following methods can be used to obtain information on *tables*:

- **getTables**(String catalog, String schemaPattern, String tableNamePattern, String[] types) returns a **ResultSet** containing information (table catalog, table schema, table name, table type, and comment) on the matching tables.

- **getColumns**(String catalog, String schemaPattern, String tableNamePattern, String columnNamePattern) returns a **ResultSet** containing information (such as table catalog, table schema, table name, column name, and data type) on the matching columns.

- **getPrimaryKeys**(String catalog, String schema, String table) returns a **ResultSet** containing information (table catalog, table schema, table name, column name, key sequence, primary key name) on the primary keys.

- **getImportedKeys**(String catalog, String schema, String table) returns a **ResultSet** containing information (such as primary key table catalog, primary key table schema, primary key table name, primary key column name, foreign key table catalog, foreign key table schema, foreign key table name, and foreign key column name) on the primary keys that are referenced by a table's foreign keys.

■ **getExportedKeys**(String catalog, String schema, String table) returns a **ResultSet** containing information (primary key table catalog, primary key table schema, primary key table name, primary key column name, foreign key table catalog, foreign key table schema, foreign key table name, foreign key column name, etc.) on the foreign keys that reference a table's primary keys.

SQLException Class

A **SQLException** object contains the following information about database access errors:

■ A string describing the error
■ A "SQLState" string that follows the X/Open SQLState conventions
■ An integer error code that is vender specific

The **SQLException** interface extends the **Exception** interface.

Constructors

■ **SQLException**()

■ **SQLException**(String reason)

■ **SQLException**(String reason, String SQLState)

■ **SQLException**(String reason, String SQLState, int vendorCode)

Methods

■ **getSQLState**() returns the SQLState (**String**).

■ **getErrorCode**() returns the vendor-specific error code (int).

■ **getNextException**() returns the next (chained) **SQLException** object.

■ **setNextException**(SQLException ex) sets the next (chained) exception.

Others

The other classes included in the **java.sql** package (in addition to **Date**, **Time**, and **Timestamp,** which were discussed in Chapter 4, "Relational Databases and SQL") include:

- **DriverPropertyInfo.** This is only of interest to programmers who need to interact with a driver to discover and supply properties for connections.

- **Types.** This class defines class constants that are used to identify SQL data types. They include the nineteen listed in Table 7-1 plus NULL and OTHER.

CONCLUSION

We hope by now you have a good understanding of JDBC and a good grasp of its API. In Chapter 10, "Sample Data Access Applications," we will go over many programming examples using JDBC to define and manipulate the **ArcWorld** sample database. Therefore, if right now you feel a little hazy on how exactly you should program in JDBC, please hang on; we will clear out that haze. If you need to know the exact syntax and semantics of the JDBC API, please consult the **java.sql** package documentation that is included in the JDK.

JDBC made Java data access easy. However, it is not the only game in town. If compile-time checking and static binding are important to you, you should consider *SQLJ*, which we will introduce in the next chapter. If you have an object-oriented database, then the *ODMG Java Binding* probably is best for you; we will discuss it in Chapter 9, "Java Binding for OODB."

JDBC is evolving and it will add a rich set of functionality in *JDBC 2.0*, particularly in the area of direct support for Java objects and user-defined data types in databases. We will discuss JDBC 2.0 in Chapter 22, "Conclusion: Emerging Technologies."

Chapter 8

Introduction to SQLJ

concepts

You probably have heard of *Embedded SQL* where SQL statements are embedded in a programming language. The programming language is called the *host language*, and an embedded program is a mixture of a host language and SQL. For many languages, such as FORTRAN, it is the only mechanism you can use to access databases from that language. For other languages, such as COBOL, Embedded SQL existed before call-level interfaces such as ODBC, and it remains as the most frequently used means for accessing databases from that language. Embedded SQL can contain either *static SQL* statements or *dynamic SQL* statements. Static SQL statements are processed at program compile time, whereas dynamic SQL statements are processed at program run time.

ANSI/ISO specified rules for Embedded SQL quite some time ago for a number of languages, including ADA, C, COBOL, FORTRAN, MUMPS, and PL/I. The elements of Embedded SQL can be classified into four groups:

■ **Executable SQL statements**. These statements can be used to manipulate SQL definitions (CREATE, ALTER, and DROP; GRANT and REVOKE), data (INSERT, SELECT, UPDATE, and DELETE; OPEN, FETCH, and CLOSE), and transactions (COMMIT and ROLLBACK; SET TRANSACTION and SET CONSTRAINTS).

- *Dynamic SQL*. These statements can be used to prepare and execute SQL statements at run time (PREPARE, DESCRIBE, and EXECUTE; DEALLOCATE, GET DESCRIPTOR, and SET DESCRIPTOR).

- *Declarations*. These statements can be used to define host variables and cursors (BEGIN DECLARE SECTION and END DECLARE SECTION; DECLARE CURSOR), which allow you to transfer data between the host language and SQL.

- *Program control*. These statements can be used to manage SQL sessions (SET AUTHORIZATION, SET CATALOG, SET NAMES, SET SCHEMA, SET SESSION, and SET TIME ZONE), database connections (CONNECT, SET CONNECTION, and DISCONNECT), exceptions (WHENEVER), and diagnostics (GET DIAGNOSTICS).

SQLJ, at the time of this writing, is a proposal being made to ANSI/ISO for *Embedded SQL for Java*, sponsored by IBM, Oracle, Sybase, and Tandem. These companies decided to submit a proposal for a new and different specification for Java because of the following considerations:

- *Object-oriented languages*, such as Java, are significantly different from the procedural languages, such as C, that already have bindings. The *type systems* of object-oriented languages can represent, for example, the types of database connections, result-set cursors, and SQL exceptions, which were not representable in the type systems of procedural languages. Cursor is an example: the type system of an object-oriented language can express the attributes of a row returned by a query, and the compiler can ensure that the operations on a cursor are correct for the particular query that it represents.

- *Java* is unique in many ways and it has special benefits that deserve special considerations. Java's type safety (for example, no pointer types) and automatic storage management allow a user's programs to run safely in the address space of database servers. Also, it makes no sense for a user to pass a buffer to a SQL operation as the destination for data; instead, data returned from SQL can be materialized as values of the appropriate types. Java's notions of portability (for example, bytecodes and virtual machines), global naming (such as globally unique package names and the use of URLs to refer to programs and databases), and component software (dynamic specification, loading, and execution) mean that pre-compilers for Embedded SQL in Java will be broadly available and customizable. The *generic portion* of a pre-compiler may be written once and made universally available. And, it may call *components* that are specialized for different vendors' databases, which support vendor-specific features and extensions to SQL.

- *JDBC* is a call-level API in Java that provides dynamic SQL functionality. It makes no sense to duplicate its functionality in Embedded SQL for Java.

145

Consequently, the elements of Embedded SQL are treated differently in the SQLJ specification:

- **Executable SQL statements**. The SQLJ specification directly adopts the executable SQL statements that manipulate SQL definitions, data, and transactions.

- **Dynamic SQL**. The SQLJ specification does not address dynamic SQL for Java. That has been done in JDBC.

- **Declarations**. The SQLJ specification replaces these with declarations of Java types for cursors and other data items with SQL attributes.

- **Program control**. The SQLJ specification omits many of these statements and uses Java types to represent database connections, exceptions, and diagnostics.

OVERVIEW OF SQLJ

SQLJ is Embedded SQL for Java. It consists of a set of clauses that extend Java programs to include *static SQL*. These clauses are static because they are textually evident in the Java program and can therefore be precompiled when the containing Java program is compiled.

A *SQLJ translator* is a tool that translates *SQLJ clauses* to standard Java code that accesses databases through a call-level interface. The output of a SQLJ translator is a generated Java program that can be compiled by any Java compiler. SQLJ can be used in a client program or a server program (for example, a stored procedure). This is illustrated in Figure 8-1, which reflects the architecture used in the SQLJ Reference Implementation developed by Oracle that uses JDBC to access databases.

SQLJ allows translators to perform compile-time analysis of SQL in Java for:

- **Syntax checking** to determine that the SQL statements are legal
- **Type checking** to ensure that the data exchanged between Java and SQL have compatible types and proper type conversions
- **Schema checking** to ensure that the SQL constructs are valid in the database schema where they will be executed.

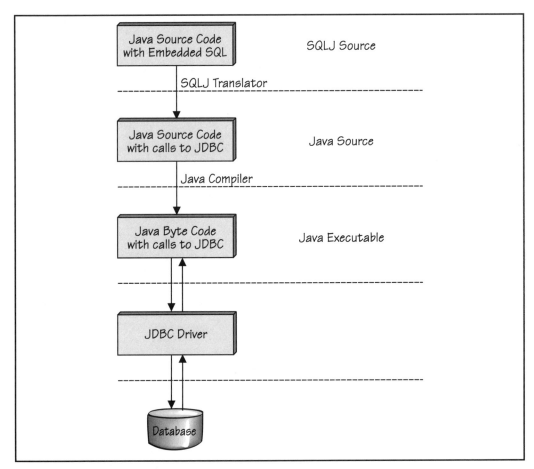

Figure 8-1. The SQLJ Translator.

SQLJ Design Goals

As is the case with JDBC, we will first look at the specific design goals of SQLJ to help us put things in perspective and understand SQLJ's following strengths and limitations:

■ **Standard Embedded SQL**. SQLJ is intended to be the ANSI/ISO standard Embedded SQL for Java. It comprises standard Java with lexically localized syntax extensions for SQL. A *SQLJ program* is a Java source program containing SQLJ clauses.

■ **SQL conformance**. SQLJ specifies a core syntax for embedding SQL in Java, which allows extensions (confined to the SQL clauses) to be supported by vendor-specific rules. Currently SQLJ only addresses *SQL-92 Entry Level*. In the future, it is expected to reach the level of SQL3.

■ *Type checking*. A SQLJ translator checks the compatibility of Java and SQL expressions at translation time.

■ *Schema checking*. Each SQLJ clause is associated with a *connection type*, which represents the kind of database schema where that clause will be executed. At translation time, an *exemplar schema* may be associated with each connection type. A SQLJ translator checks that each clause is valid in the exemplar schema corresponding to its connection type. However, it should be possible to write, translate, and compile SQLJ programs without an exemplar schema.

■ *Optimization of SQL*. A SQLJ translator can provide for the optimization of SQL queries by making them available to a database system for *pre-compilation and optimization at translation time*.

■ *Consistency with Java.* Java has some unique characteristics that significantly affect its embedding of SQL:

◆ Java has *automatic storage management* that simplifies the management of storage for data retrieved from databases.

◆ All Java types have a distinguished value, *null*, which can be used to represent the SQL NULL state.

◆ Java is designed to support programs that are *automatically portable or downloadable*. A SQLJ translator, written in Java, can call database components that are specialized by database vendors.

◆ Java is designed for *binary portability* in heterogeneous networks, which promises to enable binary portability for database applications that use static SQL.

■ *Component software*. SQLJ programs, compiled at different times, must be able to both interoperate and exchange SQL data in a type-safe and efficient manner. A Java component exports and imports *interfaces and classes* that mediate its interactions with other components. SQLJ must use those mechanisms for SQL data.

■ *Location transparency.* SQLJ is intended to be used in either client programs or server programs (for example, stored procedures). Therefore, SQLJ programs should be location transparent, which means their syntax and semantics should not depend explicitly upon their execution context.

- ***Portability.*** SQLJ programs, translated to Java calling a given SQL API, must be no less portable than Java programs written directly calling that SQL API. For instance, if a SQLJ program is translated to use JDBC, then it should run wherever JDBC runs.

SQLJ Concepts

SQLJ programs may contain the following kinds of SQL constructs:

- ***Data Definition Language (DDL)***: examples include CREATE, ALTER, and DROP
- ***Queries***: SELECT statements and expressions
- ***Data statements***: FETCH..INTO and SELECT..INTO
- ***Data Manipulation Language (DML)***: INSERT, UPDATE, and DELETE
- ***Calls to user-defined functions***
- ***Calls to stored procedures***
- ***Transaction management***: examples include COMMIT and ROLLBACK
- ***Session directives***

Host Variables

Host variables are used to pass arguments from Java to embedded SQL statements. They are Java identifiers that appear in the SQL statement, prefixed by a *colon* (:). The identifier may name a parameter, variable, or field (of an object). The following query contains host variable :y (assumed to be visible in the scope containing the query):

```
SELECT name, city FROM Building WHERE :y > yearBuilt
```

In certain SQL statements, host variables can be assigned values retrieved by SQL queries. For example:

```
SELECT name, yearBuilt INTO :n, :y FROM Building
   WHERE name = 'Lincoln Memorial'
```

SQLJ Clauses

Static SQL appears in SQLJ clauses. Each SQLJ clause begins with the token *#sql*. The simplest SQLJ clause consists of the token #sql followed by a SQL statement enclosed in *curly braces*. For example, the following SQLJ clause may appear anywhere that a Java statement appears:

```
#sql { DELETE FROM Building };
```

In a SQLJ clause, the tokens inside the curly braces are SQL tokens, except for the host variables. SQL tokens never appear outside of the single pair of curly braces.

Database Connection Context

Each SQLJ clause designates, either explicitly or implicitly, a *connection-context object* that represents the database connection where the SQL statement in that clause will execute. The connection-context object appears as a *parenthesized expression* immediately following #sql. For example, the connection-context object in the following SQLJ clause is the value of the Java variable *con*:

```
#sql (con) { DELETE FROM Building };
```

A connection-context object is an instance of a *connection-context class*, which is defined by means of a SQLJ connection clause; for example:

```
#sql context AWConnect
```

A connection-context class has methods for opening a connection to a database schema, given a URL, user name, and password. At run time, a SQLJ program must call those methods to establish a database connection before any SQLJ clauses can be executed. SQLJ allows the possibility that a Java program can manipulate multiple connection-context object connected to different databases.

The connection-context object is optional in a SQLJ clause. When it is absent from the SQLJ clause, there must be a default connection-context class for the translation unit. That default must be indicated to the translator in some manner.

Exemplar Schemas

At translation time, the connection-context class represents the kind of database schema to which the SQLJ program will connect at run time. This is made possible through the use of an *exemplar schema*, which is simply a database schema that contains the tables, views, programs, and privileges that would be required for the SQL operation in the SQLJ clause to execute successfully. An exemplar schema may be the actual run-time schema.

The invoker of a SQLJ translator must provide a mapping of connection-context classes to exemplar schemas. A SQLJ translator connects to the exemplar schema to do syntax checking, type checking, and schema checking for SQLJ clauses that will be executed on connection-contexts of the class corresponding to the exemplar schema. If no exemplar schema is provided for a connection-context class, SQLJ clauses to be executed on connections of that class will not be schema-checked at translation time.

Result-Set Iterators

SQLJ separates queries from result sets. Queries appear in program statements as SQLJ clauses. Result sets are encapsulated in first-class iterator objects. A SQLJ clause may evaluate a query and return a *result-set iterator object* containing (logically) the result set selected by that query. An iterator has one or more columns with associated Java types, which are conceptually distinct from the columns of a query that have SQL types.

SQLJ does not name individual queries or iterator objects; instead, it relies on the naming mechanism of Java to name the type of iterator objects so that iterators can be passed among SQLJ components while preserving strong type checking. Two mechanisms are supported for matching iterator columns to query columns: *bind-by-position* and *bind-by-name*. An iterator declaration clause indicates whether objects of that class use bind-by-position or bind-by-name, but not both.

Bind-by-position means that the left-to-right order of declaration of the iterator columns corresponds to the expressions selected in the query. FETCH..INTO syntax is used to retrieve data from the iterator object into Java variables. The following is an example of an iterator declaration that binds by position:

```
#sql public iterator ByPosition (String, int);
```

The iterator is used in the following query on the **Building** table to return the **name** and **yearBuilt** columns:

```
{
    ByPosition posIter;
    String name;
    int year;
    #sql posIter = { SELECT name, yearBuilt FROM Building };
    while (true) {
        #sql { FETCH :posIter INTO :name, :year };
        if (posIter.endFetch()) break;
        System.out.println(name + " was built in " + year);
    }
}
```

A SQLJ translator checks that the types of host variables in the INTO phrase match the types of the positionally corresponding iterator columns.

Bind-by-name means that the name of each iterator column is matched to the name of a query column. Named accessor methods are generated for the columns of the iterator. The name of each accessor method matches the name of a query column and its return type. The following is an example of an iterator declaration that binds by name:

```
#sql public iterator ByName (String name, int year);
```

The iterator is used in the following query on the **Building** table to return the **name** and **yearBuilt** columns:

```
{
    ByName nameIter;
    #sql nameIter = { SELECT name, yearBuilt FROM Building };
    while (nameIter.next()) {
        System.out.println(nameIter.name() + " was built in " +
            nameIter.year());
    }
}
```

Calling User-Defined Functions and Stored Procedures

A SQLJ clause may call a user-defined function by means of the SQL VALUES construct. For example, assuming a user-defined function *F1* returning an integer, the following code calls that function and assigns the result to the Java variable *x*:

```
{
    int x;
    #sql x = { VALUES( F1(35) ) };
}
```

A SQLJ clause may call a stored procedure by means of the SQL CALL statement. For example:

```
#sql { CALL Proc1(:arg) };
```

Stored procedures may have IN, OUT, or INOUT parameters.

SQLJ SPECIFICATION

A SQLJ translator takes as input one or more *Java compilation units* that may contain SQLJ clauses. A Java compilation unit is a set of classes and interfaces in the same Java package. The source text for a compilation unit is typically contained in a single text file. If the compilation units contain no SQLJ clauses, then the SQLJ translator does not affect them.

When a SQLJ translator connects to an exemplar schema, it must succeed in accepting and rewriting well-formed SQLJ clauses containing SQL constructs. The SQLJ translator then generates a Java program, which will be compiled by a Java compiler. When the resulting program executes and connects to a database, those SQL constructs must execute with the semantics ascribed to them by ANSI/ISO.

SQLJ clauses neither create Java threads nor affect the synchronization of threads. The programmer may, however, synchronize Java methods containing SQLJ clauses.

There are three kinds of SQLJ clauses:

- Connection declaration clauses
- Iterator declaration clauses
- Executable clauses

A *connection-declaration clause* declares a Java type for a database connection. An *iterator-declaration clause* declares a Java type for a result-set iterator. An *executable clause* executes a SQL construct.

Grammar Notation

The grammar for SQLJ clauses uses the following notation:

- *Terminal*. Characters in **bold** represent literals and terminal symbols.

- *Non-terminal*. Characters in *italics* represent non-terminals that are defined by the right-hand side of a production (==) or are considered to be well-known. Well-known non-terminals include *java-id*, which represents any legal Java identifier; *java-name*, which represents any legal Java name; *java-expression*, which represents any legal Java expression; and *sql-id*, which represents any legal SQL identifier.

- *Optional*. Elements between brackets ([]) are optional, which may occur zero or one time.

- *Alternative*. Alternative elements are separated by the vertical bar (|).

Host Variables

A *host variable* is a Java identifier that denotes a parameter, variable, or field (of an object); it appears in the SQL portion of a SQLJ clause, prefixed by a colon. SQLJ adopts the ANSI/SQL rules that specify where host variables may appear in static SQL statements.

```
host-variable == :java-id
```

Data Type Mappings

SQLJ allows conversions from SQL data types to Java data types identical to those specified for JDBC (see Table 7-1 on page 118). SQLJ also allows conversions from Java data types to SQL data types, as specified for JDBC (see Table 7-2 on page 119).

SQLJ Clauses

All SQLJ clauses begin with the token **#sql**. A SQLJ clause consists of these four parts:

```
#sql [connection] [glue] [sql]
```

The *connection* part is a parenthesized Java expression with a connection-context class as its type. The *glue* part consists of Java tokens and varies among the kinds of SQLJ clauses. The *sql* part is a SQL statement or expression, enclosed in curly braces. Although all three parts are shown as optional, at least one must be present in any actual SQLJ clause.

Database Connections

Database connections are represented by objects of classes that are defined by means of the *connection-declaration* clause. That clause may appear where a Java class definition may appear, and it has the following syntax:

```
#sql [modifiers] context java-id ;
```

Modifiers are Java class modifiers, such as **public**.

The effect of the clause is to generate a class named *java-id*. For example, the following clause causes the **AWConnect** class to be generated:

```
#sql context AWConnect;
```

The **AWConnect** class is defined in the following sections.

ConnectionContext Interface

The **ConnectionContext** interface is contained in the **sqlj.runtime** package. A connection context manages a set of SQL operations performed during a session with a specific database.

It has the following *class constants*:

- **CLOSE_CONNECTION** (boolean)

- **KEEP_CONNECTION** (boolean)

And, it has the following *methods*:

- **getConnectedProfile**(Object profileKey) returns the connected profile associated with the given profile key for this connection context. Collectively, the set of all connected profiles contained in a connection context represents the set of all possible SQL operations that may be performed.

- **getConnection**() returns the underlying JDBC connection object (**java.sql. Connection**) associated with this connection context.

- **getExecutionContext**() returns the default execution context (**Execution-Context**) used by this connection context.

- **close**() releases all resources used, closes any open connected profile, and closes the underlying database connection.

- **close**(boolean closeConnection) releases all resources used and closes any open connected profile. If KEEP_CONNECTION is passed, the underlying database connection is not closed. Otherwise, if CLOSE_CONNECTION is passed, the underlying database connection is closed.

- **isClosed**() returns true (boolean) if this connection context is closed.

ExecutionContext Interface

An execution context provides the context in which executable SQL operations are performed. An execution context object contains a number of operations for execution control, execution status reporting, and execution cancellation.

It has the following *class constants*:

■ **QUERY_COUNT** (boolean)

■ **EXCEPTION_COUNT** (boolean)

And, it has the following *constructor*:

■ **ExecutionContext**()

Finally, it has the following *accessor methods*:

■ **getMaxFieldSize**() returns the maximum amount (int) of data in bytes that can be returned for any field; it only applies to columns of the following types: BINARY, VARBINARY, LONGVARBINARY, CHAR, VARCHAR, and LONGVAR-CHAR.

■ **setMaxFieldSize**(int max) sets the maximum amount of data in bytes that can be returned for any field; it only applies to columns of the following types: BINARY, VARBINARY, LONGVARBINARY, CHAR, VARCHAR, and LONGVAR-CHAR.

■ **getMaxRows**() returns the maximum number (int) of rows that a result set can contain.

■ **setMaxRows**(int max) sets the maximum number of rows that a result set can contain.

■ **getQueryTimeout**() returns the number (int) of seconds this execution context will wait for this statement to execute.

■ **setQueryTimeout**(int seconds) sets the number of seconds this execution context will wait for this statement to execute.

■ **getWarnings**() returns the first warning (**java.sql.SQLWarning**) reported by the last SQL operation executed using this execution context.

■ **getUpdateCount**() returns the number (int) of rows updated by the last SQL operation executed using this execution context.

The following are additional *methods*:

■ **executeQuery**() performs an execute query on the currently registered statement.

■ **executeUpdate**() performs an execute update on the currently registered statement.

■ **cancel**() can be used by one thread to cancel a SQL operation that is currently being executed by another thread on a shared connection context.

■ **registerStatement**(java.sql.PreparedStatement stmt) sets the given statement to be the currently registered statement.

■ **releaseStatement**() releases the currently registered statement, signaling that all execution related operations have been completed.

AWConnect Class

The **AWConnect** class implements the **ConnectionContext** interface and has the following *constructors*:

■ **AWConnect**(String url) establishes a connection to the database represented by the given *url*.

■ **AWConnect**(String url, String user, String password) establishes a connection to the database represented by the given *url*; it uses the given *user* id and *password*.

■ **AWConnect**(String url, java.util.Properties info) establishes a connection to the database represented by the given *url*; it uses the given *info*.

■ **AWConnect**(ConnectionContext other) shares the same database connection with the *other* connection-context object.

■ **AWConnect**(java.sql.Connection conn) shares the same database connection with the JDBC connection, *conn*.

And, it has the following *class methods*:

■ **getDefaultContext**() returns the default connection-context (**AWConnect**) object.

- **setDefaultContext**(AWConnect ctx) sets the default connection-context object to the given *ctx* object.

- **getProfileKey**(sqlj.runtime.profile.Loader l, String profileName) returns a profile key (**Object**) for the specified profile loader and name.

- **getProfile**(Object key) returns a top-level profile (**sqlj.runtime.profile.Profile**) for the given profile key.

The Default Connection

When a SQLJ translator is run on a given compilation unit, its invocation must indicate, for each connection-class used in SQLJ clauses contained in that compilation unit, either an *exemplar schema* for that class or that no exemplar schema is provided for that class. Also, if the compilation unit contains SQLJ clauses that mention no connection-context object, the invocation must provide the *default connection-context class* and indicate either its exemplar schema or that no exemplar schema is provided.

Suppose that an invocation of a SQLJ translator indicates that the default connection-context class is the **AWConnect** class. Then SQLJ clauses that use the default connection will be translated as if they used the explicit connection-context object **AWConnect**.*getDefaultContext()*, for example:

```
#sql (AWConnect.getDefaultContext()) { UPDATE Building
  SET yearBuilt = :y WHERE name = :n };
```

Programs may install a connection-context object as the default connection by calling the *setDefaultContext()* method, for example:

```
AWConnect.setDefaultContext(new AWConnect(argv[0]));
```

Here, argv[] are argument values provided through the command line.

SQL Constructs

This section lists the kinds of SQL constructs that may appear in SQLJ clauses. Each SQL construct may appear in an *assignment clause,* which evaluates a SQL construct and assigns its value to a Java parameter, variable, or field. For example:

```
#sql posIter = { SELECT name, yearBuilt FROM Building };
```

They may also appear in a *statement clause*, which executes the SQL construct for its side effects, for example:

```
#sql { DELETE FROM Building };
```

DDL

DDL (Data Definition Language) statements include those beginning with SQL keywords such as CREATE, ALTER, and DROP. They may appear in statement clauses, and they are denoted by the non-terminal *ddl*.

Queries

A query is a SQL SELECT statement that does not contain the keyword INTO. It may appear in an assignment clause. For example:

```
#sql { SELECT name, city FROM Building WHERE :y > yearBuilt };
```

A query is denoted by the non-terminal *query*.

SELECT..INTO and FETCH..INTO

A SELECT..INTO statement is a SELECT statement that contains a list of host variables, introduced by the keyword INTO, to which the selected data is assigned. The number of host variables must match the number of selected expressions, and the SQL types of the selected expressions must be convertible to the Java types of the positionally corresponding host variables. The SELECT..INTO statement may appear in a statement clause. For example:

```
#sql { SELECT name, yearBuilt INTO :n, :y FROM Building
   WHERE name = 'Lincoln Memorial' };
```

The FETCH..INTO statement assigns the column values in the next row of a bind-by-position iterator into host variables. The number of host variables must match the number of columns in the query that evaluated to that iterator, and the host variable at position i receives the value of the selected expression at position i in the query. The FETCH..INTO statement may appear in a statement clause. An example has been shown in "Result-Set Iterators" on page 150.

Either a SELECT..INTO or a FETCH..INTO statement is denoted by the non-terminal *fetch*.

DML

DML (Data Manipulation Language) statements include SQL INSERT, UPDATE, and DELETE statements. DML statements may appear in a statement clause, and they are denoted by the non-terminal *dml*.

Calls to User-defined Functions

The SQL keyword VALUES indicates a call to a user-defined function. It may appear in an assignment clause with the following syntax:

```
VALUES( sql-name( arguments ) )
```

where

```
sql-name == [[catalog-id.]schema-id.]sql-id
catalog-id == sql-id
schema-id == sql-id
```

and where *arguments* is a list of zero or more host variables or SQL expressions, separated by commas.

The non-terminal *func* denotes a call to a user-defined function.

Calls to Stored Procedures

The SQL keyword CALL indicates a call to a stored procedure. It may appear in a statement clause with the following syntax:

```
CALL sql-name( arguments )
```

A stored procedure may have IN, OUT, or INOUT parameters. Arguments corresponding to OUT or INOUT parameters must be host variables.

The non-terminal *proc* denotes a call to a stored procedure.

Transaction Management

Transaction management statements include those beginning with SQL keywords such as COMMIT and ROLLBACK. They may appear in statement clauses, and they are denoted by the non-terminal *transaction*.

Session Directives

Session directives may appear in statement clauses. They are denoted by the non-terminal *session*.

SQL Blocks

A SQL block consists of one or more SQL constructs that may appear in a statement clause (except for a SQL block); they are terminated by semicolons and enclosed between BEGIN and END. A SQL block may appear in a statement clause. For example:

```
#sql { BEGIN
        DELETE FROM Building;
        INSERT INTO Building (name, yearBuilt) VALUES (:n, :y);
      END };
```

A SQL block is denoted by the non-terminal *block*.

Others

The following non-terminals may appear in particular SQLJ clauses:

> *expr == query | func*
>
> *stmt == simple-stmt | stmts | block*
>
> *simple-stmt == ddl | fetch | dml | proc | transaction | session*
>
> *stmts == simple-stmt | simple-stmt ; stmts*
>
> *block ==* **BEGIN** *[atomicity] stmts* ; **END**
>
> *atomicity ==* **ATOMIC** | **NOT ATOMIC**

Iterator Declarations

The SQLJ clause for declaring an iterator class has two forms, distinguishing bind-by-position from bind-by-name:

> *iterator-by-position ==*
>   **#sql** *[modifiers]* **iterator** *iterator-name* **(** *position-list* **);**

```
iterator-by-name ==
  #sql [modifiers] iterator iterator-name [implements]
    ( name-list );
```

where

```
position-list == column-type | column-type , position-list

name-list == column-pair | column-pair , name-list

column-type == java-name

column-pair == column-type column-id

column-id == java-id

implements == implements java-name-list

java-name-list == java-name | java-name , java-name-list
```

and where *modifiers* are Java class modifiers, such as **public**. An iterator declaration clause may appear where a Java class definition may appear.

From an iterator-declaration clause, a SQLJ translator generates an iterator-class. All iterator-classes implement the **ResultSetIterator** interface. For an iterator-by-position, a SQLJ translator generates an iterator class implementing the **PositionalIterator** interface; for an iterator-by-name, a SQLJ translator generates an iterator class implementing the **NamedIterator** interface. These interfaces are defined in the following sections.

ResultSetIterator Interface

The **ResultSetIterator** interface defines the shared functionality of iterators and has the following methods:

- **next**() advances this iterator to the next row, if it exists. Returns true (boolean) if advancement is successful.

- **getResultSet**() returns the JDBC result set (**java.sql.ResultSet**) associated with this iterator.

- **rowCount**() returns the number (int) of the current row. The first row is 1.

- **close**() closes this iterator, releasing any underlying resources.

- **isClosed**() returns true (boolean) if this iterator is closed.

Initially, a newly constructed iterator is positioned before the first row in the result set. An example has been given in "Result-Set Iterators" on page 150.

ForUpdate Interface

The **ForUpdate** interface must be implemented by iterators that will be used in a *positioned update or delete statement*. It has the following *method*:

■ **getCursorName**() returns the name (**String**) of the SQL cursor used by this iterator.

PositionalIterator Interface

The **PositionalIterator** interface extends the **ResultSetIterator** interface and has the following method:

■ **endFetch**() returns true (boolean) if a FETCH..INTO is attempted beyond the last row.

The FETCH..INTO statement is used for access to columns of a positional iterator. It advances the iterator to the next row in the result set and assigns its column values into host variables that are matched positionally to the expression in the query from which the iterator is obtained. An example has been given in "Result-Set Iterators" on page 150.

In addition to implementing this interface, positional iterators will provide:

■ A public constructor that takes a JDBC result set as a parameter.
■ An accessor method for each column in the expected result set. The name of the accessor method for the Nth column will be *getColN*.

NamedIterator Interface

The **NamedIterator** interface extends the **ResultSetIterator** interface.

In addition to implementing this interface, named iterators will provide:

■ A public constructor that takes a JDBC result set as a parameter.
■ An accessor method for each column in the expected result set. The name of the accessor method will match the expected name of the result column.

Executable Clauses

There are two kinds of executable clauses: the *assignment clause* and the *statement clause*. An executable clause may appear where a Java statement may appear. Java methods containing executable clauses may raise exception **java.sql.SQLException**.

Assignment Clause

An assignment clause executes a SQL operation and assigns its value to a Java parameter, variable, or field. It may appear where a Java assignment statement may appear with the following syntax:

```
#sql [connection] java-lhs = { expr };
```

Here, *java-lhs* is a Java expression that can appear on the left-hand side of a Java assignment statement.

When the value of *expr* is a result set, the type of *java-lhs* must be an iterator-class, and the number and types of columns of the query of the result set must match those of the iterator-class declaration. When the value of *expr* is not a result set, that value is produced as a value of type of *java-lhs*.

Statement Clause

A statement clause executes a SQL statement with its side effects. It may contain, in addition to SQL statements, a *call* or a *block*. A statement clause may appear where a Java statement may appear with the following syntax:

```
#sql [connection] { stmt };
```

Positioned Update and Delete

SQLJ supports positioned update and delete. In a SQLJ executable clause containing a positioned update or delete, a host variable appears in the WHERE CURRENT OF phrase:

```
WHERE CURRENT OF host-variable
```

For example:

```
#sql { UPDATE Building SET yearBuilt = :y WHERE CURRENT OF posIter };
```

Null Values

When the Java value null is passed to SQL as an input value, it denotes a SQL NULL value. For example:

```
Integer y = null;
#sql { UPDATE Building SET yearBuilt = :y WHERE name = :n };
```

When SQL NULL values are retrieved into host variables of any Java object types, those host variables are assigned the Java value null. When SQL NULL values are retrieved into host variables of any Java scalar types, **java.sql.SQLException** is raised and no assignment is made.

Exceptions

Some methods of connection-context objects and iterators may raise exception **java.sql.SQLException** as specified by JDBC (see Chapter 7, "JDBC in a Nutshell").

SQLJ RUNTIME FRAMEWORK

You may recall that in JDBC, different data sources can have different JDBC drivers, and the JDBC **DriverManager** at run time will use the first driver it finds that can successfully connect to a given data source. (The drivers must have been loaded and registered with the **DriverManager**.) Can you do the same in SQLJ? The answer is yes, and this functionality (called *portable customization*) is provided through the SQLJ runtime framework. Of course, the SQLJ runtime framework provides more functionality than this. It provides all the support needed for SQLJ code generation and runtime.

Runtime Packages

The SQLJ runtime framework consists of the following packages:

- **sqlj.runtime.** This includes classes and interfaces such as **ConnectionContext, ExecutionContext, ResultSetIterator, NamedIterator, PositionedIterator**, and **ForUpdate**, which we have discussed previously.

- **sqlj.runtime.ref.** This includes classes such as **RTPreparedStatement, RTCallableStatement**, and **RTResultSet**, which are used in SQLJ code generation (we will discuss this shortly).

- **sqlj.runtime.error.** This includes classes that contain error formatting routines.

- **sqlj.runtime.profile.** This includes classes and interfaces such as **Profile, ProfileData, EntryInfo, TypeInfo, PositionedDescriptor, ConnectedProfile**, and **Customization**, which are essential for providing the SQLJ portable customization functionality that we will discuss later.

- **sqlj.runtime.profile.ref.** This includes classes such as **JDBCProfile, PositionedProfile, TransactionControlProfile**, and **TypeRegisterProfile**, which implement the default (JDBC) connected profile that we will discuss later. It also includes classes such as **ProfileWrapper, PreparedStatementWrapper, CallableStatementWrapper**, and **ResultSetWrapper**, which you can extend to provide desired functionality for customized connected profiles.

- **sqlj.runtime.profile.util.** This includes utility classes such as **DataCustomizer**, which you can extend to provide customization of profile data, and **ProfilePrinter**, a very useful tool that can pretty-print a profile, which usually exists as a serialized object.

Executable SQL Codegen Pattern

SQLJ processing in general involves three phases: *translation, installation,* and *runtime*. At translation time, the major tasks are code generation and profile generation. We will discuss profile generation later. The code generation uses the following pattern:

- Get the *connected profile* from the connection context.
- Get the *JDBC prepared statement* or *callable statement* from the connected profile.
- Wrap the statement with the corresponding *SQLJ statement* (**RTPreparedStatement** or **RTCallableStatement**).
- Bind inputs using methods with the pattern *setXXX()*.
- Execute the statement using either *executeQuery()* or *executeUpdate()*.
- Create *iterator* (**NamedIterator** or **PositionedIterator**) if needed.
- Get outputs using methods with the pattern *getXXX()*.
- Release the statement by calling the method *close()*.

To ensure binary composition, the following requirements must be met:

- Connection contexts must implement the *getConnectedProfile()* method that takes a *profile key* as a parameter.
- Iterators must implement a public constructor that takes a *JDBC result set* as a parameter.

Connected profiles, therefore, are the means by which a SQLJ application is portably customized.

Profile Overview

In the following sections we will give a quick overview of *profile*, *connected profile*, and *customization*, which are keys to SQLJ portable customization. Each of these (and associated) constructs has a corresponding Java class or interface contained in the SQLJ runtime packages discussed previously.

Profile

A *profile* contains *profile data*, which in turn consists of one or more *entry info*. A profile is uniquely identified by its name, the associated connection context name, and a timestamp. Each entry fully describes a particular SQL statement in the SQLJ application associated with the profile, including the statement type (prepared statement or callable statement), execution type (execute query, execute update, or execute), parameters, and results. In essence, a profile fully describes its associated SQLJ application.

Connected Profile

As mentioned before, *connected profiles* are the means by which a SQLJ application is portably customized. By default, a connected profile shares the same profile data with its associated profile. It is used at run time to create executable SQL statements, as shown earlier, by using indices into "static" profile data entries. The statement returned by a connected profile obeys the following semantics:

- The SQL text is parsed and ready to execute.
- It has the same execution semantics as if JDBC had been used to dynamically execute the statement.
- Any OUT parameters have been registered.

If there is no customization, the *default connected profile* is used, which uses *standard JDBC dynamic SQL mapping* as follows:

- **Default statement creation** (provided by **JDBCProfile**)—*prepareStatement()* maps to JDBC *prepareStatement()* and *prepareCall()* maps to JDBC *prepareCall()*.
- **Default OUT parameters registration** (provided by **TypeRegisterProfile**)—JDBC *registerOutParameter()* is used.
- **Default transaction control** (provided by **TransactionControlProfile**)— JDBC *commit()*, *rollback()*, *setReadOnly()*, and *setTransactionIsolation()* are used.
- **Default positioned update/delete** (provided by **PositionedProfile**)—a new statement is dynamically created and executed as required by JDBC.

Customization

Profiles may be customized in any number of ways. Some typical examples include:

- Transformation of SQL text into a form that allows more efficient execution (for example, the use of stored procedures)
- Batch verification and/or preparation of profile entries
- Distributed and/or remote loading of custom entries
- Custom type registration of data-source-specific entry parameters
- Behavioral unification of multiple JDBC drivers

Profile Management

Profiles must be managed at all three phases of SQLJ processing:

- At translation time, profiles must be generated and packaged.
- At installation time, profiles may be customized.
- At run time, profiles must be instantiated and resolved.

We will discuss each of these tasks later. But now, we will point out the following relationships between connection context and profile (see Figure 8-2):

- At translation time, each *connection context class* manages a collection of *profile instances*.
- At run time, each *connection context instance* manages a collection of *connected profile instances*.

Profile keys are used for such management. That is, a connection context class maps profile keys to profile instances, and a connection context instance maps profile keys to connected profile instances.

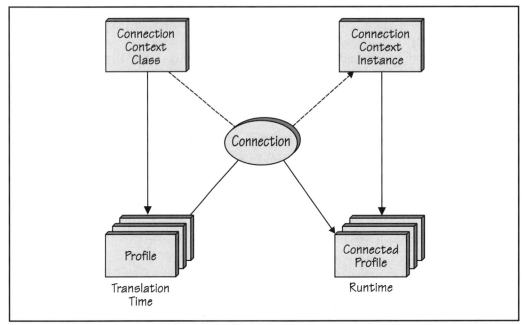

Figure 8-2. Connection Context—Profile Relationships.

Profile Generation

Profile generation occurs during SQLJ translation. Profiles are generated as *serialized objects*, and one profile is generated for each connection context. For example, if a SQLJ application contains ten SQL statements, then a profile is generated with ten entries. Each entry fully describes a particular SQL statement. Profiles are named as:

    <InputFileName>_SJProfile<N>.ser

The translator also generates a "profile keys" class with the following name:

    <InputFileName>_SJProfileKeys.class

As an example (taken from Chapter 10, "Sample Data Access Applications"), a SQLJ application contains the following SQL statement (and uses the default connection context):

    SELECT name, city, type FROM Building

The profile generated is shown in Listing 8-1. The utility class **sqlj.runtime.profile.util.ProfilePrinter**, is used to pretty-print the content of the profiles.

Listing 8-1. A Sample Profile.

```
=========================================================
printing contents of profile Select_SJProfile0
created 884150157456 (Tue Jan 06 21:15:57 PST 1998)
associated context is sqlj.runtime.ref.DefaultContext
profile loader is sqlj.runtime.profile.DefaultLoader@1ee775
contains 0 customizations
contains 1 entries
=========================================================
profile Select_SJProfile0 entry 0
#sql { SELECT name, city, type FROM Building  };
PREPARED_STATEMENT executed via EXECUTE_QUERY
role is QUERY
descriptor is null
contains 0 parameters
result set type is NAMED_RESULT
contains 3 result columns
1. mode: OUT, java type: java.lang.String (java.lang.String),
   sql type: VARCHAR, name: name
2. mode: OUT, java type: java.lang.String (java.lang.String),
   sql type: VARCHAR, name: city
3. mode: OUT, java type: java.lang.String (java.lang.String),
   sql type: VARCHAR, name: type
=========================================================
```

Profile Packaging

Profiles can be packaged in JAR files (see Chapter 3, "Java Primer"). A JAR file generally contains:

■ Client-written classes
■ SQLJ-generated classes
■ SQLJ-generated serialized profiles

The JAR manifest file contains an entry for each profile used by the application as shown in the following:

```
Name: <path>/<profile>.ser
SQLJProfile: TRUE
```

Profile packaging allows for *"installation-time" customization,* as discussed in the next section.

Profile Customization

Profile customization takes place during SQLJ installation. Customizations are added for a particular data source, and they may occur multiple times for multiple data sources. Customizations are *serialized objects* and are packaged as part of the profile.

Customizations are added to a profile through registration, using the following methods on a **Profile** object:

- *registerCustomization()*
- *replaceCustomization()*
- *deregisterCustomization()*

The registration process is similar to that used for driver registration in JDBC. Therefore, a profile may maintain a set of customizations, much the same way that the JDBC **DriverManager** maintains a set of JDBC drivers.

Profile Instantiation

At run time, profiles are instantiated using the **Profile**.*instantiate()* method. It can instantiate serialized format, class format, or the **SerializedProfile** class format (which provides non-standard means). Profile instantiation is called automatically by the SQLJ runtime.

Profile instantiation is done using a profile loader, which is created by the SQLJ-generated profile-key object. If no profile loader is provided, the default profile loader is used.

Connected Profile Resolution

A profile may have a number of associated connected profiles, each representing a customization for a particular data source connection. The connected profile is created by a **Customization** object that has the following methods:

- *acceptConnection()*
- *getProfile()*

At run time, as we have discussed previously, *connected profiles* are used to create executable SQL statements. A connected profile is obtained from the connection context using a profile key by calling the *getConnectedProfile()* method on the **ConnectionContext** object. It returns the connected profile of the *first customization* that accepts a given connection (see Figure 8-3). This policy is similar to that used in JDBC for selecting drivers to make connections. If there is no customization, the *default connected profile* is returned, which uses standard JDBC dynamic SQL mapping.

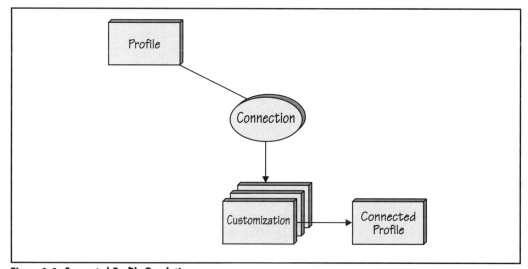

Figure 8-3. Connected Profile Resolution.

CONCLUSION

SQLJ, like JDBC, is a major milestone for Java data access. When approved by ANSI/ISO, it will become the first Embedded SQL standard for an object-oriented language, Java. This is long overdue, considering how long other object-oriented languages such as C++ and Smalltalk have been in existence. This also shows the urgency and importance the database industry has placed on standardizing Java data access.

So you have two choices when accessing SQL databases in Java: JDBC or SQLJ. JDBC is dynamic, whereas SQLJ is static. JDBC is more flexible to use, but SQLJ provides compile-time syntax, type, and schema checking. SQLJ may perform better because it can provide for the optimization of SQL queries by making them available to a database system for *pre-compilation and optimization at translation time*. For many mission-critical applications running on the mainframe accessing **DB2**, for example, this is of utmost importance. Of course, if desirable, you can use both JDBC and SQLJ in the same application.

We will give examples of SQLJ usage in Chapter 10, "Sample Data Access Applications." SQLJ is still in the proposal stage, so you should expect that changes will be made to the specification before it is finally adopted by ANSI/ISO. Also, SQLJ includes other parts that deal with Java stored procedures and Java user-defined functions (*Part 1*) as well as Java objects and user-defined data types in databases (*Part 2*). We will discuss these in Chapter 22, "Conclusion: Emerging Technologies."

Chapter 9

Java Binding for OODB

concepts

In the last two chapters, we have discussed Java access to SQL databases. Now we will turn our attention to Java binding to object-oriented databases. As the name suggests, the focus of Java binding is quite different from Java access. In the case of Java access (JDBC or SQLJ), the focus is on retrieving and manipulating in Java the data stored in SQL (or relational) databases. Such focus is *data-centric*. In the case of Java binding, on the other hand, you will see that the focus is on making Java objects transparently persistent. This focus is *programming objects-centric*.

In this chapter, we will first go over the ODMG Java binding. You may recall that ODMG 2.0 (see Chapter 5, "Object-Oriented Databases and ODMG 2.0") is the de facto standard for object-oriented databases. It consists of the following major components: Object Model, ODL, OQL, and OOPL language bindings. ODMG 2.0 does not define a common OML. Instead, the data manipulation languages are tailored to specific programming languages.

We will go over the mapping of the ODMG Object Model, Java ODL, Java OML, and Java OQL. We will then take a quick look at **POET 5.0**, which is the first commercially available object-oriented database product that conforms to the ODMG Java binding.

ODMG JAVA BINDING

The ODMG Java binding is designed based on the principle that the programmer should perceive the binding as a single language for expressing both programming and database operations. As a result:

- There is *a single unified type system* shared by the Java language and the object-oriented database. Individual instances of these types can be *transient* (Java language) or *persistent* (object-oriented database).
- The binding conforms to the *Java language syntax*. No language extension is required.
- The binding conforms to the *automatic memory management* semantics of Java. Objects become persistent when they are referenced by other persistent objects in the database. They will be removed from the database when they are no longer reachable in this manner. (Java binding, therefore, provides *persistence by reachability*. On database commit, all objects reachable from database *root objects* are stored in the database.)

In the Java binding, only instances of the so-called *persistence-capable classes* can be made persistent. These are special classes understood by the object-oriented database system, and they can have both persistent and transient instances. ODMG 2.0 does not define how a Java class becomes a persistence-capable class. This is left to the individual object-oriented database system vendor to decide. These are two of the possible implementations for providing transparent persistence support:

- **Postprocessor**. A postprocessor takes as input the Java *.class* file (bytecodes) produced by the Java compiler and produces new modified bytecodes that support persistence.
- **Preprocessor**. A preprocessor modifies the Java source to add persistence support before it goes to the Java compiler.

MAPPING OF THE ODMG OBJECT MODEL

The ODMG Object Model (see Chapter 5, "Object-Oriented Databases and ODMG 2.0") was originally designed based on the OMG Object Model. It was later extended to include features from the Java language object model (for example, classes and single inheritance among classes). Therefore, mapping of the ODMG Object Model to Java is quite straightforward. The section describes this mapping and the extensions provided by the Java binding. Please note that the following features of the ODMG Object Model are not yet supported by the Java binding:

- Extents
- Keys
- Relationships
- Access to metadata

Types

An *ODMG interface* is mapped into a Java interface, which cannot be instantiated and is not persistence-capable. An *ODMG class* is mapped into a Java class, which can be instantiated and can be made persistence-capable.

The *ODMG is-a relationship* between interfaces is mapped into the Java *extends* relationship, and the is-a relationship between classes and interfaces is mapped into the Java *implements* relationship. The *ODMG EXTENDS relationship* between classes is mapped into the Java *extends* relationship.

The ODMG atomic literal types map into their equivalent Java primitive types. These are listed in Table 9-1; also listed are the mappings for the following structured objects: **Date**, **Time**, and **Timestamp**. There are no structured literal types in the Java binding. The *ODMG array* and *sequence* map into the Java array. The *ODMG struct* maps into a Java class. No mappings are defined in ODMG 2.0 for the *ODMG enum, union,* and *interval.*

Table 9-1. Standard ODMG to Java Data Type Mapping.

ODMG Data Type	Java Data Type
short	short or Short
long	int or Integer
unsigned short	int or Integer
unsigned long	long or Long
float	float or Float
double	double or Double
char	char or Character
string	String
boolean	boolean or Boolean
octet	byte or Integer
Date	java.sql.Date
Time	java.sql.Time
Timestamp	java.sql.Timestamp

Objects

Objects may be *named*. These are the so-called *root objects*. Any objects *reachable* from them are *persistent*. This behavior is called *persistence by reachability*.

JAVA ODL

The Java ODL provides the description of the object-oriented database schema as a set of *Java classes* using Java syntax. Instances of these classes can be manipulated using the Java OML.

Attributes

Attribute declarations in the Java ODL are syntactically identical to *field* declarations in Java.

Operations

Operation declarations in the Java ODL are syntactically identical to *method* declarations in Java.

JAVA OML

The Java OML provides the means to create, delete, reference, get/set field values, and invoke methods on a persistent (database) object. It is designed so that the syntax is no different from that used for transient (programming) objects. A single expression may freely intermix references to persistent and transient objects.

Attributes

The Java OML uses standard Java syntax for accessing attributes, which are mapped to fields.

Operations

The Java OML uses standard Java syntax for invoking operations, which are mapped to methods. Operations on persistent objects behave identically and consistently with those on transient objects defined by Java.

Object Life Cycle

A database application generally begins processing by accessing one or more of the *root objects* that are named. These objects are persistent, and they provide entry points to the database. There is a single flat name space per database; all names in a particular database are unique. The methods for manipulating names are defined in the **Database** class (to be discussed later).

In the Java binding, persistence is neither limited to any particular part of the class hierarchy nor specified at object creation time. A transient object that is referenced by a persistent object will automatically become persistent when the transaction is committed. As mentioned before, this behavior is called *persistence by reachability*.

However, not all transient objects can become persistent. Instances of classes that are not *persistence-capable classes* are never persistent, even if they are referenced by a persistent object. Also, it is possible to declare a field to be transient using the keyword *transient* of the Java language, which means that the value of this field is not stored in the database. Furthermore, reachability from a transient field will not make an object persistent. *Static fields* (or class fields) are treated the same as transient fields. Reachability from a static field will not make an object persistent.

Modifications to persistent objects will be automatically reflected in the database when the transaction in which they took place is committed. Also, an object will be *automatically removed* from the database if it is neither named nor referenced by any other persistent object.

Collection Interfaces

The Java OML provides the following interfaces for each of the collection objects:

```
public interface Set extends Collection {...}

public interface Bag extends Collection {...}

public interface List extends Collection {...}
```

The **Collection** interface is defined as follows:

```
public interface Collection {
    public int size();
    public boolean isEmpty();

    public boolean contains(Object obj);
    public void add(Object obj);
    public Object remove(Object obj);

    public Enumeration elements();

    public Object selectElement(String predicate);
    public boolean existsElement(String predicate);

    public Enumeration select(String predicate);
    public Collection query(String predicate);
}
```

Please note that the ODMG **Iterator** interface is mapped into the Java **Enumeration** interface.

Transactions

All creation, access, and modification of persistent objects must be done within a transaction. Transient objects are not subject to transaction semantics. Transactions are implemented in the Java OML as objects of the **Transaction** class, defined as follows:

```
public class Transaction {
    public static final int READ, UPGRADE, WRITE;
    pulbic static Transaction current():

    Transaction();

    public boolean is_open();
    public void begin() ...;
    public void commit() ...;
    public void checkpoint() ...;
    public void abort() ...;

    public void join();
    public void leave();
```

```
    public void lock(Object obj, int mode);
}
```

Before performing any database operations, a thread must explicitly create a transaction object or associate itself with an existing transaction object, which must be open. (The creation of a new transaction object implicitly associates it with the caller's thread.) All subsequent operations by the thread are done under the thread's current transaction.

There are three ways in which threads can be used with transactions:

■ There is exactly one thread doing database operations, under exactly one transaction.
■ There may be multiple threads, each with its own separate transactions. Programmers must not pass objects from one thread to another thread that is running under a different transaction. ODMG 2.0 does not define the results of such a behavior.
■ Multiple threads may share one or more transactions. Programmers must take care of concurrency control using Java synchronization.

Database Operations

Databases are represented in the Java OML as objects of the **Database** class, defined as follows:

```
public class Database {
    public static final int notOpen = 0;
    public static final int openReadOnly = 1;
    public static final int openReadWrite = 2;
    public static final int openExclusive = 3;

    public static Database open(String database_name,
      int accessMode) ...;

    public void close() ...;

    public void bind(Object obj, String name);
    public Object unbind(String name) ...;
    public Object lookup(String name) ...;
}
```

Please note that there are no constructors provided. You must use the static method *open()* to create and open a database. Databases must be opened before any transactions can be started on them, and they must be closed after ending these transactions.

The *bind()* and *unbind()* methods allow you to manipulate names of objects, as mentioned previously. The same object may be bound to more than one name. Binding a transient object to a name makes that object persistent. The *lookup()* method allows you to access an object by name.

JAVA OQL

The full functionality of OQL is available through the Java binding. This can be accessed through the query methods on the **Collection** interface shown previously or through the **OQLQuery** class.

The **Collection** interface provides four methods for query; their signatures are:

```
public Object selectElement(String predicate);
public boolean existsElement(String predicate);

public Enumeration select(String predicate);
public Collection query(String predicate);
```

The *predicate* is a string with the syntax of the WHERE clause of OQL.

The **OQLQuery** class allows you to create a query, pass parameters, execute the query, and get the result:

```
class OQLQuery {
    public OQLQuery() {}
    public OQLQuery(String query) {...}

    public create(String query) {...}
    public bind(Object parameter) {...}

    pulbic Object execute() ... {...}
}
```

The *query* is a string with the syntax of OQL. It may contain parameters. A parameter in the query is noted *$i*, where *i* is the rank of the parameter. The parameters are set using the *bind()* method.

POET 5.0

The POET Java SDK complies with the ODMG Java binding. It uses the *preprocessor* approach, which modifies the Java source to add persistence support and creates the schema and database for persistent objects.

A POET database consists of two parts: the *dictionary* (or database schema) and the database. The persistent objects are stored in the database; the dictionary contains information about the structure of *persistence-capable classes*. Both the dictionary and database are created when you run the POET Java preprocessor. A dictionary may be shared by any number of databases. When you open a database, POET will also open the dictionary that is associated with the database.

The POET Java preprocessor extracts the needed information from the Java source and uses the information to register the persistence-capable classes in the dictionary. It also creates a new, empty database if one does not already exist. The preprocessor then calls the standard Java compiler to generate the *.class files*.

In order for the POET Java preprocessor to know which classes are persistence-capable classes, you must declare them in a special *configuration file*. This configuration file is read by the preprocessor. You can also specify other information, such as indexes, in the configuration file.

Extents, Keys, and Names

We mentioned earlier that ODMG 2.0 does not define the Java binding for extents. The POET Java SDK nevertheless supports it in the form of an **Extent** class. You can create an **Extent** object for any persistence-capable class that supports class extent (as declared in the configuration file). You can then navigate and retrieve its elements.

The POET Java SDK also supports keys, which ODMG Java binding does not define, in the form of *extent indexes*. You can declare the indexes in the configuration file. You can then use an index with the corresponding **Extent** object to facilitate the navigation and retrieval of desired elements.

Finally, in POET, name binding can also be used to bind objects with *"null" names*. When doing so, the objects are made persistent but cannot be accessed using names. They can, however, be accessed through extents or through other means such as navigation.

An Example

The following simple example illustrates the use of the ODMG Java binding as implemented in the POET Java SDK. First, the definition of the **Country** class (see the ODMG ODL definition in Chapter 6, "The ArcWorld Sample Database") is shown in Listing 9-1. This class has two fields, a constructor, and a *toString()* method. It looks just like any ordinary Java class. Second, the POET configuration file is shown in Listing 9-2. The configuration file specifies that the **Country** class is a persistence-capable class and it has extents. It also specifies the names of the dictionary and database files. Finally, a simple application, the **Main** class, is shown in Listing 9-3. This class creates three **Country** objects, uses name binding to make the objects persistent, and uses the POET **Extent** class to retrieve them and print them out.

Listing 9-1. The Country Class.

```java
import COM.POET.odmg.*;
import COM.POET.odmg.collection.*;
import java.util.Date;

class Country
{
    String name;
    byte[] cityMap;

    public Country(String n)
    {
        name = n;
    }

    public String toString()
    {
        return name;
    }
}
```

Listing 9-2. The POET Configuration File.

```
[schemata\country_dict]
oneFile = true

[databases\country_base]
oneFile = true
```

```
[classes\Country]
persistent = true
hasExtent = true
[indexes\CountryName]
class = Country
members = name
```

Listing 9-3. The Main Class.

```java
import COM.POET.odmg.*;

public class Main
{
    public static void main(String[] args) throws ODMGException
    {
        if (args.length<1) {
            System.out.println("Please specify database name as a " +
                "command line option.");
            System.exit(1);
        }

        Database db = Database.open(args[0], Database.openReadWrite);

        try {
            doit(db);
        } finally {
            db.close();
        }
    }

    static void doit(Database db) throws ODMGException
    {
        Transaction txn = new Transaction(db);
        txn.begin();

        try
        {
            Country obj;

            obj = new Country("USA");
            db.bind(obj, null);
            obj = new Country("France");
            db.bind(obj, null);
            obj = new Country("China");
```

```
        db.bind(obj, null);

        txn.checkpoint();

        // retrieve all stored instances of Country
        // using the Extent class
        Extent countries = new Extent(db, "Country");

        while (countries.hasMoreElements())  {
            System.out.println(countries.nextElement());
        }
    }

    catch (ObjectNameNotUniqueException exc)
    {
        txn.abort();
        throw exc;
    }

    catch (ODMGRuntimeException exc)
    {
        txn.abort();
        throw exc;
    }

    txn.commit();
    }

}
```

CONCLUSION

We hope that you now have a good understanding of the ODMG Java binding and how it is implemented (and extended) in **POET 5.0**. We will give a more detailed example of their usage in Chapter 10, "Sample Data Access Applications." In case you want to know the exact syntax and semantics of Java ODL, Java OML, or Java OQL, please consult the book by Cattell, et al. and the **POET** documentation listed at the end of this book.

We mentioned in Chapter 5, "Object-Oriented Databases and ODMG 2.0," that a major problem for object-oriented databases has been the difficulty to write an object-oriented database application that is portable across more than one object-oriented database product. We also said there that the new ODMG Java binding may change this picture, given the popularity of Java. Unfortunately, this is not going to be the case soon because a number of major features of the Java binding remain undefined in ODMG 2.0, including:

■ Persistence-capable classes
■ Extents
■ Keys
■ Relationships
■ Access to metadata

As more object-oriented database system vendors implement the ODMG Java binding in the future, all the missing pieces should be standardized.

Chapter 10

Sample Data Access Applications

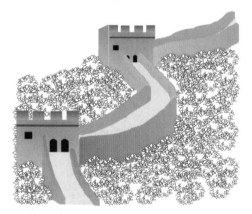

code

Now that we have studied JDBC, SQLJ, and ODMG's Java binding, we are in a position to use these to develop all sorts of data access applications for various types of databases. For the moment, we have not studied Web data access and Java client/server yet, so our applications will be local and not client/server. Our applications, then, will run on the same host where the database system runs. The database system could consist of a database client part and a database server part. In this case, the database server could run on a different host. In any case, if there is any client/server computing, it is done by the database system and is totally transparent to our applications (Figure 10-1).

In this chapter, we will go over some sample data access applications; we will not get into any complex or sophisticated applications. The complex ones, after all, are what you will be doing in your job, and we do not want to steal your thunder. Instead, we will go over some basic database administration and data access applications. We have three purposes:

- To allow you to use these applications (maybe with modifications) to build, test, and maintain the sample **ArcWorld** database
- To demonstrate some of the basic tasks you are likely to do repeatedly in real-life data access applications
- To allow us to compare and contrast the usage of JDBC, SQLJ, and ODMG's Java Binding

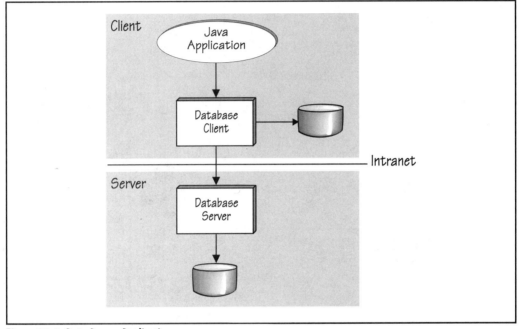

Figure 10-1. Data Access Applications.

JDBC

In the following sections, we assume that the sample **ArcWorld** database has been created by some means. Not all relational database systems allow you to create a database using JDBC. Also, it is most likely that you will create a database through a GUI tool, which allows you, for example, to assign users and passwords. Therefore, for uniformity, we assume that you have somehow created the **ArcWorld** database.

In addition, we will use the JDBC-ODBC bridge driver provided in the JDK for accessing relational databases. This driver can access any database that has an ODBC driver. Most database systems do provide ODBC drivers, so you should be able to run the sample applications with just JDK and no additional JDBC drivers.

The use of JDBC here corresponds to the first usage scenario discussed in Chapter 7, "JDBC in a Nutshell," as shown in Figure 10-2.

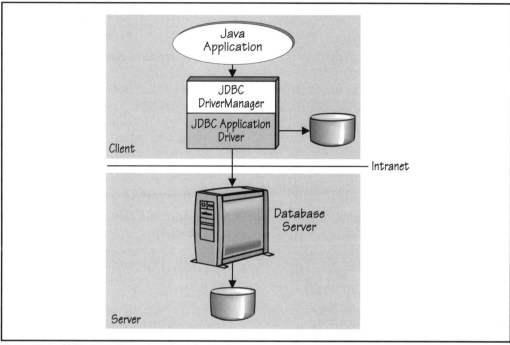

Figure 10-2. JDBC Usage Scenario—Java Applications.

Database Administration

Assuming that the **ArcWorld** database has been created, you can use one of the following two classes to initialize it (see Listings 10-1 and 10-2):

■ **InitArcWorld** will drop existing tables and create all tables.

■ **InitArcWorldData** will delete existing data.

Both classes will ask you to supply the data source name, user id, and password when invoking them. They in turn call the appropriate methods of the **ArcWorld** class to perform their tasks.

The **ArcWorld** class is designed to work with the **ArcWorld** database on any relational database system. However, neither all relational database systems nor their ODBC drivers work exactly the same way, so you may have to fine-tune it to make it work for your specific database system and ODBC driver. For example, we had to adjust the handling of the **ResultSet** in some cases to make it work for both **DB2 UDB** and **SQLServer**. The **ArcWorld** class has the following methods (see Listing 10-3):

- **init**(String ds, String uid, String pw) drops existing tables and creates new tables.

- **initData**(String ds, String uid, String pw) deletes existing data.

- **connect**(String ds, String uid, String pw) connects to the specified data source and returns a **Connection** object.

- **disconnect**(Connection con) closes the specified connection.

- **createTables**(Connection con) creates all tables. The tables are created in such an order that referential constraints are satisfied.

- **dropTables**(Connection con) drops existing tables. The tables are dropped in such an order that referential constraints are satisfied.

- **deleteData**(Conneciton con) deletes existing data. The data is deleted in such an order that referential constraints are satisfied.

Listing 10-1. The InitArcWorld Class.

```
/*
 * InitArcWorld.java
 */

public class InitArcWorld {

    public static void main(String[] args){
        if (args.length != 3){
            System.out.println("Usage: java InitArcWorld " +
              "<dataSourceName> <uid> <pw>");
            System.exit(0);
        }

        try {
            ArcWorld aw = new ArcWorld();
            aw.init(args[0], args[1], args[2]);
            System.out.println("ArcWorld database initialized");
        } catch(Exception e){
            System.err.println("Initialization of the ArcWorld " +
              "database failed");
            e.printStackTrace();
            System.exit(1);
        }
        System.exit(0);
```

```
    }
}
```

Listing 10-2. The InitArcWorldData Class.

```java
/*
 * InitArcWorldData.java
 */

public class InitArcWorldData {

    public static void main(String[] args) {
        if (args.length != 3) {
            System.out.println("Usage: java InitArcWorldData " +
                "<dataSourceName> <uid> <pw>");
            System.exit(0);
        }

        try {
            ArcWorld aw = new ArcWorld();
            aw.initData(args[0], args[1], args[2]);
            System.out.println("ArcWorld data initialized");
        } catch(Exception e) {
            System.err.println("Initialization of ArcWorld data failed");
            e.printStackTrace();
            System.exit(1);
        }
        System.exit(0);
    }
}
```

Listing 10-3. The ArcWorld Class.

```java
/*
 * ArcWorld.java
 */

import java.sql.*;

public class ArcWorld {

    public void init(String ds, String uid, String pw)
      throws Exception {
        Connection con = connect(ds, uid, pw);
```

```java
        dropTables(con);
        createTables(con);
        disconnect(con);
    }

    public void initData(String ds, String uid, String pw)
        throws Exception {
        Connection con = connect(ds, uid, pw);
        deleteData(con);
        disconnect(con);
    }

    public Connection connect(String ds, String uid, String pw)
        throws Exception {
        try {
            // Load the JDBC-ODBC driver
            Class.forName("sun.jdbc.odbc.JdbcOdbcDriver");

            String url = "jdbc:odbc:" + ds;
            System.out.println("Connecting to " + url);
            return DriverManager.getConnection(url, uid, pw);
        } catch(Exception e){
            System.err.println("Exception in connect()");
            System.err.println(e);
            throw e;
        }
    }

    public void disconnect(Connection con)
        throws Exception {
        try {
            System.out.println("Disconnecting from " +
                con.getMetaData().getURL());
            con.close();
        } catch (Exception e){
            System.err.println("Exception in disconnect()");
            System.err.println(e);
            throw e;
        }
    }

    public void createTables(Connection con)
        throws Exception {
        try {
            Statement stmt = con.createStatement();
```

```
String sql;

sql = "CREATE TABLE Country ( " +
  "name         CHAR(32) NOT NULL PRIMARY KEY, " +
  "cityMap      IMAGE)                         ";
stmt.executeUpdate(sql);

sql = "CREATE TABLE City ( " +
  "name         CHAR(32) NOT NULL PRIMARY KEY, " +
  "country      CHAR(32)                      , " +
  "archMap      IMAGE                         , " +
  "FOREIGN KEY (country) REFERENCES Country )  ";
stmt.executeUpdate(sql);

sql = "CREATE TABLE Architect ( " +
  "name         CHAR(32) NOT NULL PRIMARY KEY, " +
  "nationality  CHAR(32)                      , " +
  "picture      IMAGE )                        ";
stmt.executeUpdate(sql);

sql = "CREATE TABLE Building ( " +
  "name         CHAR(32) NOT NULL PRIMARY KEY    , " +
  "type         CHAR(32)                         , " +
  "address      VARCHAR(255)                     , " +
  "city         CHAR(32)                         , " +
  "yearBuilt    INTEGER   CHECK(yearBuilt > -300), " +
  "architect    CHAR(32)                         , " +
  "style        CHAR(32)                         , " +
  "description  TEXT                             , " +
  "picture      IMAGE                            , " +
"FOREIGN KEY (city) REFERENCES City              , " +
  "FOREIGN KEY (architect) REFERENCES Architect ) ";
stmt.executeUpdate(sql);

sql = "CREATE TABLE Church ( " +
  "name         CHAR(32) NOT NULL PRIMARY KEY    , " +
  "type         CHAR(32)                         , " +
  "address      VARCHAR(255)                     , " +
  "city         CHAR(32)                         , " +
  "yearBuilt    INTEGER   CHECK(yearBuilt > -300), " +
  "architect    CHAR(32)                         , " +
  "style        CHAR(32)                         , " +
  "description  TEXT                             , " +
  "picture      IMAGE                            , " +
  "denomination CHAR(32)                         , " +
```

```
            "pastor          CHAR(32)                      , " +
        "FOREIGN KEY (city) REFERENCES City          , " +
          "FOREIGN KEY (architect) REFERENCES Architect ) ";
        stmt.executeUpdate(sql);

        stmt.close();
    } catch (Exception e){
        System.err.println("Exception in creatTables()");
        System.err.println(e);
        throw e;
    }
}

public void dropTables(Connection con)
  throws Exception {
    try {
        DatabaseMetaData dbmd = con.getMetaData();
        Statement stmt = con.createStatement();
        ResultSet rs;
        String sql;

        rs = dbmd.getTables(null, null, "CHURCH", null);
        if (rs.next()) {
            rs.close();
            sql = "DROP TABLE Church";
            stmt.executeUpdate(sql);
        }

        rs = dbmd.getTables(null, null, "BUILDING", null);
        if (rs.next()) {
            rs.close();
            sql = "DROP TABLE Building";
            stmt.executeUpdate(sql);
        }

        rs = dbmd.getTables(null, null, "ARCHITECT", null);
        if (rs.next()) {
            rs.close();
            sql = "DROP TABLE Architect";
            stmt.executeUpdate(sql);
        }

        rs = dbmd.getTables(null, null, "CITY", null);
        if (rs.next()) {
            rs.close();
```

```java
            sql = "DROP TABLE City";
            stmt.executeUpdate(sql);
        }

        rs = dbmd.getTables(null, null, "COUNTRY", null);
        if (rs.next()) {
            rs.close();
            sql = "DROP TABLE Country";
            stmt.executeUpdate(sql);
        }

        rs.close();
        stmt.close();
    } catch(Exception e){
        System.err.println("Exception in dropTables()");
        System.err.println(e);
        throw e;
    }
}

public void deleteData(Connection con)
  throws Exception {
    try {
        Statement stmt = con.createStatement();
        ResultSet rs;
        String sql;

        sql = "SELECT count(*) FROM Church";
        rs = stmt.executeQuery(sql);
        rs.next();
        if (rs.getInt(1) > 0) {
            sql = "DELETE FROM Church";
            stmt.executeUpdate(sql);
        }


        sql = "SELECT count(*) FROM Building";
        rs = stmt.executeQuery(sql);
        rs.next();
        if (rs.getInt(1) > 0) {
            sql = "DELETE FROM Building";
            stmt.executeUpdate(sql);
        }

        sql = "SELECT count(*) FROM Architect";
```

```
        rs = stmt.executeQuery(sql);
        rs.next();
        if (rs.getInt(1) > 0) {
            sql = "DELETE FROM Architect";
            stmt.executeUpdate(sql);
        }

        sql = "SELECT count(*) FROM City";
        rs = stmt.executeQuery(sql);
        rs.next();
        if (rs.getInt(1) > 0) {
            sql = "DELETE FROM City";
            stmt.executeUpdate(sql);
        }

        sql = "SELECT count(*) FROM Country";
        rs = stmt.executeQuery(sql);
        rs.next();
        if (rs.getInt(1) > 0) {
            sql = "DELETE FROM Country";
            stmt.executeUpdate(sql);
        }

        rs.close();
        stmt.close();
    } catch(Exception e){
        System.err.println("Exception in dropTables()");
        System.err.println(e);
        throw e;
    }
  }
}
```

Data Access

Assuming that the **ArcWorld** database already exists and all its tables have been created, you can use one of the following classes to query or manipulate data in the database. These classes are simple and hard-coded; they are only for illustrative purposes. (They can be used to test the **ArcWorld** database to make sure that everything is set up correctly.) Therefore, you definitely will have to modify them to suit your purposes (see Listings 10-4 to 10-7).

- **Insert** inserts data in the database. The data must be inserted in an order satisfying referential constraints. It is inserted as a single transaction.

- **Select** queries the database.

- **Update** updates the database. All updates are done as a single transaction.

- **Delete** deletes data from the database. The data must be deleted in an order satisfying referential constraints. It is deleted as a single transaction.

All of these classes will ask you to supply the data source name, user id, and password when invoking them.

Listing 10-4. The Insert Class.

```
/*
 * Insert.java
 */

import java.sql.*;

class Insert {

    public static void main(String[] args) {
        if (args.length != 3) {
            System.out.println("Usage: java Insert " +
                "<dataSourceName> <userid> <password>");
            System.exit(0);
        }

        try {
            // Load the JDBC-ODBC driver
          Class.forName("sun.jdbc.odbc.JdbcOdbcDriver");

            String url = "jdbc:odbc:" + args[0];
            Connection con = DriverManager.getConnection(url,
                args[1], args[2]);
            Statement stmt = con.createStatement();
            con.setAutoCommit(false);

            stmt.executeUpdate("INSERT INTO Country(name) " +
                "VALUES ('USA')");
            stmt.executeUpdate("INSERT INTO City(name, country) " +
                "VALUES ('Washington', 'USA')");
            stmt.executeUpdate("INSERT INTO Building(name, city) " +
                "VALUES ('Lincoln Memorial', 'Washington')");
            stmt.executeUpdate("INSERT INTO Building(name, city) " +
```

```java
            "VALUES ('National Gallery', 'Washington')");
        stmt.executeUpdate("INSERT INTO Building(name, city) " +
            "VALUES ('The Capitol', 'Washington')");
        stmt.executeUpdate("INSERT INTO Building(name, city) " +
            "VALUES ('Washington Monument', 'Washington')");

        stmt.executeUpdate("INSERT INTO Country(name) " +
            "VALUES ('France')");
        stmt.executeUpdate("INSERT INTO City(name, country) " +
            "VALUES ('Paris', 'France')");
        stmt.executeUpdate("INSERT INTO Building(name, city) " +
            "VALUES ('Arc de Triumph', 'Paris')");
        stmt.executeUpdate("INSERT INTO Building(name, city) " +
            "VALUES ('Eiffel Tower', 'Paris')");
        stmt.executeUpdate("INSERT INTO Building(name, city) " +
            "VALUES ('Louvre', 'Paris')");

        stmt.executeUpdate("INSERT INTO Country(name) " +
            "VALUES ('China')");
        stmt.executeUpdate("INSERT INTO City(name, country) " +
            "VALUES ('Beijing', 'China')");
        stmt.executeUpdate("INSERT INTO Building(name, city) " +
            "VALUES ('Great Wall', 'Beijing')");
        stmt.executeUpdate("INSERT INTO Building(name, city) " +
            "VALUES ('Tiananmen', 'Beijing')");

        con.commit();
        System.out.println("Insert succeeded.");

        stmt.close();
        con.close();
    } catch( Exception e ) {
        e.printStackTrace();
        System.exit(1);
    }
    System.exit(0);
    }
}
```

Listing 10-5. The Select Class.

```java
/*
 * Select.java
 */
```

```java
import java.sql.*;

class Select {

    public static void main(String[] args) {
        if (args.length != 3) {
            System.out.println("Usage: java Select " +
                "<dataSourceName> <userid> <password>");
            System.exit(0);
        }

        try {
            // Load the JDBC-ODBC driver
            Class.forName("sun.jdbc.odbc.JdbcOdbcDriver");

            String url = "jdbc:odbc:" + args[0];
            Connection con = DriverManager.getConnection(url,
                args[1], args[2]);
            Statement stmt = con.createStatement();

            ResultSet rs = stmt.executeQuery(
                "SELECT name, city, type FROM Building");
            System.out.println("Got results for Building:");
            while(rs.next()) {
                String name = rs.getString("name");
                String city = rs.getString("city");
                String type = rs.getString("type");

                System.out.print(" name = " + name);
                System.out.print(" city = " + city);
                System.out.print(" type = " + type);
                System.out.print("\n");
            }

            stmt.close();
            con.close();
        } catch( Exception e ) {
            e.printStackTrace();
            System.exit(1);
        }
        System.exit(0);
    }
}
```

Listing 10-6. The Update Class.

```java
/*
 * Update.java
 */

import java.sql.*;

class Update {

    public static void main(String[] args) {
        if (args.length != 3) {
            System.out.println("Usage: java Update " +
              "<dataSourceName> <userid> <password>");
            System.exit(0);
        }

        try {
            // Load the JDBC-ODBC driver
          Class.forName("sun.jdbc.odbc.JdbcOdbcDriver");

            String url = "jdbc:odbc:" + args[0];
            Connection con = DriverManager.getConnection(url,
              args[1], args[2]);
            Statement stmt = con.createStatement();
            con.setAutoCommit(false);

            stmt.executeUpdate("UPDATE Building " +
              "SET type = 'Memorial' WHERE name = 'Lincoln Memorial'");
            stmt.executeUpdate("UPDATE Building " +
              "SET type = 'Museum' WHERE name = 'National Gallery'");
            stmt.executeUpdate("UPDATE Building " +
              "SET type = 'Government' WHERE name = 'The Capitol'");
            stmt.executeUpdate("UPDATE Building SET type = " +
              "'Monument' WHERE name = 'Washington Monument'");

            stmt.executeUpdate("UPDATE Building " +
              "SET type = 'Monument' WHERE name = 'Arc de Triumph'");
            stmt.executeUpdate("UPDATE Building " +
              "SET type = 'Tourist' WHERE name = 'Eiffel Tower'");
            stmt.executeUpdate("UPDATE Building " +
              "SET type = 'Museum' WHERE name = 'Louvre'");

            stmt.executeUpdate("UPDATE Building " +
              "SET type = 'Historic' WHERE name = 'Great Wall'");
```

```
        stmt.executeUpdate("UPDATE Building " +
            "SET type = 'Government' WHERE name = 'Tiananmen'");

        con.commit();
        System.out.println("Update succeeded.");

        stmt.close();
        con.close();
    } catch( Exception e ) {
        e.printStackTrace();
        System.exit(1);
    }
    System.exit(0);
    }
}
```

Listing 10-7. The Delete Class.

```
/*
 * Delete.java
 */

import java.sql.*;

class Delete {

    public static void main(String[] args) {
        if (args.length != 3) {
            System.out.println("Usage: java Delete " +
                "<dataSourceName> <userid> <password>");
            System.exit(0);
        }

        try {
            // Load the JDBC-ODBC driver
          Class.forName("sun.jdbc.odbc.JdbcOdbcDriver");

            String url = "jdbc:odbc:" + args[0];
            Connection con = DriverManager.getConnection(url,
                args[1], args[2]);
            Statement stmt = con.createStatement();
            con.setAutoCommit(false);

            stmt.executeUpdate("DELETE FROM Building");
```

```
        stmt.executeUpdate("DELETE FROM City");
        stmt.executeUpdate("DELETE FROM Country");

        con.commit();
        System.out.println("Delete succeeded.");

        stmt.close();
        con.close();
    } catch( Exception e ) {
        e.printStackTrace();
        System.exit(1);
    }
    System.exit(0);
    }
}
```

SQLJ

SQLJ is static, and one of its major advantages is *schema checking,* which ensures
that the SQL constructs included in SQLJ clauses are valid in the database schema
where they will be executed. Therefore, in the following listings we will not present
any sample database administration applications using SQLJ. We assume they have
been done using, for example, JDBC. We will present the same data access
applications used for JDBC, but here we do them in SQLJ. These applications are
implemented using the SQLJ Reference Implementation developed by Oracle.

Data Access

Assuming that the **ArcWorld** database already exists and all its tables have been
created, you can use one of the following classes to query or manipulate data in the
database. These classes are simple and hard-coded; they are only for illustrative
purposes. (They can be used to test the **ArcWorld** database to make sure that
everything is set up correctly.) Therefore, you definitely will have to modify them to
suit your purposes (see Listings 10-8 to 10-11).

■ **Insert** inserts data in the database. The data must be inserted in an order
   satisfying referential constraints. It is inserted as a single transaction.

■ **Select** queries the database.

■ **Update** updates the database. All updates are done as a single transaction.

■ **Delete** deletes data from the database. The data must be deleted in an order satisfying referential constraints. It is deleted as a single transaction.

All of these classes will ask you to supply the data source name, user id, and password when invoking them.

Please note the following:

1. All the SQLJ source files have an extension *.sqlj*.

2. You must first run a SQLJ source file through the SQLJ translator (sqlj).

3. The SQLJ translator will generate a standard Java source file with the same name and the extension *.java*.

4. You must then run the Java source file through the Java compiler (javac) to generate the class file.

5. We used *iterators-by-name* in the sample applications.

6. SQLJ is a proposal under consideration by ANSI/ISO for standardization. It is most likely that its syntax and semantics will change somewhat before it is finally adopted.

Listing 10-8. The SQLJ Insert Class.

```
import java.sql.*;
import sqlj.runtime.*; // SQLJ runtime classes
import sqlj.runtime.ref.*;

public class Insert {

    public static void main (String args[])
        throws SQLException
    {
        if (args.length != 3) {
            System.out.println("Usage: java Select " +
                "<dataSourceName> <userid> <password>");
            System.exit(0);
        }

        try {
          Class.forName("sun.jdbc.odbc.JdbcOdbcDriver");
        } catch (Exception e) {
          e.printStackTrace();
            System.exit(1);
        }
```

```
String url = "jdbc:odbc:" + args[0];
sqlj.runtime.ref.DefaultContext.setDefaultContext(
    new sqlj.runtime.ref.DefaultContext (
    url, args[1], args[2]) );

#sql {INSERT INTO Country(name)
    VALUES ('USA')};
#sql {INSERT INTO City(name, country)
    VALUES ('Washington', 'USA')};
#sql {INSERT INTO Building(name, city)
    VALUES ('Lincoln Memorial', 'Washington')};
#sql {INSERT INTO Building(name, city)
    VALUES ('National Gallery', 'Washington')};
#sql {INSERT INTO Building(name, city)
    VALUES ('The Capitol', 'Washington')};
#sql {INSERT INTO Building(name, city)
    VALUES ('Washington Monument', 'Washington')};

#sql {INSERT INTO Country(name)
    VALUES ('France')};
#sql {INSERT INTO City(name, country)
    VALUES ('Paris', 'France')};
#sql {INSERT INTO Building(name, city)
    VALUES ('Arc de Triumph', 'Paris')};
#sql {INSERT INTO Building(name, city)
    VALUES ('Eiffel Tower', 'Paris')};
#sql {INSERT INTO Building(name, city)
    VALUES ('Louvre', 'Paris')};

#sql {INSERT INTO Country(name)
    VALUES ('China')};
#sql {INSERT INTO City(name, country)
    VALUES ('Beijing', 'China')};
#sql {INSERT INTO Building(name, city)
    VALUES ('Great Wall', 'Beijing')};
#sql {INSERT INTO Building(name, city)
    VALUES ('Tiananmen', 'Beijing')};

#sql { COMMIT };
System.out.println("Insert succeeded.");

System.exit(0);
    }
}
```

Listing 10-9. The SQLJ Select Class.

```java
import java.sql.*;
import sqlj.runtime.*; // SQLJ runtime classes
import sqlj.runtime.ref.*;

#sql iterator BldgIterator (String name, String city, String type);

public class Select {

    public static void main (String args[])
        throws SQLException
    {
        if (args.length != 3) {
            System.out.println("Usage: java Select " +
                "<dataSourceName> <userid> <password>");
            System.exit(0);
        }

        try {
          Class.forName("sun.jdbc.odbc.JdbcOdbcDriver");
        } catch (Exception e) {
          e.printStackTrace();
            System.exit(1);
        }

        String url = "jdbc:odbc:" + args[0];
        sqlj.runtime.ref.DefaultContext.setDefaultContext(
            new sqlj.runtime.ref.DefaultContext (
            url, args[1], args[2]) );

        BldgIterator b;
        #sql b = { SELECT name, city, type FROM Building };

        while (b.next()) {
            System.out.print(" name = " + b.name());
            System.out.print(" city = " + b.city());
            System.out.print(" type = " + b.type());
            System.out.print("\n");
        }

        System.exit(0);
    }
}
```

Listing 10-10. The SQLJ Update Class.

```java
import java.sql.*;
import sqlj.runtime.*; // SQLJ runtime classes
import sqlj.runtime.ref.*;

public class Update {

    public static void main (String args[])
        throws SQLException
    {
        if (args.length != 3) {
            System.out.println("Usage: java Select " +
                "<dataSourceName> <userid> <password>");
            System.exit(0);
        }

        try {
          Class.forName("sun.jdbc.odbc.JdbcOdbcDriver");
        } catch (Exception e) {
          e.printStackTrace();
            System.exit(1);
        }

        String url = "jdbc:odbc:" + args[0];
        sqlj.runtime.ref.DefaultContext.setDefaultContext(
            new sqlj.runtime.ref.DefaultContext (
            url, args[1], args[2]) );

        #sql { UPDATE Building SET type = 'Memorial'
                WHERE name = 'Lincoln Memorial' };
        #sql { UPDATE Building SET type = 'Museum'
                WHERE name = 'National Gallery' };
        #sql { UPDATE Building SET type = 'Government'
                WHERE name = 'The Capitol' };
        #sql { UPDATE Building SET type = 'Monument'
                WHERE name = 'Washington Monument' };

        #sql { UPDATE Building SET type = 'Monument'
                WHERE name = 'Arc de Triumph' };
        #sql { UPDATE Building SET type = 'Tourist'
                WHERE name = 'Eiffel Tower' };
        #sql { UPDATE Building SET type = 'Museum'
                WHERE name = 'Louvre' };
```

```
        #sql { UPDATE Building SET type = 'Historic'
               WHERE name = 'Great Wall'  };
        #sql { UPDATE Building SET type = 'Government'
               WHERE name = 'Tiananmen' };

        #sql { COMMIT };
        System.out.println("Update succeeded.");

        System.exit(0);
    }
}
```

Listing 10-11. The SQLJ Delete Class.

```
import java.sql.*;
import sqlj.runtime.*; // SQLJ runtime classes
import sqlj.runtime.ref.*;

public class Delete {

    public static void main (String args[])
        throws SQLException
    {
        if (args.length != 3) {
            System.out.println("Usage: java Select " +
              "<dataSourceName> <userid> <password>");
            System.exit(0);
        }

        try {
          Class.forName("sun.jdbc.odbc.JdbcOdbcDriver");
        } catch (Exception e) {
          e.printStackTrace();
            System.exit(1);
        }

        String url = "jdbc:odbc:" + args[0];
        sqlj.runtime.ref.DefaultContext.setDefaultContext(
            new sqlj.runtime.ref.DefaultContext (
            url, args[1], args[2]) );

        #sql { DELETE FROM Building };
        #sql { DELETE FROM City };
        #sql { DELETE FROM Country };
```

```
        #sql { COMMIT };
        System.out.println("Delete succeeded.");

        System.exit(0);
    }
}
```

JAVA BINDING FOR OODB

In the following sections we use the POET Java SDK (see Chapter 9, "Java Binding for OODB") to define, create, delete, populate, and query the **ArcWorld** database. In addition to the features of POET that were discussed previously, we use the following POET facilities in our examples:

- Database administration for creating and deleting databases
- Object services for deleting persistent objects
- Query on class extents

Database Administration

The **ArcWorld** database is defined using the POET configuration file (see Listing 10-12). There are five persistence-capable classes in the database: **Country, City, Architect, Building**, and **Church** (these are contained in the package **ch10.poet.admin**). You can use one of the following two classes to initialize it (see Listings 10-13 and 10-14):

- **InitArcWorld** will delete the existing database and create a new one.

- **InitArcWorldData** will delete existing data.

Both classes will ask you to supply the data source name when invoking them. They in turn call the appropriate methods of the **ArcWorld** class to perform their tasks.

The **ArcWorld** class has the following methods (see Listing 10-15):

- **init**(String ds) deletes the existing database and creates a new database.

- **initData**(String ds) deletes existing data.

- **createDatabase**(String ds) creates the specified database using the corresponding dictionary as defined in the POET configuration file.

- **deleteDatabase**(String ds) deletes the specified database.

- **connect**(String ds) connects to the specified database and returns a **Database** object.

- **disconnect**(Database db) closes the specified database.

- **deleteData**(Connection con) deletes existing data. The data is deleted in such an order that referential constraints are satisfied.

Listing 10-12. The POET Configuration File for ArcWorld.

```
[schemata\ArcWorld_dict]
oneFile = true

[databases\ArcWorld]
oneFile = true

[classes\ch10.poet.admin.Country]
persistent = true
hasExtent = true
[indexes\CountryName]
class = ch10.poet.admin.Country
members = name

[classes\ch10.poet.admin.City]
persistent = true
hasExtent = true
[indexes\CityName]
class = ch10.poet.admin.City
members = name

[classes\ch10.poet.admin.Architect]
persistent = true
hasExtent = true
[indexes\ArchitectName]
class = ch10.poet.admin.Architect
members = name

[classes\ch10.poet.admin.Building]
persistent = true
hasExtent = true
[indexes\BuildingName]
class = ch10.poet.admin.Building
members = name
```

```
[classes\ch10.poet.admin.Church]
persistent = true
hasExtent = true
[indexes\ChurchName]
class = ch10.poet.admin.Church
members = name
```

Listing 10-13. The POET InitArcWorld Class.

```java
/*
 * InitArcWorld.java
 */

public class InitArcWorld {

    public static void main(String[] args){
        if (args.length != 1){
            System.out.println("Usage: java InitArcWorld " +
              "<dataSourceName>");
            System.exit(0);
        }

        try {
            ArcWorld aw = new ArcWorld();
            aw.init(args[0]);
            System.out.println("ArcWorld database initialized");
        } catch(Exception e){
            System.err.println("Initialization of the ArcWorld " +
              "database failed");
            e.printStackTrace();
            System.exit(1);
        }
        System.exit(0);
    }
}
```

Listing 10-14. The POET InitArcWorldData Class.

```java
/*
 * InitArcWorldData.java
 */

public class InitArcWorldData {
```

```java
    public static void main(String[] args) {
        if (args.length != 1) {
            System.out.println("Usage: java InitArcWorldData " +
                "<dataSourceName>");
            System.exit(0);
        }

        try {
            ArcWorld aw = new ArcWorld();
            aw.initData(args[0]);
            System.out.println("ArcWorld data initialized");
        } catch(Exception e) {
            System.err.println("Initialization of ArcWorld data failed");
            e.printStackTrace();
            System.exit(1);
        }
        System.exit(0);
    }
}
```

Listing 10-15. The POET ArcWorld Class.

```java
/*
 * ArcWorld.java
 */

import COM.POET.odmg.*;
import java.util.*;

public class ArcWorld {

    public void init(String ds)
      throws Exception {
        try {
            deleteDatabase(ds);
            createDatabase(ds);
        } catch (DatabaseNotFoundException e) {
            createDatabase(ds);
        }
    }

    public void initData(String ds)
      throws Exception {
        Database db = connect(ds);
```

```java
        deleteData(db);
        disconnect(db);
    }

    public void deleteDatabase(String ds)
      throws Exception {
        try {
            String url = "poet://LOCAL/" + ds;
            Database.admin(url, "delete", null);
        } catch(Exception e){
            System.err.println("Exception in delete");
            System.err.println(e);
            throw e;
        }
    }

    public void createDatabase(String ds)
      throws Exception {
        try {
            String url = "poet://LOCAL/" + ds;
            String dict = ds + "_dict";

            Properties props = new Properties();
            props.put("schema", dict);
            props.put("oneFile", "true");
            props.put("location", "same");

            Database.create(url, props);
        } catch(Exception e){
            System.err.println("Exception in create");
            System.err.println(e);
            throw e;
        }
    }

    public Database connect(String ds)
      throws Exception {
        try {
            String url = "poet://LOCAL/" + ds;
            return Database.open(url, Database.openReadWrite);
        } catch(Exception e){
            System.err.println("Exception in connect()");
            System.err.println(e);
            throw e;
        }
    }
```

```java
public void disconnect(Database db)
  throws Exception {
    try {
        System.out.println("Disconnecting from " +
          db.getURL());
        db.close();
    } catch (Exception e){
        System.err.println("Exception in disconnect()");
        System.err.println(e);
        throw e;
    }
}

public void deleteData(Database db)
  throws Exception {
    Transaction txn = new Transaction();
    txn.begin();

    Extent ex;
    Enumeration en;
    ex = new Extent(db, "ch10.poet.admin.Church");
    en = ex.select(null);
    ObjectServices.deleteAll(en);
    ex = new Extent(db, "ch10.poet.admin.Building");
    en = ex.select(null);
    ObjectServices.deleteAll(en);
    ex = new Extent(db, "ch10.poet.admin.Architect");
    en = ex.select(null);
    ObjectServices.deleteAll(en);
    ex = new Extent(db, "ch10.poet.admin.City");
    en = ex.select(null);
    ObjectServices.deleteAll(en);
    ex = new Extent(db, "ch10.poet.admin.Country");
    en = ex.select(null);
    ObjectServices.deleteAll(en);

    txn.commit();
}

}
```

Data Access

Assuming that the **ArcWorld** database already exists, you can use one of the following classes to query or manipulate data in the database. These classes are simple and hard-coded. They are only for illustrative purposes. (They can be used to test the **ArcWorld** database to make sure that everything is set up correctly.) Therefore, you definitely will have to modify them to suit your purposes (see Listings 10-16 to 10-19).

■ **Insert** inserts data in the database. The data must be inserted in an order satisfying referential constraints. It is inserted as a single transaction.

■ **Select** queries the database.

■ **Update** updates the database. All updates are done as a single transaction.

■ **Delete** deletes data from the database. The data is deleted in an order satisfying referential constraints. It is deleted as a single transaction.

All of these classes will ask you to supply the data source name when invoking them.

Listing 10-16. The POET Insert Class.

```
/*
 * Insert.java
 */

import ch10.poet.admin.*;

import COM.POET.odmg.*;

class Insert {

    public static void main(String[] args) {
        if (args.length != 1) {
            System.out.println("Usage: java Insert " +
              "<dataSourceName>");
            System.exit(0);
        }

        try {
            String url = "poet://LOCAL/" + "..\\admin\\" + args[0];
            Database db = Database.open(url, Database.openReadWrite);
```

```
        Transaction txn = new Transaction();
        txn.begin();

        Country co;
        City ci;
        Building bu;

        co = new Country("USA");
        db.bind(co, null);
        ci = new City("Washington", co);
        db.bind(ci, null);
        bu = new Building("Lincoln Memorial", ci);
        db.bind(bu, null);
        bu = new Building("National Gallery", ci);
        db.bind(bu, null);
        bu = new Building("The Capitol", ci);
        db.bind(bu, null);
        bu = new Building("Washington Monument", ci);
        db.bind(bu, null);

        co = new Country("France");
        db.bind(co, null);
        ci = new City("Paris", co);
        db.bind(ci, null);
        bu = new Building("Arc de Triumph", ci);
        db.bind(bu, null);
        bu = new Building("Eiffel Tower", ci);
        db.bind(bu, null);
        bu = new Building("Louvre", ci);
        db.bind(bu, null);

        co = new Country("China");
        db.bind(co, null);
        ci = new City("Beijing", co);
        db.bind(ci, null);
        bu = new Building("Great Wall", ci);
        db.bind(bu, null);
        bu = new Building("Tiananmen", ci);
        db.bind(bu, null);

        txn.commit();
        System.out.println("Insert succeeded.");

        db.close();
    } catch( Exception e ) {
```

```
        e.printStackTrace();
        System.exit(1);
    }
    System.exit(0);
    }
}
```

Listing 10-17. The POET Select Class.

```
/*
 * Select.java
 */

import ch10.poet.admin.*;

import COM.POET.odmg.*;

class Select {

    public static void main(String[] args) {
        if (args.length != 1) {
            System.out.println("Usage: java Insert " +
              "<dataSourceName>");
            System.exit(0);
        }

        try {
            String url = "poet://LOCAL/" + "..\\admin\\" + args[0];
            Database db = Database.open(url, Database.openReadWrite);

            Transaction txn = new Transaction();
            txn.begin();

            Extent exbu = new Extent(db, "ch10.poet.admin.Building");
            while ( exbu.hasMoreElements() ) {
                Building bu = (Building) exbu.nextElement();

                System.out.print(" name = " + bu.name);
                System.out.print(" city = " + bu.city.name);
                System.out.print(" type = " + bu.type);
                System.out.print("\n");
            }

            txn.commit();
```

```
            System.out.println("Select succeeded.");

            db.close();
        } catch( Exception e ) {
            e.printStackTrace();
            System.exit(1);
        }
        System.exit(0);
    }
}
```

Listing 10-18. The POET Update Class.

```
/*
 * Update.java
 */

import ch10.poet.admin.*;

import COM.POET.odmg.*;

class Update {

    public static void main(String[] args) {
        if (args.length != 1) {
            System.out.println("Usage: java Insert " +
                "<dataSourceName>");
            System.exit(0);
        }

        try {
            String url = "poet://LOCAL/" + "..\\admin\\" + args[0];
            Database db = Database.open(url, Database.openReadWrite);

            Transaction txn = new Transaction();
            txn.begin();

            Extent exbu = new Extent(db, "ch10.poet.admin.Building");
            while ( exbu.hasMoreElements() ) {
                Building bu = (Building) exbu.nextElement();

                if (bu.name.equals("Lincoln Memorial"))
                    bu.type = "Memorial";
                if (bu.name.equals("National Gallery"))
```

```
            bu.type = "Museum";
        if (bu.name.equals("The Capitol"))
          bu.type = "Government";
        if (bu.name.equals("Washington Monument"))
          bu.type = "Monument";

        if (bu.name.equals("Arc de Triumph"))
          bu.type = "Monument";
        if (bu.name.equals("Eiffel Tower"))
          bu.type = "Tourist";
        if (bu.name.equals("Louvre"))
          bu.type = "Museum";

        if (bu.name.equals("Great Wall"))
          bu.type = "Historic";
        if (bu.name.equals("Tiananmen"))
          bu.type = "Government";
      }

      txn.commit();
      System.out.println("Update succeeded.");

      db.close();
    } catch( Exception e ) {
        e.printStackTrace();
        System.exit(1);
    }
    System.exit(0);
  }
}
```

Listing 10-19. The POET Delete Class.

```
/*
 * Delete.java
 */

import ch10.poet.admin.*;

import COM.POET.odmg.*;
import java.util.*;

class Delete {
```

```java
public static void main(String[] args) {
    if (args.length != 1) {
        System.out.println("Usage: java Insert " +
          "<dataSourceName>");
        System.exit(0);
    }

    try {
        String url = "poet://LOCAL/" + "..\\admin\\" + args[0];
        Database db = Database.open(url, Database.openReadWrite);

        Transaction txn = new Transaction();
        txn.begin();

        Extent ex;
        Enumeration en;
        ex = new Extent(db, "ch10.poet.admin.Building");
        en = ex.select(null);
        ObjectServices.deleteAll(en);
        ex = new Extent(db, "ch10.poet.admin.City");
        en = ex.select(null);
        ObjectServices.deleteAll(en);
        ex = new Extent(db, "ch10.poet.admin.Country");
        en = ex.select(null);
        ObjectServices.deleteAll(en);

        txn.commit();
        System.out.println("Delete succeeded.");

        db.close();
    } catch( Exception e ) {
        e.printStackTrace();
        System.exit(1);
    }
    System.exit(0);
    }
}
```

Part 3
Web Data Access

An Introduction to Part 3

In Part 3, we will switch our attention from Java data access to Web data access. Earlier, we mentioned that the Web has become the universal client/server data access infrastructure. Without the Web, Java data access is localized and restricted. With the Web, Java data access becomes global and universal. We will now go over the basics of Web data access, including:

- Dynamic Web pages
- Java applets and servlets
- Dynamic HTML

Here is what we will be covering in Part 3:

- *Chapter 11* discusses the need and approaches for building dynamic Web pages. We then give an overview of the specific approach taken by **Net.Data**, a Web gateway tool. This tool provides a framework for building dynamic Web pages that present live data to users based on their interaction with the pages.

- *Chapter 12* reviews Java applets and Java servlets and discusses their use in Web data access. Java applets can be used to access data from the Web client. Java servlets can be used to access data from the Web server and to generate dynamic Web pages based on the data access results.

- *Chapter 13* introduces dynamic HTML, which allows you to manipulate any Web page element on the client and change its styles, positioning, and content without a round-trip to the server. A key component of dynamic HTML is data binding, which allows you to present, manipulate, and update data on the client.

So Part 3 is another must, particularly Chapter 12, and should be refreshing. You will learn how to access data on the Web, and you will get a good feel for some of the pros and cons in using Web gateway tools, Java applets, Java servlets, and dynamic HTML for data access on the Web.

Chapter 11

Dynamic Web Pages

product

We now start exploring Web data access. In Chapter 2, "Web Basics," we mentioned that HTML is static; which means that once it is defined, the text and the format of its display remain constant and cannot be changed at run time. What if you want to tailor the text and display format based on the result of data access? How do you go about doing it? In fact, how do you go about doing data access in the first place? The key is that you need to be able to execute a server program from an (input) HTML form and then to generate an (output) HTML report based on the result of that program execution. The *Common Gateway Interface (CGI)* lets you do that. Major Web servers provide their own proprietary APIs, which also let you do that. CGI is portable, but it can be slow. The Web-server unique APIs are fast, but they are not portable.

In the following sections, we will first discuss the CGI process, which is quite involved. You will also have to write a separate CGI program for each different data access, unless you get real clever. This leads us to **Net.Data**, a Web gateway tool. **Net.Data** does most of the grunt work for you and makes your job much easier when creating dynamic Web pages. There are many Web gateway tools available on the market. Here, we use **Net.Data** for illustrative purpose. **Net.Data** supports major Web server APIs in addition to CGI, provides access to a rich set of databases, and includes some important performance enhancement features. Therefore, it serves as a good case study that illustrates many of the major issues (and their solutions) one faces when designing and implementing a dynamic Web page generation tool. We will give some examples of accessing **ArcWorld** in **Net.Data**.

CGI

In a nutshell, CGI allows you to invoke a program from a Web server that normally only knows how to process HTML documents. This can be done through a URL directly from a Web browser, as an HTML anchor reference, or as an action attribute of an HTML form. In each of these three cases, the URL has the following format:

```
http://server-name/cgi-directory-name/cgi-program
```

When receiving such a URL, the Web server sets up some environment variables and invokes the CGI program. The program then reads the environment variables and starts executing. It further reads input data from the Web server through the standard input pipe, and it writes result data to the Web server through the standard output pipe. The Web server treats the results as a normal HTML document and returns it to the Web browser for display. The Web server therefore acts as a conduit between the Web client and the CGI program.

Figure 11-1 shows the common architecture for Web data access using CGI. Typically, *two passes* are involved during a user session. In the *first pass*, from a Web browser, the user downloads an HTML form using a URL. The user then fills in the input data. In the *second pass*, the user submits the HTML form whose action attribute contains a URL that specifies the name of a CGI program. The Web server invokes the program that contains a SQL query on a database. The program collects the query results and generates a standard HTML report to be returned by the Web server for display to the user. This second pass is further illustrated in Figure 11-2.

Figure 11-1. Web Data Access Using CGI.

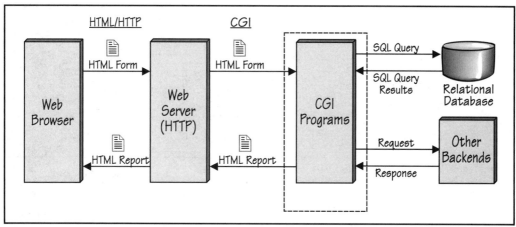

Figure 11-2. HTTP Process Flow Calling CGI.

As a developer of a CGI-based data access application, you must therefore develop or handle the (input) HTML form, the CGI program that accesses databases, the passing of input data from the HTML form to the CGI program, and the generation of an HTML report based on the data access results. All these are tailored for the specific application, so if another application comes along, you will have to repeat the whole cycle again for that application. Also, CGI can be slow, so you will have to worry about replacing CGI with Web server unique APIs, and so on and so forth. In the following section, we will see how **Net.Data** can do all this grunt work for you so that you can focus on what you really care about in the first place: Web data access.

NET.DATA

Net.Data is a Web gateway tool (see Figure 11-3). It provides a robust and scalable framework for creating dynamic Web pages with data originating from a variety of sources. It is easy to use, extendable, and fast. The development of **Net.Data** followed the evolution of Web data access, as shown in Figure 11-4. **Net.Data** was first introduced in 1995 to enable Web-based, server-side applications. It used static CGI processes and provided access to mainly DB2 databases (not surprisingly, it was then called **DB2 WWW Connection**). In 1996, it added support for access to multiple data sources (and therefore the name change to **Net.Data**), Web server APIs, live connections, the use of Java applets and JavaScript on the client, and server-side JDBC processing. The major action items planned for future releases include visual programming tools, Fast CGI support, Java servlets (server-side includes), performance improvements, additional data sources, and additional platforms.

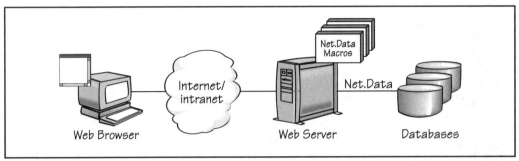

Figure 11-3. Web Data Access Using Net.Data.

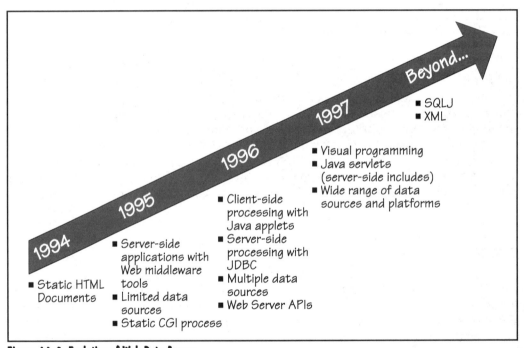

Figure 11-4. Evolution of Web Data Access.

The Net.Data Architecture

Net.Data applications have a *3-tier architecture*, as shown in Figure 11-5. Net.Data itself resides on Tier 2, a Web server. It is a Web server program that can be invoked through CGI, a Web-server specific API, or as Java servlets. (We discussed CGI earlier, we will touch upon Web-server specific APIs shortly, and we will discuss Java servlets in Chapter 12, "Java Applets and Servlets.") Net.Data applications appear in the form of *macro files*, which contain HTML forms, SQL queries, and optional function calls (in Java, REXX, Perl, or C). The user of an application invokes it from the client, Tier 1, by using a URL that specifies the Net.Data executable, the name of a macro file, and the (input) HTML form. When the user submits the form, its action causes a certain SQL query to be executed on the database server, Tier 3. The result of the query is used to generate an (output) HTML report for display to the user. (The page may contain Java applets.)

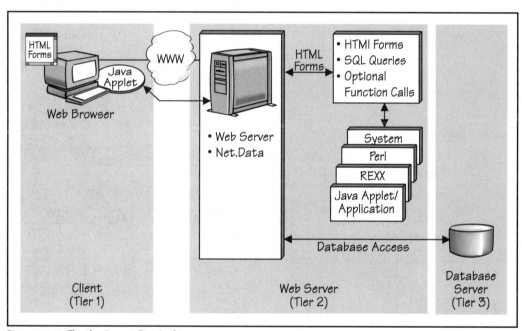

Figure 11-5. The Net.Data 3-Tier Architecture.

The component architecture of **Net.Data** is illustrated in Figure 11-6. **Net.Data** consists of the following major components (we will discuss each in more detail later):

- *Macro processor*. This is the heart and soul of **Net.Data**. It processes macro files, invokes function calls, links to language environments, and generates HTML pages.

- *Macro files*. These are **Net.Data** applications written by users.

- *Function library*. This contains **Net.Data**'s built-in functions.

- *Language environments*. These are **Net.Data**'s (external) backends or databases.

■ **Live connection**. This is a separate executable. It can be used to maintain and manage live connections to databases and Java virtual machines.

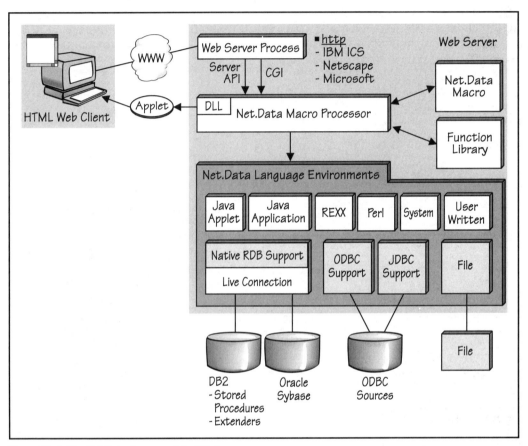

Figure 11-6. The Net.Data Component Architecture.

Macro Processing

In a typical application scenario, a **Net.Data** macro file is processed twice by the macro processor during a user session. In the *first pass*, from a Web browser, the user invokes the macro processor using a URL that specifies the macro processor, the name of the macro file, and the name of an HTML section that defines the (input) HTML form. The macro processor processes the macro file—specifically, the named HTML section—then generates a standard HTML form to be returned by the Web server for display to the user.

In the *second pass*, the user submits the HTML form, whose action attribute contains a URL that specifies the macro processor, the name of the macro file, and the name of an HTML section that defines the (output) HTML report. The macro processor again processes the macro file—specifically, the named HTML section— that contains a function call executing a SQL query on a database or invoking a procedure on other backends. The macro processor makes the function call, collects the result, and generates a standard HTML report to be returned by the Web server for display to the user. This second pass is illustrated in Figure 11-7.

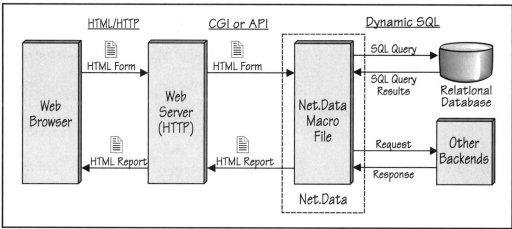

Figure 11-7. Net.Data Macro Processing: Report Generation.

The Macro Processor

The macro processor can be invoked by a Web server via a URL, as discussed before. This can be done directly by a user as an HTML anchor reference, or as an action attribute of an HTML form. When invoked as a CGI or *ICAPI (IBM's Internet Connection API)* application, the URL has the following form:

```
http://server-name/cgi-directory-name/db2www.exe/
      macro-filename/macro-block-name
```

where *db2www.exe* is the name of the macro processor executable. When invoked as an *NSAPI (Netscape Server API)* or *ISAPI (Microsoft's Internet Server API)* application, the URL has the following form:

```
http://server-name/
      macro-filename/macro-block-name
```

The macro processor processes macro files and performs the following tasks:

- Includes files, defines variables, and defines functions
- Resolves variable references and invokes function calls
- Loads in appropriate (language environment) libraries
- Generates standard HTML pages

The Macro File

If the macro processor is the heart and soul of **Net.Data**, then the macro file (or what you can express in the macro file) is its meat. The macro file provides you with the means to add logic, variables, function calls, and reports to otherwise static HTML. A macro file consists of *macro statements* which are denoted by a special *macro symbol (% or @)*. The following are the major types of macro statements:

- **Blocks**. These are used to define HTML forms and reports, variables, functions and their reports. They have the following format:

  ```
  %block-type[(...)] { ... %}
  ```

- **Function calls.** These are used to invoke functions. They have the following format:

  ```
  @function-name(...)
  ```

- **Control statements**. These can be used to control the flow of macro execution. They have the following format:

  ```
  %if ... [%elif ...] [%else ...] %endif
  ```

- **Comments**. These are included within "%{" and "%}".

There are three major types of macro blocks:

- **HTML**. This is used to define input HTML forms and output HTML reports. Typically, the action attribute of an input HTML form would reference an output HTML block, and an output HTML block would call some function(s) and perform report formatting. As discussed before, a specific (and only one) HTML block must be specified when invoking **Net.Data**. This normally would be an input HTML block.

- **Define**. This can be used to define variables. Once defined, a variable can be referenced in other macro blocks.

- **Function**. This can be used to define language-environment specific functions. Once defined, a function can be invoked in an HTML block. The **Function** block may include a ***Report*** block that defines the report to be generated, and a ***Message*** block that defines the message to be displayed in case an error occurs.

A sample macro file is shown in Figure 11-8. The corresponding browser screens displayed when invoking the macro file are also shown. From this sample you can

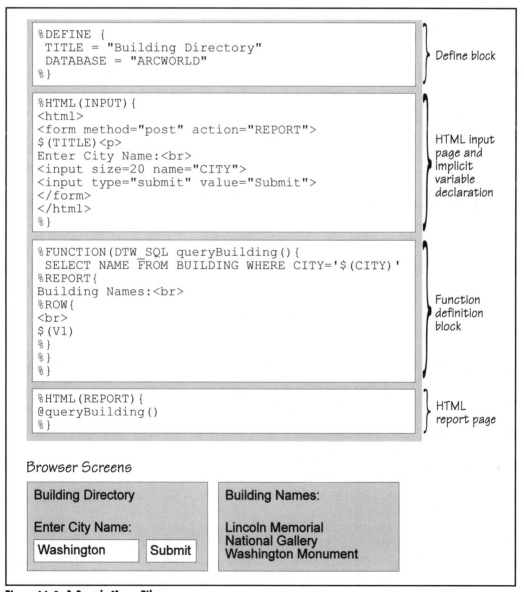

```
%DEFINE {
 TITLE = "Building Directory"
 DATABASE = "ARCWORLD"
%}
```
Define block

```
%HTML(INPUT){
<html>
<form method="post" action="REPORT">
$(TITLE)<p>
Enter City Name:<br>
<input size=20 name="CITY">
<input type="submit" value="Submit">
</form>
</html>
%}
```
HTML input page and implicit variable declaration

```
%FUNCTION(DTW_SQL queryBuilding(){
 SELECT NAME FROM BUILDING WHERE CITY='$(CITY)'
%REPORT{
Building Names:<br>
%ROW{
<br>
$(V1)
%}
%}
%}
```
Function definition block

```
%HTML(REPORT){
@queryBuilding()
%}
```
HTML report page

Browser Screens

Building Directory	Building Names:
Enter City Name: Washington Submit	Lincoln Memorial National Gallery Washington Monument

Figure 11-8. A Sample Macro File.

see that the macro file provides three major expressive capabilities:

■   Variable definition and passing
■   Function definition and invocation
■   Report definition

We will discuss these next.

Variables

Net.Data variables can be used to pass values within a macro file or between a macro file and a language environment. As is the case with HTML, all variables are character strings, which means they have no data types. The following are the major kinds of variables:

■   *Implicit*. These contain data returned from SQL queries and from function calls.
■   *Report*. These can be used to customize report format.
■   *SQL*. These can be used to tailor access to databases.
■   *User-defined*. These are user-defined variables.

User-defined variables can be defined in the Define block, defined in an HTML form's INPUT or SELECT statement, or passed in as URL data. Once defined, they can be referenced as *$(variable-name)* anywhere in the macro file.

Implicit variables are among the most useful ones provided by **Net.Data.** They include:

■ $(N$n$), $(N_columnName), $(NLIST) contain column names.
■ $(V$n$), $(V_columnName), $(VLIST) contain column values in the current row.
■ $(ROW_NUM) contains the row number of the current row.
■ $(NUMBER_COLUMN) contains the number of columns in the result table.
■ $(TOTAL_ROWS) contains the number of rows in the result table.
■ $(RETURN_CODE) contains the return code for use in the Message block.

SQL variables are useful when accessing databases. The most commonly used ones include:

■   DATABASE specifies the database to connect to. This must be set.
■   LOGIN specifies the user id.
■   PASSWORD specifies the password to be used with the user id.
■   TRANSACTION_SCOPE specifies the transaction scope for SQL statements. The default is MULTIPLE, which means all SQL statements in an HTML block are within the same scope and will commit or rollback together. Specifying SINGLE means to commit each SQL statement separately.

Functions

Net.Data functions can be used to add logic, access databases, or interact with external programs during macro execution. The following are the major types of functions:

- **Math**. These are standard mathematical functions such as *add, subtract, multiply,* and *divide.*

- **String manipulation**. These are standard string and word manipulation functions such as *concat, substr, lowercase,* and *uppercase.*

- **Table**. These are functions that can be used with *table variables.* Table variables are the ones defined using the *%TABLE* construct. They contain an array of values and the associated column names.

- **User-defined**. These are user-defined functions written for a specific language environment.

User-defined functions are specified in the Function blocks. Each contains the following information:

- Language environment
- Name
- IN, OUT, and INOUT parameters
- Return variable
- Executable statements
- Report block
- Message block

Among these, only language environment and name are required. All others are optional.

Reports

Within a Function block you can use the Report block and Message block to define the report and message(s) (in case of errors) to be generated, respectively. The Report block consists of the following:

- Header
- *ROW* block
- Footer

The Row block displays HTML formatted data once for each row of data returned from the function call. You can use Implicit variables to specify the data to be displayed. You can also use Report variables to customize the report.

The Message block allows you to associate a message with each return code value generated by the function call and to specify the action (*exit* or *continue*) for **Net.Data** to take in each case.

Language Environments

Net.Data provides a rich set of language environments (or backends), including:

- SQL/DB2, Oracle, and Sybase with native access
- ODBC
- Java Applet and Java Application
- REXX and Perl
- System (C)

Users can also build and plug in their own language environment (such as COBOL). To do so, they must conform to the Language Environment Interface and follow the required procedures.

In the sample macro file shown previously, you have already seen how straightforward it is to access databases (SQL/DB2, Oracle, Sybase, or ODBC). You simply specify the SQL statement to be executed within a function body and then call the function. If you want to execute more than one SQL statement, you can do so with multiple function definitions and then call them in the sequence you desire.

If you want to have more control over data access, you can use the Java Applet (from the client side) or the Java Application (from the server side) language environment. These are shown in Figures 11-9 and 11-10, respectively, where as can be expected, JDBC is used for data access.

The Java Applet language environment is noteworthy because it can dynamically generate the following parameter specifications for an applet:

- NUMBER_OF_TABLES
- TABLE_<i>_NAME
- NUMBER_OF_COLUMNS
- NUMBER_OF_ROWS
- COLUMN_NAME_<i>
- <column_name>_VALUE_<i>

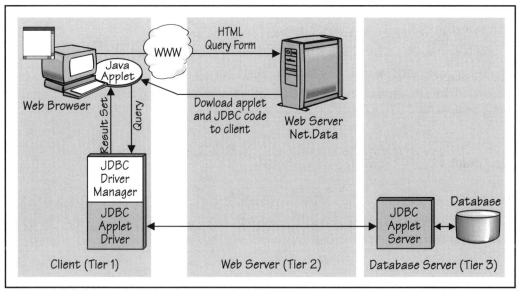

Figure 11-9. Client-Side Application with Java Applet.

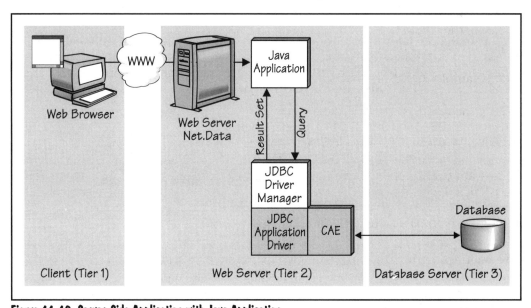

Figure 11-10. Server-Side Application with Java Application.

You can then access these values from an applet (if it inherits from the **Net.Data** built-in **DTW_Applet** class) using the following corresponding methods:

- **getNumberOfTables**() returns an int.
- **getTableNames**() returns a **String**[ ].
- **getNumberOfColumns**(String tableName) returns an int.
- **getNumberOfRows**(String tableName) returns an int.
- **getColumnNames**(String tableName) returns a **String**[ ].
- **getTable**(String tableName) returns a **String**[ ][ ].

We will discuss Java applets in Chapter 12, "Java Applets and Servlets," so we will refrain from giving an example until then. Please hold on to your raincheck and redeem it later.

Live Connection

When accessing databases (SQL/DB2, Oracle, Sybase, or ODBC), **Net.Data** normally establishes a connection to a database at the beginning of macro execution and then closes the connection at the end of macro execution. It also allows only one database connection per macro execution.

Live connection allows you to create and maintain persistent connections. It consists of a connection manager and *cliettes*. The connection manager is a separate executable from **Net.Data**. Cliettes are single-threaded processes that the connection manager starts, and they run continuously to service requests. Cliettes are:

- Made to handle specific language environments
- Pre-started at Web server initialization
- Configurable with a minimum and maximum number of processes
- Pre-connected to specified databases or backends
- Reusable for the same type of connection

Live connection therefore provides two major advantages:

- *Improved performance*. Live connection reuses connections; it does not make new connections. This can significantly improve performance when the connection time is long (for example, to a remote database server).

- *Multiple database access*. Live connection lets you connect to multiple databases during a macro execution. This is possible because each database has its unique cliettes.

SAMPLE DATA ACCESS MACROS

In the following listing, we take the JDBC **Select** class example (see Listing 10-5 on page 198) and redo it in **Net.Data**. The **Select.mac** example (see Listing 11-1) has about the sample amount of code (one page), but it has the following added functionality:

- A user can enter the data source, user id, and password information from an input panel, and the password entered is hidden. (In the case of the JDBC **Select** class, these are entered from the command line, all visible.)

- On the same panel, the user can enter a **City** name and submit the query (see Figure 11-11). If the user enters "*" for the **City** name, then all buildings will be selected, just like the JDBC **Select** class.

- The report is generated using the column names from the result set. The column names are hard-coded in the case of the JDBC **Select** class.

- The report is presented in a tabular format, with border, caption, heading, and data (see Figure 11-12). In the case of the JDBC **Select** class, it is a simple line printout.

- A user can perform the query from any Web browser. (In the case of the JDBC **Select** class, the query can only be done locally.)

Of course, the JDBC **Select** class can be extended to provide all of the functionality listed here, but it will require much more programming. We will show how it can be done with Java applets and Java servlets, respectively, in Chapter 12, "Java Applets and Servlets."

Listing 11-1. The Select Macro.

```
%{
  Select.mac
%}

%DEFINE {
 TITLE = "ArcWorld buildings query: "
%}

%FUNCTION(DTW_ODBC) queryBuilding(where) {
  SELECT name, type, city FROM Building $(where)
%REPORT {
<table border="border">
  <caption> Buildings in the ArcWorld database: </caption>
```

```
    <tr> <th>$(N1) <th>$(N2) <th>$(N3)
%ROW {
    <tr> <td>$(V1) <td>$(V2) <td>$(V3)
%}
</table>
%}
%}


%HTML(INPUT) {
<html>
<form method="post" action="REPORT">
$(TITLE)<p>
Enter the data source, user id, and password information:<br>
<input size=20 name="DATABASE"> <input size=20 name="LOGIN">
    <input size=20 type="PASSWORD" name='PASSWORD'><br>
<br>
Select the city that you would like to query:<br>
<input type="radio" name="CITY" value="*"> All cities <br>
<input type="radio" name="CITY" value="Washington"> Washington <br>
<input type="radio" name="CITY" value="Paris"> Paris <br>
<input type="radio" name="CITY" value="Beijing"> Beijing <p>
<input type="submit"> <input type="reset">
</form>
</html>
%}


%HTML(REPORT) {
%IF ($(CITY) == "*")
    @DTW_ASSIGN(where, "")
%ELSE
    @DTW_CONCAT("WHERE city = ", "'", where)
    @DTW_CONCAT(where, CITY, where)
    @DTW_CONCAT(where, "'", where)
%ENDIF
@queryBuilding(where)
%}
```

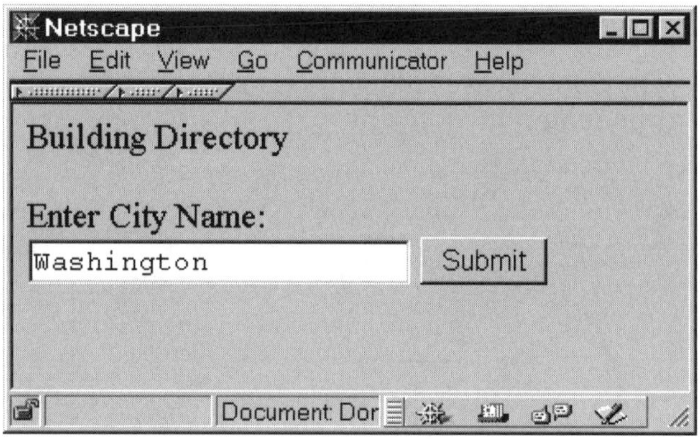

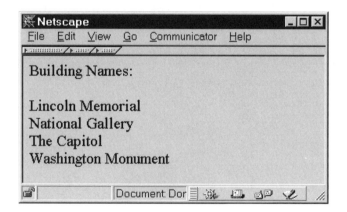

Figure 11-11. ArcWorld Building Query: Input Panel.

Figure 11-12. ArcWorld Building Query: Report Panel.

CONCLUSION

We now have taken a first, but important, step in Web data access. We have seen how **Net.Data** takes the grunt work out of CGI programming and makes life much easier for you in generating dynamic Web pages based on live data. We have also shown that **Net.Data** can be used with Java applets or Java applications. If **Net.Data** provides the functionality needed by your application, it is the way to go because it is easy to use and requires little programming effort. For detailed information on **Net.Data**, please refer to the reference listed in the back of this book, which contains a programming guide, a reference guide, and a language environment guide.

If your application requires additional functionality—such as maintaining state information across Web sessions—or flexibility, we have treats waiting for you. In the next chapter, we will discuss *Java applets* and *Java servlets*. But these will require more programming effort on your part.

Chapter 12

Java Applets and Servlets

concepts

By now we are all familiar with the phenomenal success of Java and the main reasons why it has been successful: object-orientation, simplicity, portability, safety, and dynamicity. However, before Java became prominent, there were many other programming languages that had similar characteristics like Java but never had much success. These included Eiffel and Modula-3, among the better known ones. Smalltalk did have some success, but nothing comparable to Java.

So why was Java so special? The single most important reason for Java's success was that it came out with a "killer application" in the right place at the right time. The killer application was *applets* and the HotJava browser that demonstrated the utility of applets. Before applets, HTML pages were static and dull. With applets, HTML pages became alive and were fun. Before applets (and the Web), Microsoft was about to take over the computer industry. (Windows 95 just knocked out OS/2.) With applets (and the Web), the computer industry is bursting with new energy and fierce competition. *Long live applets*!

Servlets are the new, much less known, invisible, but eventually more important siblings of applets. Applets are designed for Web clients; servlets are designed for Web servers. Applets can have all sorts of pretty faces (GUIs); servlets are either faceless or have a straight face (HTML). Applets are light, particularly for use in network computers or devices; servlets could be heavy, doing all sorts of "mundane work" behind the scene. Both can be mobile: mobile code, that is, not mobile objects.

In this chapter, we will go over Java applets and servlets, their APIs, and their use for data access on the Web. Java applets are part of the JDK; Java servlets come in the form of *Java Servlet Development Kit (JSDK)*, which can be installed over popular Web servers or as part of Sun's Java Web Server.

JAVA APPLETS

In Chapter 3, "Java Primer," we mentioned that the Java Platform enables developers to create two different kinds of programs: Java applets and Java applications. Java applets are programs that require a *Web browser* to run. As discussed in Chapter 2, "Web Basics," this is done using the *<APPLET> tag* that is embedded in a Web page that identifies the applet to run. When the Web page is accessed by a user, the applet is automatically downloaded from the Web server and runs on the client machine. Because applets are downloaded, they tend to be small and modular to avoid large download times and to accommodate thin clients.

The major benefit of using applets is that the Web browser provides a *universal client* environment. In addition, applets provide:

- Protocol-independent and platform-independent client-side components
- A common API (the Applet API that we will discuss later)
- Dynamic loading over the net (we mentioned this already in the above)
- Security (the applet security model)

Applet Programming Model

An applet must extend the **java.applet.Applet** class. As mentioned earlier, the *APPLET* element (or <APPLET> tag) allows you to embed the applet in an HTML document. Its major attributes include:

- *codebase*—the base URL for the applet
- *code*—the relative URL for the applet's class file
- *name*—useful for applets on the same page to communicate with each other
- *width*—the initial width of the applet display area
- *height*—the initial height of the applet display area
- *archive*—.*zip* or .*jar* files (for example, for the JDBC Applet Driver)

You can further use the *PARAM* element to supply initial values to the applet. It specifies a name/value pair through the *name* and *value* attributes. You can include any number of *PARAM* elements.

To use the initial values in the applet, you can call the *getParameter()* or *getParameterInfo()* method. Usually, you would do so in the *init()* method to be discussed in the following section.

Applet Life Cycle

Once the class file of an applet is downloaded by the Web browser, an instance of the applet is automatically created. The applet will go through a life cycle, supported by its life-cycle methods, and these methods are automatically called by the Web browser. You can override them, as needed, to provide desired behavior or to perform required tasks.

The life-cycle methods include:

- *init()* for initializing the applet. This method is called when the applet is first loaded or reloaded. It is called only once.

- *start()* for starting the applet. This method is called after initialization or stopping (to re-start the applet).

- *stop()* for stopping the applet. This method is called when the user leaves the Web page where the applet is embedded.

- *destroy()* for destroying the applet. This method is called after stopping. It can be used for cleanup.

The **java.applet.Applet** class is a subclass of the **java.awt.Panel** class, so another method you can override to provide desired behavior (particularly for display) is:

- *paint*(Graphics g) is for painting the screen. The input graphics object is automatically created and passed by the Web browser.

THE APPLET API

The following sections describe the classes and interfaces in the Applet API. These are all part of the **java.applet** package.

Applet Class

The **Applet** class provides a standard interface for applets. All applets are sub-classes of the **Applet** class. The **Applet** class extends the **java.awt.Panel** class.

Constructors

■ **Applet**() is the default constructor.

Methods

The following are *life-cycle methods*:

■ **init**() informs this applet that it has been loaded into the system. It is called by the browser once before the *start()* method is called.

■ **start**() informs this applet to start its execution. It is called by the browser after the *init()* method, and each time this applet is revisited in a Web page.

■ **stop**() informs this applet to stop its execution. It is called by the browser when the Web page containing this applet has been replaced by another page, and just before the *destroy()* method is called.

■ **destroy**() informs this applet that it is being reclaimed. It is called by the browser.

■ **isActive**() returns true if this applet is active. An applet is marked active just before its *start()* method is called. It is marked inactive immediately after its *stop()* method is called.

The following methods can be used to *get and manipulate its data*:

■ **getParameter**(String name) returns the value (**String**) of the named parameter in the HTML tag.

■ **getParameterInfo**() returns information (**String**[][]) about parameters that are understood by this applet. Each element consists of three strings containing the name, the type, and a description of a parameter.

■ **getAudioClip**(java.net.URL url) returns an **AudioClip** object, identified by the given url.

- **getAudioClip**(java.net.URL url, String name) returns an **AudioClip** object, identified by the given url and name.

- **play**(java.net.URL url) plays the audio clip identified by the given url.

- **play**(java.net.URL url, String name) plays the audio clip identified by the given url and name.

- **getImage**(java.netl.URL url) returns a **java.awt.Image** object, identified by the given url, that can be painted on the screen.

- **getImage**(java.net.URL url, String name) returns a **java.awt.Image** object, identified by the given url and name, that can be painted on the screen.

The following methods can be used to *obtain information about this applet* and to *manipulate it*:

- **getAppletContext**() returns an **AppletContext** object that contains this applet's context.

- **getAppletInfo**() returns information (**String**) about this applet.

- **getCodeBase**() returns the URL (**java.util.URL**) of this applet.

- **getDocumentBase**() returns the URL (**java.net.URL**) of the document where this applet is embedded.

- **getLocale**() returns the locale (**java.util.Locale**) for this applet.

- **resize**(java.awt.Dimension d) requests that this applet be resized.

- **resize**(int width, int height) requests that this applet be resized.

- **setStub**(AppletStub stub) sets this applet's stub. This is done automatically by the system.

- **showStatus**(String msg) requests that the given message be displayed on the browser's status window.

AppletContext Interface

The **AppletContext** interface gives applets access to information about their environment, the document containing the applets, and the other applets in the same document.

Methods

- **getApplet**(String name) returns the **Applet** with the specified name in the document represented by this applet context.

- **getApplets**() returns an **Enumeration** of the **Applet** objects in the document represented by this applet context.

- **getAudioClip**(java.net.URL url) returns an **AudioClip** object, identified by the given url.

- **getImage**(java.netl.URL url) returns a **java.awt.Image** object, identified by the given url, that can be painted on the screen.

- **showDocument**(java.net.URL url) requests that the browser show the Web page indicated by the given url.

- **showDocument**(java.net.URL url, String target) requests that the browser show the Web page indicated by the given url. The target argument indicates where to show it.

- **showStatus**(String msg) requests that the given message be displayed on the browser's status window.

AppletStub Interface

When an applet is first created, an applet stub is attached to it. This stub serves as the interface between the applet and its browser environment.

Methods

- **isActive**() returns true if the applet is active. An applet is marked active just before its *start()* method is called. It is marked inactive immediately after its *stop()* method is called.

- **getParameter**(String name) returns the value (**String**) of the named parameter in the HTML tag.

- **getAppletContext**() returns an **AppletContext** object that contains the applet's context.

- **getCodeBase**() returns the URL (**java.util.URL**) of the applet.

- **getDocumentBase**() returns the URL (**java.net.URL**) of the document where the applet is embedded.

- **appletResize**(int height, int weight) requests that the applet be resized.

AudioClip Interface

The **AudioClip** interface is a simple abstraction for playing an audio clip.

Methods

- **loop**() starts playing this audio clip in a loop.

- **play**() starts playing this audio clip.

- **stop**() stops playing this audio clip.

SAMPLE DATA ACCESS APPLETS

In this section, we take the **Net.Data Select.mac** example (see Listing 11-1 on page 237) and redo it using applets and JDBC (see Figure 12-1). The **SelectApplet** example (see Listings 12-1 and 12-2) has the same functionality but requires much more programming effort in Java to process the user input, make JDBC calls, and display the query result:

- A user can enter the data source, user id, and password information from an input panel, and the password entered is hidden.

- On the same panel, the user can enter a **City** name and submit the query (see Figure 12-2). The query is performed using JDBC.

- The report is generated using the column names from the result set returned by JDBC.

- The report is presented in a tabular format, with border, caption, heading, and data (see Figure 12-3).

- A user can perform the query from any Web browser supporting Java.

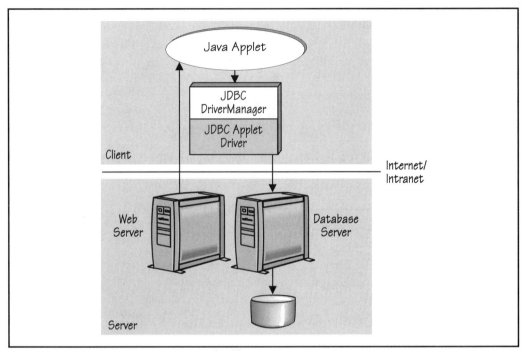

Figure 12-1. JDBC Usage Scenario—Java Applet (I).

Listing 12-1. The SelectApplet HTML File.

```
#
# SelectApplet.html
#

<html>
    <applet code=SelectApplet.class width=525 height=475
     archive="../db2java.zip">
        <param name=server value='woodview3.stl.ibm.com'>
        <param name=port value='9191'>
    </applet>
</html>
```

Listing 12-2. The SelectApplet Class.

```
/**
 * SelectApplet.java
 */

import java.awt.*;
import java.awt.event.*;
import java.applet.*;
import java.util.Vector;

import java.sql.*;

public class SelectApplet
  extends Applet implements ActionListener
{
    static {
        try {
            Class.forName("COM.ibm.db2.jdbc.net.DB2Driver");
        } catch (Exception e) {
            e.printStackTrace();
        }
    }

    public void init() {
       super.init();

       server = getParameter("server");
       port = getParameter("port");

       setLayout(null);
       addNotify();
       setSize(450,340);

       //set applet layout
       mainCardPanel = new Panel();
       mainCardPanel.setLayout(new CardLayout(0,0));
       mainCardPanel.setBounds(0,0,450,340);
       add(mainCardPanel);

       //add input panel
       inputPanel = new Panel();
       inputPanel.setLayout(null);
       inputPanel.setBounds(0,0,450, 340);
       mainCardPanel.add(" ", inputPanel);
```

```java
label1 = new java.awt.Label("ArcWorld buildings query:");
label1.setBounds(12,10,324,40);
inputPanel.add(label1);

label2 = new java.awt.Label("Enter data Source, user id, and " +
                            "password information:");
label2.setBounds(12,45,324,40);
inputPanel.add(label2);
textField1 = new java.awt.TextField();
textField1.setBounds(12,84,132,24);
textField1.requestFocus();
inputPanel.add(textField1);
textField3 = new java.awt.TextField();
textField3.setBounds(156,84,132,24);
inputPanel.add(textField3);
textField4 = new java.awt.TextField();
textField4.setBounds(300,84,132,24);
inputPanel.add(textField4);

label3 = new Label("Select the city that you would like to query:");
label3.setBounds(12,120,240,12);
inputPanel.add(label3);
Group1 = new CheckboxGroup();
radioButton1 = new java.awt.Checkbox("All cities", Group1, false);
radioButton1.setBounds(12,144,100,24);
inputPanel.add(radioButton1);
radioButton2 = new java.awt.Checkbox("Washington", Group1, false);
radioButton2.setBounds(12,168,100,24);
inputPanel.add(radioButton2);
radioButton3 = new java.awt.Checkbox("Paris", Group1, false);
radioButton3.setBounds(12,192,100,24);
inputPanel.add(radioButton3);
radioButton4 = new java.awt.Checkbox("Beijing", Group1, false);
radioButton4.setBounds(12,216,100,24);
inputPanel.add(radioButton4);

button1 = new java.awt.Button("Submit");
button1.setBounds(12,252,108,24);
inputPanel.add(button1);
button2 = new java.awt.Button("Reset");
button2.setBounds(132,252,96,24);
inputPanel.add(button2);

// add result panel
```

```
        resultPanel = new Panel();
        resultPanel.setLayout(null);
        resultPanel.setBounds(0,0,792,390);
        mainCardPanel.add(" ", resultPanel);
        label5 = new java.awt.Label("Buildings in the ArcWorld Database:");
        label5.setBounds(84,12,276,24);
        button3 = new java.awt.Button("Input");
        button3.setBounds(228,310,96,24);
        button4 = new java.awt.Button("Result");
        button4.setBounds(108,310,96,24);
        resultPanel.add(button3);
        resultPanel.add(button4);
        resultPanel.add(label5);

        mainCardLayout = new CardLayout();
        mainCardPanel.setLayout(mainCardLayout);
        mainCardLayout.addLayoutComponent("input", inputPanel);
        mainCardLayout.addLayoutComponent("result", resultPanel);
        mainCardLayout.show(mainCardPanel,"input");

        // register components' event listener
        AddListener();
    }

    private void AddListener()
    {
        button1.addActionListener(this);
        button2.addActionListener(this);
        button3.addActionListener(this);
        button4.addActionListener(this);
    }

    public void actionPerformed(ActionEvent event)
    {
        if(event.getSource() == button1)
        {
            dataSource = textField1.getText();
            userid = textField3.getText();
            password = textField4.getText();

            if (radioButton1.getState())
                city = "*";
            else if (radioButton2.getState())
                city = "Washington";
            else if (radioButton3.getState())
```

```
            city = "Paris";
        else if (radioButton4.getState())
            city = "Beijing";
        if (city.equals("*"))
            where = "";
        else
            where = " WHERE city = " + "'" + city + "'";
        sql = "SELECT name, type, city FROM Building" + where;

        submitButton_Clicked(event);
    }
    if (event.getSource() == button2)
        resetButton_Clicked(event);
    if (event.getSource() == button3)
        inputButton_Clicked(event);
    if (event.getSource() == button4)
        resultButton_Clicked(event);
}

public void submitButton_Clicked(ActionEvent event)
{
    mainCardLayout.show(mainCardPanel,"result");
}

public void resetButton_Clicked(ActionEvent event)
{
    textField1.setText("");
    textField3.setText("");
    textField4.setText("");
    radioButton1.setState(false);
    radioButton2.setState(false);
    radioButton3.setState(false);
    radioButton4.setState(false);
}

public void inputButton_Clicked(ActionEvent evnet)
{
    mainCardLayout.show(mainCardPanel,"input");
}

public void resultButton_Clicked(ActionEvent event)
{
    Graphics g = resultPanel.getGraphics();
    drawTable(g);
    query();
```

```
   }

   public void drawTable(Graphics g)
   {
      g.drawString("NAME", 75,55);
      g.drawString("TYPE", 230,55);
      g.drawString("CITY", 350,55);

      g.drawLine(10,40,420,40);
      g.drawLine(10,65,420,65);
      g.drawLine(10,90,420,90);
      g.drawLine(10,115,420,115);
      g.drawLine(10,140,420,140);
      g.drawLine(10,165,420,165);
      g.drawLine(10,190,420,190);
      g.drawLine(10,215,420,215);
      g.drawLine(10,240,420,240);
      g.drawLine(10,265,420,265);
      g.drawLine(10,290,420,290);

      g.drawLine(10,40,10,290);
      g.drawLine(420,40,420,290);
      g.drawLine(180,40,180,290);
      g.drawLine(310,40,310,290);
   }

   public void query()
   {
       try
       {
           String url = "jdbc:db2://" + server + ":" + port + '/' +
             dataSource;
           con = DriverManager.getConnection(url, userid, password);

           stmt = con.createStatement();
           rs = stmt.executeQuery(sql);

           Vector bnameVector = new Vector();
           Vector btypeVector = new Vector();
           Vector bcitynameVector = new Vector();

           int h = 80;
           Graphics g = resultPanel.getGraphics();

           while(rs.next()) {
```

```java
            String name = rs.getString(1);
            String type = rs.getString(2);
            String city = rs.getString(3);
            bnameVector.addElement(name);
            btypeVector.addElement(type);
            bcitynameVector.addElement(city);
        }

        String bname = null;
        for (int i = 0; i < bnameVector.size(); i++)
        {
            bname = bnameVector.elementAt(i).toString();
            g.drawString(bname, 20, h);
            String btype = btypeVector.elementAt(i).toString();
            g.drawString(btype, 190, h);
            String bcityname =
                        bcitynameVector.elementAt(i).toString();
            g.drawString(bcityname, 330, h);
            h += 25;

        }

        rs.close();
        stmt.close();
        con.close();

    } catch (Exception e)
    {
        e.printStackTrace();
        System.exit(0);
    }


}

// variables

    java.awt.Button button1;
    java.awt.Button button2;
    java.awt.Button button3;
    java.awt.Button button4;

    CheckboxGroup Group1;
    java.awt.Checkbox radioButton1;
    java.awt.Checkbox radioButton2;
    java.awt.Checkbox radioButton3;
```

```
java.awt.Checkbox radioButton4;

java.awt.TextField textField1;
java.awt.TextField textField3;
java.awt.TextField textField4;

java.awt.Label label1;
java.awt.Label label2;
java.awt.Label label3;
java.awt.Label label4;
java.awt.Label label5;

CardLayout mainCardLayout;
java.awt.Panel inputPanel;
java.awt.Panel resultPanel;
java.awt.Panel mainCardPanel;

String dataSource;
String userid;
String password;

String server;
String port;
Connection con;
Statement stmt;
ResultSet rs;

String sql;
String city = "";
String where;
}
```

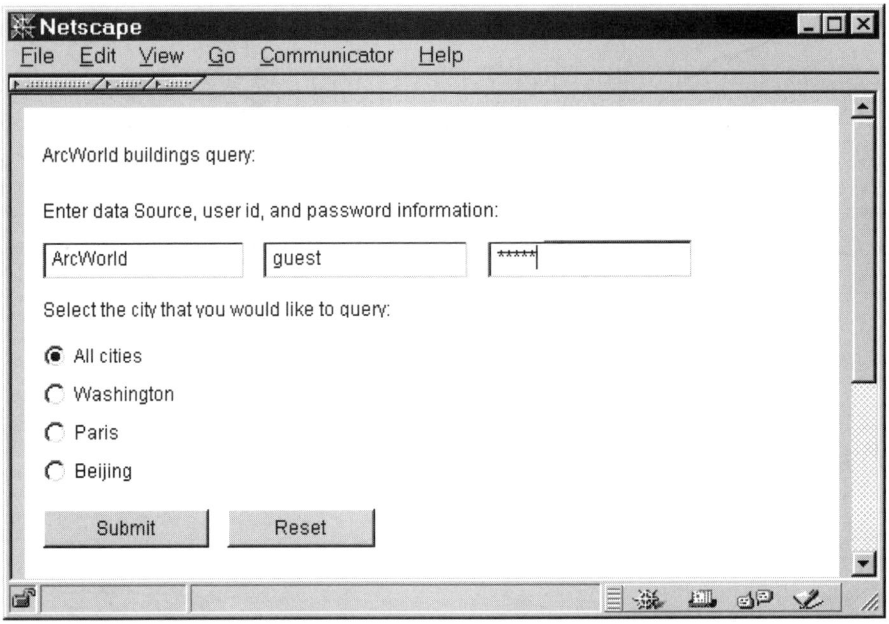

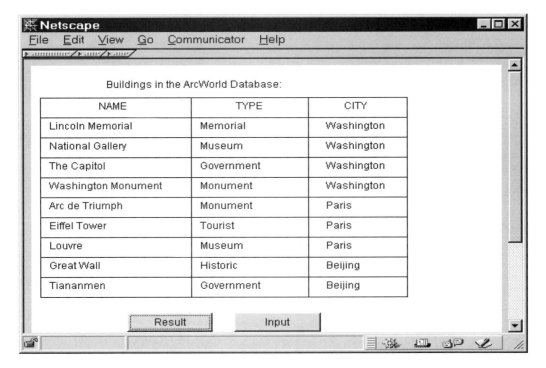

Figure 12-2. ArcWorld Building Query: Input Panel.

Figure 12-3. ArcWorld Building Query: Report Panel.

Net.Data and Applets

In this section, as promised in Chapter 11, "Dynamic Web Pages" we have added to the **Net.Data Select.mac** example (see Listing 11-1 on page 237) the use of applets (see Listing 12-3) to display the query result in bar charts, line charts, and pie charts (see Figure 12-4). These cannot be done in HTML.

Listing 12-3. The SelectChart Macro.

```
%{
  SelectChart.mac
%}

%DEFINE {
 TITLE = "ArcWorld buildings query: "
 DTW_HTML_TABLE = "yes"
 DTW_SAVE_TABLE_IN = "buildingTable"
%}

%DEFINE {
 ChartType = "3D Pie"
 ChartUI2.codebase = {http://@DTW_rGETENV("SERVER_NAME"):
   @DTW_rGETENV("SERVER_PORT")/code/chart%}
 ChartUI2.height = "250"
 ChartUI2.width = "400"
 field = "35"
 name = "$(N2)"
 numrow = "$(ROW_NUM)"
%}

%FUNCTION(DTW_APPLET) ChartUI2();

%FUNCTION(DTW_ODBC) queryBuilding(where) {
   SELECT type, count(type) FROM Building $(where) GROUP BY type
%REPORT {
<table border=2 cellspacing=40 cellpadding=0>
  <tr> <th colspan=2 bgcolor='a7a7ff'>Percentage of Buildings by Type
  <tr> <th bgcolor='ffaacc'>Query result <th bgcolor='ffaacc'> Chart
  <tr>
  <td align=center>
  <table border=1>
    <tr> <th>Type <th># of Buildings
%ROW {
    <tr> <td>$(V1) <td align=center>$(V2)
```

```
%}
  </table>
  <td>
  @DTWA_ChartUI2(ChartUI2.codebase, ChartUI2.width, ChartUI2.height,
    ChartType, numrow, buildingTable, name)
</table>
%}
%}


%HTML(INPUT) {
<html>
<form method="post" action="REPORT">
$(TITLE)<p>
Enter the data source, user id, and password information:<br>
<input size=20 name="DATABASE"> <input size=20 name="LOGIN">
  <input size=20 type="PASSWORD" name='PASSWORD'><br>
<br>
Select the city that you would like to query:<br>
<input type="radio" name="CITY" value="*"> All cities <br>
<input type="radio" name="CITY" value="Washington"> Washington <br>
<input type="radio" name="CITY" value="Paris"> Paris <br>
<input type="radio" name="CITY" value="Beijing"> Beijing <p>
<input type="submit"> <input type="reset">
</form>
</html>
%}


%HTML(REPORT) {
%IF ($(CITY) == "*")
  @DTW_ASSIGN(where, "")
%ELSE
  @DTW_CONCAT("WHERE city = ", "'", where)
  @DTW_CONCAT(where, CITY, where)
  @DTW_CONCAT(where, "'", where)
%ENDIF
<p>The following are the results of your query:
@queryBuilding(where)
%}
```

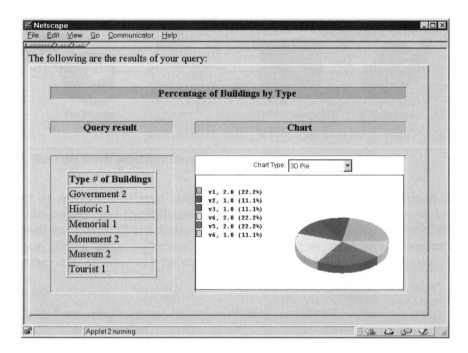

Figure 12-4. ArcWorld Building Query: Report Panel with Chart Display.

JAVA SERVLETS

Java servlets, specifically the HTTP servlets, are special kinds of Java applications that run on a *Web server*. As we will discuss later, there are many ways to load and invoke servlets. One of these is using the *<SERVLET> tag* that is embedded in a Web page, which identifies the servlet to run. When the Web page is accessed by a user, the servlet is loaded and runs on the Web server. It accepts input data from the Web server and passes output results to the Web server. Unlike applets, servlets run on the server, so they can be large and can perform all kinds of tasks without worrying too much about machine resources or network performance.

Like applets, the major benefit of using servlets is that the Web browser can provide a *universal client* environment. In addition, servlets provide:

- Protocol-independent and platform-independent server-side components
- A common API (the Servlet API which we will discuss later)
- Dynamic loading, either locally or over the net
- Security (the servlet security model)

Servlets can be used to generate dynamic HTML content (see Figure 12-5). When they are used for this purpose, they are faster and safer than CGI scripts. Servlets are faster because they use only lightweight threads to handle client requests. Servlets are safer because of automatic memory management and the servlet security model.

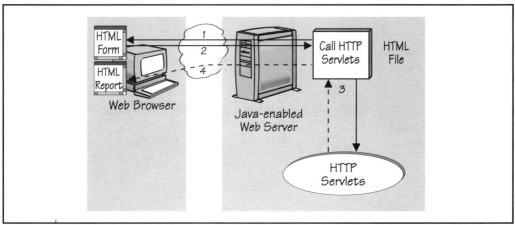

Figure 12-5. Dynamic HTML Generation Using HTTP Servlets.

Servlet Programming Model

A servlet must implement the **javax.servlet.Servlet** interface or extend a class that implements this interface, such as **javax.servlet.GenericServlet** or **javax.servlet.http.HttpServlet**. The latter is specifically designed to handle HTTP requests and to generate HTTP responses. Servlets follow this request-service-response programming model:

- Request—represented by a **java.servlet.ServletRequest** object
- Service—performed by invoking the *service()* method
- Response—represented by a **java.servlet.ServletResponse** object

Servlet Life Cycle

Once invoked (we will discuss the mechanisms in the next section), a servlet will go through a life cycle, supported by its life-cycle methods. These methods are automatically called by the Web server. You can override them, as needed, to provide desired behavior or to perform required tasks.

The life-cycle methods include:

- *init()* for initializing the servlet. This method is called when the servlet is first loaded. It is called only once.

- *service()* for performing the service. This method is called after initialization.

- *destroy()* for destroying the servlet. This method is called before unloading and is called only once. It can be used to perform cleanup operations.

For HTTP servlets, there are two additional methods:

- *doGet()* for processing the HTTP GET method. This method is called after initialization.

- *doPost()* for processing the HTTP POST method. This method is called after initialization.

Loading and Invoking Servlets

We mentioned earlier that there are many ways to load and invoke servlets. We will discuss these in the following sections. Most of them require the use of Java Web Server. One of them requires only the use of the Java Servlet Development Kit, which you can install on most existing Web servers.

Loading and Invocation

A servlet can be loaded and invoked:

- **From the /servlets/ directory.** In this case, the servlet class name is used for invocation (*http://host:port/servlet/<servlet_class>*).

Or, a servlet can be loaded and invoked using the Java Web Server:

- **From a remote location.** In this case, a URL is used for invocation (*http://host:port/servlet/<servlet-URL>*).
- **By setting up Server Side Includes**. This will be discussed in the following section.
- **By configuring the Admim Tool.** In this case, a "live" document (*.html*) is used for invocation.
- **By defining a Filter Chain.**

Server Side Includes

The *<SERVLET>* tag allows you to embed a servlet in an HTML document, which must have the special file extension *.shtml*. Its major attributes include:

- *codebase*—the base URL for the servlet
- *code*—the relative URL for the servlet's class file

You can use the *PARAM* element to supply initial values to the servlet. It specifies a name/value pair through the *name* and *value* attributes. You can include any number of *PARAM* elements.

To use the initial values in the servlet, you can call the *getInitParameter()* method. Usually you would do so in the *init()* method.

THE SERVLET API

The following describes the classes and interfaces in the Servlet API. These are all part of the **javax.servlet** package.

Servlet Interface

All servlets implement the **Servlet** interface. A servlet can be loaded into and runs inside a network service, such as a Web server. A servlet receives and responds to requests from clients.

Methods

The following are *life-cycle methods*:

- **init**(ServletConf config) initializes this servlet. It is called once, automatically, by the network service when it loads this servlet.

- **service**(ServletRequest req, ServletResponse resp) performs a single request from the client. The request object contains information about the service request, including parameters provided by the client, and the response object is used to return information to the client. Service requests are not handled until servlet initialization has completed.

- **destroy**() cleans up whatever resources are being held by this servlet. It is called once, automatically, by the network service when it unloads the servlet.

The following methods can be used to *obtain information about this servlet*:

■ **getServletConfig**() returns a **ServletConfig** object, which contains initialization parameters and start-up configuration for this servlet.

■ **getServletInfo**() returns a **String** containing information about this servlet.

ServletConfig Interface

The **ServletConfig** interface is implemented by network services or servlets to pass configuration information to a servlet when it is first loaded.

Methods

■ **getInitParameter**(String name) returns a **String** containing the value of the named initialization parameter of the servlet.

■ **getInitParameterNames**() returns an **Enumeration** containing the names of initialization parameters of the servlet.

■ **getServletContext**() returns a **ServletContext** object that contains the context for the servlet.

ServletContext Interface

The **ServletContext** interface is implemented by network services. It gives servlets access to information about their environment and allows them to log significant events. Different virtual hosts have different servlet context.

Methods

■ **getServlet**(String name) returns the **Servlet** object with the specified name. The servlet returned is initialized and ready to handle service requests.

■ **getServlets**() returns an **Enumeration** of the **Servlet** objects in this server that are within the same name space of the servlet. The enumeration always includes the servlet itself.

■ **getServerInfo**() returns information (**String**) about the network service under which the servlet is running.

- **getAttribute**(String name) returns the value (**Object**) of the named attribute of the network service.

- **getRealPath**(String path) returns the real path (**String**) corresponding to the given virtual path.

- **getMimeType**(String file) returns the mime type (**String**) of the specified file.

- **log**(String msg) writes the given message to the servlet log file.

ServletRequest Interface

The **ServletRequest** interface provides the means for getting information from the client to the servlet for a service request.

Methods

The following methods can be used to *obtain information on this request*:

- **getProtocol**() returns the protocol (**String**) of this request in the form <protocol>/<major version>.<minor version>.

- **getScheme**() returns the scheme (**String**) of the URL used in this request; for example "http".

- **getParameterNames**() returns an **Enumeration** containing the names of the parameters for this request.

- **getParameter**(String name) returns the single value (**String**) of the named parameter for this request.

- **getParameterValues**(String name) returns the values (**String[]**) of the named parameter for this request.

- **getAttribute**(String name) returns the value (**Object**) of the named attribute for this request.

- **getContentLength**() returns the size (int) of the request entity data.

- **getContentType**() returns the media type (**String**) of the request entity data.

- **getInputStream**() returns an **ServletInputStream** for reading the request body.

The following methods can be used to *obtain information on the sender and receiver*:

- **getRemoteAddr**() returns the IP address (**String**) of the agent that sent this request.

- **getRemoteHost**() returns the host name (**String**) of the agent that sent this request.

- **getServerName**() returns the host name (**String**) of the server that received this request.

- **getServerPort**() returns the port number (int) on which this request was received.

- **getRealPath**(String path) returns the real path (**String**) corresponding to the given virtual path.

ServletResponse Interface

The **ServletResponse** interface provides the means for sending response data from the servlet to the client.

Methods

- **setContentLength**(int len) sets the content length of this response.

- **setContentType**(String type) sets the content type of this response.

- **getOutputStream**() returns a **ServletOutputStream** for writing the response data.

GenericServlet Class

The **GenericServlet** class is an abstract class that simplifies writing servlets. It implements the **Servlet** and **ServletConfig** interfaces. Servlet developers may extend **GenericServlet** and, in doing so, must override the *service()* and *getServletInfo()* methods.

Constructors

- **GenericServlet**() is the default constructor that does no work.

Methods

The following are *life-cycle methods*:

- **init**(ServletConf config) initializes this servlet. It is called once, automatically, by the network service when it loads this servlet.

- **service**(ServletRequest req, ServletResponse resp) performs a single request from the client. The request object contains information about the service request, including parameters provided by the client, and the response object is used to return information to the client. Service requests are not handled until servlet initialization has completed.

- **destroy**() cleans up whatever resources are being held by this servlet. It is called once, automatically, by the network service when it unloads the servlet.

The following methods can be used to *obtain information about this servlet*:

- **getInitParameter**(String name) returns a **String** containing the value of the named initialization parameter of this servlet.

- **getInitParameterNames**() returns an **Enumeration** containing the names of initialization parameters of this servlet.

- **getServletContext**() returns a **ServletContext** object, which contains the context for this servlet.

- **getServletConfig**() returns a **ServletConfig** object, which contains initialization parameters and startup configuration for this servlet.

- **getServletInfo**() returns a **String** containing information about this servlet.

The following are additional methods:

- **log**(String msg) writes the class name of this servlet and the given message to the servlet log file.

ServletInputStream Class

The **ServletInputStream** class is an abstract class for reading servlet request data. It extends the **java.io.InputStream** class.

Constructors

■ **ServletInputStream**() is the default constructor that does no work.

Methods

■ **readLine**(byte[] b, int off, int len) reads data into the given array of bytes, starting at the offset, until the specified length of bytes have been read or "\n" is encountered. It returns the actual number (int) of bytes read, or −1 if the end of stream is reached.

ServletOutputStream Class

The **ServletOutputStream** class is an abstract class for writing servlet response data. It extends the **java.io.OutputStream** class.

Constructors

■ **ServletOutputStream**() is the default constructor that does no work.

Methods

■ **print**(int i) prints the integer provided.

■ **print**(long l) prints the long provided.

■ **print**(float f) prints the float provided.

■ **print**(double d) prints the double provided.

■ **print**(char c) prints the char provided.

■ **print**(String s) prints the **String** provided.

- **print**(boolean b) prints the boolean provided.

- **println**() prints a CRLF.

- **println**(int i) prints the integer provided, followed by a CRLF.

- **print**(long l) prints the long provided, followed by a CRLF.

- **print**(float f) prints the float provided, followed by a CRLF.

- **print**(double d) prints the double provided, followed by a CRLF.

- **print**(char c) prints the char provided, followed by a CRLF.

- **print**(String s) prints the **String** provided, followed by a CRLF.

- **print**(boolean b) prints the boolean provided, followed by a CRLF.

THE HTTP SERVLET API

The following sections describe the classes and interfaces in the HTTP Servlet API. These are all part of the **javax.servlet.http** package.

HttpServlet Class

The **HttpServlet** class is an abstract class that simplifies writing HTTP 1.0 servlets. It extends the **GenericServlet** class and provides a framework for handling the HTTP protocol. Servlet developers may extend it and, in doing so, must override the *doGet* (if HTTP GET methods are supported), *doPost* (if HTTP POST methods are supported), and *getServletInfo()* methods. To support HTTP 1.1 methods such as PUT, you must override the *service()* method and handle those additional methods directly.

Constructors

- **HttpServlet**() is the default constructor that does no work.

Methods

- **service**(HttpServletRequest req, HttpServletResponse resp) is an HTTP-specific version of the **Servlet**.*service()* method.

- **service**(ServletRequest req, ServletResponse resp) implements the high-level **Servlet**.*service()* method by delegating to the HTTP-specific *service()* method. This method is not normally overridden.

- **doGet**(HttpServletRequest req, HttpServletResponse resp) performs the HTTP GET method. When overridding this method, servlet developers should write the response headers first, and then write the response data using the servlet output stream from the response.

- **doPost**(HttpServletRequest req, HttpServletResponse resp) performs the HTTP POST method. When overridding this method, servlet developers should write the response headers first, and then write the response data using the servlet output stream from the response.

- **getLastModified**(HttpServletRequest req) returns the time (long) the requested entity was last modified.

HttpServletRequest Interface

The **HttpServletRequest** interface extends the **ServletRequest** interface and represents an HTTP servlet request. It allows the HTTP-protocol specified header information to be accessed.

Methods

The following methods can be used to *obtain information on this request*:

- **getAuthType**() returns the authentication scheme (**String**) of this request.

- **getHeaderNames**() returns an **Enumeration** representing header names of this request.

- **getHeader**(String name) returns the value (**String**) of the named header field.

- **getDateHeader**(String name) returns the value (long) of the named date header field, or −1 if not found.

- **getIntHeader**(String name) returns the value (int) of the named integer header field, or −1 if not found.

- **getMethod**() returns the method (**String**) with which this request was made.

- **getQueryString**() returns the query string part (**String**) of the request URI.

The following methods can be used to *obtain information on the sender and receiver*:

- **getRemoteUser**() returns the name (**String**) of the user making this request.

- **getRequestURI**() returns the request URI as a URL (**String**).

- **getServletPath**() returns the part of the request URI (**String**) that refers to the servlet being invoked.

- **getPathInfo**() returns extra path information (**String**) following the servlet path, but preceding the query string.

- **getPathTranslated**() returns extra path information (**String**) translated to a real path.

HttpServletResponse Interface

The **HttpServletResponse** interface extends the **ServletResponse** interface and represents an HTTP servlet response. It allows the HTTP-protocol specified header information to be manipulated.

Class Constants

- **SC_OK** (int)
- **SC_CREATED** (int)
- **SC_ACCEPTED** (int)
- **SC_NO_CONTENT** (int)
- **SC_MOVED_PERMANENTLY** (int)
- **SC_MOVED_TEMPORARILY** (int)
- **SC_NOT_MODIFIED** (int)
- **SC_BAD_REQUEST** (int)
- **SC_UNAUTHORIZED** (int)
- **SC_FORBIDDEN** (int)
- **SC_NOT_FOUND** (int)
- **SC_INTERNAL_SERVER_ERROR** (int)
- **SC_NOT_IMPLEMENTED** (int)
- **SC_BAD_GATEWAY** (int)
- **SC_SERVICE_UNAVAILABLE** (int)

Methods

■ **containsHeader**(String name) returns true if the response header has a field with the specified name.

■ **setHeader**(String name, String value) adds (or replaces) a field to the response header with the given name and value.

■ **setDateHeader**(String name, long value) adds (or replaces) a field to the response header with the given name and date value. The date is in milliseconds.

■ **setIntHeader**(String name, int value) adds (or replaces) a field to the response header with the given name and integer value.

■ **setStatus**(int sc) sets the status code for this response.

■ **setStatus**(int sc, String msg) sets the status code and message for this response.

■ **sendError**(int sc) sends an error response to the client with the specified status code.

■ **sendError**(int sc, String msg) sends an error response to the client with the specified status code and message.

■ **sendRedirect**(String location) sends a redirect response to the client using the specified location URL. The URL must be absolute.

HttpUtils Class

The **HttpUtils** class contains utility methods useful to HTTP servlets.

Class Methods

■ **getRequestURL**(HttpServletRequest req) reconstructs the URL used by the client to make the given request. The URL does not include query strings. It returns a **StringBuffer**, which can be modified.

■ **parsePostData**(int ServletInputStream) parses FORM data that is posted to the server using the HTTP POST method and the application/x-www-form-url encoded mime type. It returns a **Hashtable** of key/value pairs.

■ **parseQueryString**(String s) parses a query string and returns a **Hashtable** of key/value pairs.

Constructors

■ **HttpUtils**() is the default constructor.

SAMPLE DATA ACCESS SERVLETS

In the following section, we take the **Net.Data Select.mac** example (see Listing 11-1 on page 237) and redo it using servlets and JDBC (see Figure 12-6). The **SelectServlet** example (see Listings 12-4 and 12-5) has the same functionality and requires not much more programming effort. Both input panel and report panel remain unchanged.

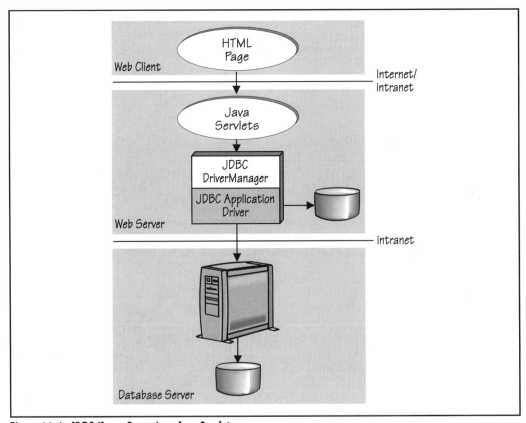

Figure 12-6. JDBC Usage Scenario—Java Servlet.

Listing 12-4. The SelectServlet Page.

```
#
# SelectServlet.html
#

<html>
  <form method="post"
   action="http://woodview2.stl.ibm.com:8080/servlet/SelectServlet">
    ArcWorld building query:<p>
    Enter the data source, user id, and password information:<br>
      <input size=20 name="DATABASE"> <input size=20 name="LOGIN">
      <input size=20 type="PASSWORD" name='PASSWORD'><br>
      <br>
    Select the city that you would like to query:<br>
      <input type="radio" name="CITY" value="*"> All cities <br>
     <input type="radio" name="CITY" value="Washington"> Washington<br>
      <input type="radio" name="CITY" value="Paris"> Paris <br>
      <input type="radio" name="CITY" value="Beijing"> Beijing <p>
      <input type="submit"> <input type="reset">
  </form>
</html>
```

Listing 12-5. The SelectServlet Class.

```
/*
 * SelectServlet.java
 */

import javax.servlet.*;
import javax.servlet.http.*;

import java.sql.*;

import java.io.*;
import java.util.*;

public
class SelectServlet extends HttpServlet {

    public void doPost (HttpServletRequest req, HttpServletResponse res)
        throws ServletException, IOException
    {
        res.setContentType("text/html");
```

```
ServletOutputStream out = res.getOutputStream();
out.println("<html>");
out.println("<head><title>Select Servlet</title></head>");
out.println("<body>");

String database = req.getParameter("DATABASE");
String login = req.getParameter("LOGIN");
String password = req.getParameter("PASSWORD");
String city = req.getParameter("CITY");

String where;
if (city.equals("*"))
    where = "";
else
    where = " WHERE city = " + "'" + city + "'";
String sql = "SELECT name, type, city FROM Building" + where;

try {
    // Load the JDBC-ODBC driver
    Class.forName("sun.jdbc.odbc.JdbcOdbcDriver");

    String url = "jdbc:odbc:" + database;
    Connection con = DriverManager.getConnection(url,
        login, password);
    Statement stmt = con.createStatement();

    ResultSet rs = stmt.executeQuery(sql);

    out.println("<table border='border'>");
    out.println("<caption> Buildings in the " +
                "ArcWorld database: </caption>");

    ResultSetMetaData rsmd = rs.getMetaData();
    String n1 = rsmd.getColumnName(1);
    String n2 = rsmd.getColumnName(2);
    String n3 = rsmd.getColumnName(3);
    out.println("<tr> <th>" + n1 + " <th>" + n2 +
        " <th>" + n3);

    while(rs.next()) {
        String v1 = rs.getString(1);
        String v2 = rs.getString(2);
        String v3 = rs.getString(3);
        out.println("<tr> <td>" + v1 +" <td>" + v2 +
            " <td>" + v3);
```

```
        }

        out.println("</table>");

        stmt.close();
        con.close();
    } catch( Exception e ) {
        e.printStackTrace();
    }

    out.println("</body></html>");
    }

    public String getServletInfo() {
        return "A servlet that performs Building queries on the " +
            "ArcWorld database";
    }
}
```

CONCLUSION

In this chapter, we have discussed the essence of Java applets and servlets and demonstrated their use for data access on the Web. Java applets are easy to use. They also allow you to develop more sophisticated GUIs than HTML pages for data presentation. However, this comes at a cost. It requires major programming effort, a fat client, and it has performance problems. The use of JavaBeans as reusable components can relieve the programming effort (we will discuss this in Chapter 20, "JavaBeans"). Nevertheless, the other issues remain.

Java servlets are also easy to use. They require much less programming effort, only a thin client, and they have fewer performance problems. Currently, they can be used to generate only HTML pages for display and therefore have only limited GUI support. However, this will change in the future (see Chapter 17, "Introduction to XML"). Therefore, *the importance of Java servlets for client/server data access is increasing.* With the development of Enterprise JavaBeans as the reusable server components (see Chapter 21, "Enterprise JavaBeans"), Java servlets will also be indispensable when using these components from the Web.

Java applets was the "killer application" for Java and the most visible component. It brought dynamic behavior to otherwise static HTML pages. However, for various reasons (the lack of uniform and in-time support among Web browser vendors, the restricted communication channel between applets and HTML pages, and performance issues), *the importance of Java applets for data access on the Web client is diminishing.* The fact that Microsoft removed all applets (where possible) from its Web sites also hurt its case. In the next chapter, we will discuss dynamic HTML, an alternate and more powerful way to bring dynamic behavior, including data access, to HTML pages on the client.

Chapter 13

Dynamic HTML

product

Dynamic HTML is a term used by many people, but with different meanings. Some people use it to mean the generation of dynamic HTML pages—for example, through server-side scripting. Most people use it to mean the provision of dynamic behavior on Web pages on the client. Even in this case, what Netscape means by Dynamic HTML is different from what Microsoft means by Dynamic HTML. Within the W3C, there is no standardization effort going on for Dynamic HTML. *Dynamic HTML is really just a concept.* It is not one specific technology. In this chapter, we will discuss what Microsoft provides in terms of Dynamic HTML, which consists of a rich set of features that allow you to manipulate any HTML document element and change styles, positioning, and content at any time (even after an HTML document has been loaded into a browser).

Key features of Dynamic HTML include:

■ **Object Model.** Dynamic HTML provides a comprehensive object model for HTML, which represents all document elements as objects and their attributes as properties of the objects. Users can manipulate these objects at any time by changing their *properties* or applying *methods* to them. The object model also provides support for keyboard and mouse *events* on all document elements.

■ *Style Sheets.* Dynamic HTML supports *Cascading Style Sheets (CSS)*. Any CSS attribute, including color and font, can be updated at any time. Also, CSS positioning coordinates can be changed at any time.

■ *Data Binding.* Data binding allows you to treat HTML in a Web page as a *template* for data to be supplied by a *data source object*. The data actually supplied by the data source object at run time is merged with the HTML template, which produces a complete Web page.

■ *Scriptlets.* A *scriptlet* is a Web page that you can use as a component in building Web applications.

Adding dynamic behavior to Web pages on the client formerly required writing complex Java applets. Dynamic HTML made this easy. Dynamic HTML is also language neutral. You can use Java applets or client-side scripting (for example, JavaScript) to control a Web page. In the following section, we will discuss these features in depth; some will be discussed in detail more than others because our focus is on client/server data access. (For simplicity, we will use *JavaScript* in the examples. Even though we have not introduced JavaScript so far, its syntax is similar to that of Java and its use in the examples should be self-explanatory.)

DYNAMIC HTML OBJECT MODEL

The core of Dynamic HTML is its object model. The object model makes HTML *changeable* by providing the following key features:

■ Access to all document elements
■ Instant page update
■ Full event model

The Dynamic HTML object model is known as an *element* model. This means that every element in the HTML document is accessible as an object, and all of its *properties*, *methods*, and *events* are exposed. The object model additionally provides various *collections* to facilitate access to document elements.

The following are major types of *objects* in the object model that are relevant to our discussion in this chapter:

■ **window** represents an open window in the browser. You use the **window** object to retrieve information about the state of the window and to gain access to the document in the window, to the events that occur in the window, and to features of the browser that affect the window.

■ **document** represents the HTML document in a given browser window. You use the **document** object to retrieve information about the document, to examine and modify the HTML elements and text within the document, and to process events.

■ **all** represents the collection of elements contained by an element.

■ **children** represents the collection of direct descendants of an element.

■ **event** represents the state of an event, such as the element in which the event occurred, the state of the keyboard keys, the location of the mouse, and the state of the mouse buttons.

■ **style** represents the current settings of all possible inline styles for a given element. Inline styles are CSS style assignments that an author applies directly to individual HTML elements.

■ **stylesheet** represents a single style sheet in the document. You use the object to retrieve information about the style sheet, such as the URL of the source file for the style sheet and the element in the document that defines the style sheet, and also to modify the style sheet.

The **document** object features an **all** collection object that contains all of the elements in the HTML document. This collection is indexed by name. For example, to get the element with ID MyHeading, you call:

```
document.all("MyHeading")
```

Or, you simply refer to its ID directly:

```
MyHeading
```

You can *add*, *delete*, and *replace* any element in the collection at any time. Once you have access to an element, you can modify its attributes and styles, among other things. For example, to change the font style of MyHeading, you enter:

```
MyHeading.style.fontStyle = "Italic"
```

In addition, you can also change the content of an element using the following properties:

■ innerHTML
■ innerText
■ outerHTML
■ outerText

For example, you can set the content of Myheading as:

```
MyHeading.innerText = "Dynamic HTML"
```

Or, another way to set it is:

```
MyHeading.innerHTML = "<A> Dynamic HTML </A>"
```

Event Model

Dynamic HTML provides events on every element in the HTML document. The common events that every element generates include the following *keyboard events*:

- **onkeypress** presses and releases a key.
- **onkeydown** presses a key.
- **onkeyup** releases a key.

And, these *mouse events* are generated:

- **onmouseover** moves the mouse over an element.
- **onmouseout** moves the mouse off an element.
- **onmousedown** presses any of the mouse buttons.
- **onmouseup** releases any of the mouse buttons.
- **onmousemove** moves the mouse over an element.
- **onclick** clicks the left mouse button on an element.
- **ondblclick** double-clicks the left mouse button on an element.

You can write scripts that interact with users through these events. You do this by providing *event handlers* for the events of interest to you. The event handler takes control when the event corresponding to the handler occurs. In general, the flow of events takes the following steps:

1. The user presses a key or clicks with the mouse.

2. An event is fired. The element affected by the event gets to handle it via its event handler.

3. The event will be passed up to successive parent elements (known as *event bubbling*) until it gets to the **document** object or until one of the event handlers cancels event bubbling.

4. Finally, a *default action* occurs unless you explicitly cancel it.

The following example shows the use of the **onmouseover** and **onmouseout** events to change the font style of MyHeading from "Normal" to "Italic" and back as the user moves the mouse over MyHeading:

```
<H1 id=MyHeading style="font-weight: normal"
    onmouseover="makeItalic();"
    onmouseout="makeNormal();">
    Dynamic HTML</H1>

<SCRIPT language=JavaScript>
    function makeItalic() {
        MyHeading.style.fontStyle = "Italic";
    }
    function makeNormal() {
        MyHeading.style.fontStyle = "Normal";
    }
</SCRIPT>
```

The **event** object, which was mentioned earlier, allows you to retrieve information about an element or to perform certain actions through the event's properties. Some of the most commonly used properties include:

- *type*—the event name
- *srcElement*—the element that fired the event
- *toElement*—the element the mouse moved to during an **onmouseover** or **onmouseout** event
- *returnValue*—the return value from the event
- *cancelBubble*—used to stop event from bubbling up the parent hierarchy
- *reason*—used on a data source object (which we will discuss later) to give the reason for completion of the data transfer

As can be expected, you can cancel event bubbling by setting:

```
window.event.cancelBubble = true
```

To cancel the default action, you set:

```
window.event.returnValue = false
```

DYNAMIC STYLES AND POSITIONING

You can dynamically change the style of any element in an HTML document. You can change colors, typefaces, indentation, and even the visibility of text. Dynamic HTML allows you to take advantage of CSS in the following ways:

■ *Inline styles*. Inline styles let you make style changes to a specific area of the document or element. Because all document elements expose a *style* property, and therefore CSS attributes, you can change the inline style based on user events. This was exactly what we showed in the earlier example.

■ *Element class*. Defining element classes allows you to change the style for more than one element using *global style sheets*. The *class* attribute on every element lets you associate any element with any class name. You can change the *className* property for any element based on user events as shown in the following example. This sample uses the **onmouseover** and **onmouseout** events to change the color of MyHeading from "textBlue" to "textRed" and back as the user moves the mouse over MyHeading. We assume that global rules for two classes, "textBlue" and "textRed", have been defined.

```
<H1 class=textBlue
    onmouseover="this.className='textRed'"
    onmouseout="this.className="textBlue">
    Dynamic HTML</H1>
```

■ *Style sheet management*. You can add new style rules to style sheets on the fly. In addition, through methods on the **styleSheet** object, you can add, change, and disable style sheets at any time.

When the font style or color of an element is changed dynamically, it still fits into the same physical space in the document as it did before the change. However, there are other styles, such as font size, that, when changed, actually change the size of the element and the amount of space required to display that element. In this case, the browser must *reflow* the document to ensure that all the elements fit.

Positioning

Dynamic HTML supports CSS positioning. You can position HTML elements using *top*, *left*, and *z-order* attributes. By assigning objects different z-orders, you can cause the objects to overlap, specifying which element should be on top of which. Two types of positioning are supported in CSS positioning:

■ *Absolute positioning*. The absolute position is always relative to the top of the document. It can be assigned by using the *style* attribute to set the position to "absolute" and to assign values to the *left* and *top* style attributes, as follows:

```
<IMG src="sample.gif" style="position:absolute; left:0; top:0">
```

■ *Relative positioning*. The relative position is always based on the element's natural position, which is determined by the parent element and any preceding and following elements. It can be assigned by using the *style* attribute to set the position to "relative" and to assign values to the *left*, *top*, *width*, and *height* style attributes.

DATA BINDING

We mentioned in the beginning that the core of Dynamic HTML is its object model because the object model makes HTML changeable. But, it is data binding that makes Dynamic HTML interesting and powerful from the client/server data access perspective. *Data binding* allows you to integrate data with native HTML elements on the client. As a result, you can create applications that *present, manipulate, and update data on the client*.

Basically, data binding allows you to treat HTML in a Web page as a *template* for data to be supplied by a *data source object*. The data actually supplied by the data source object at run time is merged with the HTML template which produces a complete Web page. Data source objects can supply their data (downloaded to the client if necessary) *asynchronously* to the page, allowing pages to render quickly and provide immediate interactivity. Also, data source objects can be implemented with the ability to update the data they expose.

Data binding is based on an architecture that consists of four major components (see Figure 13-1):

- **Data source objects** provide the data to a page. We will discuss these in more detail later.

- **Data consumers** (HTML elements) display the data. Elements include those intrinsic to HTML as well as custom objects implemented as Java applets. We will discuss these in more detail later.

- **Data binding agent** maintains the synchronization of data flow between data source objects and data consumers. When a page is first loaded, the binding agent finds the data source objects and data consumers among those elements on the page. It then maintains the synchronization of the data that flows between them.

- **Table repetition agent** works with tabular data consumers to repeat the entire data set supplied by a data source object. Individual elements in the table are synchronized through interaction with the binding agent.

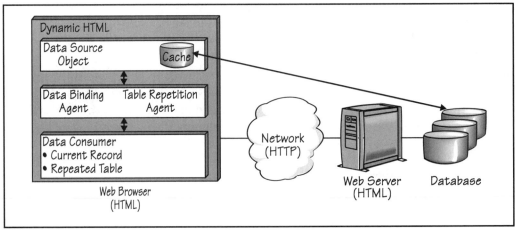

Figure 13-1. Dynamic HTML Data Binding Architecture.

Data Source Objects

Data source objects supply data to the Web page and can be implemented as Java applets. They implement an open specification that leaves it to the developer to decide on the following:

■ How the data set is specified—for example, using a JDBC connection and a SQL SELECT statement

■ How the data is transmitted to the page, including the transport protocol used and whether the transmission occurs synchronously or asynchronously

■ How the data is manipulated through scripts—for example, sorting or filtering

■ Whether the data can be updated

A data source object typically exposes its functionality through an object model accessible to scripts. This model is in the form of a standard set of properties, methods, and events. The data source specification, however, imposes no requirements regarding the object model it exposes.

The following are data source objects that come with **Internet Explorer 4.0**:

■ *JDBC Data Source Object*. This applet implements a JavaBeans-compliant interface. Data is retrieved through JDBC using SQL. We will discuss this in more detail later.

■ *HTML Data Source Object*. This allows you to define read-only data sets within an HTML document and have them included in another HTML document.

- **XML Data Source Object**. This supports the display of XML data within a Web page in nested, repeated tables. We will discuss XML in Chapter 17, "Introduction to XML."

- **Remote Data Service**. This enables you to access data from and transmit data to ODBC-compliant databases using SQL.

- **Tabular Data Control**. This supplies data that is stored in a delimited text file to the page.

You can also develop your own data source objects to be used with data binding by implementing the data source object specification.

The *JDBC Data Source Object* retrieves and stores data in a local cache. Therefore, even though JDBC provides only a scroll-forward cursor, the applet can provide random access to data. This applet, however, does not provide the ability to update data. You can extend the applet to add update functionality.

To use the JDBC Data Source Object, you embed it in an *APPLET* tag. The following properties of the object can be specified using the *PARAM* tags:

- *cabbase*—specifies the location of the code for the applet.
- *dbURL*—specifies the database URL.
- *showURL*—indicates whether a user interface should be displayed (optional).
- *sqlStatement*—provides the SQL statement to be used for accessing the database.
- *allowInsert*—indicates whether new rows can be inserted.
- *allowDelete*—indicates whether existing rows can be deleted.
- *allowUpdate*—indicates whether existing rows can be updated.
- *user*—identifies the user (optional).
- *password*—identifies the user's password (optional).

This is shown in the following example:

```
<APPLET code=JDC.class id="jds1" width=0 height=0>
    <PARAM name=cabbase
        value="http://woodview2.stl.ibm.com/code/dhtml">
    <PARAM name=dbURL value="jdbc:odbc:ArcWorld">
    <PARAM name=showURL value="false">
    <PARAM name =sqlStatement value="SELECT name, city, type
        FROM Building">
    <PARAM name=allowInsert vaule="false">
    <PARAM name=allowDelete value="false">
    <PARAM name=allowUpdate value="false">
    <PARAM name=user value="guest">
    <PARAM name=password value="guest1">
</APPLET>
```

Binding HTML Elements to Data

To display the data provided by a data source object, you must bind elements on an HTML page to its data. Bindable HTML elements fall into two categories:

- ***Single-Valued Elements***. These bind to a single field of the current row provided by the data source object.

- ***TABLE Elements***. These bind to the entire result set and use their contained elements as a template to repeat the data.

The procedure for binding a *single-valued element* to data is the same regardless of the element. Elements can be bound to data either at definition time using the *datasrc* and *datafld* attributes or at run time using the *dataSrc* and *dataFld* properties of the corresponding object in the object model. In addition, the *dataformatas* attribute can be used to indicate how the data should be rendered. Some elements, such as *BUTTON*, support read-only functionality; other elements, such as *TEXTAREA*, support updates to the data.

The *TABLE element* relies upon the elements that it contains to bind to the individual fields in the result set provided by the data source object. The contained elements serve as a template, and they are repeated once for each row in the result set. The *TABLE* element specifies the *datasrc* attribute; the contained elements specify the *datafld* attribute and inherit the *datasrc* attribute from the *TABLE* element. In addition, the *datapagesize* attribute can be used to specify the maximum number of rows that should be displayed at any one time. (This can be changed at run time using the *dataPageSize* property.)

Event Model Support for Data Binding

The data binding architecture provides a set of events that can be used in creating data-driven HTML pages. These events apply to one of the following three categories:

- ***Data source objects***—**onrowenter**, **onrowexit**, **ondataavailable**, **ondatasetcomplete**, **ondatasetchanged**, and **onreadystatechange**

- ***Bound elements***—**onbeforeupdate**, **onafterupdate**, and **onerrorupdate**

- ***Window***—**onbeforeunload**

SCRIPTLETS

Scriptlets are Web pages that are written using HTML and script according to certain conventions. By following simple conventions to expose well-defined interfaces, you can let others *reuse* the scriptlets, through the *OBJECT* tag, within other Web pages and applications. They can also customize existing scriptlet content without having to understand implementation details.

You can define a scriptlet interface (which consists of its properties and methods) by either of the following mechanisms:

- *JavaScript Public_Description Object*. This convention enables you to declare explicitly what properties and methods the scriptlet will make available.

- *Default Interface Description*. With this convention, you do not need to explicitly declare properties or methods. Instead, any variables and functions that are prefixed with *public_* become available as properties and methods.

CONCLUSION

This is the last chapter on Web data access. By now, you have seen the various ways you can use to access data on the Web. *Web gateway tools* and *Java servlets* allow you to access data from the server and then transmit the data back to the client in the form of HTML pages. *Java applets* and *dynamic HTML*, on the other hand, allow you to access data directly from the client. Each of these mechanisms has trade-offs regarding, for example, functionality, performance, portability, and ease of development.

In all of these mechanisms, the client/server computing piece is transparent to you. That is, it is done automatically for you, and you have little control over it. For example, if you use Java applets, client/server computing is taken care of by the JDBC applet driver that you use. It decides how the result set should be pre-fetched or cached, if at all. If you need explicit control over the client/server computing piece, either for an application specific reason or for performance reasons, you can use the mechanisms to be discussed in Part 4, "Java Client/Server Computing."

Dynamic HTML has a close relationship to the family of XML technologies that we will discuss in Part 5, "Web Data Interchange." For example, the Dynamic HTML object model was one of the bases (the so-called Level 0) of the Document Object Model. Also, CSS is closely related to XSL (the Extensible Stylesheet Language).

Part 4
Java Client/Server Computing

An Introduction to Part 4

When we discussed Java data access in Part 2, our focus was on data access and particularly on the Java APIs or Java language binding. We did not discuss client/server computing, except on occasions, because it was orthogonal to the main discussion.

Client/server computing is an integral part of Web data access, which we discussed in Part 3. Whether you use Web gateway tools or Java servlets to generate dynamic Web pages based on live data, HTTP is used as the protocol and mechanism for client/server computing. On the other hand, if you use Java applets or dynamic HTML with JDBC to access data, client/server computing is handled for you by the JDBC applet drivers. In all cases, client/server computing is done automatically, and you have little control over it.

There will be many occasions when you are developing sophisticated client/server data access applications that you want to have explicit control over the client/server computing piece, either for application-specific reasons or for performance reasons. In Part 4, we will discuss a few facilities that help or allow you to do so in Java:

- Java streams and object serialization
- Java RMI
- Java ORBs

Here is what we will be covering in Part 4:

- *Chapter 14* reviews Java streams and object serialization, which are important for Java client/server computing. They allow you to pass objects, not just data, by value across a network.

- *Chapter 15* reviews Java RMI, which is part of the Java Enterprise API and which provides an easy-to-use, all-Java mechanism for doing client/server computing.

- *Chapter 16* introduces Java ORBs, a more involved but CORBA-compliant mechanism for doing client/server computing in Java. Java ORBs have the benefit of using a standard protocol (IIOP) for transport and of ready interoperability with non-Java systems.

Java client/server is powerful, flexible, and fun. But it is definitely not for casual programmers. Nevertheless, once you master these facilities, you can build very sophisticated client/server data access applications. They are also integral parts of the so-called Java Platform for the Enterprise that we will discuss in Part 6, "Java Component Architectures."

Chapter 14

Java Streams and Object Serialization

concepts

Before JDK 1.1, trying to serialize a Java object was a difficult proposition (this is still the case today for, say, C++ objects). To start with, you must be able to access the object's *state*. This includes the values of not only its public instance variables, which are readily accessible, but also its protected, package-visible, and private instance variables, which may not be accessible at all. Then, for each value you must properly handle its data type. For basic data types, such as integer and float, this is easy. However, for more advanced data types, such as array, this can become messy. When it comes to object references, it can be downright tricky. You have to follow the object reference to serialize the target object, and the target object can reference other objects that you must also serialize recursively. To make matters worse, the objects can reference each other and form a cycle (or web), so you have to do cycle detection as well. There are also other issues, such as class evolution and security. So the task is daunting.

Fortunately, JDK 1.1 provides native support for object serialization. (When this is done within the JVM, many things become easier, like accessing private instance variables of an object.) So now, in most cases, object serialization is transparent. You don't even have to think about it. You just take it for granted.

Object serialization is useful in many cases. A major use is to transmit Java objects across the network, the so-called *passing objects by value*. Java RMI (Remote

Method Invocation), which we will discuss in the next chapter, does this in an automatic, transparent way. Another use is to make Java objects persistent. When used for persistence, unfortunately, object serialization is an all-or-nothing proposition that often does not scale up and is of limited use. The reason is that it generally requires that an object be saved or restored in its entirety and in serialized form.

In the following we will give an in-depth discussion of object serialization. But first, we need to give a quick overview of Java streams, particularly the API, because they are the base for object serialization. You will see examples of their usage when we discuss object serialization.

JAVA STREAMS

Java streams can be used to represent any source or destination of data in the form of a sequence of bytes, including network connections, files, and memory blocks. A key characteristic of Java streams is that their read and write operations are *synchronous* and *blocking*. This means that you must first establish a connection to the source (when reading) or destination (when writing) and that the connection remains open until the read or write operation is complete. Also, when reading data, if the data is not available immediately, the thread in which the read operation takes place is blocked until the data becomes available.

The major types of Java streams include:

- ■ *IO Streams*. These are the foundations of all Java streams. Input streams allow you to read data from a source; output streams allow you to write data to a destination. Specifically, the **InputStream** class is an abstract class that defines the fundamental ways you can read a stream of bytes from some source. The **OutputStream** class is an abstract class that defines the fundamental ways you can write a stream of bytes to some destination.

- ■ *Filter Streams*. These allow you to carry out additional processing—for example, filtering—when reading or writing data. The **FilterInputStream** class provides a "pass-through" for all the standard methods of **InputStream**. A **FilterInputStream** object holds inside itself another input stream to which it forwards all method calls. Additional processing can be performed after method forwarding. The **FilterOutputStream** class provides a pass-through for all the standard methods of **OutputStream**. A **FilterOutputStream** object holds inside itself another output stream to which it forwards all method calls. Additional processing can be performed before method forwarding.

- ■ *Data Streams*. These provide methods for you to read or write primitive Java data types without having to convert them into byte format. The **DataInput** interface and **DataInputStream** class provide methods for reading primitive Java data types from an input stream. The **DataOutput** interface and **DataOutputStream** class provide methods for writing primitive Java data types to an output stream.

■ *File Streams*. These can be used to read data from a file or write data to a file. The **FileInputStream** class represents an input stream for reading data from a file or a file descriptor. The **FileOutputStream** class represents an output stream for writing data to a file or a file descriptor.

THE STREAMS API

The Java Streams (or I/O) API is contained in the **java.io** package. It has over 70 interfaces, classes, and exceptions. In the following sections, we will discuss only the ones that are of relevance to object serialization. (The ones that are directly part of the Object Serialization API will be discussed in a later section.)

InputStream Class

The **InputStream** class is abstract and is the superclass of all classes representing an input stream of bytes.

It has the following constructor:

■ **InputStream**()

And, it has the following methods:

■ **read**() reads the next byte of data from this input stream. It returns the value (int) of the data read. If the end of the stream is reached, −1 is returned.

■ **read**(byte[ ] b) reads up to b.length() bytes of data from this input stream into the buffer *b*. It returns the number (int) of bytes read. If the end of the stream is reached, −1 is returned.

■ **read**(byte[ ] b, int off, int len) reads up to *len* bytes of data from this input stream into the buffer *b*, starting from the *off* position. It returns the number (int) of bytes read. If the end of the stream is reached, −1 is returned.

■ **skip**(long n) skips over and discards *n* bytes of data from this input stream. It returns the actual number of bytes skipped.

- **available**() returns the number (int) of bytes that can be read from this input stream without blocking.

- **markSupported**() returns true if this input stream supports the *mark()* and *reset()* methods.

- **mark**(int readlimit) marks the current position in this input stream. The *readlimit* argument corresponds to the number of bytes to be read before the mark gets invalidated.

- **reset**() repositions this input stream to the position marked.

- **close**() closes this input stream and releases any system resources associated with the stream. Once the stream is closed, it cannot be re-opened.

OutputStream Class

The **OutputStream** class is abstract and is the superclass of all classes representing an output stream of bytes.

It has the following constructor:

- **OutputStream**()

And, it has the following methods:

- **write**(int b) writes the specified byte to this output stream.

- **write**(byte[ ] b) writes b.length() bytes from the buffer *b* to this output stream.

- **write**(byte[ ] b, int off, int len) writes *len* bytes from the buffer *b*, starting at the *off* position, to this output stream.

- **flush**() flushes this output stream and forces any buffered output bytes to be written out.

- **close**() closes this output stream and releases any system resources associated with the stream. Once the stream is closed, it cannot be re-opened.

FilterInputStream Class

The **FilterInputStream** class is the superclass of all classes that filter input streams. It sits on top of an underlying input stream and provides additional functionality.

The **FilterInputStream** class extends the **InputStream** class and has the following constructor:

■ **FilterInputStream**(InputStream in) creates an input stream filter built on top of the specified input stream.

FilterOutputStream Class

The **FilterOutputStream** class is the superclass of all classes that filter output streams. It sits on top of an underlying output stream and provides additional functionality.

The **FilterOutputStream** class extends the **OutputStream** class and has the following constructor:

■ **FilterOutputStream**(OutputStream in) creates an output stream filter built on top of the specified output stream.

DataInput Interface

The **DataInput** interface provides methods for reading primitive Java data types from an input stream in a machine-independent manner. It has the following methods:

■ **readFully**(byte[ ] b) reads up to b.length() bytes of data from this input stream into the buffer *b*.

■ **readFully**(byte[ ] b, int off, int len) reads up to *len* bytes of data from this input stream into the buffer *b*, starting from the *off* position.

■ **skipBytes**(lint n) skips and discards *n* bytes of data from this input stream.

■ **readBoolean**() reads and returns a boolean value from this input stream.

■ **readByte**() reads and returns a byte value from this input stream.

- **readUnsignedByte**() reads and returns an unsigned 8-bit value (int) from this input stream.

- **readShort**() reads and returns a short value from this input stream.

- **readUnsignedShort**() reads and returns an unsigned 16-bit value (int) from this input stream.

- **readChar**() reads and returns a Unicode char value from this input stream.

- **readInt**() reads and returns an int value from this input stream.

- **readLong**() reads and returns a long value from this input stream.

- **readFloat**() reads and returns a float value from this input stream.

- **readDouble**() reads and returns a double value from this input stream.

- **readLine**() reads the next line of text from this input stream and returns a **String**.

- **readUTF**() reads and returns a **String** that has been encoded using a modified UTF-8 format from this input stream.

DataOutput Interface

The **DataOutput** interface provides methods for writing primitive Java data types to an output stream in a machine-independent manner. It has the following methods:

- **write**(int b) writes the specified byte to this output stream.

- **write**(byte[] b) writes b.length() bytes from the buffer *b* to this output stream.

- **write**(byte[] b, int off, int len) writes *len* bytes from the buffer *b*, starting at the *off* position, to this output stream.

- **writeBoolean**(boolean v) writes a boolean value to this output stream.

- **writeByte**(int v) writes an 8-bit value to this output stream.

- **writeShort**(int v) writes a 16-bit value to this output stream.

- **writeChar**(int v) writes a char value to this output stream.

■ **writeInt**(int v) writes an int value to this output stream.

■ **writeLong**(long v) writes a long value to this output stream.

■ **writeFloat**(float v) writes a float value to this output stream.

■ **writeDouble**(double v) writes a double value to this output stream.

■ **writeBytes**(String s) writes a String to this output stream.

■ **writeChars**(String s) writes a **String** to this output stream.

■ **writeUTF**(String s) writes a Unicode **String**, by encoding it using a modified UTF-8 format, to this output stream.

DataInputStream Class

A data input stream lets a user read primitive Java data types from an underlying input stream. Data input streams represent Unicode strings in a format that is a slight modification of UTF-8.

The **DataInputStream** class extends the **FilterInputStream** class and implements the **DataInput** interface. It has the following constructor:

■ **DataInputStream**(InputStream in) creates a new data input stream to read data from the specified input stream.

And, it has the following static method:

■ **readUTF**(DataInput in) reads and returns a **String** from the specified data input stream. The **String** has been encoded using a modified UTF-8 format.

DataOutputStream Class

A data output stream lets a user write primitive Java data types to an underlying output stream. Data output streams represent Unicode strings in a format that is a slight modification of UTF-8.

The **DataOutputStream** class extends the **FilterOutputStream** class and implements the **DataOutput** interface. It has the following constructor:

- **DataOutputStream**(OutputStream out) creates a new data output stream to write data to the specified input stream.

And, it has the following method:

- **size**() returns the number (int) of bytes written to this data output stream.

FileInputStream Class

A file input stream is an input stream for reading data from a file or a file descriptor. The **FileInputStream** class extends the **InputStream** class. It has the following constructors:

- **FileInputStream**(String name) creates an input file stream to read from a file with the specified name.

- **FileInputStream**(File file) creates an input file stream to read from the specified **File** object.

- **FileInputStream**(FileDescriptor fd) creates an input file stream to read from the specified **FileDescriptor** object.

And, it has the following method:

- **getFD**() returns the opaque FileDescriptor object associated with this input file stream.

FileOutputStream Class

A file output stream is an output stream for writing data to a file or a file descriptor. The **FileOutputStream** class extends the **OutputStream** class. It has the following constructors:

- **FileOutputStream**(String name) creates an output file stream to write to a file with the specified name.

- **FileOutputStream**(String name, boolean append) creates an output file stream to write to or append to a file with the specified name.

- **FileOutputStream**(File file) creates an output file stream to write to the specified **File** object.

- **FileOutputStream**(FileDescriptor fd) creates an output file stream to write to the specified **FileDescriptor** object.

And, it has the following method:

- **getFD**() returns the opaque FileDescriptor object associated with this output file stream.

IOException Class

The **IOException** class signals that an I/O exception of some sort has occurred. It extends the **Exception** class and has the following constructors:

- **IOException**()

- **IOException**(String s)

OBJECT SERIALIZATION

Object Serialization extends the core Java streams classes with support for objects. It supports the encoding of objects and the objects reachable from them (the so-called *object graph*) into a stream of bytes and the complementary reconstruction of the object graph from the stream. The default encoding of objects not only protects (private) *transient* data but also supports the *evolution of the classes*.

Object Serialization involves saving the *state* of objects in a serialized form into a stream sufficient to reconstruct the objects. Objects to be saved in the stream may support either the **Serializable** or the **Externalizable** interface. The serialized form must be able to identify and verify the *Java class* from which the object's state was saved and to restore the state to a new instance of that class. For **Serializable** objects, the serialized form automatically includes sufficient information to restore the object's state to a compatible version of the class. For **Externalizable** objects, the class is solely responsible for the content of the serialized form.

For example, to write a primitive data type (such as *int*) and an object to a file, you code the following:

```
FileOutputStream fos = new FileOutputStream("tmp");
ObjectOutput oos = new ObjectOutputStream(fos);
oos.writeInt(1);
oos.writeObject(obj);
oos.flush();
```

Objects are written with the *writeObject()* method of the **ObjectOutput** interface, and primitive data types are written using the corresponding methods of the **DataOutput** interface.

To read the primitive data type (such as *int*) and the object back from the file, you code the following:

```
FileInputStream fis = new FileInputStream("tmp");
ObjectInput ois = new ObjectInputStream(fis);
int i = ois.readInt();
Object obj = ois.readObject();
```

Objects are read with the *readObject()* method of the **ObjectInput** interface, and primitive data types are read using the corresponding methods of the **DataInput** interface. As can be expected, primitive data types and objects must be read from an input stream in the same order that they were written to an output stream.

Object Streams

The preceding examples show that Object Serialization produces and consumes a stream of bytes that contain one or more primitive data types and objects. The container for the stream implements interfaces that allow primitive data types and objects to be written into it or read from it. These are the **ObjectOutput** and **ObjectInput** interfaces, which extend the **DataOutput** and **DataInput** interfaces, respectively.

The **ObjectOutputStream** class implements the **ObjectOutput** interface and default Object Serialization. The **ObjectInputStream** class implements the **ObjectInput** interface and default object deserialization. The default mechanism serializes and deserializes all fields (public, protected, package-visible, and private) except for *transient* fields and *static* fields.

The *writeObject()* method of the **ObjectOutputStream** class serializes a given object and traverses its references to other objects in the object graph recursively. This creates a complete serialized representation of the graph. Within a stream, the first reference to any object results in the object being serialized and the assignment of a handle for that object. Subsequent references to that object are encoded as the handle. Using object handles preserves sharing and circular references that may happen in object graphs.

The *readObject()* method of the **ObjectInputStream** class deserializes the next object in a stream and traverses its references (through handles) to other objects recursively. This creates a complete object graph from the serialized object.

Serializable and Externalizable

Each object that is to be saved in a stream must explicitly allow itself to be saved by implementing the protocols needed to save and restore its state. Object Serialization specifies two such protocols: **Serializable** and **Externalizable**. For a **Serializable** class, Object Serialization can automatically save and restore fields of each class of an object and automatically handle classes that evolve. A **Serializable** class may declare which of its fields are *transient* (not saved or restored), and then write and read optional values and objects. For an **Externalizable** class, Object Serialization delegates to the class complete control over its external format and how the state of its superclass is saved and restored.

Serializable

Classes that require special handling during the serialization and deserialization process must implement the following methods:

- **writeObject**(java.io.ObjectOutputStream out)

- **readObject**(java.io.ObjectInputStream in)

If a class does not implement these methods, the default serialization provided by *defaultWriteObject()* and the default deserialization provided by *defaultReadObject()* will be used. When implemented, the class is only responsible for saving and restoring its own fields, not those of its supertypes or subtypes.

The *writeObject()* method is responsible for saving the state of the object for the particular class so that the corresponding *readObject()* can restore it later. The default mechanism for saving the object's state can be invoked by calling the *defaultWriteObject()* method. The *writeObject()* method does not need to concern itself with the state belonging to its superclass. State is saved by writing the individual fields to the **ObjectOutputStream** using the *writeObject()* method or, for primitive data types, using the methods supported by **DataOutput**.

The *readObject()* method is responsible for restoring the state of the object for the particular class. The default mechanism for restoring the object's state can be invoked by calling the *defaultReadObject()* method. The *readObject()* method does not need to concern itself with the state belonging to its superclass. State is restored by reading the individual fields from the **ObjectInputStream** using the *readObject()* method or, for primitive data types, using the methods supported by **DataInput**.

The following example shows the use of these methods to save and restore transient fields—with special encoding and decoding, respectively—that are not automatically handled by the default mechanism:

```
public class PurchaseOrder implements Serializable {
    private String userid;
    private transient String password;
    ...
    public void writeObject(ObjectOutputStream oos)
      throws IOException {
        oos.defaultWriteObject();
        String s = encode(password);
        oos.writeObject(s);
    }
    public void readObject(ObjectInputStream ois)
      throws IOException, ClassNotFoundException {
        ois.defaultReadObject();
        String s = (String) ois.readObject();
        password = decode(s);
    }
}
```

Externalizable

All classes must implement the following methods to implement their own serialization and deserialization:

■ **writeObject**(java.io.ObjectOutput out)

■ **readObject**(java.io.ObjectInput in)

The *writeObject()* method is responsible for saving the state of the object for the particular class so that the corresponding *readObject()* can restore it later. There is no default mechanism for saving the object's state. Consequently, the *writeObject()* method must write out all state information.

The *readObject()* method is responsible for restoring the state of the object for the particular class. There is no default mechanism for restoring the state of the object. Consequently, the *readObject()* method must read in all state information.

The following example shows the use of these methods to save and restore all fields:

```
public class PurchaseOrder implements Externalizable {
    private String userid;
```

```
private transient String password;
...
public void writeExternal(ObjectOutput oo)
  throws IOException {
    oo.writeObject(userid);
    String s = encode(password);
    oo.writeObject(s);
}
public void readExternal(ObjectInput oi)
  throws IOException, ClassNotFoundException {
    userid = (String) oi.ReadObject();
    String s = (String) oi.readObject();
    password = decode(s);
}
}
```

Versioning of Serializable Objects

When Object Serialization is used to save the state of Java objects in files or databases, the version of the class restoring the state could be different from the version that originally saved the state. Object Serialization provides a mechanism for automatic handling of classes that evolve. Versioning, however, applies only to **Serializable** classes. **Externalizable** classes are responsible for their own versioning.

Versioning is designed to support bidirectional communication between different versions of a class operating in different Java virtual machines:

■ Java classes can read streams written by older, compatible versions of the same class.

■ Java classes can write streams intended to be read by older, compatible versions of the same class.

Versioning is achieved through the use of **ObjectStreamClass** and *serialization version UID (Unique IDentifier)*. The **ObjectStreamClass** provides information about classes that are saved in a serialized stream. It provides the fully qualified name of the class and its serialization version UID. A *serialization version UID* identifies the unique original class version for which this class is capable of writing streams and from which it can read. Each versioned class must declare a serialization version UID; for example:

```
static final long SerialVersionUID = 3487496895819393L;
```

The serialization version UID is a 64-bit hash of the class name, interface class names, methods, and fields. It must be declared in all versions of a class, except the first. It is fixed for all compatible classes.

Evolved classes are compatible with the original class if they contain none of the following changes:

- Deleting fields
- Moving classes up or down the hierarchy
- Changing a non-static field to static or a non-transient field to transient
- Changing the declared type of a primitive field
- Changing the *writeObject()* or *readObject()* method
- Changing a class from **Serializable** to **Externalizable**, or vice-versa

Security

When a Java object is serialized, the question arises as to whether the resulting byte stream can be examined and changed, which injects viruses into the object when it is restored. Object Serialization is designed with the following security provisions:

- Only objects implementing the **Serializable** or **Externalizable** interfaces can be serialized. There are mechanisms provided for *not serializing* certain classes and certain fields.
- Object Serialization cannot be used to recreate the *same* object or to overwrite the *original* object. It can only be used to create *new* objects, which are initialized in a particular way.
- Classes loaded because of deserialization are no more or less secure than those loaded for any other reason.

Sensitive data, therefore, can be protected in a number of ways:

- Fields that contain sensitive data can be declared *transient*, which prevents them from being serialized.
- Classes that contain sensitive data can be prevented from being serialized by not implementing **Serializable** and **Externalizable** interfaces.
- The byte stream produced by Object Serialization can be *encrypted* to prevent it from being read.

THE OBJECT SERIALIZATION API

The Object Serialization API is contained in the **java.io** package.

ObjectInput Interface

The **ObjectInput** interface extends the **DataInput** interface to include the reading of objects, arrays, and Strings from an input stream. It has the following methods:

- **readObject**() reads and returns an **Object**. The class that implements this interface defines from where the object is read.

- **read**() reads the next byte of data from this input stream. It returns the value (int) of the data read. If the end of the stream is reached, −1 is returned.

- **read**(byte[ ] b) reads up to b.length() bytes of data from this input stream into the buffer *b*. It returns the number (int) of bytes read. If the end of the stream is reached, −1 is returned.

- **read**(byte[ ] b, int off, int len) reads up to *len* bytes of data from this input stream into the buffer *b*, starting from the *off* position. It returns the number (int) of bytes read. If the end of the stream is reached, −1 is returned.

- **skip**(long n) skips over and discards *n* bytes of data from this input stream. It returns the actual number of bytes skipped.

- **available**() returns the number (int) of bytes that can be read from this input stream without blocking.

- **close**() closes this input stream and releases any system resources associated with the stream. Once the stream is closed, it cannot be re-opened.

ObjectInputValidation Interface

The **ObjectInputValidation** interface is a callback interface to allow validation of objects when a complete graph of objects has been deserialized. It has the following method:

- **validateObject**() validates this object.

ObjectOutput Interface

The **ObjectOutput** interface extends the **DataOutput** interface to include the writing of objects, arrays, and Strings to an output stream. It has the following methods:

- **writeObject**(Object obj) writes the specified **Object** to this output stream. The class that implements this interface defines how the object is written.

- **write**(int b) writes the specified byte to this output stream.

- **write**(byte[] b) writes b.length() bytes from the buffer *b* to this output stream.

- **write**(byte[] b, int off, int len) writes *len* bytes from the buffer *b*, starting at the *off* position, to this output stream.

- **flush**() flushes this output stream and forces any buffered output bytes to be written out.

- **close**() closes this output stream and releases any system resources associated with the stream. Once the stream is closed, it cannot be re-opened.

Serializable Interface

Serializability of a class is automatically enabled by the class implementing the **Serializable** interface. All subclasses of a serializable class are themselves serializable. The **Serializable** interface has no fields or methods; it only identifies the semantics of being serializable.

Externalizable Interface

Externalization allows a class to specify the methods to be used for writing the state of an object to a stream and for reading it back. The **Externalizable** interface provides the methods to be implemented by a class to have complete control over the format and contents of the stream. These methods must explicitly coordinate with the superclass to save and restore its state.

The **Externalizable** interface extends the **Serializable** interface and has the following methods:

- **writeExternal**(ObjectOutput out) saves the state of this object to the output stream. The class that implements the method does so by calling the methods of **DataOutput** for its primitive data types or calling the *writeObject()* method of **ObjectOutput** for objects, strings, and arrays.

- **readExternal**(ObjectInput in) restores the state of this object from the input stream. The class that implements the method does so by calling the methods of **DataInput** for its primitive data types or calling the *readObject()* method of **ObjectInput** for objects, strings, and arrays.

ObjectInputStream Class

ObjectInputStream is used to restore objects previously serialized. It ensures that the types of all objects in the graph created from the stream match the classes present in the Java Virtual Machine. Only objects that support either the **Serializable** or **Externalizable** interface can be read from the stream.

The **ObjectInputStream** class extends the **InputStream** class and implements the **ObjectInput** interface. It has the following constructor:

■ **ObjectInputStream**(InputStream in) creates an **ObjectInputStream** that reads from the specified **InputStream**.

And, it has the following methods:

■ **defaultReadObject**() reads the non-static and non-transient fields of the current object from the input stream. This method may be called only from the *readObject()* method of the object being deserialized.

■ **readStreamHeader**() reads and verifies the magic number and version number from this input stream.

■ **resolveClass**(ObjectStreamClass v) allows classes to be fetched from an alternate source. It returns a **Class** object, and its serialVersionUID must match that of the serialized class or an exception is thrown.

■ **enableResolveObject**(boolean b) enables this input stream to allow objects read from the stream to be replaced. It returns true if the stream is trusted and allowed to enable replacement. When enabled, the *resolveObject()* method is called for every object being deserialized.

■ **resolveObject**(Object obj) allows the specified object to be replaced by another one. It returns an **Object**. This method is called after an object has been read, but before it is returned from *readObject()*. Replacing objects is disabled until *enableResolveObject()* is called.

■ **registerValidation**(ObjectInputValidation obj, int prio) registers an object to be validated before the object graph is returned. Typically, a *readObject()* method will register the object with the input stream. Then, when all of the objects are restored, a final set of validations can be performed.

ObjectOutputStream Class

ObjectOutputStream is used to save primitive data types and serialized objects. Only objects that support either the **Serializable** or the **Externalizable** interface can be written to the stream.

The **ObjectOutputStream** class extends the **OutputStream** class and implements the **ObjectOutput** and **ObjectStreamConstants** interfaces. It has the following constructor:

■ **ObjectOutputStream**(OuputStream out) creates an **ObjectOuputStream** that writes to the specified **OutputStream**.

And, it has the following methods:

■ **defaultWriteObject**() writes the non-static and non-transient fields of the current object to this output stream. This method may only be called from the *writeObject()* method of the class being serialized.

■ **writeStreamHeader**() writes the magic number and the version number to this output stream.

■ **annotateClass**(Class cl) allows the specified class data to be stored in the stream. The corresponding method in **ObjectInputStream** is *resolveClass()*.

■ **enableReplaceObject**() enables this output stream to allow objects written to the stream to be replaced. It returns true if the stream is trusted and allowed to enable replacement. When enabled the *replaceObject()* method is called for every object being serialized.

■ **replaceObject**(Object obj) allows the specified object to be replaced by another one. It returns an **Object**. Replacing objects is disabled until *enableReplace-Object()* is called.

■ **reset**() resets the state of this output stream to the same state as if it had just been created.

■ **drain**() drains any buffered data in this output stream.

ObjectStreamClass Class

An **ObjectStreamClass** describes a class that can be serialized to a stream or a class that was serialized to a stream. It contains the name and the serialVersionUID of the class.

The **ObjectStreamClass** class implements the **Serializable** interface. It has the following static method:

■ **loopup**(Class cl) returns the descriptor (**ObjectStreamClass**) for the specified class.

And, it has the following methods:

■ **getName**() returns the name of the class described by this descriptor.

■ **getSerialVersionUID**() returns the serialVersionUID (long) of the class described by this descriptor.

■ **forClass**() returns the class in the local Java Virtual Machine that is described by this descriptor.

SAVING AND LOADING THE ARCWORLD DATABASE: A SAMPLE

In the next chapter, we will show examples of using Object Serialization with Java RMI for passing objects by value. Here, we will show the use of Object Serialization for simple persistence. In particular, we will use Object Serialization to save and load the **ArcWorld** sample database.

Assuming that the **ArcWorld** database has been created, you can use the following two classes to save its data to a file or load its data from a file (see Listings 14-1 and 14-2):

■ **SaveArcWorld** will save the data of **ArcWorld** to a file.

■ **LoadArcWorld** will load the data of **ArcWorld** from a file. It will first delete the existing data.

Both classes will ask you to supply the data source name, user id, password, and file name when invoking them. They, in turn, call the appropriate methods of the **ArcWorld** class to perform their tasks.

The **ArcWorld** class (see Chapter 10, "Sample Data Access Applications") has been extended to provide the following additional methods (see Listing 14-3):

- **load**(String ds, String uid, String pw, String fn) loads the data from the given file. It first deletes the existing data.

- **save**(String ds, String uid, String pw, String fn) saves the data to the given file.

- **loadData**(Connection con, String filename) loads the data from the given file. The data is loaded in such an order that referential constraints are satisfied.

- **saveData**(Connection con, String filename) saves the data to the given file. The data is saved so that it can be properly loaded back.

Listing 14-1. The SaveArcWorld Class.

```java
/*
 * SaveArcWorld.java
 */

public class SaveArcWorld {

    public static void main(String[] args) {
        if (args.length != 4) {
            System.out.println("Usage: java SaveArcWorld " +
                "<dataSourceName> <uid> <pw> <fileName>");
            System.exit(0);
        }

        try {
            ArcWorld aw = new ArcWorld();
            aw.save(args[0], args[1], args[2], args[3]);
            System.out.println("ArcWorld data saved");
        } catch(Exception e) {
            System.err.println("Saving of ArcWorld data failed");
            e.printStackTrace();
            System.exit(1);
        }
        System.exit(0);
    }
}
```

Listing 14-2. The LoadArcWorld Class.

```
/*
 * LoadArcWorld.java
 */

public class LoadArcWorld {

    public static void main(String[] args) {
        if (args.length != 4) {
            System.out.println("Usage: java LoadArcWorld " +
                "<dataSourceName> <uid> <pw> <fileName>");
            System.exit(0);
        }

        try {
            ArcWorld aw = new ArcWorld();
            aw.load(args[0], args[1], args[2], args[3]);
            System.out.println("ArcWorld data loaded");
        } catch(Exception e) {
            System.err.println("Loading of ArcWorld data failed");
            e.printStackTrace();
            System.exit(1);
        }
        System.exit(0);
    }
}
```

Listing 14-3. The (Extended) ArcWorld Class.

```
/*
 * ArcWorld.java
 */

import java.io.*;
import java.util.*;

import java.sql.*;

public class ArcWorld {

    public void init(String ds, String uid, String pw)
      throws Exception {
        Connection con = connect(ds, uid, pw);
```

```java
        dropTables(con);
        createTables(con);
        disconnect(con);
    }

    public void initData(String ds, String uid, String pw)
        throws Exception {
        Connection con = connect(ds, uid, pw);
        deleteData(con);
        disconnect(con);
    }

    public void load(String ds, String uid, String pw, String fn)
        throws Exception {
        Connection con = connect(ds, uid, pw);
        deleteData(con);
        loadData(con, fn);
        disconnect(con);
    }


    public void save(String ds, String uid, String pw, String fn)
        throws Exception {
        Connection con = connect(ds, uid, pw);
        saveData(con, fn);
        disconnect(con);
    }


    public Connection connect(String ds, String uid, String pw)
        throws Exception {
        try {
            // Load the JDBC-ODBC driver
            Class.forName("sun.jdbc.odbc.JdbcOdbcDriver");

            String url = "jdbc:odbc:" + ds;
            System.out.println("Connecting to " + url);
            return DriverManager.getConnection(url, uid, pw);
        } catch(Exception e){
            System.err.println("Exception in connect()");
            System.err.println(e);
            throw e;
        }
    }
```

```java
public void disconnect(Connection con)
  throws Exception {
    try {
        System.out.println("Disconnecting from " +
          con.getMetaData().getURL());
        con.close();
    } catch (Exception e){
        System.err.println("Exception in disconnect()");
        System.err.println(e);
        throw e;
    }
}

public void createTables(Connection con)
  throws Exception {
    try {
        Statement stmt = con.createStatement();
        String sql;

        sql = "CREATE TABLE Country ( " +
          "name          CHAR(32) NOT NULL PRIMARY KEY, " +
          "cityMap       IMAGE)                        ";
        stmt.executeUpdate(sql);

        sql = "CREATE TABLE City ( " +
          "name          CHAR(32) NOT NULL PRIMARY KEY, " +
          "country       CHAR(32)                      " +
          "archMap       IMAGE                         " +
          "FOREIGN KEY (country) REFERENCES Country )  ";
        stmt.executeUpdate(sql);

        sql = "CREATE TABLE Architect ( " +
          "name          CHAR(32) NOT NULL PRIMARY KEY, " +
          "nationality   CHAR(32)                      " +
          "picture       IMAGE )                       ";
        stmt.executeUpdate(sql);

        sql = "CREATE TABLE Building ( " +
          "name          CHAR(32) NOT NULL PRIMARY KEY   , " +
          "type          CHAR(32)                        , " +
          "address       VARCHAR(255)                    , " +
          "city          CHAR(32)                        , " +
          "yearBuilt     INTEGER  CHECK(yearBuilt > -300), " +
          "architect     CHAR(32)                        , " +
          "style         CHAR(32)                        , " +
```

```
            "description  TEXT                                , " +
            "picture      IMAGE                                , " +
        "FOREIGN KEY (city) REFERENCES City          , " +
          "FOREIGN KEY (architect) REFERENCES Architect ) ";
        stmt.executeUpdate(sql);

        sql = "CREATE TABLE Church ( " +
            "name         CHAR(32) NOT NULL PRIMARY KEY   , " +
            "type         CHAR(32)                        , " +
            "address      VARCHAR(255)                    , " +
            "city         CHAR(32)                        , " +
            "yearBuilt    INTEGER  CHECK(yearBuilt > -300), " +
            "architect    CHAR(32)                        , " +
            "style        CHAR(32)                        , " +
            "description  TEXT                            , " +
            "picture      IMAGE                           , " +
            "denomination CHAR(32)                        , " +
            "pastor       CHAR(32)                        , " +
        "FOREIGN KEY (city) REFERENCES City          , " +
          "FOREIGN KEY (architect) REFERENCES Architect ) ";
        stmt.executeUpdate(sql);

        stmt.close();
    } catch (Exception e){
        System.err.println("Exception in creatTables()");
        System.err.println(e);
        throw e;
    }
}

public void dropTables(Connection con)
  throws Exception {
    try {
        DatabaseMetaData dbmd = con.getMetaData();
        Statement stmt = con.createStatement();
        ResultSet rs;
        String sql;

        rs = dbmd.getTables(null, null, "CHURCH", null);
        if (rs.next()) {
            rs.close();
            sql = "DROP TABLE Church";
            stmt.executeUpdate(sql);
        }
```

```java
            rs = dbmd.getTables(null, null, "BUILDING", null);
            if (rs.next()) {
                rs.close();
                sql = "DROP TABLE Building";
                stmt.executeUpdate(sql);
            }

            rs = dbmd.getTables(null, null, "ARCHITECT", null);
            if (rs.next()) {
                rs.close();
                sql = "DROP TABLE Architect";
                stmt.executeUpdate(sql);
            }

            rs = dbmd.getTables(null, null, "CITY", null);
            if (rs.next()) {
                rs.close();
                sql = "DROP TABLE City";
                stmt.executeUpdate(sql);
            }

            rs = dbmd.getTables(null, null, "COUNTRY", null);
            if (rs.next()) {
                rs.close();
                sql = "DROP TABLE Country";
                stmt.executeUpdate(sql);
            }

            rs.close();
            stmt.close();
        } catch(Exception e){
            System.err.println("Exception in dropTables()");
            System.err.println(e);
            throw e;
        }
    }
}

public void deleteData(Connection con)
    throws Exception {
        try {
            Statement stmt = con.createStatement();
            ResultSet rs;
            String sql;

            sql = "SELECT count(*) FROM Church";
```

```java
            rs = stmt.executeQuery(sql);
            rs.next();
            if (rs.getInt(1) > 0) {
                sql = "DELETE FROM Church";
                stmt.executeUpdate(sql);
            }


            sql = "SELECT count(*) FROM Building";
            rs = stmt.executeQuery(sql);
            rs.next();
            if (rs.getInt(1) > 0) {
                sql = "DELETE FROM Building";
                stmt.executeUpdate(sql);
            }

            sql = "SELECT count(*) FROM Architect";
            rs = stmt.executeQuery(sql);
            rs.next();
            if (rs.getInt(1) > 0) {
                sql = "DELETE FROM Architect";
                stmt.executeUpdate(sql);
            }

            sql = "SELECT count(*) FROM City";
            rs = stmt.executeQuery(sql);
            rs.next();
            if (rs.getInt(1) > 0) {
                sql = "DELETE FROM City";
                stmt.executeUpdate(sql);
            }

            sql = "SELECT count(*) FROM Country";
            rs = stmt.executeQuery(sql);
            rs.next();
            if (rs.getInt(1) > 0) {
                sql = "DELETE FROM Country";
                stmt.executeUpdate(sql);
            }

            rs.close();
            stmt.close();
        } catch(Exception e){
            System.err.println("Exception in dropTables()");
            System.err.println(e);
```

```
                throw e;
        }
}

void saveData(Connection con, String filename)
    throws Exception
{
        InputStream is;
        int size;

        FileOutputStream fos = new FileOutputStream(filename);
        ObjectOutputStream os = new ObjectOutputStream(fos);
        Statement stmt = con.createStatement();

        ResultSet rs;
        Vector v;
        byte[] buf = new byte[4096];
        int index;

        rs = stmt.executeQuery("SELECT * from Church");
        v = new Vector();
        while (rs.next()) {
            Church c = new Church();
            c.name = rs.getString(1);
            c.type = rs.getString(2);
            c.address = rs.getString(3);
            c.city = rs.getString(4);
            c.yearBuilt = rs.getInt(5);
            c.architect = rs.getString(6);
            c.style = rs.getString(7);

            is = rs.getAsciiStream(8);
            size = 0;
            for (;;) {
                int nread = is.read(buf);
                if (nread == -1)
                    break;
                size += nread;
            }
            is.close();
            c.description=new byte[size];
            is=rs.getAsciiStream(8);
            is.read(c.description);

            is = rs.getBinaryStream(9);
```

```
        size = 0;
        for (;;) {
            int nread = is.read(buf);
            if (nread == -1)
                break;
            size += nread;
        }
        is.close();
        c.picture = new byte[size];
        is = rs.getBinaryStream(9);
        is.read(c.picture);

        c.denomination = rs.getString(10);
        c.pastor = rs.getString(11);

        v.addElement(c);
    }
    rs = stmt.executeQuery("SELECT * from Church");
    index = 0;
    while (rs.next()) {
        Church c = (Church) v.elementAt(index++);
        is = rs.getAsciiStream(8);
        is.read(c.description);
        is = rs.getBinaryStream(9);
        is.read(c.picture);
    }
    os.writeObject(v);

    rs = stmt.executeQuery("SELECT * from Building");
    v = new Vector();
    while (rs.next()) {
        Building b = new Building();
        b.name = rs.getString(1);
        b.type = rs.getString(2);
        b.address = rs.getString(3);
        b.city = rs.getString(4);
        b.yearBuilt = rs.getInt(5);
        b.architect = rs.getString(6);
        b.style = rs.getString(7);

        is = rs.getBinaryStream(8);
        size=0;
        for (;;) {
            int nread = is.read(buf);
            if (nread == -1)
```

```
                break;
            size += nread;
        }
        is.close();
        b.description=new byte[size];
        is=rs.getAsciiStream(8);
        is.read(b.description);

        is = rs.getBinaryStream(9);
        size = 0;
        for (;;) {
            int nread = is.read(buf);
            if (nread == -1)
                break;
            size += nread;
        }
        is.close();
        b.picture = new byte[size];
        is = rs.getBinaryStream(9);
        is.read(b.picture);

        v.addElement(b);
    }
    rs = stmt.executeQuery("SELECT * from Building");
    index=0;
    while (rs.next()) {
        Building b = (Building) v.elementAt(index++);
        is=rs.getAsciiStream(8);
        is.read(b.description);
        is=rs.getBinaryStream(9);
        is.read(b.picture);
    }
    os.writeObject(v);

    rs = stmt.executeQuery("SELECT * from Architect");
    v = new Vector();
    while (rs.next()) {
        Architect a = new Architect();
        a.name = rs.getString(1);
        a.nationality = rs.getString(2);

        is = rs.getBinaryStream(3);
        size=0;
        for (;;) {
            int nread = is.read(buf);
```

```
                if (nread == -1)
                    break;
                size += nread;
            }
            is.close();
            a.picture = new byte[size];
            is=rs.getBinaryStream(3);
            is.read(a.picture);

            v.addElement(a);
        }
        rs = stmt.executeQuery("SELECT * from Architect");
        index = 0;
        while (rs.next()) {
            Architect a = (Architect) v.elementAt(index++);
            is = rs.getBinaryStream(3);
            is.read(a.picture);
        }
        os.writeObject(v);

        rs = stmt.executeQuery("SELECT * from City");
        v = new Vector();
        while (rs.next()) {
            City c = new City();
            c.name = rs.getString(1);
            c.country = rs.getString(2);

            is = rs.getBinaryStream(3);
            size = 0;
            for (;;) {
                int nread = is.read(buf);
                if (nread == -1)
                    break;
                size += nread;
            }
            is.close();
            c.archMap = new byte[size];
            is = rs.getBinaryStream(3);
            is.read(c.archMap);

            v.addElement(c);
        }
        rs = stmt.executeQuery("SELECT * from City");
        index = 0;
        while (rs.next()) {
```

```
            City c = (City) v.elementAt(index++);
            is = rs.getBinaryStream(3);
            is.read(c.archMap);
        }

        os.writeObject(v);
        rs = stmt.executeQuery("SELECT * from Country");
        v = new Vector();
        while (rs.next()) {
            Country c = new Country();
            c.name = rs.getString(1);

            is = rs.getBinaryStream(2);
            size = 0;
            for (;;) {
                int nread = is.read(buf);
                if (nread == -1)
                    break;
                size += nread;
            }
            is.close();
            c.cityMap = new byte[size];

            v.addElement(c);
        }
        rs = stmt.executeQuery("SELECT * from Country");
        index=0;
        while (rs.next()) {
            Country c=(Country) v.elementAt(index++);
            is=rs.getBinaryStream(2);
            is.read(c.cityMap);
        }
        os.writeObject(v);

}

void loadData(Connection con, String filename)
  throws Exception
{
    FileInputStream fis = new FileInputStream(filename);
    ObjectInputStream is = new ObjectInputStream(fis);
    PipedOutputStream pos = new PipedOutputStream();
    PipedInputStream pis = new PipedInputStream(pos);

    Vector v;
```

```java
PreparedStatement pstmt;

v = (Vector) is.readObject();
pstmt =
  con.prepareStatement("INSERT into Church " +
                       "values (?,?,?,?,?,?,?,?,?,?,?)");
for (int i=0; i<v.size(); i++) {
    Church c = (Church) v.elementAt(i);
    pstmt.setString(1, c.name);
    pstmt.setString(2, c.type);
    pstmt.setString(3, c.address);
    pstmt.setString(4, c.city);
    pstmt.setInt(5, c.yearBuilt);
    pstmt.setString(6, c.architect);
    pstmt.setString(7, c.style);
    pos = new PipedOutputStream();
    pis = new PipedInputStream(pos);
    pos.write(c.description);
    pstmt.setAsciiStream(8, pis, c.description.length);
    pos = new PipedOutputStream();
    pis = new PipedInputStream(pos);
    pos.write(c.picture);
    pstmt.setBinaryStream(9, pis, c.picture.length);
    pstmt.setString(10, c.denomination);
    pstmt.setString(11, c.pastor);
    pstmt.executeUpdate();
}

v = (Vector) is.readObject();
pstmt =
  con.prepareStatement("INSERT into Building " +
                       "values (?,?,?,?,?,?,?,?,?)");
for (int i=0; i<v.size(); i++) {
    Building b = (Building) v.elementAt(i);
    pstmt.setString(1, b.name);
    pstmt.setString(2, b.type);
    pstmt.setString(3, b.address);
    pstmt.setString(4, b.city);
    pstmt.setInt(5, b.yearBuilt);
    pstmt.setString(6, b.architect);
    pstmt.setString(7, b.style);
    pos = new PipedOutputStream();
    pis = new PipedInputStream(pos);
    pos.write(b.description);
    pstmt.setAsciiStream(8, pis, b.description.length);
```

```java
    pos = new PipedOutputStream();
    pis = new PipedInputStream(pos);
    pos.write(b.picture);
    pstmt.setBinaryStream(9, pis, b.picture.length);
    pstmt.executeUpdate();
}

v = (Vector) is.readObject();
pstmt =
  con.prepareStatement("INSERT into Architect values (?,?,?)");
for (int i=0; i<v.size(); i++) {
    Architect a = (Architect) v.elementAt(i);
    pstmt.setString(1, a.name);
    pstmt.setString(2, a.nationality);
    pos = new PipedOutputStream();
    pis = new PipedInputStream(pos);
    pos.write(a.picture);
    pstmt.setBinaryStream(3, pis, a.picture.length);
    pstmt.executeUpdate();
}

v = (Vector) is.readObject();
pstmt =
  con.prepareStatement("INSERT into City values (?,?,?)");
for (int i=0; i<v.size(); i++) {
    City c= (City) v.elementAt(i);
    pstmt.setString(1,c.name);
    pstmt.setString(2,c.country);
    pos = new PipedOutputStream();
    pis = new PipedInputStream(pos);
    pos.write(c.archMap);
    pstmt.setBinaryStream(3, pis, c.archMap.length);
    pstmt.executeUpdate();
}

v = (Vector) is.readObject();
pstmt =
  con.prepareStatement("INSERT into Country values (?,?)");
for (int i=0; i<v.size(); i++) {
    Country c = (Country) v.elementAt(i);
    pstmt.setString(1, c.name);
    pos.write(c.cityMap);
    pstmt.setBinaryStream(2, pis, c.cityMap.length);
    pstmt.executeUpdate();
}
```

```java
    }
}

class Country
  implements Serializable {
    String name;
    byte[] cityMap;
}

class City
  implements Serializable {
    String name;
    String country;
    byte[] archMap;
}

class Architect
  implements Serializable {
    String name;
    String nationality;
    byte[] picture;
}

class Building
  implements Serializable {
    String name;
    String type;
    String address;
    String city;
    int yearBuilt;
    String architect;
    String style;
    byte[] description;
    byte[] picture;
  }

class Church
  extends Building
  implements Serializable {
    String denomination;
    String pastor;
}
```

CONCLUSION

Object Serialization used to be a difficult and tedious task. With Java's **Serializable** objects, the task is effortless and transparent. Object Serialization is a key component of Java RMI, which we will discuss in the next chapter. It allows you to *pass objects by value* when making remote method invocations. Object Serialization is also a convenient mechanism for providing *simple persistence*. We will see its use in this way when we discuss JavaBeans and Enterprise JavaBeans (see Chapter 20, "JavaBeans" and Chapter 21, "Enterprise JavaBeans").

Object Serialization, however, is not the only way you can serialize a Java object's state or represent it in a serialized format. XML (which we will discuss in Chapter 17, "Introduction to XML") provides an alternative that is gaining popularity. Object Serialization is seamless for Java; XML, however, has a much broader applicability beyond Java.

Chapter 15

Java RMI Overview

concepts

In Chapter 7, "JDBC in a Nutshell," we stated that the introduction of JDBC in JDK 1.1 was one of the most significant events in Java data access. An equally significant event happened in JDK 1.1 from the perspective of Java client/server or distributed object computing. That was the introduction of Java *RMI (Remote Method Invocation)*. Before RMI, there was no Java distributed object computing, and it was difficult to develop client/server applications in Java. The only class library available for use was low-level sockets (**java.net**). Using sockets is tedious, error prone, and best left to experts. Among other things, it involves setting up client and server sockets to communicate with each other, designing the server socket to spawn new threads when receiving service requests, encoding method signatures, marshaling and unmarshaling arguments (not too difficult for primitive data types, but real tricky for objects because there was no Object Serialization yet), and handling exceptions.

Like JDBC, RMI is not a totally new invention. Many of its features (such as object-oriented RPC, automatic generation and usage of client stubs and server skeletons, and the naming service) came from CORBA. However, CORBA has its roots in integrating distributed, heterogeneous systems. Therefore, it had to design and use a language-neutral IDL as the central programming construct. Also, whatever CORBA does, it must do it in a language-neutral way, so it was not able to take advantage of any language-specific features. Consequently, while CORBA guarantees interoperability, but it frequently suffers from complexity. RMI, on the other hand, is specifically designed for Java. It deals only with pure distributed Java applications, and it utilizes all the native support that the Java Virtual Machine can provide and more (for example, by extending the Java Virtual Machine to support distributed garbage collection). As a result, like JDBC, RMI can be the "best" for Java distributed object computing.

In the following sections, we will first take a quick glance at RMI and go through a distributed version of the classic "Hello World" example. We will then discuss the Java distributed object model and the RMI system architecture. Finally, we will delve into the details of the RMI API and show a sample client/server data access application developed using RMI.

JAVA RMI

RMI is designed for use in the development of *distributed Java-to-Java applications* running in different Java Virtual Machines, potentially on different hosts. Unlike CORBA, which tries to provide location dependency (meaning any object that has an IDL interface can be invoked remotely), RMI makes a clear distinction between *remote objects* and *local objects*.

Only a *remote object's* methods can be invoked from another Java Virtual Machine, and all remote objects must support the **Remote** interface. In addition, remote objects must be *registered or made available* before they can be invoked remotely. When remote objects are used as arguments or results in remote method invocations, they are *passed by reference*. Remote objects can be revoked locally (within the same Java Virtual Machine); in this case they are no different from local objects.

A *local object's* methods can be invoked only from the same Java Virtual Machine. They are the "traditional" Java objects. When local objects are used as arguments or results in remote method invocations, they are *passed by value*. To do this, they must support Object Serialization, which means they must implement the **java.io.Serializable** interface.

Distributed "Hello World" Example

RMI is somewhat complex, so we will first go through a distributed version of the classic "Hello World" example and use it to illustrate the key aspects of RMI. This should give you a good feel of what RMI is and how to use it before we discuss in more depth its concepts and architecture.

The distributed "Hello World" example uses an applet (a local client) to make a remote method call to a server object (a remote object) running on the server. The applet was downloaded from the server, then invokes the server object to retrieve the message "Hello World!" and display it on the client. The example uses the following source files:

■ Hello.java (remote interface)
■ HelloImpl.java (remote object implementation)
■ HelloApplet.java (local client)
■ index.html

Remote Interface

A remote object must implement one or more remote interfaces. The remote interface has the following characteristics (see Listing 15-1):

■ The remote interface must be *public*.
■ The remote interface must extend **Remote**.
■ Each method must throw **RemoteException** in addition to any application-specific exceptions.

Listing 15-1. The Hello Interface.

```
package rmi.hello;

public interface Hello extends java.rmi.Remote {
    String sayHello() throws java.rmi.RemoteException;
}
```

Remote Object Implementation

A remote object implementation must (see Listing 15-2):

■ Specify the *remote interfaces* being implemented.
■ Optionally extend a *remote server*. (In this example, it extends **UnicastRemoteObject**, which indicates that it creates a single, non-replicated remote object that uses RMI's default sockets-based transport for communication.)
■ Define the *constructor* (with no argument) for the remote object. The constructor must throw **RemoteException**.

- Provide an implementation for each remote method. Arguments to or results from remote methods can be of any Java type, including objects. (Local objects are passed by value and remote objects are passed by reference.)
- Create and install a *security manager*, either the **RMISecurityManager** or one that you have defined. (If no security manager is specified, no class loading for RMI classes, local or otherwise, is allowed.)
- Create one or more *instances* of remote object. (The constructor of **Unicast-RemoteObject** automatically exports the remote object by listening for incoming calls on any anonymous port.)
- *Register* at least one of the remote objects with the RMI Registry for bootstrapping.

A remote object implementation may have *local methods*, which can only be invoked locally.

Listing 15-2. The HelloImpl Class.

```
package rmi.hello;

import java.rmi.*;
import java.rmi.server.UnicastRemoteObject;

public class HelloImpl
        extends UnicastRemoteObject
        implements Hello
{
    private String name;

    public HelloImpl(String s) throws java.rmi.RemoteException {
        super();
        name = s;
    }

    public String sayHello() throws RemoteException {
        return  "Hello World!";
    }

    public static void main(String args[])
    {
        // Create and install the security manager
        System.setSecurityManager(new RMISecurityManager());

        try {
            HelloImpl obj = new HelloImpl("HelloServer");
            Naming.rebind("HelloServer", obj);
```

```
        System.out.println("HelloImpl created and bound in the " +
                           "registry to the name HelloServer");

    } catch (Exception e) {
        System.out.println("HelloImpl.main: an exception occurred:");
        e.printStackTrace();
    }
  }
}
```

Local Client

A local client must (see Listings 15-3 and 15-4):

■ Look up the *remote object* and get a reference to its local stub.
■ Invoke one or more *remote methods*. This is no different from invoking a local method of a local object. That is, method invocation is location transparent.

Listing 15-3. The HelloApplet Class.

```
package rmi.hello;

import java.awt.*;
import java.rmi.*;

public class HelloApplet extends java.applet.Applet {

    String message = "";

    public void init() {

    try {
        Hello obj = (Hello)
            Naming.lookup("//" + getCodeBase().getHost() + "/HelloServer");
        message = obj.sayHello();

        } catch (Exception e) {
            System.out.println("HelloApplet: an exception occurred:");
            e.printStackTrace();
        }
    }

    public void paint(Graphics g) {
```

```
        g.drawString(message, 25, 50);
    }

}
```

Listing 15-4. The HTML File.

```
<HTML>
<title>Hello World</title>
<center> <h1>Hello World</h1> </center>

The message from the HelloServer is:
<p>
<applet codebase="../.."
        code="rmi.hello.HelloApplet"
        width=500 height=120>
</applet>
</HTML>
```

Java Distributed Object Model

We indicated that RMI was designed for use in the development of distributed Java-to-Java applications. Specifically, RMI is based on a *Java distributed object model* designed to:

■ Support seamless *remote invocation on objects* in different Java Virtual Machines.
■ Support *callback from servers to clients*.
■ Integrate the distributed object model into the Java language in a *natural* way.
■ Make *differences* between the distributed object model and local object model apparent.
■ Preserve the *safety* provided in the Java run-time environment.

The Java distributed object model is similar to the Java (local) object model in the following ways:

■ A reference to a remote object can be passed as an *argument* or returned as a *result* in any local or remote method invocation.
■ A remote object can be *cast* to any of the set of remote interfaces supported by the implementation.
■ The Java language *instanceof* operator can be used to test the remote interfaces supported by a remote object.

The Java distributed object model, however, differs from the Java (local) object model in many other ways:

- Clients of remote objects interact only with *remote interfaces*, not with the implementation classes of these interfaces.
- *Local* arguments to and results from a remote method invocation are *passed by value.*
- A remote object is *passed by reference.*
- The semantics of some of the methods defined by the *Object* class are *specialized for remote objects.*
- Clients must deal with additional *remote exceptions* that can occur during a remote method invocation.

Remote Interfaces and Classes

The interfaces and classes that are responsible for specifying the remote behavior are defined in the **java.rmi** and **java.rmi.server** packages. These packages include (see Figure 15-1):

- **Remote**. All remote interfaces extend, either directly or indirectly, the **Remote** interface. The methods in a remote interface must be defined as follows:

  - Each method must throw **RemoteException**, in addition to any application-specific exceptions.

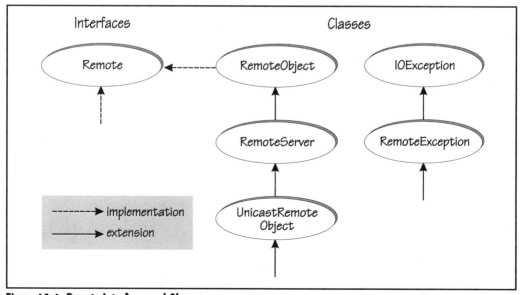

Figure 15-1. Remote Interfaces and Classes.

♦ A remote object passed as an argument or result (either directly or embedded within a local object) must be declared as its *remote interface*, not its implementation class.

- **RemoteObject**. The **RemoteObject** class and its subclasses provide the RMI server functions. In particular, the **Remote** class provides the remote semantics of **Object** by implementing methods for *equal()*, *hashCode()*, and *toString()*.

- **RemoteServer**. The **RemoteServer** class and its subclasses provide the functions needed to create objects and export them (make them available for invocation remotely). The subclasses identify the semantics of the remote reference—for example, whether the server is a single object or is a replicated object.

- **UnicastRemoteObject**. The **UnicastRemoteObject** class defines a singleton remote object whose references are valid only while the object is alive.

- **RemoteException**. The **RemoteException** class is the superclass of all exceptions that can be thrown by the RMI runtime. It is thrown when a remote method invocation fails.

Implementing a Remote Interface

A class that implements a remote interface must follow these rules:

- It usually extends **UnicastRemoteObject** or some other subclass of **RemoteServer**.
- It can implement one or more *remote interfaces*.
- It must define the *constructor* (with no argument) for the remote object. The constructor must throw **RemoteException**.
- It must provide an implementation for each *remote method*.
- It can define some *local methods* which do not appear in the remote interface and which can be used only locally.

In addition, a remote server must:

- Create and install a *security manager*, either the **RMISecurityManager** or another one.
- Create one or more *instances* of remote object.
- *Register* at least one of the remote objects with the RMI Registry for bootstrapping.

Type Equivalence of Remote Objects with Local Stubs

In the distributed object model, clients interact with the stubs of remote objects:

- The stub class has exactly the same set of *remote interfaces* defined by the remote object's class.
- The stub class does not include the local methods or local portions of the class hierarchy that constitute the object's type graph.
- The stub has the same type as the *remote portions* of the remote object's type graph.

Parameter Passing in Remote Method Invocation

An argument to or a result from a remote method invocation can be any Java type that is *serializable*. This includes:

- Primitive types, which are passed by value
- Local objects that implement the **java.io.Serializable** interface, which are passed by value
- Remote objects, which are passed by reference

Semantics of Object Methods

The default implementations in the **Object** class for the *equals()*, *hashCode()*, and *toString()* methods are not appropriate for remote objects. These are overridden by the **RemoteObject** class to provide semantics that are more appropriate for remote object:

- *equals()* determines whether two *object references* are equal, not whether the contents of the two objects are equal.
- *hashCode()* returns the *same value for all remote references* that refer to the same remote object.
- *toString()* returns a string that represents the reference of the object (for example, host name + port number + object identifier).

The following methods are declared final by the **Object** class. When used on a remote object, they have the following semantics:

- *getClass()* returns the type of the stub, which reflects the remote interfaces implemented by the object.
- *notify()*, *notifyAll()*, and *wait()* apply to the local stub, not the actual remote object.

Locating Remote Objects

A remote object must register with the RMI Registry so that clients can look it up and get a reference to its local stub. This invokes its remote methods. The **Registry** interface provides methods for *lookup, binding, rebinding, unbinding,* and *listing* the content of a registry. The **Naming** class uses the **Registry** remote interface to provide URL-based naming.

RMI System Architecture

The RMI system is designed to:

■ Support multiple *invocation mechanisms*—for example, invocation of *a single object* or of an object *replicated* at multiple locations.
■ Support various *reference semantics* for remote objects—for example, *live (transient)* references, *persistent* references, and lazy activation.
■ Provide *distributed garbage collection* of active objects.
■ Support multiple *transport mechanisms*—for example, *TCP/IP* and *UDP/IP.*

It consists of three layers (see Figure 15-2):

■ *Stub/Skeleton Layer*—client-side stubs and server-side skeletons
■ *Remote Reference Layer*—remote invocation and reference semantics
■ *Transport Layer*—connection management and remote object tracking

The Stub/Skeleton Layer

The Stub/Skeleton Layer is the interface between applications and the RMI system. It transmits data to the Remote Reference Layer via *marshal streams*, which employ Object Serialization to pass (local) objects by value.

A *stub* for a remote object is the client-side proxy for the remote object. It implements all the remote interfaces that are supported by it. It is responsible for:

■ Initiating a call to the remote object through the Remote Reference Layer
■ Marshaling arguments to a marshal stream
■ Requesting the Remote Reference Layer to invoke the call
■ Unmarshaling the result or exception from a marshal stream
■ Informing the Remote Reference Layer that the call is complete

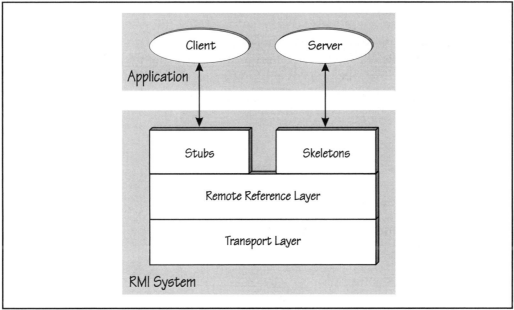

Figure 15-2. RMI System Architecture.

A *skeleton* for a remote object is the server-side proxy for the remote object. It dispatches calls to the actual remote object implementation. It is responsible for:

- Unmarshaling arguments from a marshaled stream.
- Making the up-call to the actual remote object implementation.
- Marshaling the result or exception onto a marshaled stream.

The appropriate stub and skeleton classes are determined at run time and are dynamically loaded as needed.

The Remote Reference Layer

The Remote Reference Layer deals with the lower-level transport interface. It is also responsible for carrying out a specific remote reference protocol. Various *invocation protocols* can be carried out, including:

- Unicast point-to-point invocation
- Invocation to replicated object groups
- Support for a specific replication strategy
- Support for a persistent reference to the remote object (enabling its activation)
- Reconnection strategies if the remote object becomes inaccessible

(At present, only *unicast point-to-point invocation* is supported.)

The Remote Reference Layer has two cooperating components: the *client-side* and the *server-side*. The client-side component contains information specific to the remote server and communicates via the Transport Layer to the server-side component. The server-side component implements the specific remote reference semantics before delivering a remote method invocation to the skeleton.

The Remote Reference Layer transmits data to the Transport Layer via a *stream-oriented connection*.

The Transport Layer

The Transport Layer is responsible for:

- Setting up connections to remote address spaces
- Managing connections
- Monitoring connection "liveliness"
- Listening for incoming calls
- Maintaining a table of remote objects
- Setting up a connection for an incoming call
- Locating the dispatcher for the target of the remote call and passing the connection to the dispatcher

It consists of four basic abstractions:

- *Endpoint*—a Java virtual machine or an address space
- *Channel*—a conduit between two endpoints
- *Connection*—a stream-oriented abstraction for transferring data
- *Transport*—an abstraction for setting up and managing channels, accepting calls on incoming connections, and dispatching the call to the Remote Reference Layer

Thread Usage in Remote Method Invocation

A method dispatched by the RMI runtime to a remote object implementation may or may not execute in a separate thread. Calls originating from different Java Virtual Machines will execute in different threads.

Garbage Collection of Remote Objects

Before RMI, a major characteristic of Java was that it provided automatic garbage collection of (local) objects. RMI extends this to provide automatic garbage collection of remote objects that are no longer referenced by any client. It uses a *reference counting* garbage collection algorithm. To accomplish this, the RMI runtime keeps track of all *live references* within each Java Virtual Machine. The first reference to a remote object sends a *referenced message* to the server for the remote object. Whenever a live reference enters, the reference count is incremented. As live references are found to be unreferenced, the reference count is decremented. When the last reference has been discarded, an *unreferenced message* is sent to the server.

When a remote object is not referenced by any client, the RMI runtime refers to it using a *weak reference*, which allows the Java Virtual Machine's garbage collector to discard the object if no other local references to the object exist. Thus, remote objects are only garbage collected when no more references, either local or remote, exist.

Dynamic Class Loading

RMI uses dynamic class loading to load at run time the classes required to handle method invocation on a remote object. These classes are:

- The classes of *remote objects* and their interfaces
- The *stub* and *skeleton* classes
- Other classes used in the application, such as *arguments* to or *results* from remote method invocations

In Java, the class loader that initially loads a Java class is subsequently used to load all the interfaces and classes that are used directly in the class. Specifically:

- The **AppletClassLoader** is used to download an applet and all classes used directly in that applet.
- The default class loader is used to load a class from the local CLASSPATH (client or server) and all classes used directly in that class.
- The **RMIClassLoader** is used to load those classes not directly used by the client or server application: the stub and skeleton classes, and classes of arguments and results. It looks for these classes in the following locations, in the order listed:

  - The local CLASSPATH
  - The URL encoded in the marshal stream
  - The URL specified by the local *java.rmi.server.codebase* property

The application can be configured with the property *java.rmi.server.useCodebaseOnly*, which disables the loading of classes from network hosts and forces classes to be loaded only from the locally defined codebase.

In addition to class loaders, dynamic class loading employs two other mechanisms: *Object Serialization* to transmit objects, and a *security manager* to check the classes that are loaded.

Security

In Java, when a class loader loads classes from the local CLASSPATH, they are considered trustworthy and are not restricted by a security manager. If classes are loaded from the network, there must be a security manager to ensure that loaded classes adhere to the standard Java safety guarantees:

- Applets (and all classes directly used in them) are always subject to the restrictions imposed by the **AppletSecurityManager**, which ensures that classes are loaded only from the applet host.
- Applications must either define their own security manager or use the **RMI-SecurityManager**.

RMI Through Firewalls via Proxies

The RMI Transport Layer normally attempts to open direct sockets to hosts. However, if firewalls exist in between, they do not allow this to happen. The Transport Layer provides two alternate HTTP-based mechanisms. These enable a client behind a firewall to invoke a method on a remote object that resides outside the firewall.

To get outside a firewall, the Transport Layer *embeds an RMI call within the HTTP protocol*. The RMI call is sent outside as the body of an HTTP POST request, and the return information is sent back in the body of the HTTP response. The Transport Layer will formulate the HTTP POST request in one of two ways:

- *Direct forwarding*—if the firewall proxy will forward an HTTP request directed to an arbitrary port on the host. In this case, the request is forwarded directly to the port on which the RMI server is listening. The Transport Layer on the target machine is listening with a server socket that is capable of decoding RMI calls inside HTTP POST requests.
- *Indirect forwarding*—if the firewall proxy will only forward an HTTP request directed to certain well-known HTTP ports. In this case, the request is forwarded to the HTTP server listening on port 80 of the host, and a CGI script is executed to forward the request to the target RMI server port on the same host.

The **RMISocketFactory** creates sockets that transparently provide the firewall tunneling mechanism as follows:

- *Client sockets* automatically attempt HTTP connections to hosts that cannot be connected with a direct socket.
- *Server sockets* automatically detect if a newly accepted connection is an HTTP POST request and if it is, return a socket that will expose only the body of the request and format its output as an HTTP response.

Calls transmitted via HTTP requests are at least *an order of magnitude slower* than those sent through direct sockets. Also, HTTP requests can only be initiated in *one direction through a firewall,* and a host outside of the firewall cannot initiate a remote method invocation back to the client.

THE RMI API

The RMI API is divided into the following categories:

- The RMI Client API
- The RMI Server API
- The RMI Registry API
- The RMI Stub/Skeleton API
- The RMI Garbage Collector API

The first category is used to develop RMI clients. The second and third categories are used to develop RMI servers. The last two categories are internal to RMI.

THE RMI CLIENT API

The RMI Client API is used by applets or applications to access remote objects. It is contained in the **java.rmi** package.

Remote Interface

The **Remote** interface has no fields or methods, and it serves to identify all remote objects. All remote objects must directly or indirectly implement this interface. Only those methods specified in a remote interface are available remotely. All remote interfaces and methods must be declared *public*.

RemoteException Class

All remote exceptions are subclasses of the **RemoteException** class. All remote constructors and methods must throw a remote exception.

The **RemoteException** class extends the **java.io.IOException** class and has the following constructors:

■ **RemoteException**()

■ **RemoteException**(String s) creates a remote exception with the specified string.

■ **RemoteException**(String s, Throwable ex) creates a remote exception with the specified string and exception.

And, it has the following method:

■ **getMessage**() returns the message (**String**), including the message from the nested exception, if there is one.

Naming Class

The **Naming** class provides the mechanism for obtaining references to remote objects based on names using the URL syntax: *rmi://host:port/name*. It is a final class and has the following static methods:

■ **lookup**(String name) returns the **Remote** object with the specified name.

■ **bind**(String name, Remote obj) binds the name to the specified remote object.

■ **rebind**(String name, Remote obj) rebinds the name to a new object, replacing any existing binding.

■ **unbind**(String name) unbinds the name.

■ **list**(String name) returns the names (**String**[ ]) present in the registry that match the specified name (*host:port*).

RMISecurityManager Class

The **RMISecurityManager** class defines a default security policy for RMI applications (not applets). For code loaded from a class loader, the security manager disables all functions except class definition and access.

The **RMISecurityManager** class extends the **SecurityManager** class and has the following constructor:

■ **RMISecurityManager**()

THE RMI SERVER API

The RMI Server API allows you to define, create, and export remote objects. It is contained in the **java.rmi.server** package.

RemoteObject Class

The **RemoteObject** class provides the semantics for remote objects. It is an abstract class, and implements the **Remote** and **Serializable** interfaces. It has the following constructors:

■ **RemoteObject**() creates a remote object.

■ **RemoteObject**(RemoteRef ref) creates a remote object, initialized with the specified remote reference.

It implements the remote object semantics for the following methods:

■ **hashCode**() returns the hash code (int) for this remote object. Two remote stubs that refer to the same remote object will have the same hash code.

■ **equals**(Object obj) returns true if this remote object is equivalent to the specified remote object.

■ **toString**() returns a **String** that represents the reference to this remote object.

344

RemoteServer Class

The **RemoteServer** class is the superclass to all server implementations. It provides the common framework to support a wide range of remote reference semantics. The **RemoteServer** class is abstract. It extends the **RemoteObject** class, and it has the following constructors:

- **RemoteServer**() creates a remote server object.

- **RemoteServer**(RemoteRef ref) creates a remote server object, initialized with the specified remote reference.

It has the following static methods:

- **getClientHost**() returns the host name (**String**) of the current client.

- **setLog**(java.io.OutputStream out) logs RMI calls to the specified output stream.

- **getLog**() returns the stream (**PrintStream**) containing the RMI call log.

UnicastRemoteObject Class

The **UnicastRemoteObject** class defines a non-replicated remote object whose references are valid only when the server process is alive. It provides support for point-to-point active object references (invocations, arguments, and results) using TCP/IP streams.

The **UnicastRemoteObject** class extends the **RemoteServer** class and has the following constructor:

- **UnicastRemoteObject**() creates and exports a new **UnicastRemoteObject** using an anonymous port.

It has the following static method:

- **exportObject**(Remote obj) exports the specified remote object to make it available to receive incoming calls. It returns a **RemoteStub** for the remote object. This method is used to export a unicast remote object that is not implemented by extending the **UnicastRemoteObject** class.

Unreferenced Interface

The **Unreferenced** interface allows a remote object to receive notification when there are no more remote references to it. It has the following method:

- **unreferenced**() is called when there are no current references to this remote object.

RMIClassLoader Class

The **RMIClassLoader** class provides methods for loading classes over the network. It has the following static methods:

- **loadClass**(String name) loads and returns a **Class** object with the given name from the URL specified in the **java.rmi.server.codebase** property.

- **loadClass**(java.net.URL codebase, String name) loads and returns a **Class** object with the specified name from the given URL.

- **getSecurityContext**(ClassLoader loader) returns the security context (**Object**) of the given class loader.

LoaderHandler Interface

The **LoaderHandler** interface provides the interface to implementations that can load classes over the network. The methods of **LoaderHandler** (the implementation) are used by the **RMIClassLoader** to carry out its operations.

It has the following static variable:

- **packagePrefix** contains the prefix of the package where the implementation of the **LoaderHandler** is located.

And, it has the following static methods:

- **loadClass**(String name) loads and returns a **Class** object with the given name from the URL specified in the **java.rmi.server.codebase** property.

- **loadClass**(java.net.URL codebase, String name) loads and returns a **Class** object with the specified name from the given URL.

- **getSecurityContext**(ClassLoader loader) returns the security context (**Object**) of the given class loader.

RMISocketFactory Class

The **RMISocketFactory** is used by the RMI runtime to obtain client and server sockets for RMI calls. The default implementation provides transparent RMI through firewalls using HTTP in three steps:

1. A direct socket connection to the remote server is attempted.

2. If that fails (due to a firewall), the runtime uses HTTP with the explicit port number of the server.

3. If the firewall does not allow this, then the runtime uses HTTP to a cgi-bin script on the server to POST the RMI call.

The **RMISocketFactory** class is an abstract class and has the following constructor:

- **RMISocketFactory**()

It has the following static methods:

- **setSocketFactory**(RMISocketFactory fac) sets the socket factory from which RMI creates sockets. The RMI socket factory can be set only once.

- **getSocketFactory**() returns the socket factory (**RMISocketFactory**) used by RMI.

- **setFailureHandler**(RMIFailureHandler fh) sets the failure handler to be called by the RMI runtime if socket creation fails.

- **getFailureHandler**() returns the failure handler (**RMIFailureHandler**) used by RMI.

And, it has the following methods:

- **createSocket**(String host, int port) creates and returns a client **Socket** connected to the specified host and port.

- **createServerSocket**(int port) creates and returns a **ServerSocket** on the specified port (port 0 represents an anonymous port).

RMIFailureHandler Interface

The **RMIFailureHandler** interface provides a method for specifying how the RMI runtime should respond when socket creation fails. It has the following method:

- **failure**(Exception ex) is called when the RMI runtime is unable to create a client or server socket.

THE RMI REGISTRY API

The RMI Registry API provides a well-known naming service for registering and retrieving remote objects by name. Any server process can provide its own registry, or a single registry can be used for a host.

The RMI Registry API is contained in the **java.rmi.registry** package.

Registry Interface

The **Registry** interface provides methods for lookup, binding, rebinding, unbinding, and listing the contents of a registry. A registry exists on every node that allows RMI connections to servers on that node. The registry contains a transient database that maps names to remote objects. It can be accessed through the **LocateRegistry** or **Naming** class.

The **Registry** interface extends the **Remote** interface and has the following methods:

- **lookup**(String name) returns the **Remote** object with the specified name in this registry.

- **bind**(String name, Remote obj) binds the name to the specified remote object.

- **rebind**(String name, Remote obj) rebinds the name to a new object, replacing any existing binding.

- **unbind**(String name) unbinds the name.

- **list**() returns the names (**String**[]) present in this registry.

LocateRegistry Class

The **LocateRegistry** class provides methods to obtain the **Registry** (or its stub) on a particular host (including the local host). It has the following static methods:

- **createRegistry**(int port) creates and exports a registry at the specified port. It returns the **Registry**.

- **getRegistry**() returns the **Registry** for the local host.

- **getRegistry**(int port) returns the **Registry** for the local host at the specified port.

- **getRegistry**(String host) returns the **Registry** on the specified host at the default port. If the host string is null, the local host is used.

- **getRegistry**(String host, int port) returns the **Registry** on the specified host at the specified port. If the host string is null, the local host is used. If port <= 0, the default port number is used.

RegistryHandler Interface

The **RegistryHandler** interface provides hooks to the private implementation. It has the following methods:

- **registryImpl**(int port) constructs and exports a registry on the specified port. It returns the **Registry** object.

- **registryStub**(String host, int port) returns a stub (**Registry**) for contacting a remote registry on the specified host and port.

THE RMI STUB/SKELETON API

The RMI Stub/Skeleton API is used by the stubs and skeletons generated by the *rmic* compiler. It is contained in the **java.rmi.server** package.

RemoteStub Class

The **RemoteStub** class is the superclass of all client stubs; it provides a common framework to support a wide range of remote reference semantics. Remote stubs are proxies that support exactly the same set of remote interfaces defined by the actual implementation of the remote object.

The **RemoteStub** class is an abstract class; it extends the **RemoteObject** class. It has the following constructors:

- **RemoteStub**() creates a remote stub.

- **RemoteStub**(RemoteRef ref) creates a remote stub, initialized with the specified remote reference.

And, it has the following static method:

- **setRef**(RemoteStub stub, RemoteRef ref) sets the given remote stub with the specified remote reference.

RemoteRef Interface

The **RemoteRef** interface represents the handle for a remote object. Each remote stub contains a remote reference that is used to carry out remote calls on the remote object for which it is a reference.

The **RemoteRef** interface extends the **Externalizable** interface, and it has the following field:

- **packagePrefix** contains the prefix of the package where the implementation of the **RemoteRef** is located.

And, it has the following methods:

- **newCall**(RemoteObject obj, Operation[] op, int opnum, long hash) creates and returns a **RemoteCall** object for a new method invocation on the given remote object, specified by the operation array and index.

- **invoke**(RemoteCall call) invokes the specified remote call.

- **done**(RemoteCall call) allows this remote reference to clean up (or reuse) the connection.

- **getRefClass**(ObjectOutput out) returns the name (**String**) of the reference class to be serialized onto the given output stream.

- **remoteHashCode**() returns the hash code (int) for the remote object. Two remote stubs that refer to the same remote object will have the same hash code.

- **remoteEquals**(RemoteRef ref) returns true if this remote object is equivalent to the given remote object.

- **remoteToString**() returns a **String** that represents the reference to this remote object.

RemoteCall Interface

The **RemoteCall** interface provides ways to carry out a call to a remote object. It has the following methods:

- **executeCall**() executes the remote call.

- **done**() allows cleanup after the remote call has completed.

- **getOutputStream**() returns the output stream (**ObjectOutput**) where the stub/skeleton should put the arguments and results.

- **releaseOutputStream**() releases the output stream.

- **getInputStream**() returns the input stream (**ObjectInput**) where the stub/skeleton should get the results and arguments.

- **releaseInputStream**() releases the input stream.

- **getResultStream**(boolean success) returns the output stream (**ObjectOutput**) after writing out header information relating to the success of the call. If success is true, the result is a normal return; otherwise, it is an exception.

Operation Class

The **Operation** class contains a description of a Java method. It has the following constructor:

- **Operation**(String)

And, it has the following method:

- **getOperation**() returns the description of this method.

ServerRef Interface

The **ServerRef** interface represents the server-side handle for a remote object implementation. It extends the **RemoteRef** interface, and it has the following methods:

- **exportObject**(Remote obj, Object data) exports the specified remote object and returns a client stub (**RemoteStub**).

- **getClientHost**() returns the host name (**String**) of the current client.

Skeleton Interface

All skeleton classes implement the **Skeleton** interface. A skeleton for a remote object is a server-side entity that dispatches calls to the actual remote object implementation.

The **Skeleton** interface has the following methods:

- **dispatch**(Remote obj, RemoteCall call, int opnum, long hash) unmarshals arguments, invokes the call on the actual remote object implementation, and unmarshals the result or any exception.

- **getOperations**() returns a list of method descriptors (**Operation[ ]**) for the remote object.

THE RMI GARBAGE COLLECTOR API

The RMI Garbage Collector API is used by the RMI distributed garbage collector (DGC). It is contained in the **java.rmi.dgc** package, except for the **ObjID** and **UID** classes, which are contained in the **java.rmi.server** package.

DGC Interface

The **DGC** interface is used for the server side of the distributed garbage collection algorithm. It contains two methods: *dirty* and *clean*. A *dirty* call is made when a remote reference is unmarshaled in a client. A corresponding *clean* call is made when no more references to the remote reference exist in the client.

The **DGC** interface has the following methods:

- **dirty**(ObjID[] ids, long seqNum, Lease lease) requests leases for the object references associated with the specified object identifiers. The given lease contains the client's VMID and a requested lease period. It returns a **Lease** which contains the VMID used and the lease period granted.

- **clean**(ObjID[] ids, long seqNum, VMID vmid, boolean strong) removes the VMID from the reference list of each remote object identified by the specified object identifiers.

ObjID Class

The ObjID class is used to identify remote objects uniquely in a VM. Each object identifier contains an object number and an address space identifier that is unique within a specific host. An object identifier is assigned to a remote object when it is exported.

The **ObjID** class implements the **Serializable** interface, and it has the following constructors:

- **ObjID**() creates a well-known object identifier.

- **ObjID**(int num) creates a well-known object identifier using the given object number.

And, it has the following methods:

- **write**(ObjectOutput out) writes this object identifier to the specified output stream.

- **read**(ObjectInput in) reads and returns an **ObjID** from the specified input stream.

- **hashCode**() returns a hash code (int) for this object identifier.

- **equals**(Object obj) returns true if this object identifier is equal to the specified object identifier.

- **toString**() returns a **String** representing this object identifier.

353

UID Class

A UID is an identifier that is unique with respect to the host on which it is generated. The **UID** class is a final class. It implements the **Serializable** interface, and it has the following constructor:

- **UID**() creates a well-known UID.

- **UID**(short num) creates a well-known UID with the given number.

And, it has the following methods:

- **write**(DataOutput out) writes this UID to the specified output stream.

- **read**(DataInput in) reads and returns a **UID** from the specified input stream.

- **hashCode**() returns a hash code (int) for this UID.

- **equals**(Object obj) returns true if this UID is equal to the specified UID.

- **toString**() returns a **String** representing this UID.

Lease Class

A lease contains a unique VMID and a lease duration. The **Lease** class is a final class. It implements the **Serializable** interface, and it has the following constructor:

- **Lease**(VMID vmid, long duration) creates a lease with the specified VMID and duration. The VMID may be null.

And, it has the following methods:

- **getVMID**() returns the client **VMID** associated with the lease.

- **getValue**() returns the lease duration.

VMID Class

A VMID is an identifier that is unique across all Java virtual machines. The **VMID** class is a final class. It implements the **Serializable** interface, and it has the following constructor:

- **VMID**()

It has the following static method:

- **isUnique**() returns true if an accurate address can be determined for this host.

And, it has the following methods:

- **hashCode**() returns a hash code (int) for this VMID.

- **equals**(Object obj) returns true if this VMID is equal to the specified VMID.

- **toString**() returns a **String** representing this VMID.

SAMPLE CLIENT/SERVER DATA ACCESS APPLICATIONS USING RMI

In the following sections, we take the **SelectApplet** example (see Listings 12-1 and 12-2) and redo it using RMI (see Figure 15-3). The **SelectRMIApplet/Server** example (see Listings 15-5 to 15-10) preserves the same user functionality and interface, but it performs data access on the server using JDBC. It also uses Object

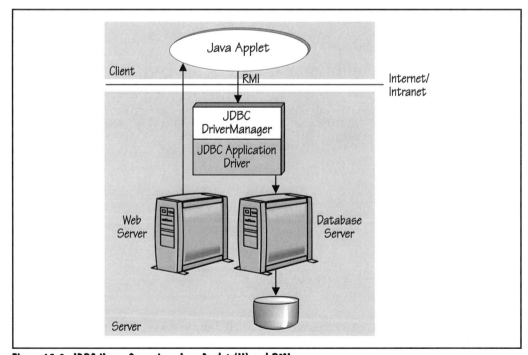

Figure 15-3. JDBC Usage Scenario—Java Applet (II) and RMI.

Serialization to pass objects (**QuerySpec** and **QueryResult**) by value, thus allowing coarse-grain communication between client and server.

Listing 15-5. The SelectRMIServer Interface.

```
/*
 * SelectRMIServer.java
 */

package rmi;

import java.rmi.*;

public interface SelectRMIServer
  extends Remote
{
    public QueryResult executeQuery(QuerySpec qs)
      throws RemoteException;
}
```

Listing 15-6. The QuerySpec Class.

```
/*
 * QuerySpec.java
 */

package rmi;

public class QuerySpec
  implements java.io.Serializable
{
    public QuerySpec(String ds, String uid, String pw, String s) {
        dataSource = ds;
        userid = uid;
        password = pw;
        sql = s;
    }

    public String getDataSource() {
        return dataSource;
    }

    public String getUserid() {
        return userid;
```

```
    }

    public String getPassword() {
        return password;
    }

    public String getSql() {
        return sql;
    }

    private String dataSource;
    private String userid;
    private String password;
    private String sql;
}
```

Listing 15-7. The QueryResult Class.

```
/*
 * QueryResult.java
 */

package rmi;

import java.util.*;

public class QueryResult
  implements java.io.Serializable
{
    public QueryResult() {
        result = new Vector();
    }

    public Vector getResult() {
        return result;
    }

    public Vector getResultRecord(int index) {
        if (index < result.size())
            return (Vector) result.elementAt(index);
        else
            return null;
    }
```

```
        private Vector result;
}
```

Listing 15-8. The SelectRMIServerImpl Class.

```java
/*
 * SelectRMIServerImpl.java
 */

package rmi;

import java.rmi.*;
import java.rmi.server.*;
import java.sql.*;

import java.io.*;
import java.util.*;

public class SelectRMIServerImpl
   extends UnicastRemoteObject
   implements SelectRMIServer
{
    public SelectRMIServerImpl()
      throws RemoteException
    {
        super();
    }

    public QueryResult executeQuery(QuerySpec qs)
        throws RemoteException
    {
        String database = qs.getDataSource();
        String login = qs.getUserid();
        String password = qs.getPassword();
        String sql = qs.getSql();
        QueryResult qr = null;

        try {
            // Load the JDBC-ODBC driver
            Class.forName("sun.jdbc.odbc.JdbcOdbcDriver");

            String url = "jdbc:odbc:" + database;
            Connection con = DriverManager.getConnection(url,
                login, password);
```

```java
            Statement stmt = con.createStatement();

            ResultSet rs = stmt.executeQuery(sql);

            qr = new QueryResult();
            Vector v1 = qr.getResult();

            while(rs.next()) {
                String s1 = rs.getString(1);
                String s2 = rs.getString(2);
                String s3 = rs.getString(3);

                Vector v2 = new Vector();
                v2.addElement(s1);
                v2.addElement(s2);
                v2.addElement(s3);

                v1.addElement(v2);
            }

            stmt.close();
            con.close();
        } catch(Exception e ) {
            e.printStackTrace();
        }

        return qr;
    }

    public static void main(String args[])
    {
        System.setSecurityManager(new RMISecurityManager());

        try {
            SelectRMIServerImpl server = new SelectRMIServerImpl();
            Naming.rebind("SelectRMIServer", server);
            System.out.println("SelectRMIServer created and bound");
        } catch(Exception e) {
            e.printStackTrace();
        }
    }
}
```

Listing 15-9. The SelectRMI HTML File.

```
<!
  SelectRMI.html
!>

<html>
    <applet codebase=".."
            code="rmi.SelectRMIApplet.class"
            width=525 height=475>
    </applet>
</html>
```

Listing 15-10. The SelectRMIApplet Class.

```java
/**
 * SelectRMIApplet.java
 */

package rmi;

import java.rmi.*;

import java.awt.*;
import java.awt.event.*;
import java.applet.*;
import java.util.Vector;

public class SelectRMIApplet
    extends Applet implements ActionListener
{
    public void init() {
        super.init();

        try {
            server = (SelectRMIServer) Naming.lookup("//" +
                getCodeBase().getHost() + "/SelectRMIServer");
        } catch(Exception e) {
            e.printStackTrace();
        }

        setLayout(null);
        addNotify();
        setSize(450,340);
```

```
//set applet layout
mainCardPanel = new Panel();
mainCardPanel.setLayout(new CardLayout(0,0));
mainCardPanel.setBounds(0,0,450,340);
add(mainCardPanel);

//add input panel
inputPanel = new Panel();
inputPanel.setLayout(null);
inputPanel.setBounds(0,0,450, 340);
mainCardPanel.add(" ", inputPanel);

label1 = new java.awt.Label("ArcWorld buildings query:");
label1.setBounds(12,10,324,40);
inputPanel.add(label1);

label2 = new java.awt.Label("Enter data Source, user id, and " +
  "password information:");
label2.setBounds(12,45,324,40);
inputPanel.add(label2);
textField1 = new java.awt.TextField();
textField1.setBounds(12,84,132,24);
textField1.requestFocus();
inputPanel.add(textField1);
textField3 = new java.awt.TextField();
textField3.setBounds(156,84,132,24);
inputPanel.add(textField3);
textField4 = new java.awt.TextField();
textField4.setBounds(300,84,132,24);
inputPanel.add(textField4);

label3 = new Label("Select the city that you " +
                   "would like to query:");
label3.setBounds(12,120,240,12);
inputPanel.add(label3);
Group1 = new CheckboxGroup();
radioButton1 = new java.awt.Checkbox("All cities",
                                     Group1, false);
radioButton1.setBounds(12,144,100,24);
inputPanel.add(radioButton1);
radioButton2 = new java.awt.Checkbox("Washington",
                                     Group1, false);
radioButton2.setBounds(12,168,100,24);
inputPanel.add(radioButton2);
```

```
            radioButton3 = new java.awt.Checkbox("Paris", Group1, false);
            radioButton3.setBounds(12,192,100,24);
            inputPanel.add(radioButton3);
            radioButton4 = new java.awt.Checkbox("Beijing", Group1, false);
            radioButton4.setBounds(12,216,100,24);
            inputPanel.add(radioButton4);

            button1 = new java.awt.Button("Submit");
            button1.setBounds(12,252,108,24);
            inputPanel.add(button1);
            button2 = new java.awt.Button("Reset");
            button2.setBounds(132,252,96,24);
            inputPanel.add(button2);

            // add result panel
            resultPanel = new Panel();
            resultPanel.setLayout(null);
            resultPanel.setBounds(0,0,792,390);
            mainCardPanel.add(" ", resultPanel);
            label5 = new java.awt.Label("Buildings in the " +
                                       "ArcWorld Database:");
            label5.setBounds(84,12,276,24);
            button3 = new java.awt.Button("Input");
            button3.setBounds(228,310,96,24);
            button4 = new java.awt.Button("Result");
            button4.setBounds(108,310,96,24);
            resultPanel.add(button3);
            resultPanel.add(button4);
            resultPanel.add(label5);

            mainCardLayout = new CardLayout();
            mainCardPanel.setLayout(mainCardLayout);
            mainCardLayout.addLayoutComponent("input", inputPanel);
            mainCardLayout.addLayoutComponent("result", resultPanel);
            mainCardLayout.show(mainCardPanel,"input");

            // register components' event listener
            AddListener();
    }

    private void AddListener()
    {
        button1.addActionListener(this);
        button2.addActionListener(this);
        button3.addActionListener(this);
```

```java
        button4.addActionListener(this);
    }

    public void actionPerformed(ActionEvent event)
    {
        if(event.getSource() == button1)
        {
            dataSource = textField1.getText();
            userid = textField3.getText();
            password = textField4.getText();

            if (radioButton1.getState())
                city = "*";
            else if (radioButton2.getState())
                city = "Washington";
            else if (radioButton3.getState())
                city = "Paris";
            else if (radioButton4.getState())
                city = "Beijing";
            if (city.equals("*"))
                where = "";
            else
                where = " WHERE city = " + "'" + city + "'";
            sql = "SELECT name, type, city FROM Building" + where;

            submitButton_Clicked(event);
        }
        if (event.getSource() == button2)
            resetButton_Clicked(event);
        if (event.getSource() == button3)
            inputButton_Clicked(event);
        if (event.getSource() == button4)
            resultButton_Clicked(event);
    }

    public void submitButton_Clicked(ActionEvent event)
    {
        mainCardLayout.show(mainCardPanel,"result");
    }

    public void resetButton_Clicked(ActionEvent event)
    {
        textField1.setText("");
        textField3.setText("");
        textField4.setText("");
```

```java
        radioButton1.setState(false);
        radioButton2.setState(false);
        radioButton3.setState(false);
        radioButton4.setState(false);
    }

    public void inputButton_Clicked(ActionEvent evnet)
    {
        mainCardLayout.show(mainCardPanel,"input");
    }

    public void resultButton_Clicked(ActionEvent event)
    {
        Graphics g = resultPanel.getGraphics();
        drawTable(g);
        query();
    }

    public void drawTable(Graphics g)
    {
        g.drawString("NAME", 75,55);
        g.drawString("TYPE", 230,55);
        g.drawString("CITY", 350,55);

        g.drawLine(10,40,420,40);
        g.drawLine(10,65,420,65);
        g.drawLine(10,90,420,90);
        g.drawLine(10,115,420,115);
        g.drawLine(10,140,420,140);
        g.drawLine(10,165,420,165);
        g.drawLine(10,190,420,190);
        g.drawLine(10,215,420,215);
        g.drawLine(10,240,420,240);
        g.drawLine(10,265,420,265);
        g.drawLine(10,290,420,290);

        g.drawLine(10,40,10,290);
        g.drawLine(420,40,420,290);
        g.drawLine(180,40,180,290);
        g.drawLine(310,40,310,290);
    }

    public void query()
    {
        try
```

```
    {
        QuerySpec qs = new QuerySpec(dataSource, userid,
                                    password, sql);
        QueryResult qr = server.executeQuery(qs);

        Vector bnameVector = new Vector();
        Vector btypeVector = new Vector();
        Vector bcitynameVector = new Vector();

        int h = 80;
        Graphics g = resultPanel.getGraphics();

        Vector v;
        int index = 0;
        while((v = qr.getResultRecord(index++)) != null) {
            String name = (String) v.elementAt(0);
            String type = (String) v.elementAt(1);
            String city = (String) v.elementAt(2);

            bnameVector.addElement(name);
            btypeVector.addElement(type);
            bcitynameVector.addElement(city);
        }

        String bname = null;
        for (int i = 0; i < bnameVector.size(); i++)
        {
            bname = bnameVector.elementAt(i).toString();
            g.drawString(bname, 20, h);
            String btype = btypeVector.elementAt(i).toString();
            g.drawString(btype, 190, h);
            String bcityname =
                bcitynameVector.elementAt(i).toString();
            g.drawString(bcityname, 330, h);
            h += 25;

        }

    } catch (Exception e)
    {
        e.printStackTrace();
        System.exit(0);
    }

}
```

```java
// variables

    java.awt.Button button1;
    java.awt.Button button2;
    java.awt.Button button3;
    java.awt.Button button4;

    CheckboxGroup Group1;
    java.awt.Checkbox radioButton1;
    java.awt.Checkbox radioButton2;
    java.awt.Checkbox radioButton3;
    java.awt.Checkbox radioButton4;

    java.awt.TextField textField1;
    java.awt.TextField textField3;
    java.awt.TextField textField4;

    java.awt.Label label1;
    java.awt.Label label2;
    java.awt.Label label3;
    java.awt.Label label4;
    java.awt.Label label5;

    CardLayout mainCardLayout;
    java.awt.Panel inputPanel;
    java.awt.Panel resultPanel;
    java.awt.Panel mainCardPanel;

    SelectRMIServer server;

    String dataSource;
    String userid;
    String password;

    String sql;
    String city = "";
    String where;
}
```

CONCLUSION

RMI made Java client/server or distributed object computing easy. It was a major breakthrough when it introduced *object pass by value* (through Object Serialization) during remote method invocation. As a result, CORBA, which used to allow only object pass by reference during remote method invocation, has since added object pass by value. The distributed garbage collection feature of RMI is also essential, though it is not applicable to heterogeneous systems.

The current implementation of RMI is not mature. It lacks many of the important features that are required to make it a robust, scalable client/server computing infrastructure. The major missing pieces include (some of these were promised by RMI and may be coming in JDK 1.2):

- Support additional *reference semantics* for remote objects—for example, *persistent references* and automatic *activation*.
- Support for *dynamic discovery* and *dynamic invocation*.
- Support *reconnection strategies* if the remote object becomes inaccessible.
- Support invocation to an object *replicated* at multiple locations.
- Support additional *transport mechanisms*—for example, UDP/IP.

RMI is a key component in the Java Platform for the Enterprise, particularly Enterprise JavaBeans (EJB). We will discuss EJB in Chapter 21, "Enterprise Java-Beans." All EJB objects support the RMI **Remote** interface.

Chapter 16

Introduction to Java ORBs

product

RMI is a simple protocol to use for development of *distributed Java-to-Java applications.* It allows you to pass objects by value, and it takes care of distributed garbage collection, among other things. However, RMI is a *pure Java solution.* If you have existing server programs written in other languages and you want to let users access them from a Java client using RMI, you can do so by developing wrapper RMI remote objects that access the existing server programs through JNI (Java Native Interface). It is not easy, but it can be done. However, if you have server programs written in Java, and you want to let users access them remotely from other languages, RMI is not a solution. *CORBA (Common Object Request Broker Architecture)* is; it has newly added Java to IDL mapping functionality. Of course, CORBA can also be used for the first scenario, with its IDL to Java mapping capability. This should not be surprising because CORBA is designed for integrating distributed, heterogeneous systems.

CORBA is a complex subject. It can be covered in more than one book and cannot be properly described in a few paragraphs. As such, we assume that you already know something about CORBA: its basic concepts and major components. If not, please consult the excellent books by Robert Orfali and Dan Harkey listed in the reference section.

In this chapter, we will delve directly into *VisiBroker for Java (VBJ)*, a complete CORBA 2.0 Object Request Broker (ORB) and one of the first ORBs implemented in Java that supports both IDL to Java and Java to IDL mappings. In particular, we will focus on its Java Ease-of-Use features, *Caffeine*, because it has a close resemblance to RMI, including support for passing objects by value through Object Serialization. Note that we purposely avoid issues such as using OSAgent vs. COSNaming, Basic Object Adapter (BOA) vs. Portable Object Adapter (POA), and using Caffeine vs. the Java to IDL Mapping and Object Pass by Value additions to the CORBA standard. You can get a complete discussion of these issues from the Orfali/Harkey books. Instead, we concentrate on using a specific vendor ORB product as an example of Java data access using a CORBA ORB. Similar examples can be developed using ORBixWeb from Iona or Java IDL, which will be part of JDK 1.2.

In the following sections, we will first take a quick glance at VBJ and, again, go through a distributed version of the classic "Hello World" example. But this time we will use VBJ (specifically Caffeine). We will then discuss in more detail the VBJ architecture and Caffeine. Finally, we will delve into some of the Java ORB API and show a sample client/server data access application developed using VBJ/Caffeine. As you can see, the presentation sequence is similar to that of RMI. This should help you make comparisons between the two.

VISIBROKER FOR JAVA (VBJ)

VBJ is a complete CORBA 2.0 ORB and supports a development environment for building, deploying, and managing *Java distributed object applications* that are interoperable across platforms. Java objects built with VBJ are easily accessed by applications (written in Java or otherwise) that communicate using the OMG's *Internet Inter-ORB Protocol (IIOP)*.

Figure 16-1 shows VBJ connecting a Java *client* (which may be an applet or application) with the *server object* it wants to use. The client does not need to know whether the server object resides on the same host or is located on a remote host. The client only needs to know the server object's name or object reference and understand how to invoke the server object's methods. The server object, on the other hand, only needs to support an *IDL interface* or the **org.omg.CORBA. Object** interface. VBJ thus provides *location transparency*.

Distributed "Hello World" Example

VBJ, like RMI, is somewhat complex, so we will first go through a distributed version of the classic "Hello World" example in VBJ/Caffeine and use it to illustrate the key aspects of VBJ. This should give you a good feel of what VBJ is and how to use it before we discuss its architecture and Caffeine in more depth.

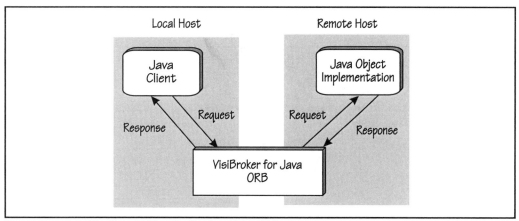

Figure 16-1. Java Distributed Object Applications Using VBJ.

The distributed "Hello World" example uses an applet (a local client) to make a remote method call to a server object (a CORBA object). The applet was downloaded and then retrieves the message "Hello World!" from the remote object and displays it on the client. The example uses the following source files:

■ Hello.java (server object interface)
■ HelloImpl.java (server object implementation)
■ HelloApplet.java (local client)
■ index.html

Server Object Interface

A server object must implement one or more CORBA object interfaces. The CORBA object interface has the following characteristics (see Listing 16-1):

■ The CORBA object interface must be *public*.
■ The CORBA object interface must extend **org.omg.CORBA.Object**.

Listing 16-1. The Hello Interface.

```
package vbj.hello;

public interface Hello extends org.omg.CORBA.Object {
    String sayHello();
}
```

Server Object Implementation

A server object implementation must (see Listing 16-2):

- Extend an *implementation base*. (The implementation base is generated using the *java2iiop* compiler, which we will discuss later.)
- Define the *constructor* (with a name as the argument) for the server object.
- Provide an implementation for each server method. Arguments to or results from server methods can be of any Java type, including objects. (Local objects are passed by value and server objects are passed by reference.)
- Initiate the ORB and BOA (Basic Object Adapter).
- Create one or more *instances* of server object.
- Activate the server object and wait for incoming client requests.

A server object implementation may have *local methods*, which can only be invoked locally.

Listing 16-2. The HelloImpl Class.

```
package vbj.hello;

public class HelloImpl
        extends _HelloImplBase
{
    public HelloImpl(String s) {
        super(s);
    }

    public String sayHello() {
        return   "Hello World!";
    }

    public static void main(String args[])
    {
        org.omg.CORBA.ORB orb = org.omg.CORBA.ORB.init(args, null);
        org.omg.CORBA.BOA boa = orb.BOA_init();
        Hello obj = new HelloImpl("HelloServer");
        boa.obj_is_ready(obj);
        System.out.println("HelloImpl created and ready " +
                        "with the name HelloServer");
        boa.impl_is_ready();
    }
}
```

Local Client

A local client must (see Listings 16-3 and 16-4):

- Initialize the ORB.
- Bind to the *remote object* and get a reference to its local stub.
- Invoke one or more *remote methods*. This is no different than invoking a local method of a local object. That is, method invocation is location transparent.

Listing 16-3. The HelloApplet Class.

```
package vbj.hello;

import java.awt.*;

public class HelloApplet extends java.applet.Applet {
    String message = "";

    public void init() {
        org.omg.CORBA.ORB orb = org.omg.CORBA.ORB.init(this);
        Hello obj = vbj.hello.HelloHelper.bind(orb, "HelloServer");
        message = obj.sayHello();
    }

    public void paint(Graphics g) {
        g.drawString(message, 25, 50);
    }
}
```

Listing 16-4. The HTML File.

```
<HTML>
<title>Hello World</title>
<center> <h1>Hello World</h1> </center>

The message from the HelloServer is:
<p>
<applet codebase="../.."  code="vbj.hello.HelloApplet"
        width=500 height=120>
<param name=ORBgatekeeperIOR
  value="http://woodview2.stl.ibm.com/code/vbj/gatekeeper.ior">
</applet>
</HTML>
```

372

VBJ ARCHITECTURE

VBJ has a rich set of features. We will not go over all of them in this chapter; instead, we will focus our attention on the following:

■ *idl2java Compiler*. It generates Java stubs and skeletons from an IDL file.

■ *Smart Binding*. This enhances performance by choosing the optimum transport mechanism whenever a client binds to a server object:

   ◆ If the object is local to the client process, the client performs a local method call.
   ◆ If the object resides in a different process, the client uses IIOP.

■ *Smart Agent*. It provides directory service functions, fault tolerance (reconnecting a client to a server if the server currently being used becomes unavailable due to a failure), and object migration facilities.

■ *Gatekeeper*. It enables clients to make calls to server objects that do not reside on the host Web server and to receive callbacks, as well as handles communication through firewalls.

■ *Java Ease-of-Use (Caffeine)*. It includes:

   ◆ *java2iiop Compiler*. It allows you to use Java, not IDL, to define the interfaces to CORBA objects.
   ◆ *java2idl Compiler*. It generates an IDL file from a Java file (byte code).
   ◆ *URL Naming*. This allows you to associate URLs with objects.

Application Development

The first step in creating an application with VBJ is to specify the server object and its interface using the OMG IDL (unless you are using Caffeine, which we will discuss later). You then use the *idl2java* compiler to generate *stubs* for the client program and *skeletons* for the server object implementation. For each IDL interface, the following Java source files are generated (assuming the IDL interface is named *Xyz*):

■ Xyz.java—Java interface
■ XyzHelper.java—helpful utility functions
■ XyzHolder.java—holder for passing parameters
■ _st_Xyz.java—stub code
■ _XyzImplBase.java—skeleton code

- ■ _tie_Xyz.java—for use with the *tie* mechanism (which we will not discuss in this chapter)
- ■ XyzOperations.java—for use with the *tie* mechanism
- ■ _example_Xyz.java—template for an example server object implementation

The stub code is used by the *client program* for method invocation. You use the skeleton code, along with the code you write, to create the *server object implementation*. When these are completed, you use the Java compiler to produce a Java applet or application and the server object. This whole process is illustrated in Figure 16-2.

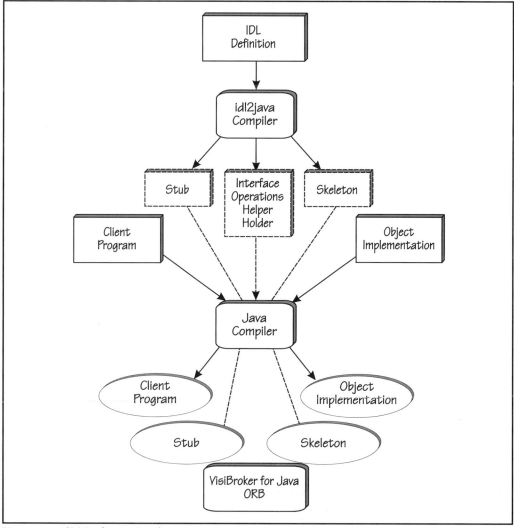

Figure 16-2. VBJ Application Development.

Naming and Binding to Objects

When creating an object, a server must specify an *object name* if the object is to be made available to client applications through the Smart Agent (which we will discuss shortly). When the server calls the **org.omg.CORBA.BOA**.*obj_is_ready()* method, the object's implementation will be registered if the object is named. Objects that are created with an object name possess *persistent object references*.

Before a client application can invoke methods on a server object, it must first obtain an object reference using the *bind()* method provided on that object's **Helper** class. There are three forms of the *bind()* method; each requires that an **org.omg.CORBA.ORB** object is supplied as the first parameter:

- The first form has no additional parameters and will result in the client being connected to any suitable server object instance.
- The second form allows you to specify an object name and will bind to the specific server object with that name.
- The third form allows you to specify an object name, a host name, and bind options.

When a client application invokes the *bind()* method, the ORB performs the following functions on behalf of the application:

- The ORB contacts the Smart Agent to locate a proper server.
- When an object implementation is located, the ORB attempts to establish a connection between the client application and the object implementation.
- If the connection is successfully established, the ORB will create a *proxy object*, if necessary, and return a reference to that object.

When a client requests a server object that resides on a remote host, the ORB will establish a TCP/IP connection between the client and the server. The ORB will instantiate a proxy object for the client to use. A method invoked on the proxy object will be marshaled and sent to the server on the remote host. The server will then unmarshal the request, invoke the method, and send the results back to the client (again through marshaling and unmarshaling). If, on the other hand, a client requests a server object that resides in the same process, the ORB will simply return a pointer to the server object itself. All methods invoked by the client on the server object will get called directly as ordinary Java methods. The ORB is involved only during the bind process. These are illustrated in Figure 16-3.

Activating Objects and Implementations

An *object implementation* provides the state and processing activities for an ORB object. An ORB object is created when its implementation class is instantiated by

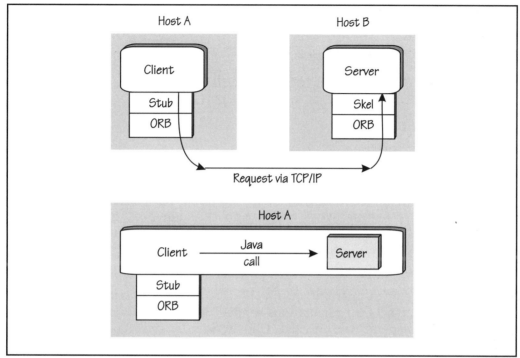

Figure 16-3. Method Invocation in VBJ.

an implementation server. As discussed previously, an object implementation may reside in the same process as its client application, or it may reside in a separate process called a server. Servers may contain a single object or multiple objects. Furthermore, servers may be activated by the BOA on demand, or they may be started explicitly by some entity external to the BOA.

The BOA provides several important functions to client applications and object implementations, including:

■ Providing several policies for activating object implementations
■ Registering object implementations with the Smart Agent

Activation policies can be set using the *BOA_init()* method on the **org.omg. CORBA.ORB** class.

Once a server has created the ORB objects, the BOA must be notified (by calling the *obj_is_ready()* method for each object) that the ORB objects are ready to receive requests from client applications. If a persistent object reference is passed to the *obj_is_ready()* method, the BOA will register the object with the Smart Agent. If the reference is transient, no such registration will occur. As mentioned previously, you create a persistent object reference when you create an object and specify an object name. Persistent object references remain valid beyond the lifetime of the process that creates them.

Once all of the ORB objects have been created and all the invocations of the *obj_is_ready()* method have been made, the server may invoke the *impl_is_ready()* method to enter an event loop. Then it waits for client requests.

The Smart Agent

The *Smart Agent* is a *dynamic, distributed directory service* that provides facilities for both client applications and object implementations. Object implementations register their objects with the Smart Agent so that client applications can locate and use those objects. When a client application invokes the *bind()* method on a server object, the Smart Agent locates the specified implementation and object so that a connection can be established between the client and the object implementation.

A Smart Agent may be started on any host. To locate a Smart Agent, client applications and object implementations send a broadcast UDP message. The first Smart Agent to respond will be used. Once a Smart Agent has been located, a point-to-point UDP connection is established for registration and look-up requests. All registration and look-up requests are dynamic, so there are no configuration files required.

When multiple Smart Agents are started on different hosts, each will recognize a subset of the server objects available and will communicate with other Smart Agents to locate server objects it cannot find. If one of the Smart Agents becomes unavailable, all object implementations registered with that Smart Agent will be automatically re-registered with another Smart Agent, and all client applications using that Smart Agent will also be automatically switched to another Smart Agent.

The Gatekeeper

The *Gatekeeper* serves as a gateway from an applet to server objects—even if a firewall is present. Web browsers generally impose two types of security restrictions on applets:

- They allow applets to only connect back to the originating host.
- They allow applets to only accept incoming connections from the originating host.

The Gatekeeper provides a way to work with these restrictions. In the first case, for any server object that is not running on the originating host, the ORB will try to communicate with the Gatekeeper; it then attempts to forward any calls from the applet to the server object. In the second case, the ORB sets up a special connection between the applet and the Gatekeeper which uses the special connection to forward the callback from the server object to the applet.

By default, the ORB runtime tries to connect directly with a server object and contacts the Gatekeeper only after determining that the server object is not reachable. You can, however, override the behavior of the ORB and cause it to always contact the Gatekeeper.

If the applet is running behind a firewall, the Gatekeeper allows it to talk to the server object through *HTTP tunneling*. If there is a client-side firewall that only allows HTTP protocol, the ORB in the client detects the failure when trying IIOP; it will automatically switch to HTTP. On the server side, the Gatekeeper listens for a message from an applet and checks to see if it is an IIOP message or an HTTP message. It then processes the message with the appropriate protocol.

As discussed in the previous chapter, HTTP tunneling is much slower than IIOP. There are two reasons for this:

- The overhead involved in wrapping and unwrapping the IIOP message inside the HTTP message.
- HTTP is a stateless protocol.

Caffeine

Caffeine provides ease-of-use features in a Java and Web environment, including the following:

- **java2iiop Compiler**—allows you to use Java, rather than IDL, to define the interfaces to CORBA objects.
- **java2idl Compiler**—generates an IDL file from a Java file (byte code).
- **URL Naming**—allows you to associate URLs with objects.

In the following sections, we will discuss the java2iiop compiler and URL naming; both are useful in an all-Java environment.

The java2iiop Compiler

The *java2iiop* compiler allows you to define *Java interfaces and data types* that can then be used as interfaces and data types in CORBA. You define the Java interface and mark them as interfaces to be used in remote method invocations. You mark them by having them extend the **org.omg.CORBA.Object** interface.

The compiler reads *Java bytecodes* and then generates IIOP-compliant stubs and skeletons needed to do all the marshaling and communication required for CORBA. In fact, the compiler generates the same files as if you had written the interface in IDL. The application development process is shown in Figure 16-4, which is essentially identical to the one starting IDL interfaces.

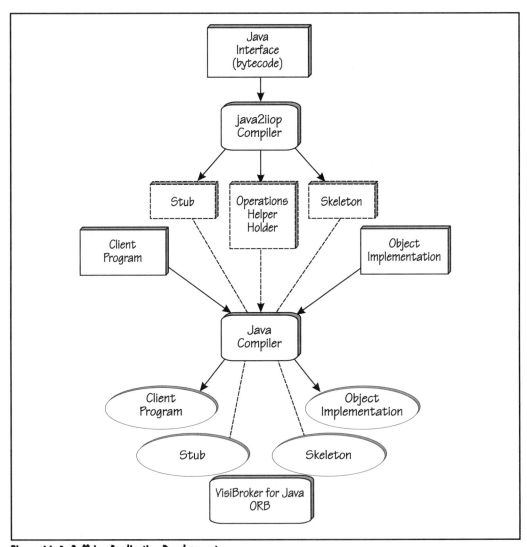

Figure 16-4. Caffeine Application Development.

Mapping of Data Types

When the java2iiop compiler generates IIOP-compliant stubs and skeletons, all Java data types must be mapped to the appropriate IDL data types for transmission by IIOP. Table 16-1 lists the mapping of Java primitive data types. The following lists the mapping of complex Java data types:

- Java packages are mapped to IDL modules.
- Java interfaces are represented as IDL interfaces, and they must extend the **org.omg.CORBA.Object** interface. Objects that implement these interfaces are *passed by reference.*
- Java arrays are mapped to IDL unbounded sequences.
- Java classes that conform to the following requirements are mapped to IDL structs (which are passed by value):
  - The class is public.
  - The class is final.
  - The class does not use implementation inheritance.
  - The data members of the class are public.
- Other Java classes are mapped to *extensible structs*. Objects belonging to these classes are *passed by value.*

VBJ uses Object Serialization to pass classes in the form of extensible structs. Therefore, all Java classes that are mapped to extensible structs must implement **java.io.Serializable**.

Table 16-1. Mapping of Java Primitive Data Types to IDL Data Types.

Java Data Type	IDL Data Type
short	short
int	long
long	long long
float	float
double	double
char	char
String	string
boolean	boolean
byte	octet
org.omg.CORBA.Any	any

Table 16-1. Mapping of Java Primitive Data Types to IDL Data Types. (Continued)

Java Data Type	IDL Data Type
org.omg.CORBA.Object	Object
org.omg.CORBA.Principal	Principal
org.omg.CORBA.TypeCode	TypeCode

URL Naming

URL Naming is a simple mechanism that allows you to associate a URL with an object's *IOR (Interoperable Object Reference)*. As a result, client applications can locate server objects without using the Smart Agent (or CORBA Naming Service). URL Naming supports any URL that the Java runtime supports, such as HTTP or FTP. With the Smart Agent, a client program can bind to persistent objects only. Using URL Naming, a server could associate a URL with a transient object's IOR.

THE JAVA ORB API

The Java ORB API consists of a comprehensive set of interfaces and classes that are defined in the IDL/Java Language Mapping Specification and that include the following packages:

- **org.omg.CORBA**
- **org.omg.CORBA.ContainedPackage**
- **org.omg.CORBA.ContainerPackage**
- **org.omg.CORBA.InterfaceDefPackage**
- **org.omg.CORBA.ORBPackage**
- **org.omg.CORBA.TypeCodePackage**
- **org.omg.CORBA.portable**

Here we will only discuss the following three classes in the **org.omg.CORBA** package that we have used directly in our example (and sample application):

- **Object**
- **ORB**
- **BOA**

Object Interface

The **Object** interface is the root of the CORBA inheritance hierarchy. All CORBA object interfaces must extend this interface. This root interface provides common functionality for all CORBA object interfaces—including network-aware runtime type information and network-aware object reference equivalence testing.

The following list contains some of its methods:

- **_object_name**() returns the object name (**String**) of this object.

- **_orb**() returns the ORB associated with this object.

- **_boa**() returns the BOA associated with this object.

- **_clone**() creates and returns a copy (**Object**) of this object reference.

- **_is_a**(String repId) returns a boolean. This method determines if this object implements the specified interface.

- **_is_bound**() returns a boolean. This method checks whether a TCP connection has been established to the object implementation.

- **_is_equivalent**(Object obj) returns a boolean. This method determines if this object is equivalent to the specified object (which means both object references refer to the same object implementation).

- **_is_local**() returns a boolean. This method determines if this object reference refers to an object implemented in a local address space.

- **_is_remote**() returns a boolean. This method determines if this object reference refers to an object implemented in a remote address space.

- **_is_persistent**() returns a boolean. This method determines if this object reference is a persistent object reference.

ORB Class

The **ORB** class provides functionality used by both clients and servers (i.e., proxy objects and object implementations). This class also provides a way to initialize the **org.omg.CORBA** infrastructure. It has this default constructor:

- **ORB**()

The following lists some of its static methods:

- **init**() returns the **ORB** singleton. This method initializes the **ORB** singleton and does it the first time the method is called.

- **init**(Applet applet) creates and returns a new **ORB** instance for an applet.

- **BOA_init**() returns the **BOA** singleton. This method initializes the **BOA** singleton and does it the first time the method is called.

- **string_to_object**(String ior) converts the string to an object reference (**Object**) and returns it.

- **object_to_string**(Object obj) converts the object reference to a **String** and returns it.

BOA Class

The **BOA** class provides the primary interface that an object implementation uses to access ORB functions. It is an abstract class, and it has the following constructor:

- **BOA**()

And, it has the following methods:

- **get_principal**(Object obj) returns the principal on whose behalf the request is made.

- **obj_is_ready**(Object obj) notifies the BOA that the specified object is ready to receive requests from client applications.

- **obj_is_ready**(Object obj, String service_name, byte[] ref_data) notifies the BOA that the specified object is ready to receive requests from client applications; it also registers the object with the service name and reference data.

- **deactivate_obj**(Object obj) notifies the BOA to deactivate the specified object.

- **impl_is_ready**() notifies the BOA to enter an event loop and wait for client requests.

SAMPLE CLIENT/SERVER DATA ACCESS APPLICATIONS USING CAFFEINE

In this section, we take the **SelectApplet** example (see Listings 12-1 and 12-2) and redo it using VBJ/Caffeine (see Figure 16-5). The **SelectORBApplet/Server** example (see Listings 16-1 to 16-6) preserves the same user functionality and interface, but it performs data access on the server using JDBC. It also uses Object Serialization to pass objects (**QuerySpec** and **QueryResult**) by value, thus allowing coarse-grain communication between client and server.

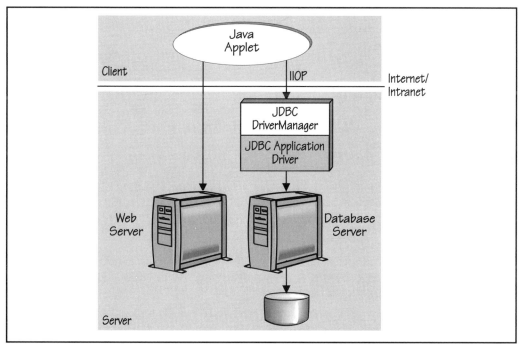

Figure 16-5. JDBC Usage Scenario—Applet (II) Using VBJ.

Listing 16-1. The SelectORBServer interface.

```
/*
 * SelectORBServer.java
 */

package vbj;

public interface SelectORBServer
  extends org.omg.CORBA.Object
{
```

```
    public QueryResult executeQuery(QuerySpec qs);
}
```

Listing 16-2. The QuerySpec Class.

```java
/*
 * QuerySpec.java
 */

package vbj;

public class QuerySpec
  implements java.io.Serializable
{
    public QuerySpec(String ds, String uid, String pw, String s) {
        dataSource = ds;
        userid = uid;
        password = pw;
        sql = s;
    }

    public String getDataSource() {
        return dataSource;
    }

    public String getUserid() {
        return userid;
    }

    public String getPassword() {
        return password;
    }

    public String getSql() {
        return sql;
    }

    private String dataSource;
    private String userid;
    private String password;
    private String sql;
}
```

Listing 16-3. The QueryResult Class.

```java
/*
 * QueryResult.java
 */

package vbj;

import java.util.*;

public class QueryResult
  implements java.io.Serializable
{
    public QueryResult() {
        result = new Vector();
    }

    public Vector getResult() {
        return result;
    }

    public Vector getResultRecord(int index) {
        if (index < result.size())
            return (Vector) result.elementAt(index);
        else
            return null;
    }

    private Vector result;
}
```

Listing 16-4. The SelectORBServerImpl Class.

```java
/*
 * SelectORBServerImpl.java
 */

package vbj;

import java.sql.*;

import java.io.*;
import java.util.*;
```

```java
public class SelectORBServerImpl
  extends _SelectORBServerImplBase
{
    public SelectORBServerImpl(String s)
    {
        super(s);
    }

    public QueryResult executeQuery(QuerySpec qs)
    {
        String database = qs.getDataSource();
        String login = qs.getUserid();
        String password = qs.getPassword();
        String sql = qs.getSql();
        QueryResult qr = null;

        try {
            // Load the JDBC-ODBC driver
            Class.forName("sun.jdbc.odbc.JdbcOdbcDriver");

            String url = "jdbc:odbc:" + database;
            Connection con = DriverManager.getConnection(url,
                login, password);
            Statement stmt = con.createStatement();

            ResultSet rs = stmt.executeQuery(sql);

            qr = new QueryResult();
            Vector v1 = qr.getResult();

            while(rs.next()) {
                String s1 = rs.getString(1);
                String s2 = rs.getString(2);
                String s3 = rs.getString(3);

                Vector v2 = new Vector();
                v2.addElement(s1);
                v2.addElement(s2);
                v2.addElement(s3);

                v1.addElement(v2);
            }

            stmt.close();
            con.close();
```

```
        } catch( Exception e ) {
            e.printStackTrace();
        }

        return qr;
    }

    public static void main(String args[])
    {
        org.omg.CORBA.ORB orb = org.omg.CORBA.ORB.init(args, null);
        org.omg.CORBA.BOA boa = orb.BOA_init();
        SelectORBServer server =
          new SelectORBServerImpl("SelectORBServer");
        boa.obj_is_ready(server);
        System.out.println("SelectORBServer created and bound");
        boa.impl_is_ready();
    }

}
```

Listing 16-5. The SelectORB HTML File.

```
<!
  SelectRMI.html
!>

<html>
    <applet codebase=".."
            code="vbj.SelectORBApplet"
            width=525 height=475>
      <param name=ORBgatekeeperIOR
        value="http://woodview2.stl.ibm.com/code/vbj/gatekeeper.ior">
    </applet>
</html>
```

Listing 16-6. The SelectORBApplet Class.

```
/**
 * SelectORBApplet.java
 */

package vbj;

import java.awt.*;
```

```java
import java.awt.event.*;
import java.applet.*;
import java.util.Vector;

public class SelectORBApplet
    extends Applet implements ActionListener
{
    public void init() {
        super.init();

        org.omg.CORBA.ORB orb = org.omg.CORBA.ORB.init(this);
        server = vbj.SelectORBServerHelper.bind(orb,"SelectORBServer");

        setLayout(null);
        addNotify();
        setSize(450,340);

        //set applet layout
        mainCardPanel = new Panel();
        mainCardPanel.setLayout(new CardLayout(0,0));
        mainCardPanel.setBounds(0,0,450,340);
        add(mainCardPanel);

        //add input panel
        inputPanel = new Panel();
        inputPanel.setLayout(null);
        inputPanel.setBounds(0,0,450, 340);
        mainCardPanel.add(" ", inputPanel);

        label1 = new java.awt.Label("ArcWorld buildings query:");
        label1.setBounds(12,10,324,40);
        inputPanel.add(label1);

        label2 = new java.awt.Label("Enter data Source, user id, " +
                                    "and password information:");
        label2.setBounds(12,45,324,40);
        inputPanel.add(label2);
        textField1 = new java.awt.TextField();
        textField1.setBounds(12,84,132,24);
        textField1.requestFocus();
        inputPanel.add(textField1);
        textField3 = new java.awt.TextField();
        textField3.setBounds(156,84,132,24);
        inputPanel.add(textField3);
        textField4 = new java.awt.TextField();
```

```
textField4.setBounds(300,84,132,24);
inputPanel.add(textField4);

label3 = new Label("Select the city that you " +
                   "would like to query:");
label3.setBounds(12,120,240,12);
inputPanel.add(label3);
Group1 = new CheckboxGroup();
radioButton1 = new java.awt.Checkbox("All cities",
                                     Group1, false);
radioButton1.setBounds(12,144,100,24);
inputPanel.add(radioButton1);
radioButton2 = new java.awt.Checkbox("Washington",
                                     Group1, false);
radioButton2.setBounds(12,168,100,24);
inputPanel.add(radioButton2);
radioButton3 = new java.awt.Checkbox("Paris", Group1, false);
radioButton3.setBounds(12,192,100,24);
inputPanel.add(radioButton3);
radioButton4 = new java.awt.Checkbox("Beijing", Group1, false);
radioButton4.setBounds(12,216,100,24);
inputPanel.add(radioButton4);

button1 = new java.awt.Button("Submit");
button1.setBounds(12,252,108,24);
inputPanel.add(button1);
button2 = new java.awt.Button("Reset");
button2.setBounds(132,252,96,24);
inputPanel.add(button2);

// add result panel
resultPanel = new Panel();
resultPanel.setLayout(null);
resultPanel.setBounds(0,0,792,390);
mainCardPanel.add(" ", resultPanel);
label5 = new java.awt.Label("Buildings in the " +
                            "ArcWorld Database:");
label5.setBounds(84,12,276,24);
button3 = new java.awt.Button("Input");
button3.setBounds(228,310,96,24);
button4 = new java.awt.Button("Result");
button4.setBounds(108,310,96,24);
resultPanel.add(button3);
resultPanel.add(button4);
resultPanel.add(label5);
```

```java
    mainCardLayout = new CardLayout();
    mainCardPanel.setLayout(mainCardLayout);
    mainCardLayout.addLayoutComponent("input", inputPanel);
    mainCardLayout.addLayoutComponent("result", resultPanel);
    mainCardLayout.show(mainCardPanel,"input");

    // register components' event listener
    AddListener();
}

private void AddListener()
{
    button1.addActionListener(this);
    button2.addActionListener(this);
    button3.addActionListener(this);
    button4.addActionListener(this);
}

public void actionPerformed(ActionEvent event)
{
    if(event.getSource() == button1)
    {
        dataSource = textField1.getText();
        userid = textField3.getText();
        password = textField4.getText();

        if (radioButton1.getState())
            city = "*";
        else if (radioButton2.getState())
            city = "Washington";
        else if (radioButton3.getState())
            city = "Paris";
        else if (radioButton4.getState())
            city = "Beijing";
        if (city.equals("*"))
            where = "";
        else
            where = " WHERE city = " + "'" + city + "'";
        sql = "SELECT name, type, city FROM Building" + where;

        submitButton_Clicked(event);
    }
    if (event.getSource() == button2)
        resetButton_Clicked(event);
```

```
        if (event.getSource() == button3)
            inputButton_Clicked(event);
        if (event.getSource() == button4)
            resultButton_Clicked(event);
    }

    public void submitButton_Clicked(ActionEvent event)
    {
        mainCardLayout.show(mainCardPanel,"result");
    }

    public void resetButton_Clicked(ActionEvent event)
    {
        textField1.setText("");
        textField3.setText("");
        textField4.setText("");
        radioButton1.setState(false);
        radioButton2.setState(false);
        radioButton3.setState(false);
        radioButton4.setState(false);
    }

    public void inputButton_Clicked(ActionEvent evnet)
    {
        mainCardLayout.show(mainCardPanel,"input");
    }

    public void resultButton_Clicked(ActionEvent event)
    {
        Graphics g = resultPanel.getGraphics();
        drawTable(g);
        query();
    }

    public void drawTable(Graphics g)
    {
        g.drawString("NAME", 75,55);
        g.drawString("TYPE", 230,55);
        g.drawString("CITY", 350,55);

        g.drawLine(10,40,420,40);
        g.drawLine(10,65,420,65);
        g.drawLine(10,90,420,90);
        g.drawLine(10,115,420,115);
        g.drawLine(10,140,420,140);
```

```java
        g.drawLine(10,165,420,165);
        g.drawLine(10,190,420,190);
        g.drawLine(10,215,420,215);
        g.drawLine(10,240,420,240);
        g.drawLine(10,265,420,265);
        g.drawLine(10,290,420,290);

        g.drawLine(10,40,10,290);
        g.drawLine(420,40,420,290);
        g.drawLine(180,40,180,290);
        g.drawLine(310,40,310,290);
    }

    public void query()
    {
        try
        {
            QuerySpec qs = new QuerySpec(dataSource, userid,
                                         password, sql);
            QueryResult qr = server.executeQuery(qs);

            Vector bnameVector = new Vector();
            Vector btypeVector = new Vector();
            Vector bcitynameVector = new Vector();

            int h = 80;
            Graphics g = resultPanel.getGraphics();

            Vector v;
            int index = 0;
            while((v = qr.getResultRecord(index++)) != null) {
                String name = (String) v.elementAt(0);
                String type = (String) v.elementAt(1);
                String city = (String) v.elementAt(2);

                bnameVector.addElement(name);
                btypeVector.addElement(type);
                bcitynameVector.addElement(city);
            }

            String bname = null;
            for (int i = 0; i < bnameVector.size(); i++)
            {
                bname = bnameVector.elementAt(i).toString();
                g.drawString(bname, 20, h);
```

```
                  String btype = btypeVector.elementAt(i).toString();
                  g.drawString(btype, 190, h);
                  String bcityname =
                              bcitynameVector.elementAt(i).toString();
                  g.drawString(bcityname, 330, h);
                  h += 25;

             }

        } catch (Exception e)
        {
            e.printStackTrace();
            System.exit(0);
        }

    }

// variables

    java.awt.Button button1;
    java.awt.Button button2;
    java.awt.Button button3;
    java.awt.Button button4;

    CheckboxGroup Group1;
    java.awt.Checkbox radioButton1;
    java.awt.Checkbox radioButton2;
    java.awt.Checkbox radioButton3;
    java.awt.Checkbox radioButton4;

    java.awt.TextField textField1;
    java.awt.TextField textField3;
    java.awt.TextField textField4;

    java.awt.Label label1;
    java.awt.Label label2;
    java.awt.Label label3;
    java.awt.Label label4;
    java.awt.Label label5;

    CardLayout mainCardLayout;
    java.awt.Panel inputPanel;
    java.awt.Panel resultPanel;
    java.awt.Panel mainCardPanel;
```

```
    SelectORBServer server;

    String dataSource;
    String userid;
    String password;

    String sql;
    String city = "";
    String where;
}
```

CONCLUSION

Thanks to VBJ, using Java with CORBA is very easy, almost as easy as using RMI. It can also have major benefits. Java allows you to write portable objects and easily distribute them; CORBA allows you to integrate them with applications written in other languages. With IDL to Java mapping, you can develop an object implementation in any language and have it accessed by a Java applet or application through IIOP. With Java to IDL mapping, you can develop an object implementation in Java (without an IDL interface) and have it accessed by an application written in any language through IIOP. With Caffeine, you can even develop pure Java distributed applications that pass objects by value using Object Serialization, but communicate through IIOP.

IIOP brings some major advantages that RMI currently lacks. Key among them are IOR (Interoperable Object Reference), transmission of transaction context, and transmission of security context. As a result, there is an ongoing effort to develop an RMI implementation that will use IIOP as the protocol, the so-called *RMI/IIOP*. This will become very important as it is an integral part of Enterprise JavaBeans (EJB)—which we will discuss in Chapter 21, "Enterprise JavaBeans."

So you have two mechanisms to choose from for Java client/server computing: Java RMI and Java/CORBA (VBJ/Caffeine is an example of it). Java RMI has an advantage in the ease-of-use category because it can explore the full capabilities of the Java language. Java/CORBA has the advantage of working with code written in other languages and what is provided by the CORBA infrastructure. The following table gives a comparison of some of the major features (as they are available today):

Table 16-2. Comparison of Java RMI and Java/CORBA Features.

Features	Java RMI	Java/CORBA
Language independence	No	Yes
Pass by value	Yes (Object Serialization)	Yes (State only)
Distributed garbage collection	Yes	No
Persistent object reference	No	Yes
URL Naming	Yes	No (VBJ: yes)
Firewall proxy (HTTP tunneling)	Yes	No (VBJ: yes)
Dynamic discovery	No	Yes
Dynamic invocation	No	Yes
Language-neutral wire protocol	No	Yes (IIOP)
Wire-level transaction	No	Yes (via CORBA OTS)
Wire-level security	No	Yes (via CORBA Security)

Part 5

Web Data Interchange

An Introduction to Part 5

In the previous part, we discussed and illustrated the use of Java Object Serialization for passing objects by value in Java client/server computing (using either Java RMI or Java ORB). The process is very transparent. However, it only works for Java, and the serialized Java object is opaque. In Part 5, we will switch our attention to XML, a new way of passing objects by value in client/server computing. XML has much broader applicability than Java Object Serialization. It is not restricted to Java objects. In fact, it can be used to represent any object, even virtual ones (for example, objects composed on the fly at run time). Also, XML can be used to represent data, not just objects. And, a serialized XML representation can be self-describing (with metadata) and is generally human readable.

We will go over the basics of XML and will focus on Web data interchange, including:

- XML (and Namespaces, XLink, and XPointer)
- DOM (and SAX)
- XML for metadata interchange

Here is what we will be covering in Part 5:

- **Chapter 17** introduces XML, a newly adopted standard for describing and exchanging data and metadata on the Web. With XML, structured data is cleanly separated into three parts: content, structure, and presentation. XML and its family of technologies promise to revolutionize the Web and helps solve its current problem of information glut. In addition to XML and Namespaces, we will also discuss XLink and XPointer, which provide linking and locating functionality for XML documents.

- **Chapter 18** describes the Document Object Model (DOM)—specifically, the Core and XML parts. DOM provides a Java API that allows you to either access an existing XML document as a tree of Java objects, or to construct such a tree of Java objects from scratch and generate a new XML document from it. We will also touch upon SAX, an event-based API for accessing XML documents.

- **Chapter 19** discusses XML for metadata interchange. In particular, we discuss the MOF (Meta Object Facility), a standard adopted by the OMG for defining metamodels, and XMI (XMI Metadata Interchange), a proposal submitted to the OMG for automatic generation of XML DTDs for a (MOF-compliant) metamodel and for XML documents for any metadata that conform to the metamodel.

XML and its family of technologies are a new, exciting, and fast-moving area with tremendous importance to client/server data access. In Part 5, you will get a good peek into the future when the Web will become an interchange and repository of all sorts of valuable, structured information as a result of XML, XLink, XPointer, DOM, and XMI.

Chapter 17

Introduction to XML

concepts

HTML is ubiquitous. HTML files exist on every Web server. They can be downloaded to any Web client and then displayed. Whenever anyone accesses anything on the Web, HTML is involved. It is hard to imagine, right now, that one day HTML may disappear altogether or play a much less important role. However, this is a distinct possibility and the reason is *XML (eXtensible Markup Language)* and its family of technologies.

We said in Chapter 2, "Web Basics," that HTML is an "application" of SGML, which is a language for defining markup languages. As such, HTML has a fixed set of tags defined by a single SGML specification. Freezing a single small set of tags allows the SGML specification to be left out of any HTML document, because it is well known to users and tools. However, this ease-of-use and convenience come at the price of several severe limitations:

- *Lack of extensibility*. HTML does not allow you to define your own tags or attributes (any extension must be approved by the W3C or adopted by the Web browser vendors).

- *Lack of structure*. HTML is designed for displaying information on a Web browser (for example, <H1> to <H2> tags). It has no provision for specifying the structure of that information (for example, a book with a title and three sections, each section with its own title).

■ *Lack of description.* HTML does not allow you to include metadata (or schema) to describe your data (for example, each book must have a title and one or more sections, and each section must have a title). There is only one SGML specification and it is fixed (unless extended by the W3C or a Web browser vendor).

■ *No support for validation.* Without support for structure and description, HTML does not support the checking of data for structural validity (for example, a book missing a title).

XML comes from the same origin as HTML, in SGML, but is very different. Whereas HTML is an application of SGML, XML is a subset (with slight modifications) of SGML. Like SGML, XML is a *meta language*—a language for defining markup languages. However, XML is specifically designed for the Web: It has 80% of the functionality of SGML, but only 20% of its complexity. XML is designed to be the standard format for *describing and exchanging structured data* on the Web. With XML, a document (or a piece of data) is separated into three parts: *structure*, *content*, and *style*. XML specifies the structure, *XSL (eXtensible Style Language)* addresses the style, and the user defines the content.

XML therefore removes all the severe limitations of HTML that were mentioned previously:

■ *Extensibility.* XML allows you to define your own tags or attributes. Better yet, XML Namespaces allow you to use and mix more than one set of tags and attributes, including reusing existing, well-designed ones (for example, the ones that have been standardized for a given industry or domain).

■ *Structure.* XML is designed for describing structured data. The structure can be nested and to any level deep (for example, a book with a title and three sections, each section with its own title).

■ *Description.* XML allows you to include metadata to describe your data (for example, each book must have a title and one or more sections, and each section must have a title). XML Namespaces further allow you to include more than one set of metadata.

■ *Validation.* If the metadata is included, XML supports the checking of data for structural validity (the so-called *valid* XML document).

In the following section we will first give an overview of XML. We will then discuss XML Namespaces, XLink, and XPointer. XLink and XPointer provide linking and locating functionality for XML documents, respectively.

EXTENSIBLE MARKUP LANGUAGE (XML)

XML describes a class of data objects called *XML documents* and partially describes the behavior of computer programs that process them. XML documents consist of storage units called *entities* that contain either parsed or unparsed data. *Parsed data* consists of characters, some of which form *markup*; the rest form *character data*. Markup encodes a description of the document's logical structure. *Unparsed data* is a resource whose content may or may not be text; if it is text, it may not be XML. A software module called an *XML processor* is used to process XML documents and provide access to their structure and content.

XML Documents

A data object is an XML document if it is *well-formed*. A well-formed XML document may in addition be *valid* if it meets certain additional constraints. Each XML document has both a *physical structure* and a *logical structure*. Physically, the document is composed of units called *entities*, as discussed previously. Logically, the document is composed of *declarations*, *elements*, *comments*, *character references*, and *processing instructions*, all of which are indicated by explicit markup.

Comments may appear anywhere in a document outside other markup; in addition, they may appear within the document type declaration (to be discussed later) at places allowed by the grammar. The following is an example of a comment:

```
<!-- This is a comment. -->
```

Processing instructions (PIs) allow documents to contain instructions for applications. They are of the form:

```
<?name ... ?>
```

We will discuss declarations, elements, and character references as we go along.

An XML document is *well-formed* if:

- It contains one or more *elements*.
- There is exactly one element, called the *root* or *document* element, and no part of it can appear in the content of any other element. For all other elements, the elements, delimited by *start-tags* and *end-tags*, nest properly within each other.
- It meets all *well-formedness constraints*.
- Each of the parsed entities that is referenced directly or indirectly within the document is well-formed.

The following is an example of a complete XML document, well-formed but not valid:

```
<?xml version="1.0:?>
<greeting>Hello, world!</greeeting>
```

As this example shows, XML documents may, and should, begin with an *XML declaration* that specifies the version of XML being used.

Document Type Declarations

The function of the markup in an XML document is to describe its logical structure and storage layout and to associate attribute-value pairs with its logical structure. XML provides a mechanism, the *document type declaration*, to define constraints on the logical structure and to support the use of predefined storage units. An XML document is *valid* if it has an associated document type declaration and if the document complies with the constraints expressed in it. The document type declaration must appear before the first element in the document.

The XML document type declaration contains or points to *markup declarations* that provide a grammar for a class of documents. This grammar is known as a *Document Type Definition (DTD)*. The document type declaration can point to an *external subset* containing markup declarations, or it can contain the markup declarations directly in an *internal subset*; it can also do both. The DTD for a document consists of both subsets.

A markup declaration is an *element type declaration*, an *attribute-list declaration*, an *entity declaration*, or a *notation declaration*. An element type declaration constrains the element's content. An attribute-list declaration specifies the name, data type, and default value (if any) of each attribute associated with a given element type. Entity declarations define storage units. Notation declarations provide names for the notations, which identify by name the format of unparsed entities, the format of elements that have a notation attribute, or the application to which a processing instruction is addressed. We will discuss element type declaration, attribute-list declaration, and entity declaration in more detail shortly.

The following is an example of an XML document with an internal document type declaration:

```
<?xml version="1.0:?>
<!DOCTYPE greeting [
    <!ELEMENT greeting (#PCDATA)>
]>
```

```
<greeting>Hello, world!</greeting>
```

The declaration can also be given externally:

```
<?xml version="1.0:?>
<!DOCTYPE greeting  SYSTEM "hello.dtd">
<greeting>Hello, world!</greeting>
```

Logical Structures

Each XML document contains one or more *elements*, which are either delimited by *start-tags* and *end-tags* or, for empty elements, by an *empty-element tag*. The text between the start-tag and end-tag is called the element's *content*. Each element has a *type*, identified by name, and may have a set of attributes. Each *attribute* has a name and a value. The following is an example of an element with two attributes:

```
<City name="Washington" country="USA"/>
```

The element structure of an XML document may, for validation purposes, be constrained using *element type declarations* and *attribute-list declarations*. As mentioned previously, an element type declaration constrains the element's content:

- *EMPTY*—the element has no content.
- *Element content*—the element has *child elements* (no character data). The constraint governs the allowed types of the child element, the order in which they may appear, and their multiplicities (zero to one "?", one " ", zero or more "?", and one or more "+").
- *ANY*—the element has child elements (no character data). Their types, order, and multiplicities are not constrained.
- *Mixed*—the element contains *character data*, optionally interspersed with child elements. The types of child elements may be constrained, but not their order or their number of occurrences.

An attribute-list declaration specifies the name, data type, and default value (if any) of each attribute associated with a given element type. It may appear only within start-tags and empty-element tags. XML attribute types are of three kinds:

- *String type*—CDATA
- *Tokenized types*—ID, IDREF, IDREFS, ENTITY, ENTITIES, NMTOKEN, and NMTOKENS
- *Enumerated types*

Each attribute declaration provides information on whether the attribute's presence is required, and if not, how an XML processor should react:

- *#REQUIRED*—the attribute must always be provided.
- *#IMPLIED*—no default value is provided.
- *Default value*—the default value is used if the attribute is not provided.
- *#FIXED default value*—the attribute must always have the default value.

The following is the complete element type declaration for the element example shown previously:

```
<!ELEMENT City EMPTY>
<!ATTLIST City
    name CDATA #REQUIRED
    country CDATA #IMPLIED>
```

Physical Structures

An XML document consists of one or more storage units, which, as mentioned, are called *entities*. Entities have content and are identified by name (except for the document entity and the external DTD subset). Each XML document has one entity called the *document entity*, which serves as the starting point for the XML processor.

Entities may be either parsed or unparsed. A *parsed entity* consists of markup and character data. Its content is referred to as its *replacement text*, which is considered an integral part of the document. An *unparsed entity* is a resource whose content may or may not be text, and, if text, may not be XML. Each unparsed entity has an associated *notation*, identified by name. XML places no constraints on the content of an unparsed entity.

There are two types of parsed entities: general entities and parameter entities. *General entities* are for use within the document content; *parameter entities* are for use within the DTD. These two types of entities occupy different namespaces. These also use different forms of reference and are recognized in different contexts. An *entity reference* refers to the content of a named entity. References to general entities use ampersand (&) and semicolon (;) as delimiters; references to parameter entities use percent-sign (%) and semicolon (;) as delimiters.

The following is an example of an external general-entity reference:

```
<!DOCTYPE book SYSTEM "book.dtd" [
    <!ENTITY toc SYSTEM "toc.xml">
]>
<book><head>&toc;</head>
</book>
```

The following is an example of parameter-entity references:

```
<!ENTITY % pattern "CDATA">
<!ENTITY % actions "#PCDATA">
<!ELEMENT rule %actions;>
<!ATTLIST rule
    pattern %pattern; #REQUIRED>
```

Sample XML Documents

We said in the beginning of this chapter that XML was designed to be the standard format for *describing and exchanging structured data* on the Web. To illustrate its usage, we have taken both the definitions of the **ArcWorld** relational database and the ArcWorld object-oriented database (see Chapter 6, "The ArcWorld Sample Database") and encoded them in DTD (see Listings 17-1 and 17-3, respectively). We have also taken the corresponding sample data (see Listing 10-4 on page 197 and Listing 10-16 on page 214) and encoded it in XML (see Listings 17-2 and 17-4, respectively). For simplicity, we have omitted the image data.

It can be seen that XML/DTD is suitable for representing both the relational data model (which consists of tables and is flat) and the object-oriented data model (which consists of classes and is hierarchical). However, DTD is quite simple, so the following features of the relational data model cannot be directly represented in DTD:

- Primary keys and secondary keys
- Data types other than strings
- Constraints

For the same reason, the following features of the object-oriented data model cannot be directly represented in DTD:

- Keys
- Data types other than strings
- Inheritance

However, XML has a hierarchical, containment-based data model; consequently it can be used to advantage when representing an object-oriented data model. For example, we can easily represent the fact that a **Country** may contain **Cities** and that, when it does, the **City** that it contains can reference it.

Listing 17-1. ArcWorld.dtd.

```xml
<?xml version="1.0" encoding="UTF-8"?>
<!-- ArcWorld.dtd -->

<!ELEMENT ArcWorld (Country*, City*, Architect*, Building*, Church*) >

<!ELEMENT Country EMPTY>
<!ATTLIST Country
  name CDATA #REQUIRED>

<!ELEMENT City EMPTY>
<!ATTLIST City
  name CDATA #REQUIRED
  country CDATA #IMPLIED>

<!ELEMENT Architect EMPTY>
<!ATTLIST Architect
  name CDATA #REQUIRED
  nationality CDATA #IMPLIED>

<!ELEMENT Building EMPTY>
<!ATTLIST Building
  name CDATA #REQUIRED
  type CDATA #IMPLIED
  address CDATA #IMPLIED
  city CDATA #IMPLIED
  yearBuilt CDATA #IMPLIED
  architect CDATA #IMPLIED
  style CDATA #IMPLIED
  description CDATA #IMPLIED>

<!ELEMENT Church EMPTY>
<!ATTLIST Church
  name CDATA #REQUIRED
  type CDATA #IMPLIED
  address CDATA #IMPLIED
  city CDATA #IMPLIED
  yearBuilt CDATA #IMPLIED
  architect CDATA #IMPLIED
  style CDATA #IMPLIED
  description CDATA #IMPLIED
  denomination CDATA #IMPLIED
  pastor CDATA #IMPLIED>
```

Listing 17-2. ArcWorld.xml.

```
<?xml version="1.0" ?>
<!-- ArcWorld.xml -->

<!DOCTYPE ArcWorld SYSTEM "ArcWorld.dtd">

<ArcWorld>

<Country name="USA"/>
<Country name="France"/>
<Country name="China"/>

<City name="Washington" country="USA"/>
<City name="Paris" country="France"/>
<City name="Beijing" country="China"/>

<Building name="Lincoln Memorial" city="Washington"/>
<Building name="National Gallery" city="Washington"/>
<Building name="The Capitol" city="Washington"/>
<Building name="Washington Monument" city="Washington"/>
<Building name="Arc de Triumph" city="Paris"/>
<Building name="Eiffel Tower" city="Paris"/>
<Building name="Louvre" city="Paris"/>
<Building name="Great Wall" city="Beijing"/>
<Building name="Tiananmen" city="Beijing"/>

</ArcWorld>
```

Listing 17-3. ArcWorldOO.dtd.

```
<?xml version="1.0" encoding="UTF-8" ?>
<!-- ArcWorldOO.dtd -->

<!ELEMENT ArcWorldOO (Country*)>

<!ELEMENT Country (City*)>
<!ATTLIST Country
  id ID #REQUIRED
  name CDATA #REQUIRED>

<!ELEMENT City (Building | Church)*>
<!ATTLIST City
  id ID #REQUIRED
```

```
  name CDATA #REQUIRED
  country IDREF #IMPLIED>

<!ELEMENT Architect EMPTY>
<!ATTLIST Architect
  id ID #REQUIRED
  name CDATA #REQUIRED
  nationality IDREF #IMPLIED>

<!ELEMENT Building EMPTY>
<!ATTLIST Building
  id ID #REQUIRED
  name CDATA #REQUIRED
  type CDATA #IMPLIED
  address CDATA #IMPLIED
  city IDREF #IMPLIED
  yearBuilt CDATA #IMPLIED
  architect IDREF #IMPLIED
  style CDATA #IMPLIED
  description CDATA #IMPLIED>

<!ELEMENT Church EMPTY>
<!ATTLIST Church
  id ID #REQUIRED
  name CDATA #REQUIRED
  type CDATA #IMPLIED
  address CDATA #IMPLIED
  city IDREF #IMPLIED
  yearBuilt CDATA #IMPLIED
  architect IDREF #IMPLIED
  style CDATA #IMPLIED
  description CDATA #IMPLIED
  denomination CDATA #IMPLIED
  pastor CDATA #IMPLIED>
```

Listing 17-4. ArcWorldOO.xml.

```xml
<?xml version="1.0" ?>
<!-- ArcWorldOO.xml -->

<!DOCTYPE ArcWorldOO SYSTEM "ArcWorldOO.dtd">

<ArcWorldOO>

<Country id="C1" name="USA">
```

```
<City id="C1c1" name="Washington" country="C1">
<Building id="C1c1b1" name="Lincoln Memorial" city="C1c1"/>
<Building id="C1c1b2" name="National Gallery" city="C1c1"/>
<Building id="C1c1b3" name="The Capitol" city="C1c1"/>
<Building id="C1c1b4" name="Washington Monument" city="C1c1"/>
</City>
</Country>

<Country id="C2" name="France">
<City id="C2c1" name="Paris" country="C2">
<Building id="C2c1b1" name="Arc de Triumph" city="C2c1"/>
<Building id="C2c1b2" name="Eiffel Tower" city="C2c1"/>
<Building id="C2c1b3" name="Louvre" city="C2c1"/>
</City>
</Country>

<Country id="C3" name="China">
<City id="C3c1" name="Beijing" country="C3">
<Building id="C3c1b1" name="Great Wall" city="C3c1"/>
<Building id="C3c1b2" name="Tiananmen" city="C3c1"/>
</City>
</Country>

</ArcWorldOO>
```

XML NAMESPACES

Writing schemas (DTDs) from scratch is hard, so it will be beneficial if we can re-use parts from existing, well-designed schemas. Also, there are many occasions when an XML document needs to use markups defined in multiple schemas, which may have been developed independently. Both considerations require that document constructs (tags and attributes) have universally unique names. *XML namespaces* provides the mechanism to accomplish this.

XML namespaces provide a simple way for qualifying names used in XML documents by associating them with namespaces identified by URI. XML namespaces are based on the use of *qualified names*, which consists of a *namespace prefix* and the *local name*, separated by a single colon. The prefix, which is mapped to a URI, selects a namespace. The combination of the universally managed URI namespace and the local name produces names that guarantee universal uniqueness.

A namespace is declared using a reserved processing instruction as shown here:

```
<?xml:namespace ns='urn:uuid:C4ED1820-6207-11d1-A29F-00AA00C14882/'
                src='http://www.w3.org' prefix='w3c' ?>
```

The *ns* attribute contains the URI that functions as a *namespace name* to identify the namespace, the *src* attribute contains an optional URI that may be used to retrieve the schema (if one exists), and the *prefix* attribute gives the namespace prefix used to associate names in an XML document with this namespace.

Namespace declarations must be located in the prolog of an XML document, after the XML Declaration (if any), and before the DTD (if any). This means that the scope of namespace prefixes is global to the whole document, including the DTD. A namespace prefix may not be declared more than once; it must be unique within an XML document. The namespace prefix *xml* is reserved. No other prefix beginning with the three-letter sequence xml, in any case combination, is allowed.

Once declared, a namespace prefix can be used in qualified names. The following names may be given as qualified names:

- Element types
- Attribute names
- Processing instruction targets

Therefore, in an XML document:

- All element types, attribute names, and processing instruction targets contain either zero or one colon.
- No entity names or notation names contain any colons.

An attribute whose name is not qualified, but which is attached to an element whose type is qualified, is in the namespace of the element type prefix. Element types and attribute names are also given as qualified names when they appear in declarations in the DTD.

The following example shows the use of a "data type" namespace to specify data types:

```
<?xml:namespace ns='urn:uuid:C2F41010-65B3-11d1-A29F-00AA00C14882/'
                prefix='dt' ?>
```

```
<Date dt:baseType="date.iso8601">1997-03-17</Date>
```

XML LINKING LANGUAGE (XLINK)

XLink specifies constructs that may be inserted into XML resources to describe links between data objects. It uses XML syntax to create structures that can describe not only simple unidirectional links but also more comprehensive multidirectional and typed links.

A *link* is an explicit relationship between two or more data objects or portions of data objects. A *linking element* is used to assert link existence and describe link characteristics. Linking elements are recognized based on the use of a designated attribute named *xml:link*. Possible values are *simple* and *extended* (as well as *locator*, *group*, and *document*, which identify other related types of elements). An element that includes such an attribute should be treated as a linking element of the indicated type. The following is an example similar to the HTML A link:

```
<A xml:link="simple" href="http://www.w3.org/">The W3C</A>
```

Linking Elements

XLink defines two types of linking element:

- A *simple link* that is usually inline and always one-directional.
- An *extended link* that may be either inline or out-of-line and must be used for multidirectional links, links originating from read-only resources, and so on.

Both kinds of links can have various types of information associated with them:

- One or more *locators* to identify the *remote resources* participating in the link; a locator is required for each remote resource.
- Semantics of the link.
- Semantics of the remote resource.
- Semantics of the *local resource*, if the link is *inline*. (An inline link is a link which serves as one of its own resources. A local resource is the content of an inline linking element not pointed to by a locator.)

This information is supplied in the form of attributes on linking elements.

The locator for a resource is typically provided by means of a URI. *XPointer* (which we will discuss later) can be used with the URI structure, as fragment identifiers, to specify a more precise *sub-resource*. A locator takes the form of an attribute called *href*, as shown in the earlier example.

The following semantic information can be provided for a link:

- Whether the link is inline, indicated with an attribute called *inline*. It can have the value *true* (the default) or *false*.
- The role of the link, indicated with an optional attribute called *role*.

The following semantic information can be provided for a remote resource:

- The role of the resource, provided with an optional attribute called *role*.
- A title for the resource, provided with an optional attribute called *title*.
- Behavior policies to use in traversing to this resource (we will discuss this later).

If the link is inline, the following semantic information can be provided for the local resource:

- The role of the resource, indicated with an optional attribute called *content-role*.
- A title for the resource, indicated with an optional attribute called *content-title*.

Simple Links

A simple link is like an HTML A link and has the following characteristics:

- The link is expressed at one of its ends.
- Users can only initiate traversal from that end to the other.
- The link goes to only one destination.

The simple linking element contains a locator attribute and all the link and resource semantic attributes. The *xml:link* attribute value for a simple link must be *simple*. Here is another example of a simple link:

```
<Citation xml:link="simple"
  href="http://www.xyz.com/xml/smith.xml"
  title="Smith" show="new"
  content-role="Reference">
    as discussed in Smith(1998)
</Citation>
```

Extended Links

An extended link can connect any number of resources, and it is often out-of-line. The additional capabilities are required for:

- Enabling outgoing links in documents that cannot be modified to add an inline link.

- Creating links to and from resources in formats with no native support for embedded links (such as multimedia formats).
- Applying and filtering sets of relevant links on demand.
- Enabling other advanced hypermedia capabilities.

The extended linking element contains a series of child elements that serve as locators. Attributes relevant to remote resources are expressed on the corresponding contained locator elements. The *xml:link* attribute value for a locator must be *locator*. The linking element itself retains those attributes relevant to the link as a whole and to its local resource, if any. The *xml:link* attribute value for an extended link must be *extended*. Here is an example of an out-of-line extended link:

```
<Commentary xml:link="extended" inline="false">
    <locator href="smith2.1" role="Essay"/>
    <locator href="jones1.4" role="Rebuttal"/>
    <locator href="robin3.2" role="Comparison"/>
</Commentary>
```

Link Behavior

XLink provides *behavior policies* that allow link authors to signal certain intentions as to the timing and effects of traversal. These include:

- ***Show.*** The *show* attribute is used to express a policy as to the context in which a resource that is traversed to should be displayed or processed. It may take one of three values:

  - *embed* indicates that upon traversal of the link, the designated resource should be embedded, for the purposes of display or processing, in the body of the resource and at the location where the traversal started.
  - *replace* indicates that upon traversal of the link, the designated resource should, for the purposes of display or processing, replace the resource where the traversal started.
  - *new* indicates that upon traversal of the link, the designated resource should be displayed or processed in a new context, which does not affect the resource where the traversal started.

- ***Actuate.*** The *actuate* attribute is used to express a policy as to when traversal of a link should occur. It may take one of two values:

  - *auto* indicates that the resource should be retrieved when any of the other resources of the same link is encountered, and that the display or processing of the initiating resource is not considered complete until this is done.
  - *user* indicates that the resource should not be presented until there is an explicit external request for traversal.

■ **Behavior.** The *behavior* attribute is used to provide detailed behavioral instructions.

XML POINTER LANGUAGE (XPOINTER)

XPointer specifies constructs that support addressing into the internal structures of XML documents. It provides for specific reference to elements, attributes, character strings, and other parts of XML documents. As mentioned in the previous section, XPointers can be used as fragment identifiers with the URI structure to specify a more precise *sub-resource*. Any fragment identifier that points into an XML resource must be an XPointer.

XPointers operate on the tree defined by the elements and other markup constructs of an XML document. An XPointer consists of a series of *location terms*; each one specifies a location, usually relative to the location specified by the prior location term. Also, each location term has a keyword (such as *id* and *child*), and it can have arguments such as instance number, element type, or attribute.

Many location terms locate individual nodes in an element tree. However, some location terms can locate more complex sets of data. Location terms are classified into *absolute terms*, *relative terms*, *span terms*, *attribute terms*, and *string data terms*.

Absolute Location Terms

The *absolute location terms* can be used to establish a location source or can serve as a self-contained XPointer. They include:

■ **root()**—if an XPointer begins with *root()*, the location source is the root element of the containing resource. If an XPointer omits any leading absolute location term, it is assumed to have a leading *root()* absolute location term.

■ **origin()**—if an XPointer begins with *origin()*, the location source is the sub-resource from which the user initiated traversal (such as defined in the XLink specification) instead of the default root element.

■ **id**(name)—if an XPointer begins with *id*(name), the location source is the element in the containing resource with an attribute having a declared type of *ID* and a value matching the given *name*.

Relative Location Terms

The *relative location terms* depend on the existence of a location source. If none is explicitly provided, the location source is the root element of the containing resource. The relative location terms provide facilities for navigating forward, backward, up, and down through the element tree. They include the following:

■ **child** identifies the *direct child nodes* of the location source.

■ **descendant** identifies nodes appearing anywhere within the *content* of the location source.

■ **ancestor** identifies element nodes *containing* the location source.

■ **preceding** identifies nodes that appear *before* the location source.

■ **following** identifies nodes that appear *after* the location source.

■ **psibling** identifies nodes that share the *same parent* with and appear *before* the location source.

■ **fsibling** identifies nodes that share the *same parent* with and appear *after* the location source.

All relative location terms accept the same set of potential arguments:

■ Selection by occurrence number, which can be *positive, negative,* or *all.*
■ Selection by node type, which can be *element* (the default), *pi* (process instruction), *comment, text* (inside element and CDATA section), *cdata,* or *all.*
■ Selection by attribute names and values.

The following example identifies the fifth child element of any type:

```
child(5)
```

The following example selects the last *Section* element in the content:

```
descendant(-1,Section)
```

The following example chooses the nearest ancestor element containing the location source and having an attribute called *name* with value "*3.2*":

```
ancestor(1,#element,name,"3.2")
```

Other Location Terms

The *spanning location term*, identified by the **span** keyword, locates a sub-resource starting at the beginning of the data selected by its first argument and continuing through to the end of the data selected by its second argument. Here is an example of a spanning XPointer that selects the first through third children of the element with ID *a1*:

```
id(a1).span(child(1),child(3))
```

The *attribute location term*, identified by the **attr** keyword, takes only an attribute name as a selector and returns the attribute's value. The following example returns the value of the attribute called *name* of the nearest ancestor element containing the location source:

```
ancestor(1,#element).attr(name)
```

The *string location term*, identified by the **string** keyword, selects one or more strings or positions between strings in the location source. The string location term accepts the following arguments, in sequence, to:

- Identify the occurrence (instance number) of the specified string, which can be *positive*, *negative*, or *all*.
- Identify the *candidate string* to be found within the location source. A *null string* is considered to identify the position immediately preceding each character in the location source.
- Identify the *position* (character offset) from the start of the candidate string(s) to the beginning of the desired final string match, which can be *positive*, *negative*, or *end*. The position number may not be zero; if omitted, it is assumed to be 1.
- Specify the number of characters to be selected.

The following XPointer identifies the position before the third character:

```
string(3,"")
```

The following XPointer selects the fifth exclamation mark and the character immediately following it:

```
string(5,"!",1,1)
```

CONCLUSION

XML provides a standard that can be used to encode the structure and content of all sorts of information, from simple to complex. XML can encode the representation for:

- An ordinary document
- A structured record, such as a purchase order
- A data record, such as the result set of a query
- An object, with data and methods, such as the persistent form of a Java object
- Metadata (schema) entities and types, such as XMI (which we will discuss in Chapter 19, "XML for Metadata Interchange")
- Meta-content about a Web site, such as CDF (Channel Definition Format)

In so doing, XML can encode not only the information itself but also its metadata. (In the case of metadata, it will be the meta-metadata.) As such, the XML encoding is self-describing and can be parsed, interpreted, and processed by machines—without human intervention.

XML provides a powerful and flexible format for expressing data. It can be used as:

- *Exchange format* for sharing data, such as between an application and a database
- *Wire format* for transferring data, such as between a client and a server
- *Persistence format* for storing data, such as in the case of a document repository

When used as exchange format for sharing data, XML by itself is not sufficient. Even with DTD, XML only encodes the syntactic (structural) information of that data. It does not provide any semantic information (meaning) about the data. What is needed is an XML vocabulary or DTD, commonly agreed among the parties involved. Such XML vocabularies already exist in certain domains, and many more will come in the future. Some examples are:

- Channel Definition Format (CDF), for describing Web content
- Open Financial Exchange Format (OFX), for exchanging financial data and instructions among financial institutions
- Open Software Distribution (OSD), for describing software components, their versions, their underlying structure, and their relationships to other components
- Chemical Markup Language (CML)
- Mathematical Markup Language (MML)

XML, XML Namespaces, XLink, and XPointer are the core technologies required to encode or represent data as XML documents. Additional technologies are needed to process and display them. The key technologies are *DOM (Document Object*

Model), a platform-neutral and language-neutral interface that allows programs and scripts to dynamically access and update the structure and content of XML documents, and *XSL (eXtensible Style Language)*, a mechanism for adding style (for example, fonts, colors, and spacing) to XML documents. We will discuss DOM in Chapter 18, "DOM and SAX," and XSL is covered in Chapter 22, "Conclusion: Emerging Technologies." XSL is still in the initial proposal stage; therefore, we will give it a cursory review.

Also needed are various types of tools. The most urgent ones are: XML processors, XML viewers, and XML editors. Among these, a number of XML processors are widely in use, some validating and some not. We will briefly discuss a validating XML processor, **XML for Java**, in the next chapter when we discuss DOM and *SAX (Simple API for XML)*.

Chapter 18

DOM and SAX

concepts

An XML document is not too useful if you cannot process it—for example, to display it on a Web browser, to print it out on a laser printer, to import it into a tool or repository, or to query about certain elements and/or attributes. Also, there are many occasions when you need to generate an XML document from scratch, but not by hand—for example, to export it from a tool or repository or to represent the data retrieved from a database. The most basic tool you need for these purposes is an XML processor that can parse or create XML documents and that provide a standard set (or sets) of APIs that allow you to access all parts (elements, attributes, entities, processing instructions, comments, and DTD) of the document. *XML for Java* is such a processor, and it is written in Java.

There are two major types of XML APIs:

- Tree-based API
- Event-based API

A *tree-based API* compiles an XML document into an internal tree structure and allows an application to navigate that tree. The *Document Object Model (DOM)* is such an API, which is in the process of being standardized by W3C. An *event-based API*, on the other hand, reports parsing events (such as the start and end of elements) to an application through callbacks. The application implements handlers to deal with the various events. *SAX (Simple API for XML)* is such an API. It is possible to generate events using a tree-based API, and it is possible to construct an in-memory tree using an event-based API. XML for Java supports both DOM and SAX.

In the following section, we will first discuss DOM, specifically DOM (Core) and DOM (XML). We will go over the corresponding Java DOM (Core) API and Java DOM (XML) API. We will then show a sample DOM application using XML for Java. After that, we will switch our attention to SAX, go over the Java SAX API, and show the same sample application but in SAX using XML for Java.

DOM (DOCUMENT OBJECT MODEL)

DOM is a platform-neutral and language-neutral, tree-based API that allows programs and scripts to access and manipulate the structure and content of parsed documents. All markup, as well as any document type declarations, are made available. DOM also allows the creation of entire documents in memory "from scratch."

DOM is an "abstraction," or a conceptual model of how documents are represented and manipulated in the products that support the DOM interfaces. Therefore, in general, products that support DOM merely "expose" the DOM interfaces as a means of accessing and manipulating their (potentially proprietary) internal data structures and operations.

DOM builds on the technology of Netscape Navigator 3.0 and Microsoft Internet Explorer 3.0. That functionality is referred to as *level zero*. The current specification, which is still a working draft being developed by the W3C, is referred to as *level one*. It concentrates on the core, HTML, and XML document models, and it contains functionality for document navigation and manipulation. The DOM interfaces are specified in OMG IDL, Java, and ECMAScript. In this chapter, we will focus on the core and XML document models, and we will discuss only the Java API.

DOM (Core)

DOM (Core) defines a set of object definitions that are sufficient to represent a document instance (the objects that occur within the document itself). The documents can be HTML (4.0) documents or XML (1.0) documents.

The primary types of objects that an application program will encounter when using DOM include:

■ **Node** is the base type of most objects. It has zero or more sequentially ordered child nodes. It usually has a parent node; the exception is that the root node in a document hierarchy has no parent.

■ **Element** represents the elements in a document. It contains, as child nodes, all the content between the start tag and the end tag of an element. Additionally, it has a list of **Attribute** objects, which are either explicitly specified or defined in the DTD with default values.

■ **DocFragment** is the root node of a document fragment.

■ **Document** represents the root node of a standalone document.

The following are auxiliary types of objects that an application programmer may encounter:

■ **NodeIterator** is used for iterating over a set of nodes specified by a filter.

■ **AttributeList** represents a collection of **Attribute** objects, indexed by attribute name.

■ **Attribute** represents an attribute in an **Element** object.

■ **DocumentContext** is a respository for metadata about a document.

■ **DOM** provides instance-independent document operations.

DOM (XML)

DOM (XML) extends DOM (Core) such that DTDs, entities, and CDATA marked sections can also be represented. The objects and interfaces defined in DOM (XML) are sufficient to allow XML validators and other applications that make use of a DTC to be written.

The basic XML objects include:

■ **XMLNode** is the XML specialization of the **Node** object. It has additional methods that are needed to manipulate specific features of XML documents.

The major objects that are used to represent the DTD of a document include:

■ **DocumentType** provides access to element type declarations, entity declarations, and notation declarations.

- **ElementDefinition** represents the definition of each element defined within the external or internal DTD subset.

- **AttributeDefinition** is used to access information about a particular attribute definition on a given element.

- **ModelGroup** represents the content model of an element.

- **EntityDefinition** represents the definition of an entity, either internally in a document or in an external file.

- **EntityReference** represents an entity reference.

- **Notation** represents the definition of a notation.

THE JAVA DOM (CORE) API

The Java DOM (Core) API is contained in the **org.w3c.dom** package.

DOM Interface

The **DOM** interface provides methods for performing operations that are independent of any particular instance of the document object model:

- **createDocument**(String type) creates and returns a **Document** object of the specified type.

- **hasFeature**(String feature) returns true (boolean) if the current version of DOM implements the specified feature.

DocumentContext Interface

The **DocumentContext** interface provides information about where the document came from, and any additional metadata about the document. It has the following methods:

- **getDocument**() returns the **Document** object, which is the root node of the document tree.

- **setDocument**(Document doc) sets the root node of the document tree.

Node Interface

The **Node** object is the primary data type in DOM. It represents a single node in the document tree. The **Node** interface has the following class constants:

- **DOCUMENT** (int)

- **ELEMENT** (int)

- **ATTRIBUTE** (int)

- **TEXT** (int)

- **PI** (int)

- **COMMENT** (int)

It has the following methods:

- **getNodeType**() returns the type (int) of this node, which can be DOCUMENT, ELEMENT, ATTRIBUTE, TEXT, PI, or COMMENT.

- **getParentNode**() returns the parent (**Node**) of this node.

- **hasChildNodes**() returns true (boolean) if this node has any children.

- **getChildNodes**() returns a **NodeIterator** object, which will enumerate all children of this node.

- **getFirstChild**() returns the first child (**Node**) of this node.

- **getNextSibling**() returns the node (**Node**) immediately following this node in a breadth-first traversal of the document tree.

- **getPreviousSibling**() returns the node (**Node**) immediately preceding this node in a breadth-first traversal of the document tree.

- **insertBefore**(Node newChild, Node refChild) inserts the *newChild* node before the *refChild* node in the list of children of this node, and then returns the new child (**Node**).

- **replaceChild**(Node newChild, Node oldChild) replaces the *oldChild* node with the *newChild* node in the list of children of this node, and then returns the old child (**Node**).

■ **removeChild**(Node oldChild) removes the *oldChild* node in the list of children of this node, and then returns the old child (**Node**).

NodeIterator Interface

The **NodeIterator** interface can be used to provide a linear view of the document tree. It has the following methods:

■ **getLength**() returns the number of nodes (int) that will be iterated over if the iterator is started at the beginning.

■ **getCurrentPos**() returns the current position (int) of the iterator.

■ **atFirst**() returns true (boolean) if the iterator is positioned at the beginning of the set of nodes that it will iterate over.

■ **atLast**() returns true (boolean) if the iterator is positioned at the end of the set of nodes that it will iterate over.

■ **toNextNode**() returns the node (**Node**) after the current position, and then resets the current position to be after the node returned.

■ **toPrevNode**() returns the node (**Node**) before the current position, and then resets the current position to be before the node returned.

■ **toFirstNode**() returns the first node (**Node**) of the set of nodes that the iterator will iterate over, and then resets the current position to be before the first node.

■ **toLastNode**() returns the last node (**Node**) of the set of nodes that the iterator will iterate over, and then resets the current position to be after the last node.

■ **moveTo**(int n) returns the nth node (**Node**) of the set of nodes that the iterator will iterate over, and then resets the current position to be before the nth node.

TreeIterator Interface

The **TreeIterator** interface extends **NodeIterator** and provides additional methods that are specific to tree traversal:

■ **numChildren**() returns the number (int) of children below the current node.

- **numPreviousSiblings**() returns the number (int) of siblings previous to the current node.

- **numNextSiblings**() returns the number (int) of siblings after the current node.

- **toParent**() moves the iterator to the parent of the current node, and then returns the parent (**Node**).

- **toFirstChild**() moves the iterator to the first child of the current node, and then returns the first child (**Node**).

- **toLastChild**() moves the iterator to the last child of the current node, and then returns the last child (**Node**).

- **toNthChild**(int n) moves the iterator to the nth child of the current node, and then returns the nth child (**Node**).

- **toPreviousSibling**() moves the iterator to the previous sibling of the current node, and then returns the previous sibling (**Node**).

- **toNextSibling**() moves the iterator to the next sibling of the current node, and then returns the next sibling (**Node**).

DocumentFragment Interface

The **DocumentFragment** interface provides the handle for a document fragment. Document fragments do not need to be well-formed XML documents; however, they do need to be well-formed XML parsed entities, which can have multiple top nodes. This interface extends **Node**, and it has the following methods:

- **getMasterDoc**() returns the **Document** object associated with this document fragment.

- **setMasterDoc**(Document doc) sets the **Document** object associated with this document fragment.

Document Interface

The **Document** object represents the entire document. It is the root of the document tree. The **Document** interface extends **DocumentFragment**, and it has the following methods:

- **getDocumentType**() returns the document type object (**Node**) associated with this document.

- **setDocumentType**(Node arg) sets the document type definition for this document.

- **getContextInfo**() returns the **DocumentContext** object associated with this document.

- **setContextInfo**(DocumentContext arg) sets the document context for this document.

- **getDocumentElement**() returns the root **Element** object of this document.

- **setDocumentElement**(Element arg) sets the root element for this document.

- **getElementsByTagName**(String tagName) returns a **NodeIterator** object, which will enumerate all elements with the given tag name.

- **createDocumentContext**() creates and returns a **DocumentContext** object.

- **createElement**(String tagName, AttributeList atts) creates and returns an **Element** object with the specified tag name and list of attributes.

- **createAttributeList**() creates and returns an empty **AttributeList** object.

- **createAttribute**(String name, Node value) creates and returns an **Attribute** object with the given name and value.

- **createTextNode**(String data) creates and returns a **Text** object with the given data.

- **createPI**(String name, String data) creates and returns a **PI** object with the given name and data.

- **createComment**(String data) creates and returns a **Comment** object with the given data.

- **createTreeIterator**(Node node) creates and returns a **TreeIterator** object anchored on the given node.

Element Interface

The **Element** object represents an element as well as its content. The **Element** interface extends **Node**, and it has the following methods:

■ **getTagName**() returns the name (**String**) of this element.

■ **getAttributes**() returns a **NodeIterator** object, which will enumerate all attributes of this element.

■ **getAttribute**(String name) returns the attribute value (**String)** by name of this element.

■ **setAttribute**(String name, String value) adds a new attribute/value pair to this element. If an attribute with the given name already exists, its value is changed to the given value.

■ **removeAttribute**(String name) removes the attribute with the given name.

■ **getAttributeNode**(String name) returns the **Attribute** object with the given name.

■ **setAttributeNode**(Attribute newAttr) adds a new attribute/value pair to this element. If an attribute with the given name already exists, its value is changed to the given value.

■ **removeAttributeNode**(Attribute oldAttr) removes the specified attribute/value pair from this element.

■ **getElementsByTagName**(String tagName) returns a **NodeIterator** object, which can be used to iterate over all child elements with the given tag name.

■ **normalize**() puts all text nodes of this element into a normal form.

Attribute Interface

The **Attribute** object represents an attribute in an **Element** object. The **Attribute** interface extends **Node**, and it has the following methods:

■ **getName**() returns the name (**String**) of this attribute.

■ **getValue**() returns the value (**String**) of this attribute.

- **getSpecified**() returns true (boolean) if this attribute was explicitly given a value.

- **setSpecified**(boolean arg) indicates whether this attribute was explicitly given a value.

- **toString**() returns the value (**String**) of this attribute. Character and general entity references will have been replaced with their values in the returned string.

AttributeList Interface

The **AttributeList** object represents a collection of **Attribute** objects that can be accessed by name. The **AttributeList** interface has the following methods:

- **getLength**() returns the number (int) of attributes in this list.

- **getAttribute**(String name) returns the **Attribute** object with the given name.

- **setAttribute**(Attribute attr) adds a new attribute to the end of this list, and then returns the newly added **Attribute** object.

- **item**(int index) returns the **Attribute** object with the given index.

- **remove**(String name) removes the attribute with the given name from this list, and then returns the removed **Attribute** object.

Text Interface

The **Text** object represents the non-markup content of an element. The **Text** interface extends **Node**, and it has the following methods:

- **getData**() returns the content (**String**) of this text node.

- **setData**(String data) sets the content of this text node.

- **append**(String data) appends the given data to the end of the content of this text node.

- **insert**(int offset, String data) inserts the given data at the specified character offset.

- **replace**(int offset, String data) replaces the characters at the specified character offset with the given data.

- **delete**(int offset, int count) deletes the specified number of characters starting at the given character offset.

- **splice**(Element element, int offset, int count) inserts the specified element as a sibling of this text node.

PI Interface

The **PI** object represents a processing instruction. The **PI** interface extends **Node**, and it has the following methods:

- **getName**() returns the name (**String**) of this processing instruction.

- **setName**(String name) sets the name of this processing instruction.

- **getData**() returns the content (**String**) of this processing instruction.

- **setData**(String data) sets the content of this processing instruction.

Comment Interface

The **Comment** object represents a comment. The **Comment** interface extends **Node**, and it has the following methods:

- **getData**() returns the content (**String**) of this comment.

- **setData**(String data) sets the content of this comment.

THE JAVA DOM (XML) API

The Java DOM (XML) API is contained in the **org.w3c.dom** package.

XMLNode Interface

The **XMLNode** interface is the XML extension to the **Node** interface. It has the following methods:

- **getParentXMLNode**(boolean expandEntities) returns the parent (**Node**) of this node.

- **hasChildXMLNodes**(boolean expandEntities) returns true (boolean) if this node has any children.

- **getChildXMLNodes**(boolean expandEntities) returns a **NodeIterator** object, which will enumerate all children of this node.

- **getFirstXMLChild**(boolean expandEntities) returns the first child (**Node**) of this node.

- **getNextXMLSibling**(boolean expandEntities) returns the node (**Node**) immediately following this node in a breadth-first traversal of the document tree.

- **getPreviousXMLSibling**(boolean expandEntities) returns the node (**Node**) immediately preceding this node in a breadth-first traversal of the document tree.

- **getEntityReference**() returns the entity reference (**EntityReference**) that generated a particular node when *expandedEntities* is set to true.

- **getEntityDeclaration**() returns the declaration (**EntityDeclaration**) for the entity reference that generated a particular node when *expandedEntities* is set to true.

DocumentType Interface

The **DocumentType** interface provides methods to access all of the element type declarations, entity declarations, and notation declarations. It extends **Node**, and it has the following methods:

- **getName**() returns the name (**String**) of DTD.

- **setName**(String name) sets the name of DTD.

- **getExternalSubset**() returns the external subset (**Node**) of DTD.

- **setExternalSubset**(Node arg) sets the external subset of DTD.

- **getInternalSubset**() returns the internal subset (**Node**) of DTD.

- **setInternalSubset**(Node arg) sets the internal subset of DTD.

- **getElementTypes**() returns a **Node** object supporting the **ElementDefinition** interface.

- **setElementTypes**(Node arg) sets the element type declarations.

- **getGeneralEntities**() returns a **Node** object supporting the **Entity** interface.

- **setGeneralEntities**(Node arg) sets the general entity declarations.

- **getParameterEntities**() returns a **Node** object supporting the **Entity** interface.

- **setParameterEntities**(Node arg) sets the parameter entity declarations.

- **getNotations**() returns a **Node** object supporting the **Notation** interface.

- **setNotations**(Node arg) sets the notation declarations.

ElementDefinition Interface

The **ElementDefinition** interface provides methods to access the definition of each element defined within the external or internal subset of DTD, including the name, attribute list, and content model. It extends **Node**, and it has the following class constants:

- **ANY** (int)

- **EMPTY** (int)

- **MODEL_GROUP** (int)

- **PCDATA** (int)

And, it has the following methods:

- **getName**() returns the name (**String**) of this element type.

- **setName**(String name) sets the name of this element type.

- **getAttributeDefinitions**() returns a **Node** object supporting the **Attribute-Definition** interface.

- **setAttributeDefinitions**(Node arg) sets the attribute definitions for this element type.

- **getContentType**() returns the content type (int) of this element type, which can be EMPTY, ANY, PCDATA, or MODEL_GROUP.

- **setContentType**(int arg) sets the content type of this element type.

- **getContentModel**() returns the content model **(ModelGroup)** of this element type, if the content type is MODEL_GROUP.

- **SetContentModel**(ModelGroup arg) sets the content model of this element type, if the content type is MODEL_GROUP.

AttributeDefinition Interface

The **AttributeDefinition** interface provides methods to access the definition of a particular attribute on an element. It extends **Node**, and it has the following class constants:

- **CDATA** (int)

- **ID** (int)

- **IDREF** (int)

- **IDREFS** (int)

- **ENTITY** (int)

- **ENTITIES** (int)

- **NMTOKEN** (int)

- **NMTOKENS** (int)

- **NAME_TOKEN_GROUP** (int)

- **NOTATION** (int)

- **REQUIRED** (int)

- **IMPLIED** (int)

■ **FIXED** (int)

And, it has the following methods:

■ **getName**() returns the name (**String**) of this attribute.

■ **setName**(String name) sets the name of this attribute.

■ **getAllowedTokens**() returns the list of tokens (**String**) that are allowed as values.

■ **setAllowedTokens**() sets the list of tokens that are allowed as values.

■ **getDeclaredType**() returns the type (int) of values this attribute may contain, which can be CDATA, ID, IDREF, IDREFS, ENTITY, ENTITIES, NMTOKEN, NMTOKENS, NOTATION, and NAME_TOKEN_GROUP.

■ **setDeclaredType**(int arg) sets the type of values this attribute may contain.

■ **getDefaultType**() returns the type (int) of default value for this attribute, which can be REQUIRED, IMPLIED, and FIXED.

■ **setDefaultType**(int arg) sets the type of default value for this attribute.

■ **getDefaultValue**() returns the default value (**Node**) of this attribute.

■ **setDefaultValue**(Node arg) sets the default value of this attribute.

ModelGroup Interface

The **ModelGroup** object represents the content model of an element, if the content type is MODEL_GROUP. The content model is represented as a tree. Leaf nodes in the tree are either **ElementToken** or **PCDATAToken**. The **ModelGroup** interface extends **Node**, and it has the following class constants:

■ **OPT** (int): "?"

■ **PLUS** (int): "+"

■ **REP** (int): "*"

■ **AND** (int): "??"

- **OR** (int): "|"

- **SEQ** (int): ","

And, it has the following methods:

- **getOccurrence**() returns the number (int) of times this model group can occur, which can be OPT, PLUS, or REP.

- **setOccurrence**(int arg) sets the number of times this model group can occur.

- **getConnector**() returns the connection type (int) of this model group, which can be AND, OR, and SEQ.

- **setConnector**(int arg) sets the connection type of this model group.

- **getTokens**() returns the **Node** object that defines the list of tokens in this model group.

- **setTokens**(Node arg) sets the list of tokens in this model group.

ElementToken Interface

The **ElementToken** interface represents the token type for an element declaration. It extends **Node**, and it has the following class constants:

- **OPT** (int): "?"

- **PLUS** (int): "+"

- **REP** (int): "*"

And, it has the following methods:

- **getName**() returns the name (**String**) of this element type.

- **setName**(String name) sets the name of this element type.

- **getOccurrence**() returns the number (int) of times this element can occur, which can be OPT, PLUS, or REP.

- **setOccurrence**(int arg) sets the number of times this element can occur.

PCDATAToken Interface

The **PCDATAToken** interface represents the token type for the string #PCDATA. It extends **Node**.

CDATASection Interface

The **CDATASection** interface represents a region in which most of the XML delimiter recognition does not take place. It extends **Text**.

Notation Interface

The **Notation** interface represents the definition of a notation within a DTD. It extends **Node**, and it has the following methods:

- **getName**() returns the name (**String**) of this notation.

- **setName**(String name) sets the name of this notation.

- **getIsPublic**() returns true (boolean) if a public identifier was specified in this notation declaration.

- **setIsPublic**(boolean arg) identifies whether a public identifier was specified in this notation declaration.

- **getPublicIdentifier**() returns the public identifier (**String**) of this notation.

- **setPublicIdentifier**(String arg) sets the public identifier of this notation.

- **getSystemIdentifier**() returns the system identifier (**String**) of this notation.

- **setSystemIdentifier**(String arg) sets the system identifier of this notation.

EntityDeclaration Interface

The **EntityDeclaration** interface represents an entity declaration in a DTD. It has the following methods:

- **getReplacementString**() returns the **String** that a reference to this entity is replaced with.

- **setReplacementString**(String arg) sets the string that a reference to this entity is replaced with.

- **getReplacementSubtree**() returns the parsed subtree (**DocumentFragment**) that references to this entity would logically point to.

- **setReplacementSubtree**(DocumentFragment arg) sets the parsed subtree that references to this entity would logically point to.

EntityReference Interface

The **EntityReference** interface represents an entity reference in a DTD. It has the following methods:

- **getIsExpanded**() returns true (boolean) if the default view of entities is to be expanded.

- **setIsExpanded**(boolean arg) sets whether the default view of entities is to be expanded.

- **expand**() expands this entity reference.

SAMPLE DOM APPLICATION

In the following listings, we will use a simple application to illustrate the usage of **XML for Java** and the DOM API. XML for Java is a validating XML processor written in Java. It supports and implements the DOM API. XML for Java provides a **com.ibm.xml.parser.Parser** class that can be instantiated to represent an XML parser that can parse an XML document and generate a tree of DOM nodes.

This application (see Listing 18-1) can parse any XML document and print out its elements, attributes, and character data. Using the relational **ArcWorld** XML view (see Listing 18-2 and Listing 17-2 on page 407) as input, it generates the output shown in Listing 18-3.

Listing 18-1. DOMDemo.java.

```
import com.ibm.xml.parser.*;
import org.w3c.dom.*;

import java.io.*;
```

```java
public class DOMDemo {

    public static void main(String[] argv) {
        try {
            if (argv.length != 1) {
                System.out.println("Usage: java DOMDemo " +
                                        "<document>");
                System.exit(0);
            }

            String fn = argv[0];
            InputStream is = new FileInputStream(fn);

            Parser ps = new Parser(fn);
            Document doc = ps.readStream(is);
            System.out.println("Start document");

            Element el = doc.getDocumentElement();
            printElement(el);

            System.out.println("End document");
        } catch (Exception e) {
            e.printStackTrace();
        }
    }

    public static void printElement(Element el) {
        String en = el.getTagName();
        System.out.println("Start element: " + en);

        NodeIterator ni = el.getAttributes();
        Node n = ni.toNextNode();
        while (n != null) {
            Attribute a = (Attribute) n;
            System.out.println("Attribute: " + a.getName() + "=" +
                '"' + a.toString() + '"');

            n = ni.toNextNode();
        }

        if (el.hasChildNodes()) {
            ni = el.getChildNodes();

            n = ni.toNextNode();
            while (n != null) {
```

```
                int nt = n.getNodeType();
                if (nt == Node.ELEMENT) {
                    Element e = (Element) n;
                    printElement(e);
                } else if (nt == Node.TEXT) {
                    Text t = (Text) n;
                  System.out.println("Text: " + '"' + t.getData() + '"');
                }

                n = ni.toNextNode();
            }
        }

        System.out.println("End element: " + en);
    }

}
```

Listing 18-2. ArcWorld.xml.

```xml
<?xml version="1.0" ?>
<!-- ArcWorld.xml -->

<!DOCTYPE ArcWorld SYSTEM "ArcWorld.dtd">

<ArcWorld>

<Country name="USA"/>
<Country name="France"/>
<Country name="China"/>

<City name="Washington" country="USA"/>
<City name="Paris" country="France"/>
<City name="Beijing" country="China"/>

<Building name="Lincoln Memorial" city="Washington"/>
<Building name="National Gallery" city="Washington"/>
<Building name="The Capitol" city="Washington"/>
<Building name="Washington Monument" city="Washington"/>
<Building name="Arc de Triumph" city="Paris"/>
<Building name="Eiffel Tower" city="Paris"/>
<Building name="Louvre" city="Paris"/>
<Building name="Great Wall" city="Beijing"/>
<Building name="Tiananmen" city="Beijing"/>
```

```
</ArcWorld>
```

Listing 18-3. ArcWorld.dom.

```
Start document
Start element: ArcWorld
Text: "

"
Start element: Country
Attribute: name="USA"
End element: Country
Text: "
"
Start element: Country
Attribute: name="France"
End element: Country
Text: "
"
Start element: Country
Attribute: name="China"
End element: Country
Text: "

"
Start element: City
Attribute: name="Washington"
Attribute: country="USA"
End element: City
Text: "
"
Start element: City
Attribute: name="Paris"
Attribute: country="France"
End element: City
Text: "
"
Start element: City
Attribute: name="Beijing"
Attribute: country="China"
End element: City
Text: "
```

```
"
Start element: Building
Attribute: name="Lincoln Memorial"
Attribute: city="Washington"
End element: Building
Text: "
"
Start element: Building
Attribute: name="National Gallery"
Attribute: city="Washington"
End element: Building
Text: "
"
Start element: Building
Attribute: name="The Capitol"
Attribute: city="Washington"
End element: Building
Text: "
"
Start element: Building
Attribute: name="Washington Monument"
Attribute: city="Washington"
End element: Building
Text: "
"
Start element: Building
Attribute: name="Arc de Triumph"
Attribute: city="Paris"
End element: Building
Text: "
"
Start element: Building
Attribute: name="Eiffel Tower"
Attribute: city="Paris"
End element: Building
Text: "
"
Start element: Building
Attribute: name="Louvre"
Attribute: city="Paris"
End element: Building
Text: "
"
Start element: Building
Attribute: name="Great Wall"
```

```
Attribute: city="Beijing"
End element: Building
Text: "
"
Start element: Building
Attribute: name="Tiananmen"
Attribute: city="Beijing"
End element: Building
Text: "


"
End element: ArcWorld
End document
```

SAX (SIMPLE API FOR XML)

SAX is a simple, event-based API for XML parsers. The benefit of an event-based API is that it does not require the creation of an internal tree structure to represent the parsed XML document. Therefore, you can parse XML documents much larger than your available system memory.

SAX provides events for the following structural information for XML documents:

- The start and end of the document
- Document type declaration
- The start and end of elements
- Attributes of each element
- Character data
- Unparsed entity declarations
- Notation declarations
- Processing instructions

THE JAVA SAX API

The Java SAX API is contained in the **org.xml.sax** package, and it consists of the following:

- Interfaces implemented by the XML parser: **Parser, AttributeList,** and **Locator**
- Interfaces implemented by the application: **DocumentHandler, DTDHandler, EntityResolver,** and **ErrorHandler**

■ Standard SAX classes: **HandlerBase, InputSource, SAXException,** and **SAXParseException**

There are also helper classes contained in the **org.xml.sax.helper**s package:

■ **ParserFactory, AttributeListImpl,** and **LocatorImpl**

Parser Interface

The **Parser** interface is the basic interface for SAX parsers. All SAX parsers must implement this interface and a default constructor. It has the following methods:

■ **setDocumentHandler**(DocumentHandler handler) allows an application to register a document event handler.

■ **setDTDHandler**(DTDHandler handler) allows an application to register a DTD event handler.

■ **setEntityResolver**(EntityResolver resolver) allows an application to register a custom entity resolver.

■ **setErrorHandler**(ErrorHandler handler) allows an application to register an error event handler.

■ **setLocale**(java.util.Locale locale) allows an application to request a locale for errors and warnings.

■ **parse**(InputSource source) parses an XML document.

■ **parse**(String systemId) parses an XML document from a system identifier (URI).

AttributeList Interface

The **AttributeList** interface contains an element's attribute specifications. It has the following methods:

■ **getlength**() returns the number (int) of attributes in this list.

■ **getName**(int i) returns the name (**String**) of an attribute in this list (by position).

■ **getType**(int i) returns the type (**String**) of an attribute in this list (by position).

- **getType**(String name) returns the type (**String**) of an attribute in this list (by name).

- **getValue**(int i) returns the value (**String**) of an attribute in this list (by position).

- **getValue**(String name) returns the value (**String**) of an attribute in this list (by name).

Locator Interface

The **Locator** interface associates a SAX event with a document location. It has the following methods:

- **getPublicId**() returns the public identifier (**String**) for the current document event.

- **getSystemId**() returns the system identifier (**String**) for the current document event.

- **getLineNumber**() returns the line number (int) where the current document event ends.

- **getColumnNumber**() returns the column number (int) where the current document event ends.

DocumentHandler Interface

The **DocumentHandler** interface provides callback methods to receive notification of general document events. It has the following methods:

- **setDocumentLocator**(Locator locator) receives an object for locating the origin of SAX document events.

- **startDocument**() receives notification of the beginning of a document.

- **endDocument**() receives notification of the end of a document.

- **startElement**(String name, AttributeList atts) receives notification of the beginning of an element.

- **endElement**(String name) receives notification of the end of an element.

- **characters**(char[ ] ch, int start, int length) receives notification of character data.

- **ignorableWhitespace**(char[ ] ch, int start, int length) receives notification of ignorable whitespace in the element content.

- **processingInstruction**(String target, String data) receives notification of a processing instruction.

DTDHandler Interface

The **DTDHandler** interface provides callback methods to receive notification of DTD events. It has the following methods:

- **notationDecl**(String name, String publidId, String systemId) receives notification of a notation declaration event.

- **unparsedEntityDecl**(String name, String publidId, String systemId, String notationName) receives notification of an unparsed entity declaration event.

EntityResolver Interface

If a SAX application needs to implement customized handling for external entities, it must implement the **EntityResolver** interface. It has the following method:

- **resolveEntity**(String publicId, String systemId) returns the InputSource object for the resolved external entity.

ErrorHandler Interface

If a SAX application needs to implement customized error handling, it must implement the **ErrorHandler** interface. It has the following methods:

- **error**(SAXParseException exception) receives notification of a recoverable error.

- **fatalError**(SAXParseException exception) receives notification of a non-recoverable error.

- **warning**(SAXParseException exception) receives notification of a warning.

HandlerBase Class

The **HandleBase** class implements the default behavior for four SAX interfaces: **DocumentHandler, DTDHandler, EntityResolver,** and **ErrorHandler**. It has this default constructor:

■ **HandleBase**()

And, it has the following methods:

■ **setDocumentLocator**(Locator locator) receives an object for locating the origin of SAX document events.

■ **startDocument**() receives notification of the beginning of a document.

■ **endDocument**() receives notification of the end of a document.

■ **startElement**(String name, AttributeList atts) receives notification of the beginning of an element.

■ **endElement**(String name) receives notification of the end of an element.

■ **characters**(char[ ] ch, int start, int length) receives notification of character data.

■ **ignorableWhitespace**(char[ ] ch, int start, int length) receives notification of ignorable whitespace in the element content.

■ **processingInstruction**(String target, String data) receives notification of a processing instruction.

■ **notationDecl**(String name, String publidId, String systemId) receives notification of a notation declaration event.

■ **unparsedEntityDecl**(String name, String publidId, String systemId, String notationName) receives notification of an unparsed entity declaration event.

■ **resolveEntity**(String publicId, String systemId) returns the InputSource object for the resolved external entity.

■ **error(SAXParseException exception)** receives notification of a recoverable error.

- **fatalError**(SAXParseException exception) receives notification of a non-recoverable error.

- **warning**(SAXParseException exception) receives notification of a warning.

InputSource Class

The **InputSource** class allows a SAX application to encapsulate information about an input source in a single object. It has the following constructors:

- **InputSource**()

- **InputSource**(String systemId)

- **InputSource**(java.io.InputStream byteStream)

- **InputSource**(java.io.Reader characterStream)

And, it has the following methods:

- **getPublicId**() returns the public identifier (**String**) for the current document event.

- **setPublicId**() sets the public identifier for the current document event.

- **getSystemId**() returns the system identifier (**String**) for the current document event.

- **setSystemId**() sets the system identifier for the current document event.

- **getByteStream**() returns the byte stream (**java.io.InputStream**) for this input source.

- **setByteStream**(java.io.InputStream byteStream) sets the byte stream for this input source.

- **getCharacterStream**() returns the character stream (**java.io.Reader**) for this input source.

- **setCharacterStream**(java.io.Reader characterStream) sets the character stream for this input source.

- **getEncoding**() returns character encoding (**String**) for a byte stream or URI.

- **setEncoding**(String encoding) sets the character encoding.

ParserFactory Class

The **ParserFactory** class is a helper class. It provides convenient methods for dynamically loading SAX parsers. It has the following class methods:

- **makeParser**() creates and returns a new SAX parser (**Parser**) using the "org.xml.sax.parser" system property.

- **makeParser**(String className) creates and returns a new SAX parser (**Parser**) using the given class name.

SAMPLE SAX APPLICATION

In the following listings, we will use the same application that we used earlier for DOM to illustrate the usage of XML for Java and the SAX 1.0 API. XML for Java supports and implements the SAX API. It provides a **com.ibm.xml.parser. SAXDriver** class that implements the SAX **Parser** and **AttributeList** interfaces.

This application (see Listing 18-4) again can parse any XML document and print out its elements, attributes, and character data. Using the relational **ArcWorld** XML view (see Listing 18-2 and Listing 17-2 on page 407) as input, it generates the output shown in Listing 18-5.

Listing 18-4. SAXDemo.java.

```java
import org.xml.sax.*;
import org.xml.sax.helpers.*;

import java.io.*;

public class SAXDemo implements DocumentHandler {

    public static void main(String args[])
      throws Exception
    {
        if (args.length != 1) {
            System.out.println(
              "Usage: java -Dorg.xml.sax.parser=<className> " +
              "SAXDemo <document>");
            System.exit(1);
        }

        Parser p = ParserFactory.makeParser();
```

```java
        SAXDemo demo = new SAXDemo();
        p.setDocumentHandler(demo);

        FileInputStream is = new FileInputStream(args[0]);
        InputSource source = new InputSource(is);
        source.setSystemId(args[0]);

        p.parse(source);
    }

    public void setDocumentLocator(Locator locator)
    {
        System.out.println("Document locator supplied.");
    }

    public void startDocument()
    {
        System.out.println("Start document");
    }

    public void endDocument()
    {
        System.out.println("End document");
    }

    public void startElement(String name, AttributeList attributes)
    {
        System.out.println("Start element: " + name);
        for (int i = 0; i < attributes.getLength(); i++) {
            System.out.println("Attribute: " +
                        attributes.getName(i) +
                        '=' + '"' +
                        attributes.getValue(i) +
                        '"');
        }
    }

    public void endElement(String name)
    {
        System.out.println("End element: " + name);
    }

    public void characters(char ch[], int start, int length)
    {
        System.out.println("Characters: ");
```

```
        displayCharacters(ch, start, length);
    }

    public void ignorableWhitespace(char ch[], int start, int length)
    {
        System.out.println("Ignorable whitespace: ");
        displayCharacters(ch, start, length);
    }

    public void processingInstruction(String name, String data)
    {
        System.out.println("Processing instruction: " +
                        name + ' ' + data);
    }

    private static void displayCharacters(char ch[], int start, int length)
    {
        for (int i = start; i < start + length; i++) {
            switch (ch[i]) {
                case '\n':
                    System.out.print("\\n");
                    break;
                case '\t':
                    System.out.print("\\t");
                    break;
                default:
                    System.out.print(ch[i]);
                    break;
            }
        }
        System.out.print("\n");
    }
}
```

Listing 18-5. ArcWorld.sax.

```
Start document
Start element: ArcWorld
Ignorable whitespace:
\n\n
Start element: Country
Attribute: name="USA"
End element: Country
```

```
Ignorable whitespace:
\n
Start element: Country
Attribute: name="France"
End element: Country
Ignorable whitespace:
\n
Start element: Country
Attribute: name="China"
End element: Country
Ignorable whitespace:
\n\n
Start element: City
Attribute: name="Washington"
Attribute: country="USA"
End element: City
Ignorable whitespace:
\n
Start element: City
Attribute: name="Paris"
Attribute: country="France"
End element: City
Ignorable whitespace:
\n
Start element: City
Attribute: name="Beijing"
Attribute: country="China"
End element: City
Ignorable whitespace:
\n\n
Start element: Building
Attribute: name="Lincoln Memorial"
Attribute: city="Washington"
End element: Building
Ignorable whitespace:
\n
Start element: Building
Attribute: name="National Gallery"
Attribute: city="Washington"
End element: Building
Ignorable whitespace:
\n
Start element: Building
Attribute: name="The Capitol"
Attribute: city="Washington"
```

```
End element: Building
Ignorable whitespace:
\n
Start element: Building
Attribute: name="Washington Monument"
Attribute: city="Washington"
End element: Building
Ignorable whitespace:
\n
Start element: Building
Attribute: name="Arc de Triumph"
Attribute: city="Paris"
End element: Building
Ignorable whitespace:
\n
Start element: Building
Attribute: name="Eiffel Tower"
Attribute: city="Paris"
End element: Building
Ignorable whitespace:
\n
Start element: Building
Attribute: name="Louvre"
Attribute: city="Paris"
End element: Building
Ignorable whitespace:
\n
Start element: Building
Attribute: name="Great Wall"
Attribute: city="Beijing"
End element: Building
Ignorable whitespace:
\n
Start element: Building
Attribute: name="Tiananmen"
Attribute: city="Beijing"
End element: Building
Ignorable whitespace:
\n\n
End element: ArcWorld
End document
```

CONCLUSION

DOM is still evolving. This chapter is based on the April 16, 1998 working draft. So you should expect changes before it is completed. Once DOM is adopted as a W3C standard, we are likely to see XML processors supporting the DOM API become widely available on all platforms—for example, embedded in Web browsers, embedded in XML repositories, and running on Web application servers. When this happens, it will be the birth of *universal document object model*, or *universal data object model*, and the dawn of *data-centric computing*. Just imagine that you (or any application) will be able to send to anyone (or any application) an XML document. XML will become a truly *universal data interchange format*. If needed, you can even package some Java code (based on DOM) with it so that it can sing and dance. (Sounds like *XML Beans*?)

DOM is a low-level, navigation-based API. It is complete, but you must traverse from node to node to get what you want and to do what you need to. If the document tree is big, this can be messy and time-consuming. People are already working on a higher-level, declarative language for accessing and/or retrieving the internal structures of XML documents. We discussed a pointer language, XPointer, in Chapter 17, "Introduction to XML." We will briefly discuss a pattern language in Chapter 22, "Conclusion: Emerging Technologies."

Chapter 19

XML for Metadata Interchange

concepts

Implementing effective and efficient IT-based business solutions for an enterprise—whether it is for application development, business intelligence, or content management—requires the use and integration of many tools from different vendors. This, however, is difficult to achieve because the tools often cannot easily interchange the data they use with each other. As a result, translation and manual re-entry are frequently used; both are sources of inefficiency, error, and loss.

XML can ease the problem of tool interoperability by providing a flexible and easily processed *data interchange format*. In principle, a tool needs only to be able to *export* and *import* the data it uses in XML format to interoperate with other XML-capable tools. There is no need to implement a separate export and import facility for each pair of tools that exchange data.

The extent of the *data* that can be exchanged between two tools depends on how much of the data can be understood by both tools. To facilitate understanding, *metadata* (data about data) must also be exchanged with the data. XML again provides a flexible and easily processed *metadata interchange format*, as we have mentioned in Chapter 17, "Introduction to XML."

If both tools share the same *model of metadata* (the definition of the structure and meaning of the data), commonly referred to as the *metamodel*, all of the data transferred can be understood and used. However, gaining consensus on a totally shared metamodel among all tools is difficult even within a single company and for a single domain. It is more likely that a common subset of the metamodel can be developed for a given domain and shared among all tools, with each tool adding its own extensions as needed.

In this chapter, we will discuss the *MOF (Meta Object Facility)* and *XMI (XML Metadata Interchange)*. MOF is a standard adopted by the OMG for defining metamodels. It defines a simple meta-metamodel with sufficient semantics to allow you to define metamodels in various domains. XMI is a proposal submitted to the OMG for automatic generation of XML DTDs for a (MOF-compliant) metamodel and of XML documents for any metadata that conform to the metamodel.

With MOF and XMI, the XML DTDs for a metamodel are obtained by first defining the metamodel (in compliance with MOF) and then applying the XML DTD generation rules. The generation approach ensures that a given metamodel will always map to the same set of XML DTDs. Similarly, the XML document for a metadata is obtained by first defining the metadata (in conformance with the metamodel) and then applying the XML Document generation rules. The generation approach again ensures that a given metadata will always map to the same XML document.

META OBJECT FACILITY (MOF)

MOF is the OMG's adopted standard for modeling metadata and representing it as CORBA objects. It can support any kind of metadata that is describable using object modeling. MOF can be used to represent a wide range of metadata; for example:

- Metadata to support the software analysis and design processes
- Metadata for data warehousing, data mining, and database interoperability
- Metadata for Web data sources such as on-line document collections

In the first case, the OMG has already adopted UML (Unified Modeling Language) as the metamodel for *object analysis and design (OA&D)*. UML conforms to the MOF. In the second case, the OMG is working on a proposal for a common warehouse metamodel that uses MOF as the meta-metamodel.

MOF is compatible with the OMG four-layer metamodeling architecture as shown in Figure 19-1. The lowest level, *M0*, is the instance level (for example, OA&D objects or warehouse data). The next level higher, *M1*, is the model level (for example, an OA&D model or warehouse metadata). The next level higher, *M2*, is the metamodel level (for example, the OA&D metamodel, UML, or a common warehouse metamodel yet to be standardized). The highest level, *M3*, is the meta-metamodel (for example, the MOF meta-metamodel).

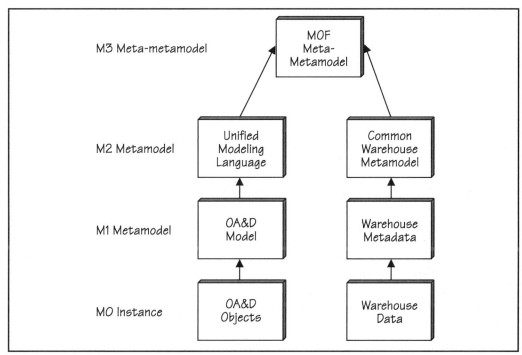

Figure 19-1. The OMG Metamodeling Architecture.

The MOF specification consists of three parts: the MOF Model, the MOF IDL Mapping, and the MOF CORBA Interfaces. We will give a brief review of each in the following, but we won't go into too much detail. Our primary focus in this chapter is on XMI, the automatic generation of XML documents and XML DTDs from metadata and its corresponding metamodel, respectively, for interchange.

The MOF Model

The *MOF Model* refers to the MOF's built-in meta-metamodel. It is an abstract language for defining MOF metamodels. The MOF uses UML notation as the graphical notation. (We assume you know something about UML, which is beyond the scope of this book. If not, please take a look at one of the many books published on UML. The UML notation is very versatile and can be used to graphically represent a meta-metamodel, metamodel, or model.)

The main metadata modeling concepts supported by the MOF are:

- **Classes** can have *Attributes* and *Operations* at both the class and instance level. Attributes are used to represent metadata. Operations are used to support metamodel specific functions on the metadata. Operations can have *Parameters*. Both Attributes and Parameters may be defined to be ordered, or to have structural constraints on their cardinality and uniqueness. Classes may inherit from other Classes. Multiple inheritance is allowed.

- **Associations** support binary links between Class instances. Each Association has two *AssociationEnds*. AssociationEnds may be defined to be ordered, or to have structural constraints on their cardinality and uniqueness. They may also be specified with aggregation (shared or composite) semantics. When a Class is the type of an AssociationEnd, the Class may contain a *Reference* that allows navigation of the Association's links from a Class instance.

- **Packages** are collections of related Classes and Associations. Packages can be composed by importing other Packages or by inheriting from them. Packages can be nested.

- **DataTypes** allow the use of non-object types for Attributes or Parameters.

- **Constraints** are used to define the well-formedness rules for the metadata described by a metamodel. Any languages may be used to express Constraints. In particular, *OCL (Object Constraint Language)*, which has been adopted as part of UML by the OMG, can be used for this purpose.

The MOF IDL Mapping

The *MOF IDL Mapping* is a standard set of templates that can be used to map a MOF metamodel onto a corresponding set of CORBA IDL interfaces. For an input to the mapping that is the metamodel for a given kind of metadata, the resulting IDL interfaces are for the CORBA objects that represent that metadata. The mapped IDL interfaces are typically used for storing and accessing the metadata in a repository.

The main correspondence between elements in a MOF metamodel (M2-level entities) and the CORBA objects that represent metadata (M1-level entities) are:

- A *Class* in the metamodel maps onto an IDL interface for *metadata objects* and a *metadata class proxy*. These interfaces support the Attributes, Operations, and References defined in the metamodel. The class proxy also provides a factory operation for metadata objects.

- An *Association* in the metamodel maps onto an IDL interface for a *metadata association proxy* that supports association queries and updates.

■ A *Package* in the metamodel maps onto an IDL interface for a *metadata package proxy* that acts as a holder for the proxies for the Classes and Associations contained in the Package.

The semantics of the mapped interfaces are defined in great detail by the MOF specification so that metadata repositories implemented by different vendors can interoperate.

In addition to the metamodel-specific interfaces for the metadata (as defined by the IDL Mapping), MOF *metadata objects* also inherit from a group of *Reflective* base interfaces, which allow a client program to access and update metadata in a generic way without either being compiled against the metamodel's generated IDL or having to use the CORBA DII (Dynamic Invocation Interface).

The MOF CORBA Interfaces

The *MOF CORBA Interfaces* are a set of IDL interfaces for the CORBA objects that represent a MOF metamodel. This is derived by using the MOF IDL Mapping to map the MOF meta-metamodel onto a corresponding set of CORBA IDL interfaces. That is, the MOF meta-metamodel is treated as the metamodel for MOF metamodels and is used as the input to the mapping. The resulting IDL interfaces are, therefore, for the CORBA objects that represent a MOF metamodel.

XML METADATA INTERCHANGE (XMI)

XMI is a submission proposed to the OMG, whose main purpose is to enable easy interchange of metadata between tools and between tools and metadata repositories (compliant with the MOF) in distributed heterogeneous environments. The XMI specification mainly consists of:

■ A set of XML DTD production rules for transforming MOF-compliant metamodels to XML DTDs
■ A set of XML Document production rules for encoding and transferring MOF-compliant metadata
■ Design principles for XMI-compliant DTDs
■ Generation principles for XMI-compliant XML documents

In the following sections, we will discuss the design principles for XMI-compliant DTDs and the generation principles for XMI-compliant XML documents. Please refer to the XMI submission listed at the end of this book for XML DTD production rules and XML document production rules.

XMI DTD Design Principles

XMI specifies the requirements that each DTD used by XML, the so-called *XMI DTD*, must satisfy. This allows some metamodel information contained in an XMI DTD to be verified through XML validations. The use of DTDs in an XML document is always optional; an XML document need not reference a DTD, even if one exists. However, it can be advantageous to use XMI DTDs and to perform XML validation. If XML validation is performed, any XML processor can perform some verification, thus relieving import/export programs of the burden of performing these checks.

Each *XMI DTD* must satisfy the following requirements:

- All elements defined by the XMI specification must be declared in the DTD.

- Each metamodel construct (class, attribute, and association) must have a corresponding element declaration. The element declaration may be defined in terms of entity declarations.

- All elements that represent extensions to the metamodel must be declared in the DTD.

XML validation can determine whether the XML elements required by the XMI specification are present in an XML document containing metadata, whether XML attributes that are required in these XML elements have values, and whether some of the values are correct. XML validation can also perform some verification that the metadata conforms to a metamodel. Because it is not currently possible to automatically encode all of the semantic constraints for a metamodel in a DTD, it is impossible to rely solely on XML validation to verify that the metadata satisfies all of a metamodel's semantic constraints. Finally, XML validation can be used to validate extensions to the metamodel.

Basic Principles

The prefix "*XMI.*" is used to distinguish all XML elements defined by the XMI specification. This is to avoid name conflicts with XML elements that are part of a metamodel. (After the XML Namespaces become a W3C recommendation, it should be possible to place all of the required XML elements in a single namespace and use the XML Namespaces mechanism to avoid name conflicts.)

In addition to required XML element declarations, there are *two attributes* that must be defined. Every XML element that corresponds to a metamodel class must have a required attribute of XML type ID. This attribute is used to associate an XML element with another XML element. The other attribute determines whether the

XML element is defined locally or whether it is a proxy for an XML element in another document.

Every *metamodel class* is represented by an XML element whose name is the class name. The element definition lists the attributes of the class, references to associations of the class, and the classes this class contains (either explicitly or through composition associations).

Every *attribute* of a metamodel class is represented by an XML element whose name is the attribute name. The attributes are listed in the content model of the XML element corresponding to the metamodel class in the order they are declared in the metamodel.

Each *association* between metamodel classes is represented by two XML elements that represent the roles of the association ends. The multiplicities of the association ends are translated to the XML multiplicities that specify the content models of the corresponding XML elements.

Any number of *XMI.extension* elements can be included in the content model of any XML element that represents a metamodel class. These extension elements have a content model of ANY. Tools that support XMI are expected to store the extension information and export it again to ensure round-trip engineering, even though in general they will not be able to process it further.

XMI DTD and Document Structure

Every *XMI DTD* consists of the following declarations (the first three are not unique to XMI):

- An XML version processing instruction
- An optional encoding declaration that specifies the character set
- Any other valid XML processing instructions
- The required XMI declarations (to be discussed later)
- Declarations for a specific metamodel
- Declarations for extensions

Every *XMI document* consists of the following declarations (none is unique to XMI):

- An XML version processing instruction
- An optional encoding declaration that specifies the character set
- Any other valid XML processing instructions
- An optional external DTD declaration with an optional internal DTD declaration

XMI Declarations

Every XMI DTD must include the declarations of the following XML attributes:

- *XML.id* is an attribute that must be included in the Attlist of an element representing a metamodel class. Here is an example:

      ```
      <!ELEMENT x ...>
      <!ATTLIST x XMI.id ID #REQUIRED ...>
      ```

- *XMI.remote* is an attribute that must be included in the Attlist of an element representing a metamodel class. Here is an example:

      ```
      <!ELEMENT x ...>
      <!ATTLIST x XMI.id ID #REQUIRED
                   XMI.remote (true|false) "false" ......>
      ```

Every XMI DTD must include the declarations of the following XML elements:

- *XMI* is the top-level element.

- *XMI.header* contains an optional element that has information about the metadata being transferred as well as elements that identify the metamodel.

- *XMI.documentation* contains information about the metadata being transferred—for example, the owner of the metadata or a contact person for the metadata. It may contain:

  - *XMI.owner*
  - *XMI.contact*
  - *XMI.longDescription*
  - *XMI.shortDescription*
  - *XMI.exporter*
  - *XMI.exporterID*
  - *XMI.exporterVersion*
  - *XMI.notice*

- *XMI.metamodel* identifies the metamodel.

- *XMI.content* contains the actual metadata being transferred.

- *XMI.extensions* contains elements that have metadata that is an extension of the metamodel.

■ *XMI.remoteContent* is used in XML elements that are proxies for XML elements in other documents.

■ *XMI.reference* is the mechanism used by XMI to associate XML elements with other XML elements, either within one XML document or between XML documents. This element is used in the content models of XML elements representing the roles of association ends, as well as with the XMI.remoteContent element to locate the XML element for which it is acting as a proxy.

■ *XMI datatype elements* represent MOF datatypes and include:

- ◆ *XML.any*
- ◆ *XML.array*
- ◆ *XML.arrayItem*
- ◆ *XML.arrayLen*
- ◆ *XML.enum*
- ◆ *XML.sequence*
- ◆ *XML.seqItem*
- ◆ *XML.struct*
- ◆ *XML.field*
- ◆ *XML.union*
- ◆ *XML.discrim*

Metamodel Class Specification

XMI uses the rules for generating a *Hierarchical Entity DTD* to represent information about metamodel classes (their attributes, associations, and containment relationships), as well as inheritance between metamodel classes. The Hierarchical Entity DTD generation rules use the XML entity substitution technique extensively. The declaration of entities for commonly used information reduces the repetition of declarations used in multiple areas. This declaration also allows regular formats for expressing copy-down inheritance in element declarations.

Every *metamodel class* consists of three parts: *properties*, *associations*, and *compositions*. Three entities are declared for every metamodel class, whose prefix is the name of the class and whose suffix is "Properties", "Associations", and "Compositions". The properties entity contains elements that represent metamodel attributes. The associations entity contains elements representing roles of association ends. The compositions entity contains elements that represent the role of associations that are aggregations. Here is an example of a metamodel class "c1" that has attributes, associations, and containment relationships:

```
<!ENTITY % c1Properties 'propertiesForC1'>
<!ENTITY % c1Associations 'AssociationsForC1'>
<!ENTITY % c1Compositions 'CompositionsForC1'>
```

```
<!ELEMENT c1 (XMI.remoteContent |
    (%c1Properties;, %c1Associations;, %c1Compositions;))>
```

XML does not have a built-in mechanism to represent inheritance. As such, XMI specifies *copy-down inheritance*—inheritance is represented by using the required properties, associations, and compositions entities for each class. Here is an example of a metamodel class "c2" with a superclass "c1" and its own attributes, associations, and containment relationships:

```
<!ENTITY % c2Properties '%c1Properties; propertiesForC2'>
<!ENTITY % c2Associations '%c1Associations; AssociationsForC2'>
<!ENTITY % c2Compositions '%c2Compositions; CompositionsForC2'>
<!ELEMENT c2 (XMI.remoteContent |
    (%c2Properties;, %c2Associations;, %c2Compositions;))>
```

In this manner, the properties, associations, and compositions are copied directly from each superclass via the substitution capability of entities. Note that the declarations of entities of superclasses must precede the declarations of entities and elements of their subclasses.

Each *attribute* of a metamodel class is represented as an XML element instead of XML attribute. This allows more complex encoding and very large values. The declaration of an attribute named "a" with a non-enumerated type is as follows:

```
<!ELEMENT a (type specification | XMI.reference)>
```

The type specification is usually one of the XMI datatypes. A modified declaration is used to represent an attribute named "a" with an enumerated type; for example:

```
<!ELEMENT a EMPTY>
<!ATTLIST a XMI.value (enum1|enum2|...) #REQUIRED>
```

Here is an example of two attributes "a1" and "a2" where "a1" is a string and "a2" is a boolean:

```
<!ELEMENT a (#PCDATA | XMI.reference)>
<!ELEMENT a EMPTY>
<!ATTLIST a XMI.value (true|false) #REQUIRED>
```

Each *association* is represented by an XML entity and an XML element. The declaration of an association named "r" with multiplicity "m" for a metamodel class "c" is:

```
<!ENTITY % cAssociations 'rm'>
<!ELEMENT r (XMI.reference)>
```

The valid multiplicities for "m" are:

- "?" for zero or one
- " " for exactly one
- "+" for one or more
- "*" for any other value

Each XML element representing the role of an association end contains an XMI.reference element that should refer to an instance of "c" or one of its subclasses.

XML Document Generation Principles

XMI specifies the manner in which a model will be represented as an XML document. XML document generation is defined as a set of rules, which when applied to a model or model elements produce an XML document. These rules can be applied to any model whose metamodel can be described by the MOF.

The MOF meta-metamodel does not require any specific construct or mechanism to be used to define, in a metamodel, what will constitute a model. Therefore, XMI provides two distinct methods of specifying the modeling elements that are used to generate an XML document.

Production by Object Containment

Most metamodels are characterized by a *composition hierarchy*. Modeling elements of some type are composed of other modeling elements. These elements in turn are composed by other elements. For example, in UML, a Model is composed of, for example, Classes, UseCases, and Packages; a Class is composed of, for example, Attributes and Operations. This composition is defined using the MOF's composite form of Association, and it must obey strict containment—an element cannot be contained in multiple compositions. To support models and model fragments as compositions, XMI provides for XML document *Production by Object Containment*. Given a composite object, XMI's production rules define the XML document that represents the composite object and all the contained objects in the composition hierarchy.

The rules for Production by Object Containment are applied to a single root object of a composition hierarchy. The rules are applied throughout the composition hierarchy by navigating through the composition links. In addition, the rules make use of the model's metamodel to represent the types of the values.

Each generated XML document begins with a prologue and the standard XMI elements that we discussed earlier. Next comes the actual model, starting with the root object. For each object, including the root object, the *element* start tags are generated from the object's *metamodel class name*. Here is an example for a root object whose metamodel class name is "Model":

```
<Model XMI.id="a1">
```

The element attribute XMI.id provides a unique identifier within the document for this element.

Next, each *attribute* of the current object is used to generate an XML element, which is defined by the name of the attribute. The attribute value is then written out as its content. Here is an example for the "Model" root object's "name" attribute whose value is "ArcWorld":

```
<name>ArcWorld</name>
```

We will go over an example of *Production by Object Containment* shortly.

Production by Package Extent

It may not always be possible or desirable to represent a set of modeling elements through a composition hierarchy. Therefore, XMI specifies a second set of rules, *Production by Package Extent*, for generating XML documents from modeling elements.

The MOF provides the *Package* element to support metamodel development. At the metamodel level, Package objects are always the topmost (uncontained) elements. A Package will contain *Classes* and *Associations* directly and possibly through nested Packages. In the IDL-generated form of a MOF metamodel, interfaces representing specific features of these Packages, Classes, and Associations, are used for model development. For each Package, there is a corresponding subtype of *RefPackage*, an interface in the MOF's Reflective module. Likewise, for each Class, there is a corresponding subtype of *RefObject*, and for each Association, a corresponding subtype of *RefAssociation*.

The *Package Extent* is the top-level RefPackage subtype object, all the RefPackage, RefObject, and RefAssociation subtype objects it contains, and all the objects and links associated with them. The rules for Production by Package Extent act upon the uncontained RefPackage instance, producing an XML document that represents all the elements in the extent of that RefPackage.

The Production by Package Extent approach is more desirable when:

- More than one composition hierarchy needs to be exchanged.
- There are interconnections among separate composition hierarchies that need to be replicated.
- It is necessary to ensure that values of classifier-level attributes are preserved, even when no instances of that class exist.

The Production by Object Containment approach, on the other hand, provides:

- Finer granularity of the units of interchange
- Less dependence upon the RefPackage, RefAssociation, and RefObject features

SAMPLE METADATA INTERCHANGE

In the following example, we have taken the **ArcWorld** sample database (see Chapter 6, "The ArcWorld Sample Database")—in fact, a very simplified version of it—and represented it as a UML model (see Figure 19-2). The choice of UML as the metamodel is for illustrative purposes, because UML is a MOF-compliant metamodel and is well-known. The same **ArcWorld** model is then represented as an instance of the UML metamodel in Figure 19-3. Figure 19-4 shows the relationships between a model and its metamodel, both graphically and in XML, as an interchange format. The XML tags are derived from the (UML) metamodel, and the actual content is derived from the (**ArcWorld**) model. Finally, the XML document fragment (which can be used for metadata interchange) generated by XMI for the **ArcWorld** model is shown in Figure 19-5. The XML document fragment is generated using Production by Object Containment.

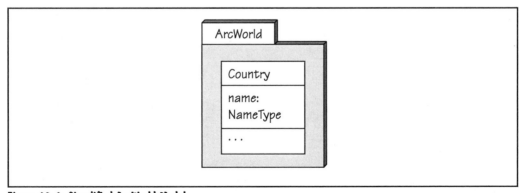

Figure 19-2. Simplified ArcWorld Model.

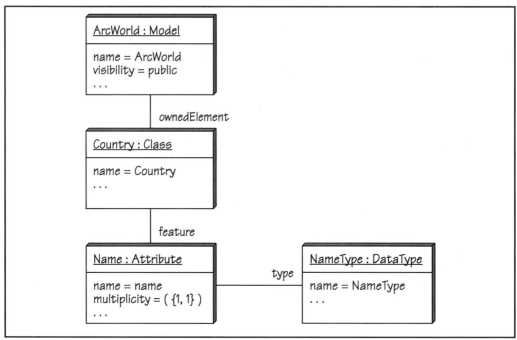

Figure 19-3. ArcWorld as a Metamodel Instance.

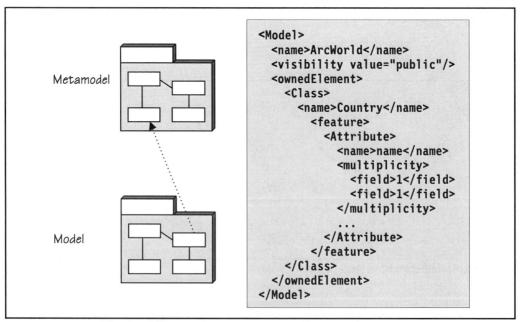

```
<Model>
  <name>ArcWorld</name>
  <visibility value="public"/>
  <ownedElement>
    <Class>
      <name>Country</name>
      <feature>
        <Attribute>
          <name>name</name>
          <multiplicity>
            <field>1</field>
            <field>1</field>
          </multiplicity>
          ...
        </Attribute>
      </feature>
    </Class>
  </ownedElement>
</Model>
```

Figure 19-4. Metamodel and Model (Tags and Content).

```
<Model XMI.id="a1">
<name>ArcWorld</name>
  <visibility XMI.value="public"/>
  <ownedElement>
    <Class XMI.id="a7">
      <name>Country</name>
        <feature>
          <Attribute>
            <name>name</name>
            <multiplicity>
              <field>1</field>
              <field>1</field>
            </multiplicity>
            <type>NameType</type>
          </Attribute>
        </feature>
    </Class>
  </ownedElement>
</Model>
```

Figure 19-5. ArcWorld as an XML Document Fragment.

CONCLUSION

We hope this chapter illustrates the feasibility and tremendous potential of using *XMI (XML for Metadata Interchange)*. In fact, metadata interchange may very well become one of the most important applications of XML. A major reason is that it is relatively easy and inexpensive. Tools and repositories that need to exchange metadata do not need to implement a new API (either Java-based, CORBA-based, or DCOM-based), which can be expensive, or to rehost to a new repository (either IBM, Microsoft, or Oracle), which can be even more costly. They need only provide an XML export and import facility. XMI provides an excellent framework to implement such a facility to exchange any kind of metadata (or model) and its MOF-compliant metamodel. As our example shows, XMI has been applied to exchange UML models and the UML metamodel. It will be soon be applied to exchange metadata and its metamodel in other domains—for example, data warehousing.

XMI currently is an OMG submission. It is likely to have many changes when it is finally adopted as an OMG standard. Also, since XML Namespaces, X-Link, and XPointer currently are not W3C adopted standards, XMI does not utilize their features. Instead, it provides its own equivalent features. Once these become W3C standards, XMI will have to be revised to remove any redundant features.

Part 6
Java Component
Architectures

An Introduction to Part 6

Up to now, we have concentrated on Java and Web data access in isolation. That is, we have assumed that your interest is in building client/server data access applications in Java on the Web, and nothing more. What happens if you are interested in building client/server data access components for sale to others to build large-scale applications, or if you are interested in building such applications yourself? In either case, data access is just one component of the application, although a most important one from our perspective. But data access must work seamlessly together with other major components, including naming, distribution, transactions, and security. How do you go about doing it? In Part 6, we will discuss a scalable component architecture, Enterprise JavaBeans (EJB), that provides you with the framework to do just that.

Here is what we will be covering in Part 6:

- *Chapter 20* introduces JavaBeans, the client component model that supports the development of portable, reusable Java components. (EJB extends the JavaBeans component model to address the needs of server components.)

- *Chapter 21* introduces EJB, a component architecture for development and deployment of object-oriented, distributed enterprise-level Java applications. EJB integrates naming, distribution, persistence, transactions, and security. It provides a high-level declarative programming model.

If you are an enterprise-level application programmer, you should be very excited about Part 6. The programming model and services discussed here will make your job that much easier and more pleasant. There is now hope that you will finally be able to concentrate on what is of most interest to you—enterprise-level business logic—and not worry about the low-level plumbing stuff.

Even if you are not an enterprise-level application programmer, you should still find it rewarding to go over Part 6. In addition to the important and fascinating new topics that we will be covering, you will see many of the "old" topics that we covered in previous parts being used here: Java reflection, Java events, Java archive, JDBC, Java servlets, Java Object Serialization, Java RMI, and Java ORBs.

Chapter 20

JavaBeans

concepts

Like JDBC and RMI, JavaBeans was a significant addition to Java; it was first introduced in JDK 1.1. *JavaBeans* is a component architecture that enables creation, assembly, and use of dynamic Java components. A component is a reusable software module that is supplied in a *binary form*. Both interface to and interaction with the component are at a binary level. JavaBeans defines a standard set of interfaces and behaviors that enable you to build reusable Java components. A Java component that conforms to the JavaBeans specification is called a *Bean.*

What makes a Java component a Bean? Not much. There is no specific interface that a Java component must implement to make it a Bean. Most Java classes could be considered Beans if appropriately packaged. Some classes, for example, define *properties* according to the JavaBeans convention and are therefore Beans. Other classes support the registration of *event-listeners* with them and are therefore also Beans. A Bean must be packaged in a *JAR file*. Within the JAR file, there is normally a manifest file listing its contents. If an entry for a class specifies the attribute *Java-Bean: True*, the class is understood to be a Bean. If there is no manifest file, all classes are assumed to be Beans. Many Beans provide **BeanInfo** objects that specify explicit information about their methods, properties, events, and other Bean-related information. If no **BeanInfo** objects are provided, the Java reflection methods can be used to find out information about the Beans.

In this chapter, we will first give an overview of JavaBeans, including its properties, events, introspection, customization, persistence, and packaging. We will then discuss the JavaBeans API and show an example of data access Beans. As you can see from the previous paragraph, JavaBeans is intimately tied to Java reflection, Java events, and Java archive. These were discussed in Chapter 3, "Java Primer." You may want to quickly review them before you proceed.

OVERVIEW OF JAVABEANS

JavaBeans is a portable, platform-independent component model written in Java. It enables developers to write reusable components once and run them anywhere—thus benefiting from the portable, platform-independent nature of Java. A *Bean* is any Java class that adheres to certain property and event interface conventions. Beans may be manipulated in a visual builder environment and composed together into applications.

There are a range of different kinds of JavaBean components. Some Beans will be used as *building blocks* in composing applications. So a developer may use a builder tool to connect together and customize a set of Beans to act as an application. An example of such a Bean is an AWT button. Other Beans will be more like *regular applications* that may then be composed together to form compound documents. An example is a spreadsheet Bean that is embedded inside a Web page.

Fundamentals

Individual Beans will vary in the functionality they support, but the typical features that distinguish a Bean are:

- *Events* as a communication mechanism that can be used to connect Beans

- *Properties* both for customization and programmatic use

- *Introspection* so that a builder tool can analyze a Bean's events, properties, and methods

- *Customization* so that a user can use a builder tool to customize the appearance and behavior of a Bean

- *Persistence* so that a Bean can have its state saved away and restored later

- *Packaging*, including class files, serialized-object files, and resource files

Design Time vs. Run Time

A Bean can run inside an application builder. This is referred to as the *design-time* environment. Within this environment, the Bean should provide design information to the application builder thus allowing the end user to *customize* the appearance and behavior of the Bean.

A Bean must of course be usable at *run time* within the generated application. In this environment there is much less need for design information or customization. The design information and customization code may potentially be quite large. Therefore, the JavaBeans architecture supports the *design-time interfaces* (those that pertain to introspection and customization) in separate classes from the *run-time interfaces*.

Visibility

Many Beans will have a GUI appearance and are *visible*. However, it is possible to implement *invisible* Beans that have no GUI appearance. In either case, the Beans are able to perform such functions as firing events, calling methods, and saving persistent state. They are also editable in a GUI builder using either standard property sheets or customizers (we will discuss these later).

Some Beans may be able to run either with or without a GUI appearance, depending on where they are instantiated. For example, if a given Bean is run in a server, it may be invisible. But if it is run on a user's desktop, it may have a GUI appearance. The **Visibility** interface can be used to query a Bean not only to determine whether it absolutely needs a GUI but also to advise the Bean whether a GUI is available.

Security

Beans are subject to the standard Java security model. Specifically, when a Bean runs as part of an untrusted applet, it will be subject to the standard applet security restrictions. However, when a Bean runs as part of a Java application or a signed applet, it will be treated as a normal Java application and allowed normal access to files and network hosts.

Network Access

The JavaBeans API is designed for use *within a Java Virtual Machine*. That is, Beans by themselves are not distributed objects. Several network access mechanisms (see Figure 20-1) can be used to connect Beans to network servers. The three primary network access mechanisms are (as we have discussed in previous chapters):

- Java RMI
- Java ORBs
- JDBC

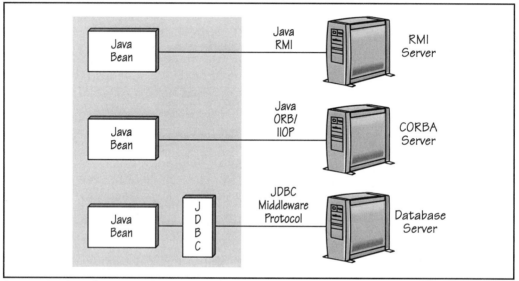

Figure 20-1. Network Access Mechanisms.

Events

Events are one of the core features of the JavaBeans architecture. Events provide a convenient mechanism for allowing components to be plugged together in an application builder. This allows some components to act as sources for event notifications that can then be caught and processed by other components. Please refer back to Chapter 3, "Java Primer" for a quick review. In the following sections, we will see their use with properties to provide change notification and verification.

Properties

A *property* is a single public attribute. Properties can be read/write, read-only, or write-only. There are several types of properties: simple, indexed, bound, and constrained. Properties are accessible in a number of ways:

- Properties can be accessed programmatically by other components calling their *getter* and *setter* methods.
- Properties may be presented in a *property sheet* for a user to edit.
- Properties tend to be *persistent* and will be saved as part of the persistent state of the Bean.
- Properties may be exposed in *scripting environments* as though they were fields of objects.

Simple Properties

A *simple property* represents a single value and, following a simple design pattern, can be defined with a pair of *get/set methods*. A property's name is derived from the method names. For example, the method names *getX()* and *setX()* indicate a property named "X". A method named *isX()* by convention indicates that "X" is a boolean property.

Indexed Properties

An *indexed property* represents an array of values. It can be defined with a pair of *get/set methods* that take an integer index parameter to access the individual value. The property may also support getting and setting the entire array at once.

Bound Properties

A *bound property* notifies other objects that support the **PropertyChange-Listener** interface when its value changes. Each time its value changes, the property fires a **PropertyChangeEvent**, which contains the property name, its old value, and its new value. Notification granularity is per Bean.

If a Bean supports bound properties, then it should support a pair of multicast event listener registration methods:

- **addPropertyChangeListener**(PropertyChangeListener x)
- **removePropertyChangeListener**(PropertyChangeListener x)

When a property change occurs on a bound property, the Bean should call the *propertyChange()* method of the **PropertyChangeListener** class on any registered listeners, passing a **PropertyChangeEvent** object.

For programming convenience, there is a utility class called **PropertyChangeSupport** that can be used by event sources to keep track of registration and firing of events.

Constrained Properties

A *constrained property* allows other objects that support the **VetoableChange-Listener** interface to veto its value change. Constrained property listeners can veto a change by throwing a **PropertyVetoException**. In general, constrained properties should also be bound. The property should notify any registered **Veto-ableChangeListeners** that a vetoable change has been proposed. If the change is acceptable, the property notifies any registered **PropertyChangeListeners** that the change has completed.

If a Bean supports constrained properties, then it should support a pair of multicast event listener registration methods:

- **addVetoableChangeListener**(VetoableChangeListener x)
- **removeVetoableChangeListener**(VetoableChangeListener x)

When a property change occurs on a constraint property, the Bean should call the *vetoableChange()* method of the **VetoableChangeListener** class on any registered listeners, passing a **PropertyChangeEvent** object. If the event recipient does not want the requested update to be performed, it may throw a **PropertyVeto-Exception**. It is the event source's responsibility to catch this exception, revert to the old value, and issue a new *vetoableChange()* method call to report the reversion.

For programming convenience, there is a utility class called **VetoableChangeSupport** that can be used by event sources to keep track of the registration and firing of events.

Introspection

Introspection allows you to discover at run time or in the builder environment what events, properties, and methods a Bean supports. It is a composite mechanism. By default, a low-level *reflection* mechanism (see Chapter 3, "Java Primer") is used to study the methods supported by a Bean, and then simple *design patterns* are applied to deduce from those methods what events, properties, and public methods are supported. However, if a Bean implementer chooses to provide a **BeanInfo** class to describe the Bean, the **BeanInfo** class will be used to discover the Bean's behavior.

By default, the following design patterns are used to determine which *events* a Bean multicasts:

```
public void add<EventListenerType>(<EventListenerType> a);
```

```
public void remove<EventListenerType>(<EventListenerType> a);
```

For *simple properties*, the following design patterns are used:

```
public <PropertyType> get<PropertyName>();
public set<PropertyName>(<PropertyType> a);
```

In addition, for *boolean properties*, a getter method with the following pattern is used:

```
public boolean is<PropertyName>();
```

The following design patterns are used to determine *indexed properties*:

```
public <PropertyType> get<PropertyName>(int a);
public set<PropertyName>(int a, <PropertyType> b);
```

By default, all public methods of a Bean are exposed as external *methods*.

The **Introspector** class is provided to simplify the introspection process and to ensure that all tools apply the same inspection rules. It walks over the class/super-class hierarchy of the target class. At each level, it checks if there is a matching **BeanInfo** class that provides explicit information about the Bean. If so, it uses that information. Otherwise, it uses the low-level reflection APIs to study the target class, and it uses the design patterns already mentioned to analyze its behavior.

Customization

You can provide customization of how a Bean appears and behaves within a visual builder environment in two different ways. First, if a Bean exports a set of properties, then an application builder can use these properties to construct a GUI *property sheet* that lists the properties. It also provides a *property editor* that implements the **PropertyEditor** interface for each property. The user can then use this property sheet to update the properties of the Bean.

For large components that offer a number of different ways of being configured, however, it may be more appropriate to provide a specialized class for customizing the Bean. These classes are called *customizers*, and they implement the **Customizer** interface.

Persistence

To make a Bean persistent, you can simply define its class as implementing **java.io.Serializable** (see Chapter 14, "Java Streams and Object Serialization").The state of the Bean will automatically be saved. To prevent selected fields from being saved, you can mark them *transient* or *static*. In general, you should save the state of all exposed properties of the Bean. Selected internal state variables may also be saved. You should not, however, save references to external Beans or event listeners.

Packaging

Beans are packaged and distributed through *JAR files* (see Chapter 3, "Java Primer"). A JAR file may contain the following entries:

- A set of class files to provide behavior for a Bean. These entries must have names ending in ".*class*".
- Optionally, a serialized prototype of a Bean to be used to initialize the Bean. These entries must have names ending in ".*ser*".
- Other *resource* files needed by the Bean—including images, sound, text, and video.
- Optional help files in HTML format to provide documentation for the Bean.
- Optional internationalization information to be used by the Bean to localize itself.

The *name* of a Bean is a string that is a sequence of names separated by periods (.). Beans that are instantiated from classes have the same name as the corresponding class. These are mapped to JAR entries by replacing each period (.) with a forward slash (/) and adding ".class" at the end. Beans that are based on serialized prototypes have names similar to class names. These are mapped to JAR entries by replacing each period (.) with a forward slash (/) and adding ".ser" at the end.

A JAR file may include a *manifest file* to describe its content. Three manifest header tags are defined for use with JavaBeans:

- The *Java-Bean* tag is used to identify entries that represent Beans. If an entry for a class specifies the attribute *Java-Bean: True*, the class is understood to be a Bean. If there is no manifest file, all classes are assumed to be Beans.

- The *Depends-On* tag is used to specify other entries that it depends on. If the list is empty, then there are no dependencies. If the tag is missing, the dependency is unknown.

- The *Design-Time* tag is used to specify whether the entry is only needed at design time. It should be followed by a value of either "True" or "False".

THE JAVABEANS API

The JavaBeans API is contained in the **java.beans** package. It contains the following interfaces and classes:

- General: **Beans, Visibility**
- Properties: **PropertyChangeListener, VetoableChangeListener, PropertyChangeEvent, PropertyChangeSupport, VetoableChangeSupport**
- Introspection: **Introspector, BeanInfo, SimpleBeanInfo, FeatureDescriptor, BeanDescriptor, EventSetDescriptor, MethodDescriptor, ParameterDescriptor, PropertyDescriptor, IndexedPropertyDescriptor**
- Customization: **Customizer, PropertyEditor, PropertyEditorManager, PropertyEditorSupport**

Beans Class

The **Bean** class provides some general-purpose bean-control methods. It has this default constructor:

- **Beans**()

And, it has the following static methods:

- **instantiate**(ClassLoader cls, String name) instantiates and returns a Bean (**Object**). The Bean is created based on a name relative to a class loader.

- **getInstanceOf**(Object bean, Class targetType) returns an **Object** representing a specified type view of a Bean.

- **isInstanceOf**(Object bean, Class targetType) returns true (boolean) if a Bean can be viewed as a given target type.

- **isDesignTime**() returns true (boolean) if the Bean is running in an application builder environment.

- **setDesignTime**(boolean isDesignTime) indicates whether or not the Bean is running in an application builder environment.

- **isGUIAvailable**() returns true (boolean) if we are running in an environment where an interactive GUI is available.

- **setGUIAvailable**(boolean isGUIAvailable) indicates whether or not the Bean is running in an environment where an interactive GUI is available.

Visibility Interface

The **Visibility** interface can be used to query a Bean to determine whether it absolutely needs a GUI, and to advise the Bean whether a GUI is available. It has the following methods:

- **needsGui**() returns true (boolean) if this Bean absolutely needs a GUI.

- **avoidingGui**() returns true (boolean) if this Bean is currently avoiding use of a GUI.

- **okToUseGui**() instructs this Bean that it is OK to use a GUI.

- **dontUseGui**() instructs this Bean that it should not use a GUI.

PropertyChangeListener Interface

An object supporting the **PropertyChangeListener** interface can be registered with a source Bean so it can be notified of any bound property updates. This interface extends the **java.util.EventListener** interface, and it has the following method:

- **propertyChange**(PropertyChangeEvent evt) gets called when a bound property is changed to perform whatever task is desired.

VetoableChangeListener Interface

An object supporting the **VetoableChangeListener** interface can be registered with a source Bean so as to be notified of any constrained property updates. This interface extends the **java.util.EventListener** interface and has the following method:

- **vetoableChange**(PropertyChangeEvent evt) gets called when a constrained property is changed. If the recipient wants the property change to be rolled back, it can throw a **PropertyVetoException**.

PropertyChangeEvent Class

A PropertyChange event gets delivered whenever a Bean changes a bound or constrained property. A **PropertyChangeEvent** object is sent as an argument to the **PropertyChangeListener** and **VetoableChangeListener** methods. This class extends the java.util.EventObject class, and it has the following constructor:

- **PropertyChangeEvent**(Object source, String propertyName, Object oldValue, Object newValue)

And, it has the following methods:

- **getPropertyName**() returns the name (**String**) of the property that was changed.

- **getNewValue**() returns the new value (**Object**) for the property.

- **getOldValue**() returns the old value (**Object**) for the property.

PropertyChangeSupport Class

The **PropertyChangeSupport** class is a utility class that can be used by Beans that support bound properties. It implements **java.io.Serializable**, and it has the following constructor:

- **PropertyChangeSupport**(Object sourceBean)

And, it has the following methods:

- **addPropertyChangeListener**(PropertyChangeListener listener) adds a **PropertyChangeListener** to the listener list.

- **removePropertyChangeListener**(PropertyChangeListener listener) removes a **PropertyChangeListener** from the listener list.

- **firePropertyChange**(String propertyName, Object oldValue, Object newValue) reports a bound property update to any registered listeners.

VetoableChangeSupport Class

The **VetoableChangeSupport** class is a utility class that can be used by Beans that support constrained properties. It implements **java.io.Serializable**, and it has the following constructor:

- **VetoableChangeSupport**(Object sourceBean)

And, it has the following methods:

- **addVetoableChangeListener**(VetoableChangeListener listener) adds a **VetoableChangeListener** to the listener list.

- **removeVetoableChangeListener**(VetoableChangeListener listener) removes a **VetoableChangeListener** from the listener list.

- **fireVetoableChange**(String propertyName, Object oldValue, Object newValue) reports a constrained property update to any registered listeners. If the recipient wants the property change to be rolled back, it can throw a **PropertyVetoException**.

Introspector Class

The **Introspector** class provides a standard way for tools to learn about the properties, events, and methods supported by a target Bean. It has the following static methods:

- **getBeanInfo**(Class beanClass) introspects a Bean and returns a **BeanInfo** object that describes all of its properties, exposed methods, and events.

- **getBeanInfo**(Class beanClass, Class stopClass) introspects a Bean and returns a **BeanInfo** object that describes all of its properties, exposed methods, and events. The introspection stops at the stopClass.

- **getBeanInfoSearchPath**() returns the array of package names (**String**[ ]) that will be searched to find **BeanInfo** classes.

- **setBeanInfoSearchPath**(String[ ] path) sets the list of package names that will be searched to find **BeanInfo** classes.

BeanInfo Interface

A Bean implementer who wants to provide explicit information about a Bean may provide a class that implements the **BeanInfo** interface and provides explicit information about, for example, methods, properties, and events of that Bean. The **BeanInfo** interface has the following methods:

- **getBeanDescriptor**() returns a **BeanDescriptor** that provides overall information about this Bean, such as its displayName and customizer.

- **getPropertyDescriptors**() returns an array of **PropertyDescriptors** describing the editable properties supported by this Bean.

- **getMethodDescriptors**() returns an array of **MethodDescriptors** describing the externally visible methods supported by this Bean.

- **getEventSetDescriptors**() returns an array of **EventSetDescriptors** describing the kinds of events fired by this Bean.

- **getDefaultPropertyIndex**() returns the index of the default property in the **PropertyDescriptor** array.

- **getDefaultEventIndex**() returns the index of the default event in the **EventSetDescriptor** array.

- **getAdditionalBeanInfo**() returns an arbitrary collection of other **BeanInfo** objects that provide additional information on this Bean.

- **getIcon**(int iconKind) returns an **Image** object that can be used to represent the Bean in, for example, toolboxes and toolbars.

SimpleBeanInfo Class

The **SimpleBeanInfo** class is a support class to make it easier for people to provide **BeanInfo** classes. It defaults to providing "noop" information, and it can be selectively overridden to provide more explicit information on chosen topics. When the introspector sees the noop values, it will apply low-level introspection and design patterns to automatically analyze the target Bean.

This class implements the **BeanInfo** interface, and has this default constructor:

- **SimpleBeanInfo**()

And, it has the following methods:

- **getBeanDescriptor**() returns a **BeanDescriptor** that provides overall information about this Bean, such as its displayName and customizer.

- **getPropertyDescriptors**() returns an array of **PropertyDescriptors** describing the editable properties supported by this Bean.

- **getMethodDescriptors**() returns an array of **MethodDescriptors** describing the externally visible methods supported by this Bean.

- **getEventSetDescriptors**() returns an array of **EventSetDescriptors** describing the kinds of events fired by this Bean.

- **getDefaultPropertyIndex**() returns the index of the default property in the **PropertyDescriptor** array.

- **getDefaultEventIndex**() returns the index of the default event in the **Event-SetDescriptor** array.

- **getAdditionalBeanInfo**() returns an arbitrary collection of other **BeanInfo** objects that provide additional information on this Bean.

- **getIcon**(int iconKind) returns an **Image** object that can be used to represent the Bean in toolboxes, toolbars, etc.

- **loadImage**(String resouceName) loads and returns an **Image** object that can be used to represent the Bean in, for example, toolboxes and toolbars.

FeatureDescriptor Class

The **FeatureDescriptor** class is the common base class for such classes as **PropertyDescriptor, EventSetDescriptor,** and **MethodDescriptor**. It supports some common information that can be set and retrieved for any of the introspection descriptors. In addition it provides an extension mechanism so that arbitrary attribute/value pairs can be associated with a design feature. It has this default constructor:

- **FeatureDescriptor**()

And, it has the following methods:

- **getName**() returns the name (**String**) of this feature.

- **setName**(String name) sets the name of this feature.

- **getDisplayName**() returns the localized display name (**String**) of this feature.

- **setDisplayName**(String name) sets the localized display name of this feature.

- **getShortDescription**() returns the localized short description (**String**) of this feature.

- **setShortDescription**(String name) sets the localized short description of this feature.

- **isExpert**() returns true (boolean) if this feature is intended for expert users.

- **setExpert**(boolean expert) sets whether or not this feature is intended for expert users.

- **isHidden**() returns true (boolean) if this feature is intended for tools.

- **setHidden**(boolean expert) sets whether or not this feature is intended for tools.

- **setValue**(String attributeName, Object value) associates a named attribute with this feature.

- **getValue**(String attributeName) returns the value (Object) of the named attribute.

- **attributeNames**() returns an enumeration (**java.util.Enumeration**) of attribute names associated with this feature.

BeanDescriptor Class

The **BeanDescriptor** class provides global information about a Bean—including its Java class and displayName. It extends the **FeatureDescriptor** class, and it has the following constructors:

- **BeanDescriptor**(Class beanClass)

- **BeanDescriptor**(Class beanClass, Class customizerClass)

And, it has the following methods:

- **getBeanClass**() returns the **Class** object for this Bean.

- **getCustomizerClass**() returns the **Class** object for this Bean's customizer.

EventSetDescriptor Class

The **EventSetDescriptor** class describes a group of events that a given Bean fires. It extends the **FeatureDescriptor** class, and it has the following constructors:

- **EventSetDescriptor**(Class sourceClass, String eventSetName, Class listener-Type, String listenerMethodName)

- **EventSetDescriptor**(Class sourceClass, String eventSetName, Class listener-Type, String[ ] listenerMethodNames, String addListenerMethodName, String removeListenerMethodName)

- **EventSetDescriptor**(String eventSetName, Class listenerType, String[ ] listenerMethodNames, String addListenerMethodName, String removeListenerMethodName)

- **EventSetDescriptor**(String eventSetName, Class listenerType, MethodDescriptor[ ] listenerMethodDescriptors, String addListenerMethodName, String removeListenerMethodName)

And, it has the following methods:

- **getListenerType**() returns the **Class** object for the listener of this event set.

- **getListenerMethods**() returns an array of **Methods** for the listener of this event set.

- **getListenerMethodDescriptors**() returns an array of **MethodDescriptors** for the listener of this event set.

- **getAddListenMethod**() returns the method used to register a listener at the event source.

- **getRemoveListenMethod**() returns the method used to remove a listener at the event source.

- **getUnicast**() returns true (boolean) if the event source is unicast.

- **setUnicast**(boolean unicast) marks the event source as unicast (or not).

- **isInDefaultEventSet**() returns true (boolean) if this event set is in the default event set.

- **setInDefaultEventSet**() marks this event set as in the default event set.

MethodDescriptor Class

The **MethodDescriptor** class describes a particular method that a Bean supports for external access from other components. It extends the **FeatureDescriptor** class, and it has the following constructors:

■ **MethodDescriptor**(Method method)

■ **MethodDescriptor**(Method method, ParameterDescriptor[] paramDesc)

And, it has the following methods:

■ **getMethod**() returns the low-level description (**Method**) of this method.

■ **getParameterDescriptors**() returns the array of **ParameterDescriptors** of this method.

ParameterDescriptor Class

The **ParameterDescriptor** class allows Bean implementers to provide additional information on each of its parameters. It extends the **FeatureDescriptor** class, and it has the default constructor:

■ **ParamenterDescriptor**()

PropertyDescriptor Class

The **PropertyDescriptor** class describes one property that a Bean exports via a pair of accessor methods. It extends the **FeatureDescriptor** class, and it has the following constructors:

■ **PropertyDescriptor**(String propertyName, Class beanClass)

■ **PropertyDescriptor**(String propertyName, Class beanClass, String getterName, String setterName)

■ **PropertyDescriptor**(String propertyName, Method getter, Method setter)

And, it has the following methods:

- **getPropertyType**() returns a **Class** object that describes the type information for this property.

- **getReadMethod**() returns a **Method** object that describes the method that should be used to read the property value.

- **getWriteMethod**() returns a **Method** object that describes the method that should be used to write the property value.

- **isBound**() returns true (boolean) if this property is a bound property.

- **setBound**(boolean bound) marks this property as bound (or not).

- **isConstrained**() returns true (boolean) if this property is a constrained property.

- **setConstrained**(boolean constrained) marks this property as constrained (or not).

- **getPropertyEditorClass**() returns any explicit **PropertyEditor** class that has been registered for this property.

- **setPropertyEditorClass**(Class propertyEditorClass) associates an explicit **PropertyEditor** class with this property.

IndexedPropertyDescriptor Class

The **IndexedPropertyDescriptor** class describes one indexed property that a Bean exports via a pair of indexed accessor methods. It extends the **PropertyDescriptor** class, and it has the following constructors:

- **IndexedPropertyDescriptor**(String propertyName, Class beanClass)

- **IndexedPropertyDescriptor**(String propertyName, Class beanClass, String getterName, String setterName, String indexedGetterName, String indexedSetterName)

- **PropertyDescriptor**(String propertyName, Method getter, Method setter, Method indexedGetter, Method indexedSetter)

And, it has the following methods:

- **getIndexedPropertyType**() returns a **Class** object that describes the type information for this indexed property.

- **getIndexedReadMethod**() returns a **Method** object that describes the method that should be used to read an indexed property value.

- **getIndexedWriteMethod**() returns a **Method** object that describes the method that should be used to write an indexed property value.

Customizer Interface

A customizer class provides a complete custom GUI for customizing a target Bean. Customizers must implement the **Customizer** interface, and they should inherit from the **java.awt.Component** class so it can be instantiated inside an AWT dialog or panel. Each customizer should have a null constructor.

The **Customizer** interface has the following methods:

- **setObject**(Object bean) sets the Bean to be customized.

- **addPropertyChangeListener**(PropertyChangeListener listener) adds a **PropertyChangeListener** to the listener list.

- **removePropertyChangeListener**(PropertyChangeListener listener) removes a **PropertyChangeListener** from the listener list.

PropertyEditor Interface

A **PropertyEditor** class provides support for GUIs that want to allow users to edit a property value of a given type. Each class must implement the **PropertyEditor** interface, and it should have a null constructor.

The PropertyEditor interface has the following methods:

- **getValue**() returns the value (**Object**) of this property.

- **setValue**(Object value) sets the value of this property.

- **isPaintable**() returns true (boolean) if the class will honor the *paintValue*() method.

- **paintValue**(java.awt.Graphic gfx, java.awt.Rectangle box) paints a representation of this property value into a given area of screen real estate.

- **getJavaInitializationString**() returns a fragment of Java code that can be used to initialize a variable with this property value.

- **getAsText**() returns this property value as a user-editable string.

- **setAsText**(String text) sets this property value by parsing a given string.

- **getTags**() returns the tag values for this property.

- **supportsCustomEditor**() returns true (boolean) if the **PropertyEditor** can provide a custom editor.

- **getCustomEditor**() returns a **java.awt.Component** that will allow a user to directly edit this property value.

- **addPropertyChangeListener**(PropertyChangeListener listener) adds a **PropertyChangeListener** to the listener list.

- **removePropertyChangeListener**(PropertyChangeListener listener) removes a **PropertyChangeListener** from the listener list.

PropertyEditorManager Class

The **PropertyEditorManager** class can be used to locate a property editor for any given type name. It has the following static methods:

- **registerEditor**(Class targetType, Class editorClass) registers a property editor of the specified editor class for the given target type.

- **findEditor**(Class targetType) returns a PropertyEditor for the given target type.

- **getEditorSearchPath**() returns the array of package names (**String**[ ]) that will be searched to find property editors.

- **setEditorSearchPath**(String[ ] path) changes the list of package names that will be searched to find property editors.

PropertyEditorSupport Class

The **PropertyEditorSupport** class is a utility class. It implements the **Property-Editor** interface, and it has the following constructors:

- **PropertyEditorSupport**()

- **PropertyEditorSupport**(Object source)

And, it has the following methods:

- **getValue**() returns the value (**Object**) of this property.

- **setValue**(Object value) sets the value of this property.

- **isPaintable**() returns true (boolean) if the class will honor the *paintValue()* method.

- **paintValue**(java.awt.Graphic gfx, java.awt.Rectangle box) paints a representation of this property value into a given area of screen real estate.

- **getJavaInitializationString**() returns a fragment of Java code that can be used to initialize a variable with this property value.

- **getAsText**() returns this property value as a user-editable string.

- **setAsText**(String text) sets this property value by parsing a given string.

- **getTags**() returns the tag values for this property.

- **supportsCustomEditor**() returns true (boolean) if the **PropertyEditor** can provide a custom editor.

- **getCustomEditor**() returns a **java.awt.Component** that will allow a user to directly edit this property value.

- **addPropertyChangeListener**(PropertyChangeListener listener) adds a **Prop-ertyChangeListener** to the listener list.

- **removePropertyChangeListener**(PropertyChangeListener listener) removes a **PropertyChangeListener** from the listener list.

- **firePropertyChange**() reports to any interested listeners that this property has been modified.

SAMPLE DATA ACCESS BEANS

In this section, we take the **SelectServlet** example (see Listings 12-4 and 12-5) and redo it using JavaBeans (see Figure 20-2). The **SelectServletBean** example (see Listings 20-1 to 20-3) preserves the same user functionality and interface, but it performs data access on the server using JavaBeans. We have intentionly used an event adapter for communication between **SelectServletBean** and **DataAccessBean** for illustrative purpose.

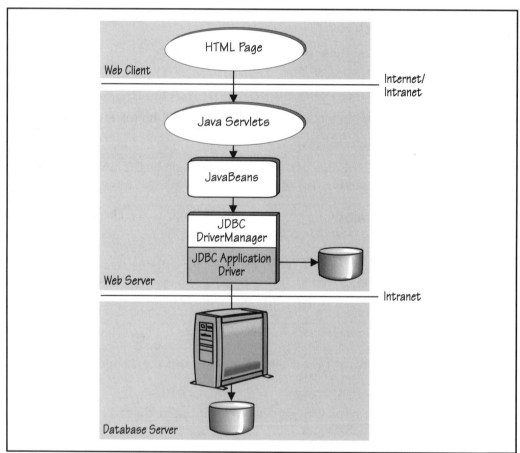

Figure 20-2. JDBC Usage Scenario—Java Servlets/JavaBeans.

Listing 20-1. The SelectServletBean HTML Page.

```
<!
  SelectServletBean.html
!>

<html>
```

```
    <form method="post"

action="http://woodview2.stl.ibm.com:8080/servlet/SelectServletBean">
    ArcWorld building query:<p>
    Enter the data source, user id, and password information:<br>
      <input size=20 name="DATABASE"> <input size=20 name="LOGIN">
      <input size=20 type="PASSWORD" name='PASSWORD'><br>
      <br>
    Select the city that you would like to query:<br>
      <input type="radio" name="CITY" value="*"> All cities <br>
     <input type="radio" name="CITY" value="Washington"> Washington <br>
      <input type="radio" name="CITY" value="Paris"> Paris <br>
      <input type="radio" name="CITY" value="Beijing"> Beijing <p>
      <input type="submit"> <input type="reset">
  </form>
</html>
```

Listing 20-2. The SelectServletBean Class.

```
/*
 * SelectServletBean.java
 */

import java.beans.*;

import javax.servlet.*;
import javax.servlet.http.*;

import java.sql.*;

import java.io.*;
import java.util.*;

public class SelectServletBean
  extends HttpServlet
{
    public DataAccessBean daBean = null;
    public PropertyChangeAdapter adapter = new PropertyChangeAdapter();
    public boolean queryStatus = false;

    public synchronized void setQueryStatus(boolean b)
    {
        queryStatus = b;
    }
```

```java
public synchronized boolean getQueryStatus()
{
    return queryStatus;
}

public void doPost (HttpServletRequest req, HttpServletResponse res)
    throws ServletException, IOException
{
    int index;

    res.setContentType("text/html");
    ServletOutputStream out = res.getOutputStream();
    out.println("<html>");
    out.println("<head><title>SelectServletBean</title></head>");
    out.println("<body>");

    String database = req.getParameter("DATABASE");
    String login = req.getParameter("LOGIN");
    String password = req.getParameter("PASSWORD");
    String city = req.getParameter("CITY");

    String where;
    if (city.equals("*"))
        where = "";
    else
        where = " WHERE city = " + "'" + city + "'";
    String sql = "SELECT name, type, city FROM Building" + where;

    daBean = new DataAccessBean(database, login, password, sql);
    daBean.addPropertyChangeListener(adapter);
    daBean.execQuery();

    if (getQueryStatus()) {
        out.println("<table border='border'>");
        out.println("<caption> Buildings in the ArcWorld database: " +
            "</caption>");

        String n1 = daBean.getColArray(0);
        String n2 = daBean.getColArray(1);
        String n3 = daBean.getColArray(2);
        out.println("<tr> <th>" + n1 + " <th>" + n2 +
            " <th>" + n3);

        int numElements = daBean.getMaxResultArrayLen();
        int currentElement = 0;
```

```java
            index = 0;

            while(currentElement < numElements &&
              daBean.getResultArray(currentElement) != null) {
                String v1 = daBean.getResultArray(currentElement++);
                String v2 = daBean.getResultArray(currentElement++);
                String v3 = daBean.getResultArray(currentElement++);
                out.println("<tr> <td>" + v1 +" <td>" + v2 +
                    " <td>" + v3);
            }

        } else {
            out.println(daBean.getErrorMsg());
        }

        out.println("</table>");
      out.println("</body></html>");
    }

    public String getServletInfo() {
        return "A servlet that performs Building queries on the " +
            "ArcWorld database";
    }

    class PropertyChangeAdapter implements PropertyChangeListener
    {
        public void propertyChange(PropertyChangeEvent e)
        {
            String status = new String(e.getNewValue().toString());

            if(status.equals("true"))
            {
                if( daBean.getErrorMsg() != null)
                {
                    setQueryStatus(false);
                }
                else{
                    setQueryStatus(true);
                }
            }
        }
    }

    }
}
```

Listing 20-3. The DataAccessBean Class.

```java
/*
 * DataAcessBean.java
 */

import java.beans.*;

import java.sql.*;

import java.io.*;

public class DataAccessBean
{

    public DataAccessBean(String db, String login, String pw, String query)
    {
        database = db;
        user = login;
        password = pw;
        sql = query;

        resultArray = new String[getMaxResultArrayLen()];
        colArray = new String[getMaxColArrayLen()];
        numColumns = 0;
        fillStatus = false;

        changes = new PropertyChangeSupport(this);
    }

    public void execQuery()
    {
        String url = "jdbc:odbc:" + database;
        String driver = "sun.jdbc.odbc.JdbcOdbcDriver";

        Connection con = null;
        Statement stmt = null;
        ResultSet rs = null;
        ResultSetMetaData rsmd = null;

        String result;
        int index = 0;
        int numCols = 0;
        String colValue = null;
```

```java
    try {
        Class.forName(driver);

        con = DriverManager.getConnection(url, user, password);
        stmt = con.createStatement();

        rs = stmt.executeQuery(sql);

        rsmd = rs.getMetaData();
        numCols = rsmd.getColumnCount();
        setNumColumns(numCols);

        for (int i = 1; i <= numCols; i++)
        {
            colValue = new String("");
            colValue = rsmd.getColumnLabel(i);
            setColArray(index, colValue);
            index++;
        }

        index = 0;
        while (rs.next())
        {
            for (int i = 1; i <= numCols; i++)
            {
                result = rs.getString(i);
                setResultArray(index, result);
                index++ ;
            }
        }

        setFillStatus(true);

        rs.close();
        stmt.close();
        con.close();

    } catch (Exception e) {
        errMessage = e.getMessage();
        return;
    }

}

public void addPropertyChangeListener(PropertyChangeListener l)
```

```java
{
    changes.addPropertyChangeListener(1);
}

public void removePropertyChangeListener(PropertyChangeListener 1)
{
    changes.removePropertyChangeListener(1);
}

public synchronized boolean getFillStatus()
{
    return fillStatus;
}

public void setFillStatus(boolean newValue)
{
    boolean oldValue = fillStatus;
    fillStatus = newValue;

    Boolean oldObj = new Boolean(oldValue);
    Boolean newObj = new Boolean(newValue);

    changes.firePropertyChange("fillStatus", oldObj, newObj);
}

public String getColArray(int index){
    return this.colArray[index];
}

public void setColArray(int index, String value)
{
    this.colArray[index] = value;
}

public String getResultArray(int index){
    return this.resultArray[index];
}

public void setResultArray(int index, String value)
{
    this.resultArray[index] = value;
}

public void setNumColumns(int n)
{
```

```
    numColumns = n;
}

public int getNumColumns()
{
    return numColumns;
}

public int getMaxResultArrayLen()
{
    return maxResultArrayLen;
}

public void setMaxResultArrayLen(int i)
{
    maxResultArrayLen = i;
}

public int getMaxColArrayLen()
{
    return maxColArrayLen;
}

public void setMaxColArrayLen(int i)
{
    maxColArrayLen = i;
}

public String getErrorMsg() {
    return errMessage;
}

//bean properties
private String database;
private String user;
private String password;
private String sql;

// bean properties associated with query results
private String[] resultArray = null;
private String[] colArray = null;
private int maxResultArrayLen = 1000;
private int maxColArrayLen = 30;
private boolean fillStatus = false;
private int numColumns;
```

```
private String errMessage = null;

// used for firing events
private PropertyChangeSupport changes = null;

}
```

CONCLUSION

The JavaBeans architecture provides a powerful mechanism to build reusable software components. It has the potential to break up the traditional monolithic application development paradigm. A Bean is essentially a *plug-and-play* software component. Our sample data access Beans provide an inkling of what is going to come. Very soon, you should be able to use your favorite Beans for each aspect of your application—for example, network connection, data access, and report generation. All you need to do is to use a builder tool to connect Beans together and, *voila*, you have a full-fledged application in place—at least in principle.

In the next chapter, we will discuss Enterprise JavaBeans, the sibling of JavaBeans both in name and by design. JavaBeans are generic and lightweight. These Beans may be visible or invisible, but they are more likely to be visible. They can run on the client or server, but they are more likely to be seen on the client (our sample data access Beans, nonetheless, were server Beans). Enterprise JavaBeans, on the other hand, are specific and heavyweight. Enterprise Beans are invisible, with no GUI whatsoever. They are designed to run on the server. In fact, they are designed to be accessed remotely, as we shall see.

Chapter 21

Enterprise JavaBeans

concepts

The publication of the Enterprise JavaBeans (EJB) Specification Version 1.0 was the most significant event in the Java scene since JDK 1.1. In JDK 1.1, Java for enterprise client/server computing was enabled with the introduction of JDBC, RMI, and JavaBeans. JDBC made data access in Java possible. RMI brought Java distributed object computing. And JavaBeans provided the Java component model and thus plug-and-play and reuse. All of these are important to enterprise client/server computing. However, by themselves, they have helped mainly in building client-side applications or components. Little support is provided for building robust and scalable server components.

EJB is designed specifically to facilitate the building of robust and scalable server components. It provides support for some of the key missing functionality required for server components: global naming, distributed transactions, transparent persistence, and security. EJB does this by adopting and integrating the services provided by a number of existing and new Java facilities. The facilities include Java Naming and Directory Interfaces (JNDI), Java Transaction Services (JTS), and Java Security.

EJB is much more than a collection of these integrated services: JNDI, RMI, JTS, and Java Security. It actually provides a *new and high-level programming paradigm* for building enterprise server components and enterprise client/server applications. EJB provides declarative policies on transaction, state management, and security. It therefore separates the concerns of system programming (such as naming, distribution, transaction, persistence, and security) from those of business programming (business methods). It provides a framework whereby all system programming tasks are automatically taken care of, given a few simple rules. This allows server component builders to concentrate on building *business objects*.

In the following sections, we will first give an overview of EJB and the EJB architecture. We will then discuss in detail the two types of enterprise Beans: *Session Beans* and *Entity Beans*. We will finish by examining the EJB APIs and presenting two sample enterprise Beans.

OVERVIEW OF EJB

EJB defines a component model for the development, deployment, and execution of Java applications based on a *multitier, distributed object architecture*. It extends the JavaBeans component model to support *server components*. The multitier approach supports a *thin-client* application architecture required by Web-based business applications. It increases the application's flexibility, manageability, performance, reliability, reusability, and scalability.

Enterprise Beans execute within an *EJB server* that provides a set of runtime services such as *threading, transaction control, state management, security,* and *resource sharing*. Enterprise Beans are *portable* across any EJB server and can run on any platform. An EJB server provides a container for the enterprise Bean, called the *EJB container*, that implements the services for one or more classes of enterprise Beans. A typical EJB server is shown in Figure 21-1. It can be accessed through IIOP from a client (either through RMI/IIOP from a Java client or through CORBA/IIOP from a non-Java client).

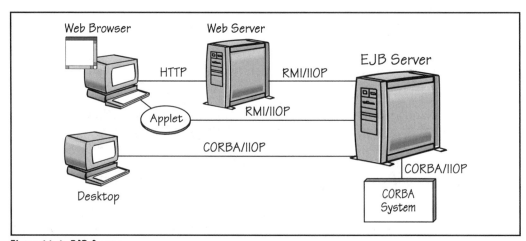

Figure 21-1. EJB Server.

Session Beans and Entity Beans

EJB defines two types of enterprise Beans:

- Session Bean
- Entity Bean

Support for session Beans is mandatory for an EJB 1.0-compliant container. Support for entity Beans is optional for an EJB 1.0-compliant container.

A typical *session Bean* has the following characteristics:

- Does not represent data in a database
- May update *shared data* in an underlying database
- Executes on behalf of *a single client*
- Can be *transaction-aware*
- Is relatively *short-lived*
- Is *removed* when the EJB server crashes

A typical *entity Bean* has the following characteristics:

- Represents *data* in a database
- Allows *shared access* from multiple clients
- Is *transactional*
- Can be *long-lived* (as long as the data is in the database)
- Survives crashes of the EJB server

EJB Developer Roles

The EJB component architecture means that there is not one single type of EJB developer constructing monolithic applications. Instead, there are various types of EJB developers; each plays an important *role* in developing and deploying applications. These roles include:

- ***EJB server provider.*** The server provider implements the *EJB server*, which handles distributed object, distributed transaction, and other system services for enterprise Beans managed by containers. Potential EJB server implementations may be based on CORBA platforms, database systems, transaction processing monitors, and Web servers. The EJB server provider usually implements containers for use with its EJB server.

- ***EJB container provider.*** The container provider produces an *EJB container*, which manages and interfaces with enterprise Beans at run time. The container can implement the *session Bean* contract or the *entity Bean* contract for one or more data sources. EJB specifies a standard API (the *EJB API)* between the container and enterprise Beans that it manages. The container provider also makes *tools* available for the deployer to use in deploying enterprise Beans in the runtime environment.

■ **Enterprise Bean provider.** The enterprise Bean provider develops *enterprise Beans* to implement specific *business tasks*. It relies on the EJB container provider for providing distribution, transactions, persistence, and security services. The enterprise Bean provider must package enterprise Beans and related items into an *ejb-jar* file.

■ **Deployer.** The deployer takes enterprise Beans produced by an enterprise Bean provider and *deploys* them in a specific operational environment. It may also *customize* the functionality of an enterprise Bean. Typically, it uses tools provided by an EJB container provider to modify the required *deployment descriptors* and *environment properties*.

■ **Application assembler.** The application assembler uses the client view contract of the enterprise Beans deployed at the server to assemble *client applications*. The application assembler may also produce new enterprise Beans by combining existing ones. The new enterprise Beans and related items must be packaged into an *ejb-jar* file.

Enterprise Beans as Components

An enterprise Bean is created and managed at run time by a *container*. Client access is mediated by the container and the *EJB server*. A client always uses the *same API for object creation, lookup, and destruction*, regardless of how an enterprise Bean is implemented and what function it provides.

A client's view of an enterprise Bean, however, is defined by the *enterprise Bean provider*; it is not affected by the container and the EJB server. An enterprise Bean can represent a *stateless* service, a conversational (*stateful*) session with a particular client, or a persistent *entity* object shared among multiple clients.

An enterprise Bean can be customized at deployment time by editing its *deployment descriptors* and *environment properties*.

EJB Contracts

EJB specifies the contracts (see Figure 21-2) between a client and a container, between a container and the enterprise Beans that it manages, and for ejb-jar files.

These contracts must be fulfilled to ensure that the product of each EJB developer role is compatible with the product of the other roles.

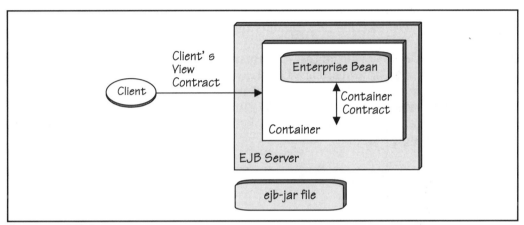

Figure 21-2. EJB Contracts.

Client's View Contract

This is a contract between a client and a container. It provides a uniform *programming model* for client applications using enterprise Beans as components. Both the enterprise Bean provider and the EJB container provider have obligations to fulfill the contract. This contract includes:

- **Object identity.** A client expects that an EJB object (a proxy object that represents an enterprise Bean, to be discussed later) has a unique identifier. The container provider is responsible for generating a unique identifier for each session EJB object. For entity Beans, the enterprise Bean provider is responsible for supplying a unique primary key that the container embeds into the EJB object's identifier.

- **Home interface.** An enterprise Bean provider is responsible for supplying an enterprise Bean's home interface, which extends **javax.ejb.EJBHome**. A home interface defines zero or more *create()* methods. A home interface for entity Beans optionally defines *find<METHOD>* methods. A client locates an enterprise Bean's home interface through JNDI.

  The enterprise Bean provider is responsible for the implementation of the *ejbCreate* methods in the enterprise Bean class, whose signatures must match those of the *create* methods. The container is responsible for delegating a client-invoked *create* method to the matching *ejbCreate* method on an enterprise Bean.

The entity Bean provider is responsible for the implementation of the *ejbFind<METHOD>* methods in the entity Bean class, whose signature must match those of the *find<METHOD>* methods. The container is responsible for delegating a client-invoked *find<METHOD>* method to the matching *ejbFind<METHOD>* method on an entity Bean.

- **Method invocation.** An enterprise Bean defines a remote interface, which extends **java.rmi.Remote**. This interface defines the business methods callable by a client. The enterprise Bean provider is also responsible for the implementation of the business methods in the enterprise Bean class. The container is responsible for delegating a client-invoked business method to its implementation in the enterprise Bean class.

Container Contract

This is a contract between an enterprise Bean and its container. Both the enterprise Bean provider and the EJB container provider have obligations to fulfill the contract. This contract includes:

- **State management callbacks.** For a session Bean, this includes the state management callbacks defined by the **javax.ejb.SessionBean** and the **javax.ejb.SessionSynchronization** interfaces. For an entity Bean, this includes the state management callbacks defined by the **javax.ejb.EntityBean** interface. The container invokes the callback methods defined by these interfaces at the appropriate times to notify the instance of any important events.

- **EJB context.** The container passes a **javax.ejb.SessionContext** interface to a session Bean instance when it is created. The instance uses it to obtain various information and services from its container. Similarly, an entity Bean instance uses the **javax.ejb.EntityContext** interface to communicate with its container.

- **Environment properties.** These include the environment properties (**java. util.Properties**) that a container makes available to its enterprise Bean.

- **Services.** These include the list of services a container provides for its enterprise Bean.

Ejb-jar File

An *ejb-jar* file is a standard format used by EJB tools for packaging enterprise Beans. Both the enterprise Bean provider and the application assembler have obligations to fulfill the contract. This contract includes:

- JAR file manifest entries that describe the contents of the ejb-jar file
- Java class files for the enterprise Beans
- Enterprise Bean deployment descriptors that the container needs to manage the enterprise Beans
- Enterprise Bean environment properties that the enterprise Beans require at run time

EJB ARCHITECTURE

The key components of the EJB architecture are shown in Figure 21-3. These apply to both session Beans and entity Beans, except that, for session Beans, there are no *find* methods. These components include (many have already been mentioned):

- **EJB server.** The EJB server provides an environment to support the execution of applications developed using enterprise Beans. It manages and coordinates the allocation of system resources. An EJB server may have multiple EJB containers.

- **EJB container.** The EJB container provides a *naming context* for the enterprise Bean. It manages the *life cycle* and *state* (if applicable) of the enterprise Bean. It also coordinates distributed *transactions* and implements *security*.

- **Enterprise Bean.** The enterprise Bean implements *a specific set of methods* that allow the EJB container to manage and invoke the object.

- **EJB context.** The EJB context is used by both the enterprise Bean and the EJB container to coordinate, for example, *transactions, persistence,* and *security.*

- **EJB object.** The EJB object is an *external representation* of the enterprise Bean, generated by the EJB container, that client applications interact with. It exposes only *application-related interfaces*. All client requests are *intercepted by the EJB container* to insert transaction, state, and security rules on all operations.

- **EJBHome.** The EJB home provides methods to *create* and *remove* EJB objects. For entity Beans, it also provides methods to *find* EJB objects based on primary keys.

- **Deployment descriptor.** The deployment descriptor is used to establish the runtime service settings for an enterprise Bean, including the environment properties. They can be set at application deployment or application assembly time.

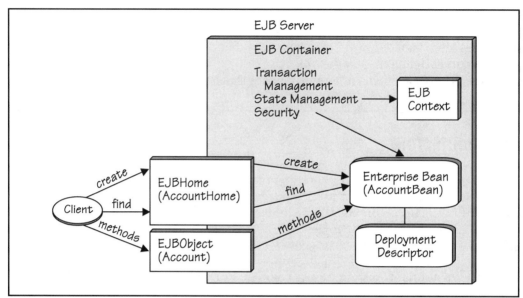

Figure 21-3. EJB Architecture.

Support for Naming

EJB relies on *JNDI* to locate the *home interface* for an enterprise Bean. For example, the home interface for *Account* EJB objects can be located using the following code segment:

```
Context ctx = new InitialContext();
AccountHome accountHome = (AccountHome)
    ctx.lookup("containerManaged.AccountHome");
```

Support for Distribution

Support for *remote client access* to an enterprise Bean is through *RMI*. RMI allows a client to invoke an enterprise Bean using distributed object protocols, including the industry-standard *IIOP* protocol. RMI makes access to an enterprise Bean *location independent* to a client programmer.

The objects involved in client/server access are shown in Figure 21-4. The following objects are present in the client's JVM (Java Virtual Machine):

- A stub for the enterprise Bean's home object
- A stub for the EJB object

The following objects are present in the EJB container's JVM (both objects are RMI remote objects):

■ The enterprise Bean's home object
■ The EJB object, which is a proxy for the enterprise Bean

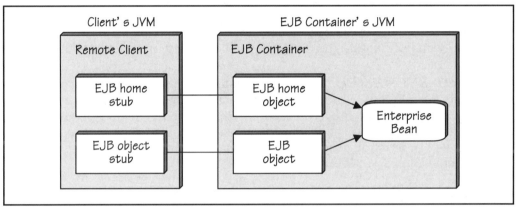

Figure 21-4. EJB Support for Distribution.

Support for Transactions

Support for distributed transactions is one of the key features of EJB. EJB allows an application developer to write an application that atomically updates data in multiple databases that are possibly distributed across multiple sites. The sites may use EJB servers and EJB containers from different vendors.

The burden of managing transactions is put on the EJB container and the EJB server—not on the enterprise Bean. The EJB container implements the *declarative transaction scope* that we will discuss later. The EJB server implements the necessary low-level transaction protocols, such as the *distributed two-phase commit protocol* and transaction context propagation. EJB supports *flat transactions*, which is modeled after the OMG Object Transaction Service (OTS). An enterprise Bean that is transaction-enabled corresponds to the **Transactional-Object** described in OTS.

EJB is a high-level component architecture that is designed to hide complexity from application developers. Therefore, most clients and enterprise Beans do not need to access transaction management programmatically. The clients and enterprise Beans that have to programmatically control transaction scope should use the **javax.jts.UserTransaction** interface, which is part of the Java Transaction Service (JTS) API and is the only JTS interface that the EJB container provider must implement.

Declarative Transaction Management

As mentioned before, every client method invocation on an enterprise Bean is interposed by the EJB container. The interposition allows for delegating the transaction management responsibility to the EJB container. The declarative transaction management is controlled by a *transaction attribute* associated with each enterprise Bean's container. The transaction attribute is specified in the enterprise Bean's deployment descriptor. It can be associated with an individual method or the entire enterprise Bean. EJB defines the following values for the transaction attribute:

- *TX_NOT_SUPPORTED.* The container must always invoke an enterprise Bean that has the TX_NOT_SUPPORTED transaction attribute without a transaction scope. If a client calls with a transaction scope, the container suspends it before delegating the method call to the enterprise Bean. The container resumes the suspended transaction scope when the method call on the enterprise Bean has completed.

- *TX_BEAN_MANAGED.* An enterprise Bean with the TX_BEAN_MANAGED attribute can use the **javax.jts.UserTransaction** interface to demarcate transaction scope.

- *TX_REQUIRED.* The container must always invoke an enterprise Bean that has the TX_REQUIRED transaction attribute within a transaction scope. If a client calls with a transaction scope, the container invokes the enterprise Bean's method in the client's transaction scope. If the client calls without a transaction scope, the container automatically starts a new transaction before delegating the method call to the enterprise Bean. It then attempts to commit the transaction when the method call on the enterprise Bean has completed and before the method result is sent to the client.

- *TX_SUPPORTS.* An enterprise Bean that has the TX_SUPPORTS attribute is invoked in the client's transaction scope. If the client does not have a transaction scope, the enterprise Bean is also invoked without a transaction scope.

- *TX_REQUIRES_NEW.* The container must always invoke an enterprise Bean that has the TX_REQUIRES_NEW transaction attribute within a new transaction scope. The container starts a new transaction before delegating the method call to the enterprise Bean. The container attempts to commit the transaction when the method call on the enterprise Bean has completed and before the method result is sent to the client. If a client calls with a transaction scope, the transaction is suspended before the new transaction is started and is resumed when the new transaction has completed.

- *TX_MANDATORY.* An enterprise Bean that has the TX_MANDATORY attribute is always invoked in the scope of the client's transaction. If the client calls without a transaction scope, the container throws the **TransactionRequired** exception.

Transaction Isolation Levels

The enterprise Bean provider must specify the transaction isolation level in the deployment descriptor. The possible isolation levels are:

- **TRANSACTION_READ_UNCOMMITTED**
- **TRANSACTION_READ_COMMITTED**
- **TRANSACTION_REPEATABLE_READ**
- **TRANSACTION_SERIALIZABLE**

These isolation levels correspond to the ones specified in JDBC (see Chapter 7, "JDBC in a Nutshell"). The EJB container uses the transaction isolation level information in the following way:

- For session Beans and entity Beans with Bean-managed persistence (to be discussed shortly), the container ensures that the specified transaction isolation level is set on the database connections used by the enterprise Bean at the start of each transaction.
- For entity Beans with container-managed persistence (to be discussed shortly), the database access calls generated by the container tools must achieve the specified isolation level.

Support for Security

The EJB architecture puts most of the burden of implementing security management on the EJB container and the EJB server—not on the enterprise Bean. Support for security includes the following components:

- Java Security API defined in the **java.security** package. Specifically, the EJB architecture uses the **java.security.Identity** class as the API to describe a user identity for security purposes. The identity can describe a specific user or a security role.

- Security-related methods in the **javax.ejb.EJBContext** interface. These allow an enterprise Bean to obtain the identity of the client that invoked the current method:

  - **getCallerIdentity()**
  - **isCallerInRole**(java.security.Identy ident)

- Security-related attributes specified in the deployment descriptor. The deployment descriptor includes access control entries that allow the container to perform run-time security management on behalf of the enterprise Bean. Each entry can be for an individual method or for the entire enterprise Bean. The entry consists of a list of identities of the type **java.security.Identity**.

At run time, when an enterprise Bean makes a call to an underlying resource manager or invokes another enterprise Bean, this security identity will be associated with the call. The identity consists of two parts:

◆ *RunAsMode*—specifies whether a method should execute with the identity of the client (CLIENT_IDENTITY), the identity of a system account (SYSTEM_IDENTITY), or the identity of a specified user account (SPECIFIED_IDENTITY).

◆ *RunAsIdentity*—specifies the user identity if the value of *RunAsMode* is SPECIFIED_IDENTITY.

EJB-CORBA Mapping

The EJB-CORBA mapping is specified to ensure interoperability for multi-vendor EJB environments (see Figure 21-5). The mapping covers:

■ *Mapping of naming*—specifies how COS Naming is used to locate the **EJB-Home** objects.

■ *Mapping of distribution*—defines the relationship between an enterprise Bean and a CORBA object, and the mapping of the Java RMI remote interfaces to OMG IDL.

■ *Mapping of transactions*—defines the mapping of the EJB transaction support to the OMG OTS (Object Transaction Service). This allows the propagation of transaction context through IIOP.

■ *Mapping of security*—defines the mapping of the security features in EJB to CORBA Security. This allows the propagation of security context through IIOP.

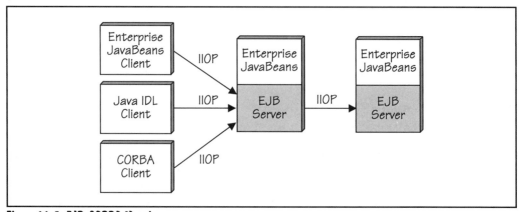

Figure 21-5. EJB-CORBA Mapping.

SESSION BEANS

A session Bean is a non-persistent object that implements some business logic running on the server. Session Beans are intended to be private resources used only by the client that created them. They are not shared among multiple clients, and they appear anonymous. A session EJB object handle can be held beyond the life of a client process by serializing the handle to persistent store. When the handle is later deserialized, the session EJB object it returns will work as long as the object still exists on the server. The home interface of the session Bean allows the client to create and remove the EJB object for a given session Bean.

An example session Bean (**AccountBean**) and the inheritance relationship between its interfaces and classes is shown in Figure 21-6. The session Bean provider is responsible for the following:

- Define a home interface (**AccountHome**) for the session Bean, which extends **javax.ejb.EJBHome**. The home interface must define one or more *create()* methods for the session Beans.
- Define the session Bean's remote interface (**Account**), which extends **javax.ejb.EJBObject.** The remote interface must define the business methods callable by a client.
- Write the business logic in the session Bean class (**AccountBean**), which extends **javax.ejb.SessionBean**. The session Bean class must define the *ejb-Create()* methods invoked at a session Bean creation.
- Specify the environment properties that the session Bean needs at run time.
- Define a deployment descriptor that specifies any deployment information that the session Bean provider wants to associate with the session Bean.

The EJB container provider (say, **DB2**) is responsible for supplying:

- The **DB2Home** class that provides the implementation of the **javax.ejb.EJB-Home** interface.
- The **DB2Remote** class that provides the implementation of the **javax.ejb. EJBObject** interface.
- The **DB2Bean** class that provides additional methods to allow the container to manage its session Beans.
- The **DB2MetaData** class that provides the implementation of the **javax.ejb. EJBMetaData** interface.

The tools provided by the EJB container provider (say, **DB2**) are responsible for the following:

- Generate the class (**DB2AccountHome**) that implements the session Bean's home interface.

- Generate the class (**DB2AccountRemote**) that implements the session Bean's remote interface. The tools also generate the associated stubs and skeletons.
- Generate the implementation of the session Bean class suitable for the container (**DB2AccountBean**).
- Generate the class (**DB2AccountMetaData**) that implements **javax.ejb.EJB-MetaData** interface for the session Bean.

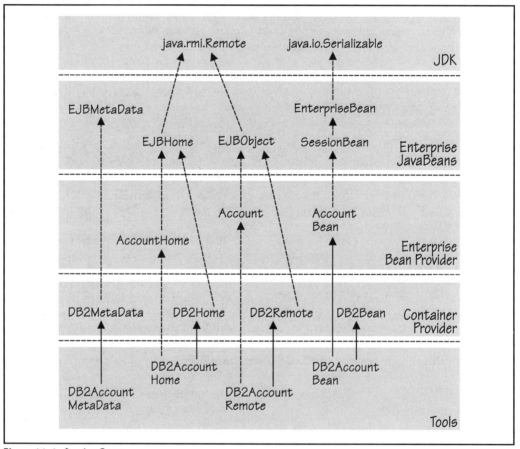

Figure 21-6. Session Beans.

The session Bean container manages the life cycle of the session Bean. To efficiently manage the size of its working set, the container may need to temporarily transfer the state of an idle session Bean to some form of secondary storage. The transfer from the working set to secondary storage is called *passivation*. The transfer back is called *activation*. The container may only passivate a session Bean when it is not in a transaction.

To help its container manage its state, a session Bean specifies in its deployment descriptor one of the following state management modes:

■ *STATELESS*—the session Bean contains no conversational state between methods; any instance can be used for any client.

■ *STATEFUL*—the session Bean contains conversational state that must be retained across methods and transactions.

In advanced cases, a session Bean's conversational state may contain open resources. In such cases, the session Bean developer must close and open the resources using the *ejbPassivate* and *ejbActivate* callback methods (part of the **javax.ejb.SessionBean** interface). A session Bean's conversational state is not transactional. To ensure a session Bean's conversational state is consistent with the state of its underlying database, the session Bean developer must use the callback methods of the **javax.ejb.SessionSynchronization** interface.

ENTITY BEANS

An entity Bean is a persistent object that represents an object view of an entity stored in a persistent storage. Multiple clients can access an entity Bean concurrently. The container that manages the entity Bean properly synchronizes access to the entity Bean using transactions. Each entity Bean has an identity—its primary key—that survives a crash and restart of its container. An entity EJB object handle can be held beyond the life of a client process by serializing the handle to persistent store. When the handle is later deserialized, the entity EJB object it returns will work as long as the entity still exists in persistent storage. The home interface of the entity Bean allows the client to create, loop up, and remove EJB objects for a given entity Bean.

An example entity Bean (**AccountBean**) and the inheritance relationship between its interfaces and classes is shown in Figure 21-7. The entity Bean provider is responsible for the following:

■ Define a home interface (**AccountHome**) for the entity Bean, which extends **javax.ejb.EJBHome**. The home interface must define one or more *create* and *find<METHOD>* methods for the entity Beans.
■ Define the entity Bean's remote interface (**Account**), which extends **javax.ejb.EJBObject.** The remote interface must define the business methods callable by a client.
■ Write the business logic in the entity Bean class (**AccountBean**), which extends **javax.ejb.EntityBean**. The Entity Bean class must define the *ejbCreate()* methods which are invoked when an Entity Bean is created.
■ Specify the environment properties that the entity Bean needs at run time.

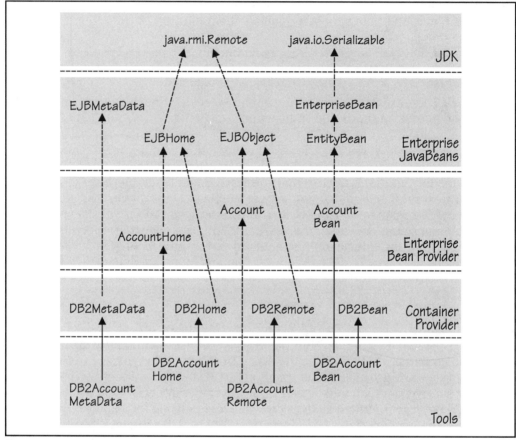

Figure 21-7. Entity Beans.

■ Define a deployment descriptor that specifies any deployment information that the entity Bean provider wants to associate with the entity Bean.

The EJB container provider (say, **DB2**) is responsible for supplying:

■ The **DB2Home** class that provides the implementation of the **javax.ejb.EJB-Home** interface.

■ The **DB2Remote** class that provides the implementation of the **javax.ejb. EJBObject** interface.

■ The **DB2Bean** class that provides additional methods to allow the container to manage its entity Beans.

■ The **DB2MetaData** class that provides the implementation of the **javax.ejb. EJBMetaData** interface.

The tools provided by the EJB container provider (say, **DB2**) are responsible for the following:

- Generate the class (**DB2AccountHome**) that implements the entity Bean's home interface.
- Generate the class (**DB2AccountRemote**) that implements the entity Bean's remote interface. The tools also generate the associated stubs and skeletons.
- Generate the implementation of the entity Bean class suitable for the container (**DB2AccountBean**).
- Generate the class (**DB2AccountMetaData**) that implements the **javax.ejb. EJBMetaData** interface for the entity Bean.

We mentioned that an entity Bean implements an object view of an entity stored in an underlying database. The protocol for transferring the state of the entity between the entity Bean's instance variables and the underlying database is referred to as *persistence*. EJB allows the entity Bean provider either to implement the entity Bean's persistence directly in the enterprise Bean's class (the so-called *Bean-managed persistence*) or to delegate the enterprise Bean's persistence to the container (the so-called *container-managed persistence*).

In the Bean-managed persistence case, the entity Bean provider writes database access calls (using, for example, JDBC or SQLJ) directly in the methods of the entity Bean class. The database access calls are performed in the *ejbCreate*, *ejbRemove*, *ejbFind<METHOD>*, *ejbLoad*, and *ejbStore* callback methods of the **javax.ejb. EntityBean** interface.

In the container-managed persistence case, the entity Bean provider does not write the database access calls in the enterprise Bean class. Instead, the EJB container provider's tools generate the database access calls at the enterprise Bean's deployment time. The enterprise Bean provider must specify in the *containerManaged-Fields* properties (of the **javax.ejb.EntityDescriptor** interface) the list of instance fields for which the EJB container provider tools must generate database access calls.

THE EJB API

The EJB API consists of interfaces and classes contained in the following three packages:

- javax.ejb: **EJBHome, EJBMetaData, EJBObject, Handle, EnterpriseBean, SessionBean, EntityBean, EJBContext, SessionContext, SessionSynchronization, EntityContext**
- javax.ejb.deployment: **DeploymentDescriptor, SessionDescriptor, Entity-Descriptor, AccessControlEntry, ControlDescriptor**
- javax.jts: **UserTransaction**

EJBHome Interface

The **EJBHome** interface is extended by each enterprise Bean's home interface. An enterprise Bean's home interface defines the methods that allow a client to create, find, and remove EJB objects. The **EJBHome** interface extends **java.rmi.Remote**, and it has the following methods:

- **getEJBMetaData**() returns the **EJBMetaData** object for the enterprise Bean, which allows the client to obtain metadata information about the enterprise Bean.

- **remove**(Handle handle) removes an EJB object identified by its handle.

- **remove**(Object primaryKey) removes an EJB object identified by its primary key.

EJBMetaData Interface

The **EJBMetaData** interface allows a client to obtain the enterprise Bean's metadata information. The class that implements this interface must be serializable. The **EJBMetaData** interface has the following methods:

- **getEJBHome**() returns the home (**EJBHome**) interface of the enterprise Bean.

- **getHomeInterfaceClass**() returns the **Class** object for the enterprise Bean's home interface.

- **getRemoteInterfaceClass**() returns the **Class** object for the enterprise Bean's remote interface.

- **isSession**() returns true (boolean) if the enterprise Bean's type is "session".

- **getPrimaryKeyClass**() returns the **Class** object for the enterprise Bean's primary key class.

EJBObject Interface

The **EJBObject** interface is extended by an enterprise Bean's remote interface. An enterprise Bean's remote interface provides the client's view of an EJB object. It defines the business methods callable by a client. The **EJBObject** interface extends **java.rmi.Remote**, and it has the following methods:

- **getEJBHome**() returns the enterprise Bean's home (**EJBHome**) interface.

- **getHandle**() returns a **Handle** for this EJB object.

- **getPrimaryKey**() returns the primary key (**Object**) of this EJB object.

- **isIdentical**(EJBObject bean) returns true (boolean) if the given EJB object is identical to this EJB object.

- **remove**() removes this EJB object.

Handle Interface

The **Handle** interface is implemented by all EJB object handles. A handle is an abstraction of a persistent reference to an EJB object. The implementation class for the handle must be serializable. The **Handle** interface has the following method:

- **getEJBObject**() returns the **EJBObject** represented by this handle.

EnterpriseBean Interface

The **EnterpriseBean** interface must be implemented by every enterprise Bean class. It extends **java.io.Serializable**, and it is a tagging interface.

SessionBean Interface

The **SessionBean** interface is implemented by every session enterprise Bean class. The container uses the **SessionBean** methods to notify the enterprise Bean instances of the instance's life cycle events. The **SessionBean** interface extends **EnterpriseBean**, and it has the following methods:

- **setSessionContext**(SessionContext ctx) sets the associated session context. The container calls this method after the instance creation.

- **ejbActivate**() is called by the container when the instance is activated from its "passive" state.

- **ejbPassivate**() is called by the container before the instance enters the "passive" state.

- **ejbRemote**() is called by the container before it terminates this session Bean. This happens either as a result of a client's invoking a remove operation or when the container decides to terminate the session Bean after a time-out.

EntityBean Interface

The **EntityBean** interface is implemented by every entity enterprise Bean class. The container uses the **EntityBean** methods to notify the enterprise Bean instances of the instance's life cycle events. The **EntityBean** interface extends **Enterprise-Bean**, and it has the following methods:

- **setEntityContext**(EntityContext ctx) sets the associated entity context. The container calls this method after the instance creation.

- **unsetEntityContext**() unsets the associated entity context. The container calls this method before removing the instance.

- **ejbActivate**() is called by the container when the instance is activated from its "passive" state.

- **ejbPassivate**() is called by the container before the instance enters the "passive" state.

- **ejbRemote**() is called by the container before it ends the life of this entity Bean. This happens as a result of a client's invoking a remove operation.

- **ejbLoad**() is called by the container to instruct the instance to synchronize its state by loading its state from the underlying database.

- **ejbStore**() is called by the container to instruct the instance to synchronize its state by storing it to the underlying database.

EJBContext Interface

The **EJBContext** interface provides an enterprise Bean instance with access to the container-provided, run-time context.

- **getEJBHome**() returns the enterprise Bean's home (**EJBHome**) interface.

- **getUserTransaction**() returns the transaction demarcation interface (**javax. jts.UserTransaction**).

■ **getRollbackOnly**() returns true (boolean) if the transaction has been marked for rollback only.

■ **setRollbackOnly**() marks the current transaction for rollback.

■ **getEnvironment**() returns the enterprise Bean's environment properties (**java.util.Properties**).

■ **getCallerIdentity**() returns the **java.security.Identity** of the caller.

■ **isCallerInRole**(java.security.Identity role) returns true (boolean) if the caller has the given role.

SessionContext Interface

The **SessionContext** interface provides access to the run-time session context that the container provides for a session enterprise Bean instance. The **SessionContext** interface extends **EJBContext,** and it has the following method:

■ **getEJBObject**() returns the **EJBObject** that is currently associated with this instance.

SessionSynchronization Interface

The **SessionSynchronization** interface allows a session Bean instance to be notified by its container of transaction boundaries.

■ **afterBegin**() notifies a session Bean instance that a new transaction has started, and that the subsequent business methods on the instance will be invoked in the context of the transaction.

■ **beforeCompletion**() notifies a session Bean instance that a transaction is about to be committed.

■ **afterCompletion**(boolean committed) notifies a session Bean instance that a transaction commit protocol has completed; it also tells the instance whether the transaction has been committed or rolled back.

EntityContext Interface

The **EntityContext** interface provides an entity enterprise Bean instance with access to the container-provided run-time context. The **EntityContext** interface extends **EJBContext** and has the following methods:

- **getEJBObject**() returns the **EJBObject** that is currently associated with this instance.

- **getPrimaryKey**() returns the primary key (**Object**) of the EJB object that is currently associated with this instance.

DeploymentDescriptor Class

The **DeploymentDescriptor** class is the common base class for the **SessionDe-scriptor** and **EntityDescriptor** deployment descriptor classes. It implements **java.io.Serializable** and has the default constructor:

- **DeploymentDescriptor**()

And, it has the following methods:

- **getEnterpriseBeanClassName**() returns the enterprise Bean's full class name (**String**).

- **setEnterpriseBeanClassName**(String value) sets the enterprise Bean's full class name.

- **getHomeInterfaceClassName**() returns the full name (**String**) of the enterprise Bean's home interface.

- **setHomeInterfaceClassName**(String value) sets the full name of the enterprise Bean's home interface.

- **getRemoteInterfaceClassName**() returns the full name (**String**) of the enterprise Bean's remote interface.

- **setRemoteInterfaceClassName**(String value) sets the full name of the enterprise Bean's remote interface.

- **getBeanHomeName**() returns the name (**String**) to associate with the enterprise Bean in the JNDI name space.

- **setBeanHomeName**(String value) sets the name to associate with the enterprise Bean in the JNDI name space.

- **getControlDescriptor**() returns the array of the enterprise Bean's control descriptors (**ControlDescriptor[ ]**).

- **setControlDescriptor**(ContorlDescriptor[ ] values) sets the array of the enterprise Bean's control descriptors.

- **getControlDescriptor**(int index) returns the enterprise Bean's control descriptor (**ControlDescriptor**) at the specified index.

- **setControlDescriptor**(int index, ContorlDescriptor value) sets the enterprise Bean's control descriptor at the specified index.

- **getAccessControlEntries**() returns the array of **AccessControlEntry** objects for the enterprise Bean.

- **setAccessControlEntries**(AccessControlEntry[ ] values) sets the **AccessControlEntry** objects for the enterprise Bean.

- **getAccessControlEntries**(int index) returns the **AccessControlEntry** object at the specified index for the enterprise Bean.

- **setAccessControlEntries**(int index, AccessControlEntry value) sets the **AccessControlEntry** object at the specified index for the enterprise Bean.

- **getEnvironmentProperties**() returns the enterprise Bean's environment properties (**java.util.Properties**).

- **setEnvironmentProperties**(java.util.Properties value) sets the enterprise Bean's environment properties.

SessionDescriptor Class

The **SessionDescriptor** class defines the deployment descriptor for a session enterprise Bean. It extends **DeploymentDescriptor**, and it has the following class constants:

- **STATELESS_SESSION** (int)

- **STATEFULL_SESSION** (int)

It has this default constructor:

■ **SessionDescriptor**()

And, it has the following methods:

■ **getSessionTimeout**() returns the session time-out value (int) in seconds.

■ **setSessionTimeout**(int value) sets the session time-out value in seconds.

■ **getStateManagementType**() returns the session Bean's state management type (int).

■ **setStateManagementType**(int value) sets the session Bean's state management type. Its value must be either STATEFUL_SESSION or STATELESS_SESSION.

EntityDescriptor Class

The **EntityDescriptor** class defines the deployment descriptor for an entity enterprise Bean. It extends **DeploymentDescriptor**, and it has this default constructor:

■ **EntityDescriptor**()

And, it has the following methods:

■ **getPrimaryKeyClassName**() returns the full class name (**String**) of the enterprise Bean's primary key.

■ **setPrimaryKeyClassName** (String value) sets the full class name of the enterprise Bean's primary key.

■ **getContainerManagedFields**() returns the array of the container-managed fields (**Field**[ ]).

■ **setContainerManagedFields**(Field[ ] values) sets the array of the container-managed fields.

■ **getContainerManagedFields**(int index) returns the container-managed fields (**Field**) at the specified index.

■ **setContainerManagedFields**(int index, Field value) sets the container-managed field at the specified index.

ControlDescriptor Class

The **ControlDescriptor** class defines the transaction and security attributes to be associated with the run-time execution of an enterprise Bean method. It implements **java.io.Serializable**, and it has the following constants:

- **TX_NOT_SUPPORTED** (int)
- **TX_BEAN_MANAGED** (int)
- **TX_REQUIRED** (int)
- **TX_SUPPORTS** (int)
- **TX_REQUIRES_NEW** (int)
- **TX_MANDATORY** (int)
- **TRANSACTION_READ_UNCOMMITTED** (int)
- **TRANSACTION_READ_COMMITTED** (int)
- **TRANSACTION_REPEATABLE_READ** (int)
- **TRANSACTION_SERIALIZABLE** (int)
- **CLIENT_IDENTITY** (int)
- **SPECIFIED_IDENTITY** (int)
- **SYSTEM_IDENTITY** (int)

It has the following constructors:

- **ControlDescriptor**()

- **ControlDescriptor**(Method method)

And, it has the following methods:

- **getMethod**() returns the **Method** associated with this control descriptor.

- **setMethod**(Method method) sets the method to which this control descriptor applies.

- **getTransactionAttribute**() returns the value (int) of the transaction attribute.

- **setTransactionAttribute**(int value) sets the value of the transaction attribute. It must be one of the following: TX_NOT_SUPPORTED, TX_BEAN_MANAGED, TX_REQUIRED, TX_REQUIRES_NEW, and TX_MANDATORY.

- **getIsolationLevel**() returns the value (int) of the isolation level.

- **setIsolationLevel**(int value) sets the value of the isolation level. The value must be one of the following: TRANSACTION_READ_UNCOMMITTED, TRANS-ACTION_READ_COMMITTED, TRANSACTION_REPEATABLE_READ, and TRANSACTION_SERIALIZABLE.

- **getRunAsMode**() returns the value (int) of the runAsMode security attribute.

- **setRunAsMode**(int value) sets the value of the runAsMode security attribute. The value must be one of the following: CLIENT_IDENTITY, SPECI-FIED_IDENTITY, and SYSTEM_IDENTITY.

- **getRunAsIdentity**() returns the value of the runAsIdentity security attribute (**java.security.Identity**).

- **setRunAsIdentity**(java.security.Identity value) sets the value of the runAsIdentity security attribute.

AccessControlEntry Class

The **AccessControlEntry** class associates a list of security identities with an enterprise Bean's method. It implements **java.io.Serializable**, and it has the following constructors:

- **AccessControlEntry**()

- **AccessControlEntry**(Method method)

- **AccessControlEntry**(Method method, java.security.Identity)

And, it has the following methods:

- **getMethod**() returns the **Method** associated with this access control entry.

- **setMethod**(Method method) sets the method to which this access control entry applies.

- **getAllowedIdentities**() returns the array of identities (**java.security.Identy**[]) that are permitted to invoke this method.

- **setAllowedIdentities**(java.security.Identity[] values) sets the array of identities that are permitted to invoke this method.

- **getAllowedIdentities**(int index) returns the identity (**java.security.Identy**) at the specified index that are permitted to invoke this method.

- **setAllowedIdentities**(java.security.Identity value) sets the identity at the specified index that are permitted to invoke this method.

UserTransaction Interface

The **UserTransaction** interface defines the methods that allow an application to explicitly manage transaction boundaries. It has the following class constants:

- **STATUS_ACTIVE** (int)
- **STATUS_MARKED_ROLLBACK** (int)
- **STATUS_PREPARED** (int)
- **STATUS_COMMITTED** (int)
- **STATUS_ROLLEDBACK** (int)
- **STATUS_UNKNOWN** (int)
- **STATUS_NO_TRANSACTION** (int)
- **STATUS_PREPARING** (int)
- **STATUS_COMMITTING** (int)
- **STATUS_ROLLING_BACK** (int)

And, it has the following methods:

- **begin**() creates a new transaction and associates it with the current thread.

- **commit**() completes the transaction associated with the current thread. When this method completes, the thread becomes associated with no transaction.

- **rollback**() rolls back the transaction associated with the current thread. When this method completes, the thread becomes associated with no transaction.

- **setRollbackOnly**() modifies the transaction associated with the current thread such that the only possible outcome of the transaction is to roll back the transaction.

- **setTransactionTimeout**(int seconds) modifies the value of the time-out value that is associated with the transactions started by the current thread with the begin method.

- **getStatus**() returns the status (int) of the transaction associated with the current thread.

SAMPLE ENTERPRISE BEANS

In the following sections, we develop two Enterprise JavaBeans using WebLogic's Tengah application server. Figure 21-8 illustrates the Tengah development process for enterprise Beans. The development process follows these steps:

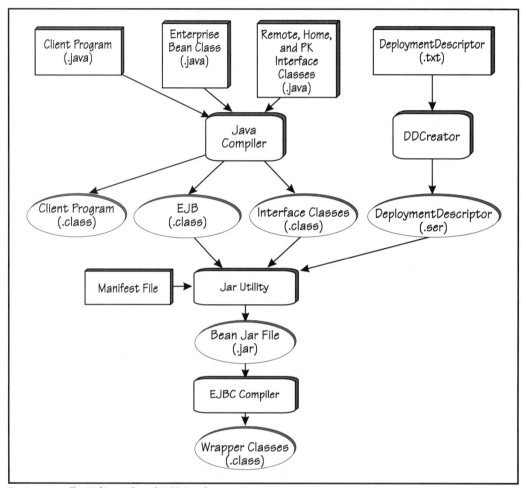

Figure 21-8. The WebLogic Tengah EJB Development Process.

1. ***Write Remote and Home interfaces.*** These interfaces define the methods you will use to create, find, and interact with your enterprise Bean. If you are developing an entity Bean, you will also need to define a *Primary Key* interface.

2. ***Write enterprise Bean class.*** This is the meat of your enterprise Bean. You implement the methods defined in the remote and home interfaces.

3. ***Write deployment descriptor text.*** This file contains the details necessary to deploy your enterprise Bean. You create it using a text editor.

4. ***Write client program.*** With the definition of your enterprise Bean's interfaces and the deployment details defined, you are now ready to write your client program.

5. ***Compile Java programs.*** Compile the Java source for all of the classes and interfaces you have created.

6. ***Create the DeploymentDescriptor serialization files.*** Using the Tengah *DDCreator* utility, create the serialized class file that contains the deployment descriptor data.

7. ***Package all of the classes into a JAR file.*** Using the Java *jar* utility, package all of enterprise Bean *.class* and *.ser* files into a *.jar* file.

8. ***Create wrapper classes using the Tengah EJBC compiler.*** As a final step in deploying your enterprise Bean on a Tengah server, you must run the EJBC compiler against the JAR file containing your enterprise Bean. This creates *wrapper classes* that the Tengah Enterprise JavaBean Server uses to run your enterprise Bean.

These eight steps are a quick overview of the Tengah EJB development process. The complete details for the Tengah development process are located on your CD-ROM in the Tengah documentation. After completing the development of your enterprise Bean, you must register it with the Tengah Server. This is done with text entries in the *weblogic.properties* file. Figure 21-9 is a screen capture of the Tengah console; it shows that the five example enterprise Beans provided with Tengah and the two enterprise Beans developed for this book have been registered with the Tengah Server.

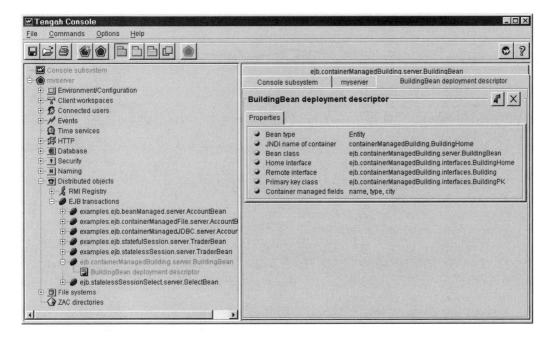

Figure 21-9. The Tengah Server Console.

A Sample Stateless Session EJB

In the following section, we take the **SelectRMI** example (see listings starting on page 355) and redo it using a stateless session enterprise Bean that runs on the **WebLogic Tengah** EJB server. The **SelectApplet** example preserves the same user functionality and interface as the RMI example, but it performs data access on the server using a stateless session EJB that makes JDBC calls on the client's behalf. As in the RMI example, this example also uses Object Serialization to pass objects by value (**QuerySpec** and **QueryResult**). We don't repeat these classes here, so see Listings 15-6 and 15-7. The use of these classes allows coarse-grain communication between client and server. Listings 21-1 through 21-6 shows the Bean implementation, Home interface, Remote interface, DeploymentDescriptor text file, manifest file, and the client applet for the Select stateless session example.

Listing 21-1. The Stateless Session EJB: SelectBean.

```
package ejb.statelessSessionSelect.server;

import javax.ejb.*;
import java.io.*;
import java.util.*;
import java.sql.*;

import ejb.statelessSessionSelect.interfaces.*;

public class SelectBean implements SessionBean {

  // private variables
  private transient SessionContext ctx;
  private transient Properties     props;


  public void ejbActivate()  {
      System.out.println("ejbActivate called");
  }

  public void ejbRemove() {
      System.out.println("ejbRemove called");
  }

  public void ejbPassivate() {
      System.out.println("ejbPassivate called");
  }
```

```java
public void setSessionContext(SessionContext ctx) {
    System.out.println("setSessionContext called");
  this.ctx = ctx;
  props    = ctx.getEnvironment();
}

public void ejbCreate () {
    System.out.println("ejbCreate called");
}

public QueryResult executeQuery(QuerySpec qs)
{
    String database = qs.getDataSource();
    String login = qs.getUserid();
    String password = qs.getPassword();
    String sql = qs.getSql();
    QueryResult qr = null;

    try {
        // Load the JDBC-ODBC driver
        Class.forName("sun.jdbc.odbc.JdbcOdbcDriver");

        String url = "jdbc:odbc:" + database;
        Connection con = DriverManager.getConnection(url,
            login, password);
        Statement stmt = con.createStatement();

        ResultSet rs = stmt.executeQuery(sql);

        qr = new QueryResult();
        Vector v1 = qr.getResult();

        while(rs.next()) {
            String s1 = rs.getString(1);
            String s2 = rs.getString(2);
            String s3 = rs.getString(3);

            Vector v2 = new Vector();
            v2.addElement(s1);
            v2.addElement(s2);
            v2.addElement(s3);

            v1.addElement(v2);
        }
```

```
            stmt.close();
            con.close();
        } catch( Exception e ) {
            e.printStackTrace();
        }

        return qr;
    }

    public String getDatabaseName() {
        return (String)props.get("jdbcPoolName");
    }

}
```

Listing 21-2. The Stateless Session EJB Home Interface: SelectHome.

```
package ejb.statelessSessionSelect.interfaces;

import javax.ejb.*;
import java.rmi.RemoteException;

public interface SelectHome extends EJBHome {

    Select create() throws CreateException, RemoteException;
}
```

Listing 21-3.The Stateless Session EJB Remote Interface: Select.

```
package ejb.statelessSessionSelect.interfaces;

import javax.ejb.*;
import java.rmi.RemoteException;
import java.rmi.Remote;

public interface Select extends EJBObject, Remote {

    public  QueryResult executeQuery(QuerySpec qs)
        throws ProcessingErrorException, RemoteException;

}
```

Listing 21-4. The Stateless Session DeploymentDescriptor.txt File.

```
(SessionDescriptor

  beanHomeName
       statelessSessionSelect.SelectHome
  enterpriseBeanClassName
       ejb.statelessSessionSelect.server.SelectBean
  homeInterfaceClassName
       ejb.statelessSessionSelect.interfaces.SelectHome
  remoteInterfaceClassName
       ejb.statelessSessionSelect.interfaces.Select
  isReentrant                 false

  ; Session EJBean-specific properties:
  stateManagementType               STATELESS_SESSION
  sessionTimeout                    5; seconds
  ; end session EJBean-specific properties

  (accessControlEntries
  ); end accessControlEntries

  (controlDescriptors
    (DEFAULT
       isolationLevel             TRANSACTION_SERIALIZABLE
       transactionAttribute       TX_REQUIRED
       runAsMode                  CLIENT_IDENTITY
    ); end Default
  ); end controlDescriptors

  (environmentProperties
    maxBeansInFreePool           100
    maxBeansInCache              100
    idleTimeoutSeconds           5
  ); end environmentProperties
); end SessionDescriptor
```

Listing 21-5. The Stateless Session EJB Manifest File.

```
Name: ejb/statelessSessionSelect/deployment/SelectBeanDD.ser
Enterprise-Bean: True
```

Listing 21-6. The Stateless Session SelectApplet Class.

```java
/**
 * SelectApplet.java
 */

package ejb.statelessSessionSelect.client;

import java.rmi.*;
import javax.ejb.*;
import javax.naming.*;

import java.awt.*;
import java.awt.event.*;
import java.applet.*;
import java.util.Vector;
import java.util.Properties;

import ejb.statelessSessionSelect.interfaces.*;

public class SelectApplet
  extends Applet implements ActionListener
{
    public void init() {
        super.init();

        try {
        Context ctx = getInitialContext();
        SelectHome ejbSelectHome =
            (SelectHome) ctx.lookup(
                "statelessSessionSelect.SelectHome");

        ejbSelect = ejbSelectHome.create();
        }
        catch (ProcessingErrorException pe) {
          System.out.println("Processing Error: " + pe);
        }
        catch (Exception e) {
          System.out.println("System Error: ");
          e.printStackTrace();
        }

        setLayout(null);
        addNotify();
        setSize(450,340);
```

```java
//set applet layout
mainCardPanel = new Panel();
mainCardPanel.setLayout(new CardLayout(0,0));
mainCardPanel.setBounds(0,0,450,340);
add(mainCardPanel);

//add input panel
inputPanel = new Panel();
inputPanel.setLayout(null);
inputPanel.setBounds(0,0,450, 340);
mainCardPanel.add(" ", inputPanel);

label1 = new java.awt.Label("ArcWorld buildings query:");
label1.setBounds(12,10,324,40);
inputPanel.add(label1);

label2 = new java.awt.Label("Enter data Source, user id, " +
                            "and password information:");
label2.setBounds(12,45,324,40);
inputPanel.add(label2);
textField1 = new java.awt.TextField();
textField1.setBounds(12,84,132,24);
textField1.requestFocus();
inputPanel.add(textField1);
textField3 = new java.awt.TextField();
textField3.setBounds(156,84,132,24);
inputPanel.add(textField3);
textField4 = new java.awt.TextField();
textField4.setBounds(300,84,132,24);
inputPanel.add(textField4);

label3 = new Label("Select the city that you would " +
                   "like to query:");
label3.setBounds(12,120,240,12);
inputPanel.add(label3);
Group1 = new CheckboxGroup();
radioButton1 = new java.awt.Checkbox("All cities",
                                     Group1, false);
radioButton1.setBounds(12,144,100,24);
inputPanel.add(radioButton1);
radioButton2 = new java.awt.Checkbox("Washington",
                                     Group1, false);
radioButton2.setBounds(12,168,100,24);
inputPanel.add(radioButton2);
```

```java
        radioButton3 = new java.awt.Checkbox("Paris",
                                             Group1, false);
        radioButton3.setBounds(12,192,100,24);
        inputPanel.add(radioButton3);
        radioButton4 = new java.awt.Checkbox("Beijing",
                                             Group1, false);
        radioButton4.setBounds(12,216,100,24);
        inputPanel.add(radioButton4);

        button1 = new java.awt.Button("Submit");
        button1.setBounds(12,252,108,24);
        inputPanel.add(button1);
        button2 = new java.awt.Button("Reset");
        button2.setBounds(132,252,96,24);
        inputPanel.add(button2);

        // add result panel
        resultPanel = new Panel();
        resultPanel.setLayout(null);
        resultPanel.setBounds(0,0,792,390);
        mainCardPanel.add(" ", resultPanel);
        label5 = new java.awt.Label("Buildings in the " +
                                    "ArcWorld Database:");
        label5.setBounds(84,12,276,24);
        button3 = new java.awt.Button("Input");
        button3.setBounds(228,310,96,24);
        button4 = new java.awt.Button("Result");
        button4.setBounds(108,310,96,24);
        resultPanel.add(button3);
        resultPanel.add(button4);
        resultPanel.add(label5);

        mainCardLayout = new CardLayout();
        mainCardPanel.setLayout(mainCardLayout);
        mainCardLayout.addLayoutComponent(inputPanel, "input");
        mainCardLayout.addLayoutComponent(resultPanel, "result");
        mainCardLayout.show(mainCardPanel,"input");

        // register components' event listener
        AddListener();
    }

private void AddListener()
{
        button1.addActionListener(this);
```

```java
    button2.addActionListener(this);
    button3.addActionListener(this);
    button4.addActionListener(this);
}

public void actionPerformed(ActionEvent event)
{
    if(event.getSource() == button1)
    {
        dataSource = textField1.getText();
        userid = textField3.getText();
        password = textField4.getText();

        if (radioButton1.getState())
            city = "*";
        else if (radioButton2.getState())
            city = "Washington";
        else if (radioButton3.getState())
            city = "Paris";
        else if (radioButton4.getState())
            city = "Beijing";
        if (city.equals("*"))
            where = "";
        else
            where = " WHERE city = " + "'" + city + "'";
        sql = "SELECT name, type, city FROM Building" + where;

        submitButton_Clicked(event);
    }
    if (event.getSource() == button2)
        resetButton_Clicked(event);
    if (event.getSource() == button3)
        inputButton_Clicked(event);
    if (event.getSource() == button4)
        resultButton_Clicked(event);
}

public void submitButton_Clicked(ActionEvent event)
{
    mainCardLayout.show(mainCardPanel,"result");
}

public void resetButton_Clicked(ActionEvent event)
{
    textField1.setText("");
```

```java
        textField3.setText("");
        textField4.setText("");
        radioButton1.setState(false);
        radioButton2.setState(false);
        radioButton3.setState(false);
        radioButton4.setState(false);
    }

    public void inputButton_Clicked(ActionEvent evnet)
    {
        mainCardLayout.show(mainCardPanel,"input");
    }

    public void resultButton_Clicked(ActionEvent event)
    {
        Graphics g = resultPanel.getGraphics();
        drawTable(g);
        query();
    }

    public void drawTable(Graphics g)
    {
        g.drawString("NAME", 75,55);
        g.drawString("TYPE", 230,55);
        g.drawString("CITY", 350,55);

        g.drawLine(10,40,420,40);
        g.drawLine(10,65,420,65);
        g.drawLine(10,90,420,90);
        g.drawLine(10,115,420,115);
        g.drawLine(10,140,420,140);
        g.drawLine(10,165,420,165);
        g.drawLine(10,190,420,190);
        g.drawLine(10,215,420,215);
        g.drawLine(10,240,420,240);
        g.drawLine(10,265,420,265);
        g.drawLine(10,290,420,290);

        g.drawLine(10,40,10,290);
        g.drawLine(420,40,420,290);
        g.drawLine(180,40,180,290);
        g.drawLine(310,40,310,290);
    }

    public void query()
```

```
{
    try
    {
        QuerySpec qs = new QuerySpec(dataSource, userid,
                                     password, sql);
        QueryResult qr = ejbSelect.executeQuery(qs);

        Vector bnameVector = new Vector();
        Vector btypeVector = new Vector();
        Vector bcitynameVector = new Vector();

        int h = 80;
        Graphics g = resultPanel.getGraphics();

        Vector v;
        int index = 0;
        while((v = qr.getResultRecord(index++)) != null) {
            String name = (String) v.elementAt(0);
            String type = (String) v.elementAt(1);
            String city = (String) v.elementAt(2);

            bnameVector.addElement(name);
            btypeVector.addElement(type);
            bcitynameVector.addElement(city);
        }

        String bname = null;
        for (int i = 0; i < bnameVector.size(); i++)
        {
            bname = bnameVector.elementAt(i).toString();
            g.drawString(bname, 20, h);
            String btype = btypeVector.elementAt(i).toString();
            g.drawString(btype, 190, h);
            String bcityname =
                    bcitynameVector.elementAt(i).toString();
            g.drawString(bcityname, 330, h);
            h += 25;
        }
    } catch (Exception e)
    {
        e.printStackTrace();
        System.exit(0);
    }
}
```

```java
static public Context getInitialContext() throws Exception {
  Properties p = new Properties();
  p.put(Context.INITIAL_CONTEXT_FACTORY,
    "weblogic.jndi.T3InitialContextFactory");
  p.put(Context.PROVIDER_URL, url);
  if (user != null) {
    System.out.println ("user: " + user);
    p.put(Context.SECURITY_PRINCIPAL, user);
    if (pw == null)
      pw = "";
    p.put(Context.SECURITY_CREDENTIALS, pw);
  }
  return new InitialContext(p);
}


// variables

static String url      = "t3://localhost:7001";
static String user     = null;
static String pw = null;

java.awt.Button button1;
java.awt.Button button2;
java.awt.Button button3;
java.awt.Button button4;

CheckboxGroup Group1;
java.awt.Checkbox radioButton1;
java.awt.Checkbox radioButton2;
java.awt.Checkbox radioButton3;
java.awt.Checkbox radioButton4;

java.awt.TextField textField1;
java.awt.TextField textField3;
java.awt.TextField textField4;

java.awt.Label label1;
java.awt.Label label2;
java.awt.Label label3;
java.awt.Label label4;
java.awt.Label label5;

CardLayout mainCardLayout;
java.awt.Panel inputPanel;
```

```
    java.awt.Panel resultPanel;
    java.awt.Panel mainCardPanel;

    Select server;
    Select ejbSelect;

    String dataSource;
    String userid;
    String password;

    String sql;
    String city = "";
    String where;
}
```

A Sample Container Managed Entity EJB

In the following example we rewrite our Building query example using a container-managed entity EJB that runs on the **WebLogic Tengah** EJB server. Unlike our previous examples that used JDBC for data access, here we depend on the data access mechanisms of our entity Bean. The use of an entity Bean causes several structural changes to our application:

■ Instead of an enterprise Bean that performs JDBC calls, a **BuildingBean** enterprise Bean is defined to represent our data. Specifically, the **BuildingBean** is a representation of the ArcWorld Building table. Public attributes are defined in the **BuildingBean** class; these are in turn mapped to Building table columns using an *attributeMap* in the DeploymentDescriptor.txt file. Finder methods are also defined in the **BuildingHome** interface and mapped to *finderDescriptors* in the DeploymentDescriptor.txt file.

■ We also take advantage of defining the source of our data in the DeploymentDescriptor.txt file. This eliminates the need for the user to enter a data source and its associated user and password in the **SelectApplet**, so those fields are eliminated. Moving the definition to the DeploymentDescriptor.txt file also makes our application more flexible and easier to deploy.

■ Instead of building a **QuerySpec** object, we use a finder method that returns an **Enumeration** of **Building** objects based on our *city* search criteria. The **QueryResult** object is also eliminated and replaced with method calls to a specific Bean that returns attribute data.

Note that with the introduction of the entity Bean, the communication between the client and the server has become more fine-grained. Unlike earlier examples where the data from an entire result set was returned to the client from the server as one serialized class, the data from each entity Bean is retrieved individually by the client. An alternative is to define a method call that returns all of the data we are interested in for a specific **Building** EJB instance. This would reduce network traffic and improve performance when accessing one Bean. However, we would still not achieve the "one query, one result set" interaction of the StatelessSession example.

Listings 21-7 through 21-13 shows the Bean implementation, Home interface, Remote interface, primary key class, DeploymentDescriptor text file, manifest file, and the client applet for the **Building** container managed entity Bean example. Note that the DeploymentDescriptor text file defines the mapping of the Building table columns to **BuildingBean** attributes.

Listing 21-7. The Container Managed Entity EJB: BuildingBean.

```
package ejb.containerManagedBuilding.server;

import java.io.Serializable;
import java.rmi.RemoteException;
import java.rmi.Remote;
import javax.ejb.*;
import java.util.*;

import ejb.containerManagedBuilding.interfaces.*;

public class BuildingBean implements EntityBean {

  // private variables
  private transient EntityContext ctx;

  // public container managed variables
  public          String        name; // also the primary Key
  public          String        type;
  public          String        city;
  private transient boolean      isDirty;

  // EntityBean implementation
  public boolean isModified() {
    return isDirty;
  }

  public String id() {
    return "" + System.identityHashCode(this) + ", PK = " +
```

```
      (String) ((ctx == null) ? "nullctx"
              : ((ctx.getPrimaryKey() == null ?
                "null" : ctx.getPrimaryKey().toString()))));
}

public void ejbActivate() throws RemoteException {
}

public void ejbPassivate() throws RemoteException {
}

public void setEntityContext(EntityContext ctx)
  throws RemoteException
{
  this.ctx = ctx;
}

public void unsetEntityContext() throws RemoteException {
  this.ctx = null;
}

public void ejbLoad() throws RemoteException {
}

public void ejbStore() throws RemoteException {
}

public void ejbRemove() throws RemoteException {
}

public void ejbCreate(String name, String type, String city) {
  this.name = name;
  this.type = type;
  this.city = city;
}

public void ejbPostCreate(String name, String type, String city) {
}

// Application defined methods
public String getCity() {
    return this.city;
}

public String getType() {
```

```
    return this.type;
  }
}
```

Listing 21-8. The Container Managed Entity EJB Home: BuildingHome.

```java
package ejb.containerManagedBuilding.interfaces;

import javax.ejb.*;
import java.rmi.Remote;
import java.rmi.RemoteException;
import java.util.*;

public interface BuildingHome extends EJBHome {

  public Building create(String name, String type, String city)
    throws CreateException, RemoteException;

  public Building findByPrimaryKey(BuildingPK primaryKey)
    throws FinderException, RemoteException;

  public Enumeration findBuildingByCity(String city)
    throws FinderException, RemoteException;

  public Enumeration findAllBuildings()
    throws FinderException, RemoteException;
}
```

Listing 21-9. The Container Managed Entity EJB Remote Interface: Building.

```java
package ejb.containerManagedBuilding.interfaces;

import java.rmi.RemoteException;
import java.rmi.Remote;
import javax.ejb.*;


public interface Building extends EJBObject, Remote {


  public String getCity()
    throws RemoteException;
```

```
  public String getType()
      throws RemoteException;
}
```

Listing 21-10. The Container Managed Entity EJB Primary Key Class: BuildingPK.

```
package ejb.containerManagedBuilding.interfaces;

public class BuildingPK implements java.io.Serializable {
  public String name;
}
```

Listing 21-11. The Container Managed Entity EJB DeploymentDescriptor.txt File.

```
(EntityDescriptor
  beanHomeName
      containerManagedBuilding.BuildingHome
  enterpriseBeanClassName
      ejb.containerManagedBuilding.server.BuildingBean
  homeInterfaceClassName
      ejb.containerManagedBuilding.interfaces.BuildingHome
  remoteInterfaceClassName
      ejb.containerManagedBuilding.interfaces.Building
  isReentrant                      false

  (accessControlEntries
  ); end accessControlEntries

  (controlDescriptors
    (DEFAULT
      isolationLevel               TRANSACTION_SERIALIZABLE
      transactionAttribute         TX_REQUIRED
      runAsMode                    CLIENT_IDENTITY
    ); end isolationLevel
  ); end controlDescriptors

  (environmentProperties
    maxBeansInFreePool             20
    maxBeansInCache                100
    idleTimeoutSeconds             10
    isModifiedMethodName           isModified

    (finderDescriptors
```

```
        "findBuildingByCity(String city)" "(= city $city)"
        "findAllBuildings()" "(= 1 1)"
    ); end finderDescriptors

    (persistentStoreProperties
        persistentStoreType          jdbc
        (jdbc
            tableName                Building
            dbIsShared               false
            poolName                 ejbPool

            (attributeMap
              ; Maps the EJBean attributes to database column names
              ; EJBean attribute      Database column name
              ; ----------------------------------------
                name                  name
                type                  type
                city                  city
            ); end attributeMap
        ); end jdbc
    ); end persistentStoreProperties
); end environmentProperties

  ; Entity EJBean-specific properties:

primaryKeyClassName
        ejb.containerManagedBuilding.interfaces.BuildingPK
containerManagedFields    [name type city]

  ; end entity EJBean-specific properties.

); end EntityDescriptor
```

Listing 21-12. The Container Managed Entity EJB Manifest File.

```
Name: ejb/containerManagedBuilding/deployment/BuildingBeanDD.ser
Enterprise-Bean: True
```

Listing 21-13. The Container Managed SelectApplet.

```
/**
 * SelectApplet.java
 */
```

```java
package ejb.containerManagedBuilding.client;

import java.rmi.*;
import javax.ejb.*;
import javax.naming.*;

import java.awt.*;
import java.awt.event.*;
import java.applet.*;
import java.util.*;

import ejb.containerManagedBuilding.interfaces.*;

public class SelectApplet
  extends Applet implements ActionListener
{
    public void init() {
        super.init();

        try {
        Context ctx = getInitialContext();
        home = (BuildingHome) ctx.lookup(
                  "containerManagedBuilding.BuildingHome");
        }
        catch (ProcessingErrorException pe) {
          System.out.println("Processing Error: " + pe);
        }
        catch (Exception e) {
          System.out.println("System Error: ");
          e.printStackTrace();
        }

        setLayout(null);
        addNotify();
        setSize(450,340);

        //set applet layout
        mainCardPanel = new Panel();
        mainCardPanel.setLayout(new CardLayout(0,0));
        mainCardPanel.setBounds(0,0,450,340);
        add(mainCardPanel);

        //add input panel
        inputPanel = new Panel();
        inputPanel.setLayout(null);
```

```java
inputPanel.setBounds(0,0,450, 340);
mainCardPanel.add(" ", inputPanel);

label1 = new java.awt.Label("ArcWorld buildings query:");
label1.setBounds(12,10,324,24);
inputPanel.add(label1);

label3 = new Label("Select the city that you would " +
                   " like to query:");
label3.setBounds(12,45,240,24);
inputPanel.add(label3);
Group1 = new CheckboxGroup();
radioButton1 = new java.awt.Checkbox("All cities",
                                     Group1, false);
radioButton1.setBounds(12,69,100,24);
inputPanel.add(radioButton1);
radioButton2 = new java.awt.Checkbox("Washington",
                                     Group1, false);
radioButton2.setBounds(12,93,100,24);
inputPanel.add(radioButton2);
radioButton3 = new java.awt.Checkbox("Paris",
                                     Group1, false);
radioButton3.setBounds(12,117,100,24);
inputPanel.add(radioButton3);
radioButton4 = new java.awt.Checkbox("Beijing",
                                     Group1, false);
radioButton4.setBounds(12,141,100,24);
inputPanel.add(radioButton4);

button1 = new java.awt.Button("Submit");
button1.setBounds(12,177,108,24);
inputPanel.add(button1);
button2 = new java.awt.Button("Reset");
button2.setBounds(132,177,96,24);
inputPanel.add(button2);

// add result panel
resultPanel = new Panel();
resultPanel.setLayout(null);
resultPanel.setBounds(0,0,792,390);
mainCardPanel.add(" ", resultPanel);
label5 = new java.awt.Label("Buildings in the " +
                            "ArcWorld Database:");
label5.setBounds(84,12,276,24);
button3 = new java.awt.Button("Input");
```

```java
    button3.setBounds(228,310,96,24);
    button4 = new java.awt.Button("Result");
    button4.setBounds(108,310,96,24);
    resultPanel.add(button3);
    resultPanel.add(button4);
    resultPanel.add(label5);

    mainCardLayout = new CardLayout();
    mainCardPanel.setLayout(mainCardLayout);
    mainCardLayout.addLayoutComponent(inputPanel, "input");
    mainCardLayout.addLayoutComponent(resultPanel, "result");
    mainCardLayout.show(mainCardPanel,"input");

    // register components' event listener
    AddListener();
}

private void AddListener()
{
    button1.addActionListener(this);
    button2.addActionListener(this);
    button3.addActionListener(this);
    button4.addActionListener(this);
}

public void actionPerformed(ActionEvent event)
{
    if(event.getSource() == button1)
    {
        if (radioButton1.getState())
            city = "*";
        else if (radioButton2.getState())
            city = "Washington";
        else if (radioButton3.getState())
            city = "Paris";
        else if (radioButton4.getState())
            city = "Beijing";
        submitButton_Clicked(event);
    }
    if (event.getSource() == button2)
        resetButton_Clicked(event);
    if (event.getSource() == button3)
        inputButton_Clicked(event);
    if (event.getSource() == button4)
        resultButton_Clicked(event);
```

```java
}

public void submitButton_Clicked(ActionEvent event)
{
    mainCardLayout.show(mainCardPanel,"result");
}

public void resetButton_Clicked(ActionEvent event)
{
    radioButton1.setState(false);
    radioButton2.setState(false);
    radioButton3.setState(false);
    radioButton4.setState(false);
}

public void inputButton_Clicked(ActionEvent evnet)
{
    mainCardLayout.show(mainCardPanel,"input");
}

public void resultButton_Clicked(ActionEvent event)
{
    Graphics g = resultPanel.getGraphics();
    drawTable(g);
    query();
}

public void drawTable(Graphics g)
{
    g.drawString("NAME", 75,55);
    g.drawString("TYPE", 230,55);
    g.drawString("CITY", 350,55);

    g.drawLine(10,40,420,40);
    g.drawLine(10,65,420,65);
    g.drawLine(10,90,420,90);
    g.drawLine(10,115,420,115);
    g.drawLine(10,140,420,140);
    g.drawLine(10,165,420,165);
    g.drawLine(10,190,420,190);
    g.drawLine(10,215,420,215);
    g.drawLine(10,240,420,240);
    g.drawLine(10,265,420,265);
    g.drawLine(10,290,420,290);
```

```
        g.drawLine(10,40,10,290);
        g.drawLine(420,40,420,290);
        g.drawLine(180,40,180,290);
        g.drawLine(310,40,310,290);
    }

    public void query()
    {
        try
        {
            // Find Buildings by city
            if (city.equals("*")) {
                e = home.findAllBuildings();
            } else {
                e = home.findBuildingByCity(city);
            }

            int h = 80;
            Graphics g = resultPanel.getGraphics();

            String name;
            while (e.hasMoreElements()) {
                building = (Building) e.nextElement();
                name = building.getPrimaryKey().toString();
                g.drawString(name, 20, h);
                g.drawString(building.getType(), 190, h);
                g.drawString(building.getCity(), 330, h);
                h += 25;
            }
        } catch (Exception e)
        {
            e.printStackTrace();
            System.exit(0);
        }
    }

    static public Context getInitialContext() throws Exception {
        Properties p = new Properties();
        p.put(Context.INITIAL_CONTEXT_FACTORY,
            "weblogic.jndi.T3InitialContextFactory");
        p.put(Context.PROVIDER_URL, url);
        if (user != null) {
            System.out.println ("user: " + user);
            p.put(Context.SECURITY_PRINCIPAL, user);
            if (pw == null)
```

```
      pw = "";
    p.put(Context.SECURITY_CREDENTIALS, pw);
  }
  return new InitialContext(p);
}


// variables
static String url       = "t3://localhost:7001";
static String user      = null;
static String pw = null;

java.awt.Button button1;
java.awt.Button button2;
java.awt.Button button3;
java.awt.Button button4;

CheckboxGroup Group1;
java.awt.Checkbox radioButton1;
java.awt.Checkbox radioButton2;
java.awt.Checkbox radioButton3;
java.awt.Checkbox radioButton4;

java.awt.Label label1;
java.awt.Label label2;
java.awt.Label label3;
java.awt.Label label4;
java.awt.Label label5;

CardLayout mainCardLayout;
java.awt.Panel inputPanel;
java.awt.Panel resultPanel;
java.awt.Panel mainCardPanel;

BuildingHome home;
Building building;

Enumeration e;
String city = "";
}
```

CONCLUSION

EJB is one of the most significant developments in enterprise computing. If successful, it will revolutionize the development, deployment, and execution of business applications. EJB provides a new, high-level programming model with integrated support for declarative transaction, state, and security management. It allows a business application developer to not worry about system programming at all and to totally focus on business programming. *EJB*, however, *is in an embryonic stage.* The EJB 1.0 specification is still fresh. Products that implement this specification are just coming out in beta form and the tool support is limited.

Although EJB is high level, it is still complex. *Tools (for example, development, deployment,* and *execution) and IDEs (Integrated Development Environments) will be critical for its success.* Debugging an EJB application, with all of its indirection, declarative transaction scopes, and declarative security attributes, will be a total nightmare without the proper tools. A simple method invocation on an enterprise Bean involves the interworking of the following objects/systems: EJB object proxy, EJB object, EJB container, enterprise Bean, and EJB server. If the enterprise Bean calls other enterprise Beans, then for each such call, more objects/systems are involved for each enterprise Bean: EJB object, EJB container, enterprise Bean, and EJB server. Each enterprise Bean involved can have different transaction, isolation, persistence, and security policies. Each EJB container and each EJB server can be from a different vendor and have different services, reliability, and performance. It will be quite a feat to figure out the reason when something goes wrong. It will likely be a feat to explain when something goes right in terms of expected results and performance.

Optimistically, it probably will take a few years for EJB to mature, judging from how long it has taken CORBA to mature, which still has nothing integrated nor a high-level programming model like EJB. Until then, it will be interesting times. We should be seeing EJB products, in all sizes and shapes, coming from all sorts of vendors (with the likely, obvious exception of Microsoft). These products will come and go. When the dust settles, will we see EJB servers running everywhere (from mainframe to mini to desktop to laptop and even smaller machines, made by different vendors)? Will they serve all sorts of EJB containers (again made by different vendors)? And, will they run all sorts of enterprise Beans (some stateless session Beans, some session Beans with state, some entity Beans managing their own persistence, and some entity Beans with transparent persistence managed by their containers)? *Only time will tell; say the year 2000?*

Chapter 22

Conclusion: Emerging Technologies

concepts

So we are now at the conclusion of our journey—*client/server data access with Java and XML*. We hope it has been a fascinating journey for you, and a rewarding learning experience. We have visited many "lands," some familiar and some quite strange (at least in the beginning). But there is one thing in common: They all have something to do with data, Java, and the Web. Also, they all are rapidly changing. Therefore, a word of caution: What you read in this "tour guide" could be outdated if you actually visit some of these "lands" now. This can be particularly true for *SQLJ*, *DOM*, *XLink*, and *XPointer*, because we knew they were still evolving when we visited them.

Before we say good-bye, we would like to give you a little treat since you have been such a wonderful reader. We will take you for a flight over the "future land" and give you a bird's-eye view of what is coming. We will give you a very brief overview of some of the key technologies that are emerging in the *client/server data access* landscape. Our purpose is to make you aware of what is coming and to wet your appetite. We hope we will be able to visit these in depth with you in a future edition of this "tour guide." The key technologies that are emerging include (organized roughly according to the parts of this book):

- WebDAV (Web)
- Jini (Java)

- Object-relational databases and SQL3 (database systems)
- JDBC 2.0, SQLJ Part 1 & Part 2 (Java data access)
- DASL (Web data access)
- JavaMail (Java client/server computing)
- XSL (Web data interchange)
- Java/Web application servers, and data warehousing and business intelligence (Java/Web component architectures)

Finally, we will ponder a bit on the question that you may have in your mind or that you may be asked by a friend or adversary: *Java or XML?*

WEB

The two key technologies of the Web, HTTP and HTML, are both facing major challenges and changes. *HTML* is being challenged by *XML* and its family of technologies (which we discussed in Part 5, "Web Data Interchange"). HTML may coexist with XML. If so, it will definitely become "XML-ized." *HTTP* is being challenged by *HTTP-NG (HTTP Next Generation)*, a new architecture based on a simple, highly extensible distributed object-oriented model. HTTP-NG, however, is still in a very early phase of development. In the following section, we will take a quick look at *WebDAV*, an extension of HTTP for distributed authoring, which relies heavily on the use of *metadata*, represented in XML.

WebDAV

WebDAV (World Wide Web Distributed Authoring and Versioning) is an extension of *HTTP/1.1* (see Chapter 2, "Web Basics") that provides a standard infrastructure for asynchronous collaborative authoring of a wide variety of *Web resources* that have associated *metadata* in the form of attributes and links. WebDAV specifies a set of methods, headers, request entity body formats, and response entity body formats that provide operations for:

- **Resource properties**. The ability to create, remove, and query information about Web resources, such as their authors and creation dates. Also provided is the ability to link resources of any media type to related resources.

- **Resource collections**. The ability to create sets of related Web resources and to retrieve a hierarchical membership listing.

- **Resource locking**. The ability to keep more than one person from working on a Web resource at the same time. This prevents the "lost update problem."

- **Namespace**. The ability to instruct the server to copy and move Web resources.

Unlike HTTP, which encodes method parameter information exclusively in HTTP headers, WebDAV encodes method parameter information either in an *XML request entity body* or in an HTTP header. In addition, *XML* is used to encode the *response entity body*.

Resource Properties

Properties are metadata that describe the state of a resource. They provide efficient discovery and management of resources. There are two categories of properties: "live" and "dead." A live property has its syntax and semantics enforced by the server. A dead property has its syntax and semantics enforced by the client.

The WebDAV property model consists of *name/value* pairs. The value of a property is, at minimum, a well-formed XML document. The name of a property identifies the syntax and semantics of the property. The XML namespace mechanism, which is based on URIs, is used to name properties. A WebDAV *link* is a special type of property value that allows typed connections to be established between resources of any media type. The property value consists of source and destination URLs; the property name identifies the link type.

Resource Collections

The *collection* is a new type of Web resource. A collection is a resource whose state consists of an unordered list of internal member resources and a set of properties. An internal member must only belong to the collection once, and it must have a URI that is immediately relative to the base URI of the collection. Properties defined on collections behave exactly as do properties on non-collection resources.

Resource Locking

WebDAV allows locks to vary over two client-specified parameters: the number of principals involved (*exclusive* vs. *shared*) and the type of access to be granted (currently only one type is specified: *write*). The most basic form of lock is an *exclusive lock*. This is a lock where the access right in question is only granted to a single principal. *Shared locks*, on the other hand, are provided for principals to indicate that they intend to exercise their access rights, but not to exclude others from exercising an excess right. A shared lock allows multiple principals to receive a lock.

New HTTP Methods

The following are some of the new HTTP methods defined by WebDAV for distributed authoring that use XML as a request and response format:

- **PROPFIND** retrieves properties defined on the request URI, if the resource does not have any internal members, or on the request URI and potentially its member resources, if the resource does have internal members.
- **PROPPATCH** processes instructions specified in the request body to set and/or remove properties defined on the resource identified by the request URI.
- **MKCOL** creates a new collection. All WebDAV-compliant resources must support the MKCOL method.
- **LOCK** requests a lock of any access type.
- **UNLOCK** removes the lock identified by the lock token from the request URI, and all other resources included in the lock.

JAVA

The most significant development in Java in the near future will be the final release of *JDK 1.2*, which will contain enhancements to many of the subjects that we have discussed in this book:

- Java Archive
- JavaBeans
- Java Reflection
- JDBC
- Object Serialization
- RMI

JDK 1.2 will also contain a number of new features of relevance to client/server data access:

- Collections
- Java IDL
- Swing

In the following section, we will take a quick look at *Jini*—a visionary, new way of doing Java distributed computing. Supposedly when Bill Joy presented a proposal to Sun in pre-1994, it consisted of three main concepts:

- A *language* that would run on all platforms
- A *virtual machine* to run this language
- A *networked system* to allow the distributed virtual machines to work as a single system

So the third concept has not materialized until Jini. (If you guessed "Java" and "Java Virtual Machine" for the first two, you are right.) In the long run, Jini may have a significant impact on client/server, distributed computing.

Jini

The *Jini* technology enables spontaneous networking of a wide variety of software and hardware—anything that can be connected to a network. A Jini system is a distributed system based on the concept of *federating* groups of *users* and the *resources* required by those users. Resources can be implemented as either software, hardware, or a combination of the two. A Jini system consists of the following parts:

- An ***infrastructure*** that consists of a set of components for federating services in a distributed system
- A ***programming model*** that supports and encourages the production of reliable distributed services
- A set of ***services*** that offer functionality to any other member of the federation

The Jini system extends the Java application environment (see Chapter 3, "Java Primer") from a single Java virtual machine to *a network of Java virtual machines*. The network supports a fluid configuration of Java objects (both code and data) that can move from place to place as needed and can call any part of the network to perform operations.

Key Concepts

The most important concept within the Jini system architecture is that of a *service*. Members of a Jini system federate so they can share access to services. A Jini federation consists of services that can be composed together to perform a particular task. The dynamic nature of the Jini system allows services to be added or withdrawn from a federation at any time. Jini systems provide mechanisms for *service construction, lookup, communication, and use*.

Services are found and resolved by a *lookup service*. A lookup service maps *interfaces* provided by a service to sets of objects that implement the service. In addition, metadata entries associated with a service allow fine-grained selection of services based on *properties*. A service is added to a lookup service by a process called *discovery*, indicating that the presence of the service is discovered by the Jini system.

Communication between services is accomplished using *RMI* (see Chapter 15, "Java RMI Overview"). RMI allows not only data to be passed from object to object around the network but also full objects (including data and code). RMI provides mechanisms to find, activate, and garbage collect object groups. It also provides the infrastructure for multicast and replication.

Access to many of the services is *lease-based*. A lease is a grant of guaranteed access over a time period. Each lease is negotiated between the user of the service and the provider of the service. If a lease is not renewed before it is freed, then both the user and the provider can conclude the service can be freed. Leases are either exclusive or non-exclusive. Non-exclusive leases allow multiple users to share a service.

The Jini security model is built on the notions of a *principal* and an *access control list*. Jini services are accessed on behalf of some entity, the principal. Whether access to a service is allowed depends on the content of the access control list associated with the service.

A series of operations, either within a single service or spanning multiple services, can be grouped in a *transaction*. The Jini transaction interfaces supply a service protocol needed to coordinate a *two-phase commit*.

The Jini system architecture supports *distributed events*. An object may allow other remote objects to register interest in events in the object and receive a notification of the occurrence of such an event.

Component Overview

As mentioned previously, the components of the Jini system are grouped into three categories: *infrastructure, programming model*, and *services*. The Jini *infrastructure* defines the minimal Jini core and includes:

- An extended version of **RMI** that is the basic mechanism of communication between components.
- A **distributed security** system, integrated into RMI, that extends the Java security model to distributed systems.
- The **discovery protocol**, a service protocol that allows services to become part of the Jini federation.
- The **lookup service**, that serves as a repository of services and the place for offering and finding services by members of the Jini federation.

The infrastructure both enables the programming model and makes use of it. The programming model rests on the ability to move code, which is supported by the infrastructure. Among the interfaces that make up the Jini *programming model* are:

- The **leasing** interface, which defines a way of accessing and freeing services using a renewable, duration-based model

- The ***event and notification*** interfaces, which is an extension of the Java event model to the distributed environment that enables event-based communication between services
- The ***transaction (two-phase commit)*** interfaces, which introduce a light-weight, object-oriented protocol enabling Jini objects to coordinate state changes

It is not required that the implementation of a service use the Jini programming model, but such services must use that model for their interaction with the Jini infrastructure. The Jini infrastructure and programming model enable services to be offered and found in the federation. The services make use of the infrastructure to announce their presence in the federation, to look up each other, and to make calls to each other.

Services appear programmatically as Java objects. A service has an interface that defines the operations that can be requested of that service. The initial Jini services include:

- A ***two-phase commit manager***, which enables groups of objects to participate in the two-phase commit protocol defined by the programming model
- ***JavaSpaces***, which can be used for simple communication and for storage of related groups of Java objects

Service Architecture

The heart of the Jini system is a pair of protocols called *discovery* and *lookup*. Discovery occurs when a service joins a Jini lookup service; lookup occurs when a client needs to locate and invoke a service. *Discovery* is the process of adding a service to a Jini system. First, the service provider locates a lookup service by broadcasting a presence announcement. Then, a proxy for the service is loaded into the lookup service. *Lookup* is the process for a client to locate an appropriate service by its type along with its properties.

The final stage is to invoke the service. The proxy code is loaded into the client from the lookup service. The ability to move code from the service provider to the lookup service—and from there to the client of the service—gives the service provider great freedom in the communication patterns between the service and its clients. This code movement also ensures that the proxy held by the client and the service for which it is a proxy are always synchronized. This occurs because the proxy is supplied by the service itself.

DATABASE SYSTEMS

Relational database vendors appear to have withstood the challenge made by object-oriented database vendors. In the process they have transformed relational databases into *object-relational databases*, which we will quickly review in the following section. With the growing importance of XML and its promise to transform the Web into a giant, universal information store, "*XML repository*" may become the next major battleground for database vendors.

Object-Relational Databases and SQL3

Relational databases were developed for traditional business applications such as banking transactions and inventory control. As discussed in Chapter 4, "Relational Databases and SQL," the relational data model is simple; it mainly views data as tables of rows and columns. Also, the types of data that can be stored in a table are basic types such as integer, numeric, and characters. Further, it does not allow users to extend the type system by adding new data types.

Object-oriented applications (such as Java applets or applications), on the other hand, make extensive use of major object-oriented features such as a user-extensible type system, encapsulation, inheritance, dynamic binding of methods, complex and composite objects, and object identity. The limitations of the relational data model need to be removed to enable the building of object-oriented, persistent applications. The challenge, therefore, is to eliminate as much as possible the so-called "*impedance mismatch*" between the relational data model and the object-oriented application model.

Object-relational databases are developed on the premise that extending, and not fundamentally changing, the relational data model is the best way to meet this challenge. They add support for object-oriented data modeling by extending both the relational data model and SQL, the query language. These extensions have become part of the new draft of the SQL standard named *SQL3*.

The major object extensions fall into the following categories:

- Extended functions
    - User-defined functions
    - Stored procedures
- Extended data types
    - Large objects
    - Distinct types
    - Structured types

Extended Functions

Relational database systems have traditionally provided a small number of built-in functions to perform simple operations such as computing an average and calculating a sum. This capability is not sufficient to represent business logic, except in very simple applications. *User-defined functions* and *stored procedures* allow users to define arbitrary business logic using popular programming languages such as Java. User-defined functions are also the fundamental mechanism needed to support extended data types.

User-defined functions are created using a statement called *CREATE FUNCTION*, which names the new function and specifies its signature and semantics. User-defined functions can be further classified into two subcategories:

- **Sourced functions.** A sourced function duplicates the semantics of another function, called its source function.
- **External functions.** An external function is a function that is written in a programming language, such as Java. The CREATE FUNCTION statement for an external function specifies the programming language and where to find the code that implements the function.

Like Java, SQL supports the concept of *function overloading*. This means that several user-defined functions may be defined to have the same name, but with different signatures. When a function is called with arguments, the system uses the *function resolution* process to choose the "best" applicable function to invoke.

A user-defined function may be specified to be *FENCED* or *UNFENCED*. The FENCED option specifies that the function must always be run in an address space that is separate from the database. This protects the integrity of the database against accidental or malicious damage that might be inflicted by the function.

Stored procedures are created using a statement called *CREATE PROCEDURE*, which names the new procedure and specifies its signature and semantics. A stored procedure is generally written in an external programming language such as Java. The CREATE PROCEDURE statement for a stored procedure specifies the programming language and where to find the code that implements the procedure.

No two identically named stored procedures within a schema are permitted to have exactly the same number of parameters. Therefore, resolution process is not needed when invoking a stored procedure. A stored procedure may have IN, OUT, and INOUT parameters, and it may return more than one result set.

A stored procedure may be specified to be *FENCED* or *UNFENCED*. The FENCED option specifies that the procedure must always be run in an address space that is separate from the database. This protects the integrity of the database against accidental or malicious damage that might be inflicted by the procedure.

User-defined functions and stored procedures are similar but different. A major difference is that a stored procedure is simply an application program managed and run by the database system. Therefore, for example, you can make JDBC calls in a stored procedure, but not in a user-defined function (assuming both are written in Java). Both JDBC and SQLJ support the usage of user-defined functions and stored procedures (see Chapter 7, "JDBC in a Nutshell" and Chapter 8, "Introduction to SQLJ," respectively).

Extended Data Types

Relational database systems have typically provided a fixed number of built-in data types designed to support traditional business applications. Increasingly, however, database applications are requiring the storage and manipulation of objects that are very large (such as images, audio, and video) and/or have complex behavior (such as components of an software design). Extended data types allow users to define arbitrarily large and complex data types including *large objects*, *distinct types*, and *structured types*.

Two new built-in data types are added in SQL3 to support large objects:

- **BLOB (Binary Large Object)**. The BLOB data type can contain, for example, up to two gigabytes of binary data. BLOBs cannot be assigned to or compared with values of any other data type.
- **CLOB (Character Large Object)**. The CLOB data type can contain, for example, up to two gigabytes of single-byte character data. CLOBs can be assigned to or compared with values of other character data types (CHAR, VARCHAR, and LONGVARCHAR).

It can be quite expensive to move large objects from one place to another, either in memory or across a network. LOBs can be manipulated in user programs by means of *locators*, which represent the values of a LOB without actually containing the LOB data. (Locators can also be used to represent structured types.)

Distinct types are provided to supplement the database systems's built-in data types. Each distinct type shares a common internal representation with one of the built-in data types, called its base type. Despite this common representation, however, the distinct type is considered to be a separate data type, distinct from all others, and thus provides strong typing. Distinct types are created using the CREATE TYPE statement. Here is an example:

```
CREATE TYPE DOLLAR AS NUMERIC(10,2)
```

Structured types are what will transform relational databases into object-relational databases. Structured types support all major object-oriented features that we mentioned earlier: a user-extensible type system, encapsulation, inheritance, dynamic binding of methods, complex and composite objects, and object identity. Structured types are created using the CREATE TYPE statement. Once created, they can be used as:

- The type of a column in a table. Structured types used in this way are sometimes called *abstract data types*.
- The type of a table. Structured types used in this way are sometimes called *row types*.

The following example shows the use of structured types as row types together with complex (embedded) and composite (referenced) objects; the latter uses the *REF* data type:

```
CREATE TYPE RESIDENCE
(    street VARCHAR(100),
     city VARCHAR(100),
     occupant REF(PERSON)
)
CREATE TYPE FULLNAME
(    first VARCHAR(50),
     last VARCHAR(50)
)
CREATE TYPE PERSON
(    name FULLNAME,
     home REF(RESIDENCE)
)

CREATE TABLE Homes OF RESIDENCE (OID REF(RESIDENCE)
     VALUES ARE SYSTEM GENERATED)
CREATE TABLE People OF PERSON (OID REF(PERSON)
     VALUES ARE SYSTEM GENERATED)
```

JAVA DATA ACCESS

Things have moved fast in the arena of Java data access. JDBC 1.0 is barely one year old, and here is the final *JDBC 2.0* specification with major enhancements. However, unlike JDBC 1.0, for which the final specification came with a running JDBC-ODBC driver implementation, JDBC 2.0 is just a specification, and it will be so for a while because of its features. The same is true with SQLJ. Part 0 (the original proposal on embedded SQL for Java) is not yet an adopted standard, and here are working drafts of *SQLJ Part 1* and *SQLJ Part 2*, dealing with Java stored procedures and Java data types, respectively. We will give a quick overview of these in the following sections. ODMG is not idling either. Its members are working on removing the current limitations of the *ODMG Java Binding* and making ODMG 2.0 (or a newer version) an ECMA standard.

JDBC 2.0

The major enhancements made by JDBC 2.0 come in the following categories:

■ *Advanced database features*. There are some important features provided by database systems that are not supported by JDBC 1.0. These include *scrollable cursors* and advanced data types, such as *large objects* and *distinct types*. All of these are supported by JDBC 2.0. In addition, JDBC 2.0 supports both databases that provide storage for *Java objects* and databases that store SQL3 *structured types*.

■ *JavaBeans*. When JDBC 1.0 was developed, there was no component model for the Java platform. With JavaBeans, JDBC should provide a foundation for developing data-aware JavaBeans components. A new **RowSet** type has been added in JDBC 2.0 to meet this goal.

■ *Other pieces of the Java platform*. Some of the new Java APIs that are important to JDBC and are supported in JDBC 2.0 include the *Java Naming and Directory Interface (JNDI)* and the *Java Transaction Service (JTS)*.

The major new features that are provided by JDBC 2.0 include:

■ *Result set enhancements*. JDBC 1.0 provided result sets that had the ability to scroll in a forward direction only. *Scrollable result sets* allow for more flexibility in the processing of results by providing both forward and backward movement through their contents. They also allow for relative and absolute positioning. JDBC 2.0 also allows result sets to be *directly updatable*.

■ *Batch updates*. The batch update feature allows an application to submit multiple update statements (INSERT/UPDATE/DELETE) in a single request to the database. This can greatly improve performance in some situations.

■ *Persistent Java objects*. JDBC 1.0 provided some support for storing Java objects and retrieving Java objects from a database via the *getObject()* and *setObject()* methods. This is enhanced by providing new *metadata* capabilities that can be used to retrieve a description of the Java objects that a database contains.

- *New SQL data types*. The new SQL data types that are supported include:

  ◆ Large objects—BLOB, CLOB
  ◆ Distinct types
  ◆ Structured types
  ◆ Constructed types—ARRAY, REF

  In addition, JDBC 2.0 provides for customizing the *mapping* of SQL distinct and structured types into Java classes.

- *JNDI for naming databases*. JNDI can be used in addition to the JDBC driver manager to obtain a connection to a database. When an application uses JNDI, it specifies a *logical name* that identifies a particular database and JDBC driver for accessing that database. This has the advantage of making the application code independent of a particular JDBC URL and JDBC driver.

- *Distributed transaction support*. This feature allows a JDBC driver to support the standard *two-phase commit* protocol used by JTS.

- *Rowsets*. A rowset encapsulates a set of rows. It may or may not maintain an open database connection. When a rowset is "disconnected" from its data source, updates performed on the rowset are propagated to the underlying database using an *optimistic concurrency control* algorithm. A rowset object is a JavaBean.

- *Connection pooling.* This feature allows for a single *connection cache* that spans the different JDBC drivers that may be in use. Creating and destroying database connections is expensive, so connection pooling is important for achieving good performance.

The JDBC 2.0 API has been factored into two complimentary components. The first component, termed the *JDBC 2.0 Core API*, consists of the updated contents of the **java.sql** package. The second component, termed the *JDBC 2.0 Standard Extension API*, consists of the contents of a new package, **javax.sql**.

The **java.sql** package contains all of the additions that have been made to the existing JDBC 1.0 interfaces and classes. It also has the following new interfaces and classes:

- **java.sql.BatchUpdateException**
- **java.sql.Array, java.sql.Blob, java.sql.Clob, java.sql.Ref, java.sql.SQLData, java.sql.SQLInput, java.sql.SQLOutput, java.sql.Struct**

The new **javax.sql** package has been introduced to contain the parts of the JDBC 2.0 API that are closely related to other pieces of the Java platform. These pieces are themselves standard extensions, such JNDI and JTS. In addition, some advanced features, such as rowsets and connection pooling, have also been added to it. The **javax.sql** package includes:

- **javax.sql.ConnectionEvent, javax.sql.ConnectionEventListener, javax.sql. ConnectionPoolDataSource, javax.sql.PooledConnection**
- **javax.sql.CursorMovedEvent, javax.sql.CursorMovedListener**
- **javax.sql.RowSet, javax.sql.RowSetImpl, javax.sql.RowSetMetaData, javax. sql.RowSetMetaDataImpl, javax.sql.RowSetUpdatedEvent, javax. sql.RowSetUpdatedListener**
- **javax.sql.DataSource, javax.sql.XAConnection, javax.sql.XADataSource**

SQLJ Part 1 & Part 2

The term SQLJ is used for a series of specifications for ways to use Java with SQL:

- ***Part 0: Embedded SQL for Java*** includes specifications for embedding SQL statements in Java methods. We discussed this in Chapter 8, "Introduction to SQLJ."
- ***Part 1: Java Stored Procedures*** includes specifications for calling Java static methods as SQL stored procedures and user-defined functions.
- ***Part 2: Java Data Types*** includes specifications for using Java classes as SQL user-defined data types.

The collection of these facilities provides a way to write Java classes whose methods invoke SQL statements. Also provided is a way to use those classes in a SQL system, including writing user-defined functions, stored procedures, and data types in Java.

SQLJ Part 1 specifies SQL extensions for installing Java classes in a SQL system, for invoking static methods of Java classes in SQL as *user-defined functions* and *stored procedures*, for obtaining specified output values of parameters, and for returning result sets.

The SQLJ Part 1 extensions to SQL include the following:

- New built-in schema, named *sqlj*, which is assumed to be in all catalogs of a SQLJ implementation and to contain all of the built-in procedures of the SQLJ facility

- New built-in procedures:

  - sqlj.install_jar—loads a set of Java classes in a SQL system.
  - sqlj.replace_jar—replaces a set of Java classes.
  - sqlj.remove_jar—deletes a previously installed set of Java classes.

- ◆ sqlj.alter_java_path—specifies a path for name resolution within Java classes

- ■ Extended statements:

  - ◆ CREATE PROCEDURE/FUNCTION—specifies a SQL name for a Java static method.
  - ◆ DROP PROCEDURE/FUNCTION—deletes the SQL name of a Java static method.
  - ◆ GRANT—grants the usage privilege on Java jars.
  - ◆ REVOKE—revokes the usage privilege on Java jars.

- ■ Conventions for returning values of OUT and INOUT parameters and for returning result sets.

SQLJ Part 2 specifies SQL extensions for installing Java classes in a SQL system, and for using those classes as *data types* in SQL. This capability of using Java classes in SQL has two different but complementary uses:

- ■ It provides a type extension mechanism for SQL.
- ■ It provides a persistence capability for Java objects.

The advantage of the SQLJ Part 2 facility over plain SQL facilities is that you don't have to map Java objects into scalar SQL data types. And you don't have to store Java objects as untyped binary strings.

SQLJ Part 2 assumes the facility of SQLJ Part 1. The SQLJ Part 2 extensions to SQL include the following:

- ■ Extended statements:

  - ◆ CREATE TYPE—specifies a SQL name for a Java class.
  - ◆ DROP TYPE—deletes the SQL name of a Java class.

  In the SQLJ Part 2 facilities, the extended statements can only be specified in deployment descriptor files.

- ■ New forms of reference—qualified references to the fields and methods of columns whose data types are defined on Java classes.

WEB DATA ACCESS

The most significant impact on Web data access in the near future will be *XML* and the use of *metadata* in search. XML and its family of technologies are still in the early stages of development, so the eventual impact is currently not clear. One glimpse is provided by *DASL*, which we will briefly discuss in the following sections. An interesting feature about DASL is that both the metadata that it is searching, which are WebDAV properties, and the query statements it uses to express the search, are all represented in XML.

DASL

DASL (DAV Searching and Locating) is an extension to the WebDAV protocol to support efficient server searching for resources based on WebDAV properties or document content (full-text search). HTTP/1.1 and WebDAV provide support for client-side search, but not server-side search. DASL provides a new HTTP method that allows servers to perform the search instead of moving all candidate resources to the client to perform the search.

DASL includes the *SEARCH* method, the DASL response header for use with the OPTIONS method, a request entity body that specifies the query, and a simple search grammar that conformant servers must support. A *query* specifies the search criteria that resources must meet to satisfy the query, search scope, result record definition, and sort specification.

DASL follows the typical HTTP/1.1 request/response chain. A client invokes the SEARCH method with an *XML request entity body* containing the query. The server responds with a *text/xml* entity body that contains the result set. The response is a typical WebDAV multistatus response containing a response element for each affected resource.

DASL specifies a *simple search grammar* a SQL-compliant server must support. This grammar is derived from existing XML elements in WebDAV. In addition, the results are returned in a WebDAV multistatus element. DASL allows any other query grammar to be used within the search request element. It is up to the server to access the type element and interpret the contents of the query appropriately.

The DASL simple search grammar uses an extensible XML syntax. It has the following major components:

- *select* provides the result record definition.
- *from* defines the search scope.
- *where* defines the search criteria.
- *sortby* defines the sort order of the result set.

The DASL *select* element defines the result record. It contains two possible types of elements, both defined in WebDAV:

- *allprops* is the result record for a given resource that includes all the properties for that resource.
- *props* is the result record for a given resource that includes only those properties named by this element.

The DASL *from* element defines the search scope. It contains one or more of the following:

- *scope*—each scope contains:
  - ◆ *uri* indicates the URI for a collection to use as a scope.
  - ◆ *depth* (optional) has a value of "0" or "infinite", indicating non-recursive and recursive searching of a scope, respectively.

The DASL *where* element defines the search criteria. It contains any XML element that defines a search operator that evaluates to True, False, or Unknown. The search operator is applied to the resource. If, and only if, the result of the operation is True, then the resource is included as a member of the result set.

The DASL *sortby* element specifies the ordering of the result set. It contains a list of properties for each resource in the result set upon which to sort.

JAVA CLIENT/SERVER COMPUTING

Java client/server computing up to this point has been done mainly using synchronous communication mechanisms: RMI or Java ORB. However, asynchronous communication mechanisms are coming in the form of *JavaMail* and *JMS (Java Messaging Service)*. In the following section, we will briefly discuss JavaMail. The specification on JMS is currently not available.

JavaMail

JavaMail is a Java-based mail and messaging framework. The JavaMail API provides a set of abstract classes defining objects that comprise a mail system. The API defines classes like **Message**, **Store**, and **Transport**. In addition, the API provides concrete subclasses of the abstract classes that implement widely used Internet mail protocols. The JavaMail API supports many different messaging system implementations—different message formats, different message stores, and different message transports.

The JavaMail architectural components are layered as follows:

- The ***Abstract Layer*** declares interfaces and classes intended to support mail-handling functions that all mail systems support. These API elements are intended to be extended and subclassed as necessary to support standard data types, and to interface with message access and message transport protocols as necessary.

- The ***Internet Mail Implementation Layer*** implements part of the Abstract Layer using Internet standards.

JavaMail clients use the JavaMail API, and service providers implement the JavaMail API. The layered architecture allows clients to use the same API to send, receive, and store a variety of messages using different data types from different message stores and using different message transport protocols.

The JavaMail API is intended to perform the following functions:

- Create a *mail message* consisting of a collection of header attributes and a block of data of some known data type, as specified in the header. JavaMail uses the **Part** interface and the **Message** class to define a mail message.
- Create a *session* object that authenticates the user and controls access to the message store and transport.
- *Send* the message to its recipient list.
- *Retrieve* a message from a message store.
- Execute a *high-level command* on a retrieved message. High-level commands like *view* and *print* are intended to be implemented via JavaBeans.

The major components comprising the JavaMail architecture include:

- ***The Message class***. The **Message** class is an abstract class that defines a set of attributes and a content for a mail message. Message attributes specify addressing information and define the structure of the content, including the content type. The **Message** class implements the **Part** interface, which defines attributes that are required to define and format the content carried by a **Message** object, and to interface successfully to a mail system. The content of a **Message** is a collection of bytes, or a reference to a collection of bytes. JavaMail has no knowledge of the data type or format of the message content. The message recipient usually knows the content data type and format; it also knows how to handle that content.

- ***Message storage and retrieval***. Messages are stored in **Folder** objects. A folder can contain subfolders as well as messages, thus providing a tree-like folder hierarchy. The **Folder** class defines methods that fetch, append, copy, and delete **Messages**. The **Store** class defines a database that holds a folder hierarchy together with its messages. It specifies methods to establish a connection to the database, to fetch folders, and to close a connection.

- ***Message composition and transport***. A client creates a new message by instantiating an appropriate **Message** subclass. It sets attributes such as the recipient addresses and the subject, inserts content into the message, and finally sends the message by invoking the *send()* method on the **Transport** class. The **Transport** class routes a message to its destination addresses. It selects the appropriate transport based on the destination addresses.

■ ***The Session class***. The **Session** class defines the global and per-user mail-related properties. JavaMail system components use the **Session** object to set and get specific properties.

WEB DATA INTERCHANGE

With XML, a document is separated into three parts: structure, content, and presentation. XML, XLink, and XPointer define the structure. In the following section, we will briefly discuss *XSL*, which defines a way to associate presentation style (for example, formatting semantics) with a document marked up using XML. XSL is still in a very early stage of development, but it is urgently needed in order for XML to be "presentable."

XSL

XSL (eXtensible Style Language) is a stylesheet language designed for use with XML. It provides functionality beyond CSS (for example, element reordering). It is expected that CSS (see Chapter 13, "Dynamic HTML") will be used to display simply structured XML documents. Also expected is that XSL will be used where more powerful formatting capabilities are required or for formatting highly structured information such as XML structured data or XML documents that contain structured data.

Web authors create content at three different levels of sophistication:

■ *Markup*—relies solely on a declarative syntax.
■ *Script*—additionally uses code "snippets" for more complex behaviors.
■ *Program*—uses a full programming language.

XSL is intended to be accessible to the *"markup"* level user by providing a declarative solution to most data description and rendering requirements. Less common tasks are accommodated through a graceful escape to a familiar scripting environment.

XSL enables formatting information to be associated with elements in the source document to produce formatted output. The formatted output is created by formatting a tree of *flow objects*. A flow object has a class that represents a kind of formatting task. A flow object also has a set of named characteristics that further specify the formatting.

The association of elements in the source tree to flow objects is through *construction rules*. The construction rules contain both a *pattern* to identify specific elements in the source tree and an *action* to specify a resulting sub-tree of flow objects. The XSL processor recursively processes source elements to produce a complete flow object tree.

In addition to construction rules, XSL also supports *style rules* that allow the merging of characteristics. While only one construction rule can be invoked for a particular source element, all applicable style rules are invoked, allowing per-characteristic merging as in CSS.

An XSL stylesheet describes this formatting process through a small set of XML elements. An XSL stylesheet contains an *XSL document element*. This element can contain both rule elements representing construction rules and style-rule elements representing style merging rules.

The powerful capabilities provided by XSL allow:

- Formatting of *source elements* based on ancestry/descendency, position, and uniqueness
- The creation of *formatting constructs*, including generated text and graphics
- The definition of reusable *formatting macros*
- Writing-direction independent stylesheets
- Extensible set of *formatting objects*

JAVA/WEB COMPONENT ARCHITECTURES

The technologies we discussed in this book are all important to client/server data access: Web, Java, database systems, Java data access, Web data access, Java client/server computing, and Web data interchange. However, individually, they are only pieces of a puzzle. They need to be put together in some fashion to provide an integrated solution to the customers. In the following sections, we will briefly look at two prominent architectures for integration:

- ***Java/Web application servers*** with focus on *objects* and *OLTP (On-line Transaction Processing)*
- ***Business intelligence and data warehousing*** with focus on *data, metadata,* and *OLAP (On-line Analytical Processing)*

Java/Web Application Servers

Java/Web application servers (JWAS) provide an integrated development and execution environment for server-side Java application components. They support remote access to the application components on the Web, and they manage resource usage to increase application scalability. They achieve scalability by distributing the processing load across multiple processors and by pooling and sharing system resources, such as operating system processes, database connections, and network sessions.

A prominent architecture for JWAS is the *Java Platform for the Enterprise (JPE)* announced by Sun. JPE defines a server component model, EJB (see Chapter 21, "Enterprise JavaBeans"), and a set of APIs that will enable the development and management of distributed applications integrating Java, Web, CORBA, relational database systems, and transaction managers. JPE provides not only platform portability but also middleware portability.

The JPE APIs consists of:

■ *Distributed communications*

  ◆ *RMI* defines Java-to-Java communication (see Chapter 15, "Java RMI Overview").
  ◆ *Java IDL* defines Java-to-CORBA communication (see Chapter 16, "Introduction to Java ORBs").
  ◆ *JMS (Java Messaging Services)* provides support for asynchronous messaging.

■ *Data access*

  ◆ *JDBC* defines a call-level interface for accessing relational databases (see Chapter 7, "JDBC in a Nutshell").
  ◆ *SQLJ* defines an embedded interface for accessing relational databases (see Chapter 8, "Introduction to SQLJ").
  ◆ *ODMG Java Binding* provides access to object-oriented databases (see Chapter 9, "Java Binding for OODB").

■ *Infrastructure*

  ◆ *JNDI (Java Naming and Directory Interfaces)* defines a standard interface for accessing disparate network naming and directory services.
  ◆ *JTS (Java Transaction Services)* defines a standard interface to heterogeneous transaction managers.
  ◆ *JMAPI (Java Management API)* provides support for distributed application management.

■ *Server components*

   ◆ *Servlets* defines a standard mechanism to invoke server-based Java applications from a Web page (see Chapter 12, "Java Applets and Servlets").

   ◆ *EJB (Enterprise JavaBeans)* defines a server component model (see Chapter 21, "Enterprise JavaBeans").

Business Intelligence and Data Warehousing

Business intelligence systems focus on improving the access and delivery of business information to both information providers (such as business analysts) and information consumers (such as business executives and business managers). They achieve this by providing both advanced Web-based and graphical *OLAP* and *information mining* tools as well as prepackaged applications that exploit the power of those tools. These applications may need to process and analyze large volumes of information using a variety of tools. Therefore, a business intelligence system must provide scalability and be able to support and integrate products from multiple vendors.

Data warehousing provides an excellent approach for transforming operational and external data into useful and reliable information to support the need of business intelligence systems. A data warehouse is a subject-oriented, integrated, time-variant, and non-volatile collection of information in support of management decisions. It involves:

■ One or more tools to extract data from any type of data source (relational, hierarchical, or object-oriented), including both operational and external data

■ The cleansing and transformation of the data into subject-oriented information with a metadata catalog

A prominent architecture for business intelligence systems is the one provided by IBM. This architecture consists of the following components:

■ *Business intelligence applications*. These applications are tailored for a specific industry and/or application domain.

■ *Decision-support tools*. These can be broken down into three categories:

   ◆ Query and reporting tools
   ◆ OLAP tools
   ◆ Information-mining tools

- **Access enablers**. These consist of APIs (such as *JDBC* and *SQLJ*) and middleware (such as **Net.Data**) that allow client tools to access and process business information managed by database systems.

- **Data management**. These are products (such as **DB2**) that are used to manage the business information of interest to end users.

- **Data warehousing modeling and construction tool**s. These tools are used to capture data from operational and external sources, clean and transform it, and load it into a data warehouse or data mart.

- **Metadata management**. This component manages the metadata associated with the business intelligence system, including the technical metadata used by developers and administrators, as well as the business metadata for supporting business users. The focus is on improving metadata interchange (for example, via *XML*) between tools and automating and synchronizing this interchange wherever possible.

- **Administration**. This component covers all aspects of business intelligence administration, including security and authorization, backup and recovery, monitoring and tuning, operations and scheduling, and auditing and accounting.

JAVA OR XML

So it is finally time to say good-bye. As promised, let us ponder a bit on the question as we leave: *Java* or *XML*?

Are both just hype? We hope this book has shown that they are not. Both are solid technologies, evolved from earlier incarnations. *Are both magic bullets?* We hope this book has shown that they are not that either. Both are good for certain things and not so good for others. Both are still young and evolving (Java may be in its adolescence, but XML is definitely in its infancy). *Is one better than the other?* Well, that depends:

- **Java** is an object-oriented programming language and virtual machine. Java is object-centric or behavior-centric and encapsulates data. Java has inherent support for networking, and one of Java's key benefits is its ability to glue together heterogeneous systems over a network through programming and object interchange.

- **XML** is a hierarchical markup language and processor. XML is data-centric or state-centric and provides no behavior. XML is inherently designed as a serialized format, and one of XML's key benefits is its ability to glue together heterogeneous systems over a network through data and metadata interchange.

So we think the answer to the question is: *Java and XML*. Java is becoming the *universal programming language*. XML will become the *universal data representation. Combining Java with XML is a powerful strategy for client/server data access going into the twenty-first century.*

Where to Go for More Information

We have compiled the following list of references to help you find more information on the topics we covered in this book.

Client/Server

- Robert Orfali, Dan Harkey, and Jeri Edwards, **The Essential Client/Server Survival Guide, Second Edition** (Wiley, 1996)

- Robert Orfali and Dan Harkey, **Client/Server Programming with Java and CORBA, Second Edition** (Wiley, 1998)

Web

- **HTML 3.2 Reference Specification** (W3C Recommendation 14-Jan-1997, http://www.w3.org/TR/REC-html32)

- **HTML 4.0 Specification** (W3C Recommendation 18-Dec-1997, http://www.w3.org/TR/REC-html40)

- **HTTP—Hypertext Transfer Protocol** (http://www.w3.org/Protocols/)

- **WWW Distributed Authoring and Versioning (WebDAV)** (http://www.ietf.org/html.charters/webdav-charter.html)

Java

- **Java** (http://www.ibm.com/java/, http://java.sun.com/)

- **Java Products and APIs** (http://java.sun.com/products/)

- **Jini** (http://java.sun.com/products/jini/)

- James Gosling, Bill Joy, and Guy Steele, **The Java Language Specification** (Addison-Wesley, 1996)

Database Systems

- C. J. Bontempo and C. M. Saracco, **Database Management Principles and Products** (Prentice Hall, 1995)

- C. J. Date, **An Introduction to Database Systems, Sixth Edition** (Addison-Wesley, 1995)

SQL

- Jim Melton and Alan R. Simon, **Understanding the New SQL: A Complete Guide** (Morgan Kaufmann, 1993)

Relational and Object-Relational Database Systems

- **DB2 Universal Database** (http://www.software.ibm.com/data/db2/)

- **Oracle8** (http://www.oracle.com/st/products/uds/oracle8/)

- **SQL Server** (http://www.microsoft.com/sql/)

- Don Chamberlin, **A Complete Guide to DB2 Universal Database** (Morgan Kaufmann, 1998)

- C. M. Saracco, **Universal Database Management: A Guide to Object/Relational Technology** (Morgan Kaufmann, 1998)

ODMG

- **ODMG Standard Overview** (http://www.odmg.org/)

- R. G. G. Cattell, et al., **The Object Database Standard: ODMG 2.0** (Morgan Kaufmann, 1997)

Object-Oriented Database Systems

■ **POET** (http://www.poet.com/)

Java and Web Data Access

■ V. Srinivasan and D. T. Chang, **Object Persistence in Object-Oriented Applications**, *IBM Systems Journal*, Vol. 36, No. 1 (1997)

Java Data Access

■ **The JDBC Database Access API** (http://splash.javasoft.com/databases/jdbc/)

■ **SQLJ** (http://www.oracle.com/st/products/jdbc/sqlj/)

Web Data Access

■ **Net.Data** (http://www.software.ibm.com/data/net.data/)

■ Josephine Cheng and Susan Malaika (eds.), **Web Gateway Tools: Connecting IBM and Lotus Applications to the Web** (Wiley, 1997)

■ **Java Web Server** (http://java.sun.com/products/webserver/)

■ **Dynamic HTML** (http://www.microsoft.com/workshop/author/default.asp)

■ **DAV Searching and Locating (DASL)** (http://www.ics.uci.edu/pub/ietf/dasl/)

Java Client/Server Computing

■ **IDL/Java Language Mapping** (OMG TC Document orbos/97-03-01)

■ **Java to IDL Mapping** (OMG TC Document orbos/98-01-07)

- **VisiBroker** (http://www.inprise.com/visibroker/)

- **JavaMail** (http://java.sun.com/products/javamail/)

XML and Web Data Interchange

- **XML** (http://www.w3.org/XML/, http://www.microsoft.com/xml/default.asp)

- **Namespaces in XML** (http://www.w3c.org/TR/WD-xml-names)

- **XML Linking Language (XLink)** (http://www.w3c.org/TR/WD-xml-names)

- **XML Pointer Language (XPointer)** (http://www.w3c.org/TR/WD-xptr)

- **eXtensible Style Language (XSL)** (http://www.w3c.org/Style/XSL/)

- **Document Object Model (DOM)** (http://www.w3.org/DOM/)

- **SAX 1.0: The Simple API for XML** (http://www.megginson.com//SAX)

- **XML for Java** (http://www.alphaworks.ibm.com/formula/xml/)

- **Meta Object Facility (MOF) Specification** (OMG TC Document ad/97-08-14)

- **XML Metadata Interchange (XMI)** (OMG TC Document ad/98-07-01)

Java/Web Component Architectures

- **JavaBeans** (http://java.sun.com/beans/)

- **Enterprise JavaBeans** (http://java.sun.com/products/ejb/)

- **Java/Web Application Servers** (http://www.software.ibm.com/webservers, http://java.sun.com/marketing/enterprise/index.html, http://www.weblogic.com/)

- **Business Intelligence and Data Warehousing** (http://www.software.ibm.com/data/busn-intel)

Index

Index

594

Index

Java(tm) Development Kit, Version 1.1.6
and BDK Version 1.x
Combined Binary Code License

This binary code license ("License") contains rights and restrictions associated with use of the accompanying software and documentation ("Software"). Read the License carefully before installing the Software. By installing the Software you agree to the terms and conditions of this License.

1. Limited License Grant. Sun grants to you ("Licensee") a non-exclusive, non-transferable limited license to use the Software without fee for evaluation of the Software and for development of Java(tm) compatible applets and applications. Licensee may make one archival copy of the Software and may re-distribute complete, unmodified copies of the Software to software developers within Licensee's organization to avoid unnecessary download time, provided that this License conspicuously appear with all copies of the Software. Except for the foregoing, Licensee may not re-distribute the Software in whole or in part, either separately or included with a product. Refer to the Java Runtime Environment Version 1.1.5 binary code license (http://java.sun.com/products/JDK/1.1/index.html) for the availability of runtime code which may be distributed with Java compatible applets and applications.

2. Java Platform Interface. Licensee may not modify the Java Platform Interface ("JPI", identified as classes contained within the "java" package or any subpackages of the "java" package), by creating additional classes within the JPI or otherwise causing the addition to or modification of the classes in the JPI. In the event that Licensee creates any Java-related API and distributes such API to others for applet or application development, Licensee must promptly publish an accurate specification for such API for free use by all developers of Java-based software.

3. Restrictions. Software is confidential copyrighted information of Sun and title to all copies is retained by Sun and/or its licensors. Licensee shall not modify, decompile, disassemble, decrypt, extract, or otherwise reverse engineer Software. Software may not be leased, assigned, or sublicensed, in whole or in part. **Software is not designed or intended for use in on-line control of aircraft, air traffic, aircraft navigation or aircraft communications; or in the design, construction, operation or maintenance of any nuclear facility. Licensee warrants that it will not use or redistribute the Software for such purposes.**

4. Trademarks and Logos. This License does not authorize Licensee to use any Sun name, trademark or logo. Licensee acknowledges that Sun owns the Java trademark and all Java-related trademarks, logos and icons including the Coffee Cup and Duke ("Java Marks") and agrees to: (i) to comply with the Java Trademark Guidelines at http://java.sun.com/trademarks.html; (ii) not do anything harmful to or inconsistent with Sun's rights in the Java Marks; and (iii) assist Sun in protecting those rights, including assigning to Sun any rights acquired by Licensee in any Java Mark.

5. Disclaimer of Warranty. Software is provided "AS IS," without a warranty of any kind. ALL EXPRESS OR IMPLIED REPRESENTATIONS AND WARRANTIES, INCLUDING ANY IMPLIED WARRANTY OF MERCHANTABILITY, FITNESS FOR A PARTICULAR PURPOSE OR NON-INFRINGEMENT, ARE HEREBY EXCLUDED.

6. Limitation of Liability. SUN AND ITS LICENSORS SHALL NOT BE LIABLE FOR ANY DAMAGES SUFFERED BY LICENSEE OR ANY THIRD PARTY AS A RESULT OF USING OR DISTRIBUTING SOFTWARE. IN NO EVENT WILL SUN OR ITS LICENSORS BE LIABLE FOR ANY LOST REVENUE, PROFIT OR DATA, OR FOR DIRECT, INDIRECT, SPECIAL, CONSEQUENTIAL, INCIDENTAL OR PUNI-TIVE DAMAGES, HOWEVER CAUSED AND REGARDLESS OF THE THEORY OF LIABILITY, ARISING OUT OF THE USE OF OR INABILITY TO USE SOFTWARE, EVEN IF SUN HAS BEEN ADVISED OF THE POSSIBILITY OF SUCH DAMAGES.

7. Termination. Licensee may terminate this License at any time by destroying all copies of Software. This License will terminate immediately without notice from Sun if Licensee fails to comply with any provision of this License. Upon such termination, Licensee must destroy all copies of Software.

8. Export Regulations. Software, including technical data, is subject to U.S. export control laws, including the U.S. Export Administration Act and its associated regulations, and may be subject to export or import regulations in other countries. Licensee agrees to comply strictly with all such regulations and acknowledges that it has the responsibility to obtain licenses to export, re-export, or import Software. Software may not be downloaded, or otherwise exported or re-exported (i) into, or to a national or resident of, Cuba, Iraq, Iran, North Korea, Libya, Sudan, Syria or any country to which the U.S. has embargoed goods; or (ii) to anyone on the U.S. Treasury Department's list of Specially Designated Nations or the U.S. Commerce Department's Table of Denial Orders.

9. Restricted Rights. Use, duplication or disclosure by the United States government is subject to the restrictions as set forth in the Rights in Technical Data and Computer Software Clauses in DFARS 252.227-7013(c) (1) (ii) and FAR 52.227-19(c) (2) as applicable.

10. Governing Law. Any action related to this License will be governed by California law and controlling U.S. federal law. No choice of law rules of any jurisdiction will apply.

11. Severability. If any of the above provisions are held to be in violation of applicable law, void, or unenforceable in any jurisdiction, then such provisions are herewith waived to the extent necessary for the License to be otherwise enforceable in such jurisdiction. However, if in Sun's opinion deletion of any provisions of the License by operation of this paragraph unreasonably compromises the rights or increase the liabilities of Sun or its licensors, Sun reserves the right to terminate the License and refund the fee paid by Licensee, if any, as Licensee's sole and exclusive remedy.

Inprise Corporation
TRIAL EDITION SOFTWARE License Statement

YOUR USE OF THE TRIAL EDITION SOFTWARE DISTRIBUTED WITH THIS LICENSE IS SUBJECT TO ALL OF THE TERMS AND CONDITIONS OF THIS LICENSE STATEMENT. IF YOU DO NOT AGREE TO ALL OF THE TERMS AND CONDITIONS OF THIS STATEMENT, DO NOT USE THE SOFTWARE.

1. This Software is protected by copyright law and international copyright treaty. Therefore, you must treat this Software just like a book, except that you may copy it onto a computer to be used and you may make archive copies of the Software for the sole purpose of backing up our Software and protecting your investment from loss. Your use of this software is limited to evaluation and trial use purposes only.

FURTHER, THIS SOFTWARE CONTAINS A TIME-OUT FEATURE THAT DIS-ABLES ITS OPERATION AFTER A CERTAIN PERIOD OF TIME. A TEXT FILE DELIVERED WITH THE SOFTWARE WILL STATE THE TIME PERIOD AND/OR SPECIFIC DATE("EVALUATION PERIOD") ON WHICH THE SOFTWARE WILL EXPIRE. Though Inprise does not offer technical support for the Software, we welcome your feedback.

If the Software is an Inprise development tool, you can write and compile applications for your own personal use on the computer on which you have installed the Software, but you do not have a right to distribute or otherwise share those applications or any files of the Software which may be required to support those applications. APPLICATIONS THAT YOU CREATE MAY REQUIRE THE SOFTWARE IN ORDER TO RUN. UPON EXPIRATION OF THE EVALUATION PERIOD, THOSE APPLICATIONS WILL NO LONGER RUN. You should therefore take precautions to avoid any loss of data that might result.

2. INPRISE MAKES NO REPRESENTATIONS ABOUT THE SUITABILITY OF THIS SOFTWARE OR ABOUT ANY CONTENT OR INFORMATION MADE ACCESSIBLE BY THE SOFTWARE, FOR ANY PURPOSE. THE SOFTWARE IS PROVIDED 'AS IS' WITHOUT EXPRESS OR IMPLIED WARRANTIES, INCLUDING WARRANTIES OF MERCHANTABILITY AND FITNESS FOR A PARTICULAR PURPOSE OR NONINFRINGEMENT. THIS SOFTWARE IS PROVIDED GRATUITOUSLY AND, ACCORDINGLY, INPRISE SHALL NOT BE LIABLE UNDER ANY THEORY FOR ANY DAMAGES SUFFERED BY YOU OR ANY USER OF THE SOFTWARE. INPRISE WILL NOT SUPPORT THIS SOFTWARE AND IS UNDER NO OBLIGA-TION TO ISSUE UPDATES TO THIS SOFTWARE.

3. While Inprise intends to distribute (or may have already distributed) a commercial release of the Software, Inprise reserves the right at any time to not release a commercial release of the Software or, if released, to alter prices, features, specifications, capabilities, functions, licensing terms, release dates, general availability or other characteristics of the commercial release.

4. Title, ownership rights, and intellectual property rights in and to the Software shall remain in Inprise and/or its suppliers. You agree to abide by the copyright law and all other applicable laws of the United States including, but not limited to,

export control laws. You acknowledge that the Software in source code form remains a confidential trade secret of Inprise and/or its suppliers and therefore you agree not to modify the Software or attempt to decipher, decompile, disassemble or reverse engineer the Software, except to the extent applicable laws specifically prohibit such restriction.

5. Upon expiration of the Evaluation Period, you agree to destroy or erase the Software, and to not re-install a new copy of the Software. This statement shall be governed by and construed in accordance with the laws of the State of California and, as to matters affecting copyrights, trademarks and patents, by U.S. federal law. This statement sets forth the entire agreement between you and Inprise.

6. Use, duplication or disclosure by the Government is subject to restrictions set forth in subparagraphs (a) through (d) of the Commercial Computer-Restricted Rights clause at FAR 52.227-19 when applicable, or in subparagraph (c) (1) (ii) of the Rights in Technical Data and Computer Software clause at DFARS 252.227-7013,and in similar clauses in the NASA AR Supplement. Contractor/manufacturer is Inprise Corporation, 100 Enterprise Way, Scotts Valley, CA 95066.

7. You may not download or otherwise export or reexport the Software or any underlying information or technology except in full compliance with all United States and other applicable laws and regulations. In particular, but without limitation, none of the Software or underlying information or technology may be downloaded or otherwise exported or reexported (i) into (or to a national or resident of) Cuba, Haiti, Iraq, Libya, Yugoslavia, North Korea, Iran, or Syria or (ii) to anyone on the US Treasury Department's list of Specially Designated Nationals or the US Commerce Department's Table of Deny Orders. By downloading the Software, you are agreeing to the foregoing and you are representing and warranting that you are not located in, under control of, or a national or resident of any such country or on any such list.

8. INPRISE OR ITS SUPPLIERS SHALL NOT BE LIABLE FOR (a) INCIDENTAL, CONSEQUENTIAL, SPECIAL OR INDIRECT DAMAGES OF ANY SORT, WHETHER ARISING IN TORT, CONTRACT OR OTHERWISE, EVEN IF INPRISE HAS BEEN INFORMED OF THE POSSIBILITY OF SUCH DAMAGES, OR (b) FOR ANY CLAIM BY ANY OTHER PARTY. THIS LIMITATION OF LIABILITY SHALL NOT APPLY TO LIABILITY FOR DEATH OR PERSONAL INJURY TO THE EXTENT APPLICABLE LAW PROHIBITS SUCH LIMITATION. FURTHERMORE, SOME STATES DO NOT ALLOW THE EXCLUSION OR LIMITATION OF INCIDENTAL OR CONSEQUENTIAL DAMAGES, SO THIS LIMITATION AND EXCLUSION MAY NOT APPLY TO YOU.

9. HIGH RISK ACTIVITIES. The Software is not fault-tolerant and is not designed, manufactured or intended for use or resale as on-line control equipment in hazardous environments requiring fail-safe performance, such as in the operation of nuclear facilities, aircraft navigation or communication systems, air traffic control, direct life support machines, or weapons systems, in which the failure of the Software could lead directly to death, personal injury, or severe physical or environmental damage ("High Risk Activities"). Inprise and its suppliers specifically disclaim any express or implied warranty of fitness for High Risk Activities.

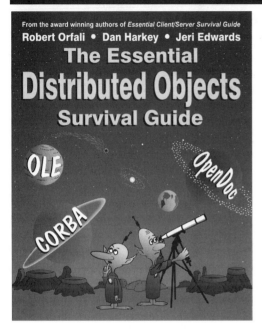

Your Instant Guide to CORBA!

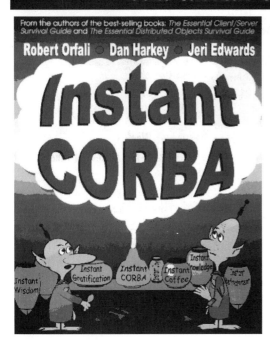

Contents at a Glance

I highly recommend it!

Distributed CORBA Objects have found their killer app. It's the Object Web—or the marriage of distributed objects and the Internet. The major computing companies—including Sun, JavaSoft, IBM, Netscape, Apple, Oracle, BEA, and HP—have chosen CORBA IIOP as the common way to connect distributed objects across the Internet and intranets. Consequently, CORBA is about to become as ubiquitous as TCP/IP. Instant CORBA is your guide to understanding this revolutionary new technology. If you're in a real hurry, the book even provides a condensed tour that will make you CORBA literate in four hours or less. Written in a gentle, witty style, this comprehensive book covers:

■ The Object Web—or how CORBA/IIOP, Java, and the Internet are coming together.
■ Everything you need to know about a CORBA 2.0 ORB.
■ The fifteen CORBA Object Services—including Transactions, Trader, Security, Naming, Events, Time, and Collections.
■ CORBA's dynamic object facilities such as callbacks, dynamic invocations, object introspection, and the interface repository.
■ Next-generation ORB technology—including CORBA 3.0's messaging, pass-by-value, and server-side frameworks.
■ The marriage of CORBA with MOM and TP Monitors.
■ Forthcoming CORBA attractions such as mobile agents, shippable places, and the business object framework.
■ Products such as Iona's OrbixWeb, Netscape/Visigenic's VisiBroker, and Sun's NEO/Joe.

WILEY

Available at Bookstores Everywhere

For more information visit **http://www.wiley.com/compbooks**
ISBN: 0471-18333-4, 314 pages, 1997, $19.99 US / $28.50 CAN

An Insider's Tour of Client/Server Applications!

3-Tier Client/Server At Work

Jeri Edwards

With Deborah DeVoe

Transactions per Second

Forward by Robert Orfali

Contents at a Glance

Part 1. 3-Tier Client/Server Fundamentals
   Why 3-Tier Client/Server is Hot
   TP Monitors: The 3-Tier Workhorse
   Tuxedo 101

Part 2. 3-Tier Client/Server at Work
   UK Employment Service Rolls Out 3-Tier in Record Time
   PeopleSoft Moves Applications to 3-Tier
   Wells Fargo Leads the Way to Internet Banking
   Apple Improves Ordering With a 3-Tier Upgrade
   MCI: A Client/Server Framework for Data Services
   3M: Data Management for Enhanced Patient Care
   3-Tier Brings Car Registration to Europe
   AT&T Takes on Order Turnaround

Part 3. The Zen of 3-Tier
   The Road to 3-Tier Nirvana

You've heard the theory behind 3-tier client/server. Now learn how to put it into practice. Jeri Edwards takes you on a rare, international tour of eight large companies' client/server applications that are at work in enterprises today.

I may not appear in this book, but I still highly recommend it!

You'll get an insider's peek at these companies' projects. Find out what went right, and what they would do differently next time. You'll learn:

✔ Why 3-tier architectures are key to successful enterprise client/server applications

✔ How to migrate from monolithic, single-tier applications to multi-tier client/server

✔ What today's middle-tier platforms are—including TP Monitors, ORBs, MOMs, and RPCs—and when to use them

✔ What the architectural trade-offs are and how to choose between them

✔ How successful projects are run and what outcomes to expect

✔ Word to the wise: tips from the architects

WILEY

Available at Bookstores Everywhere

For more information visit **http://www.wiley.com/compbooks**
ISBN: 0471-18443-8, 238 pages, 1997, $22.99 US / $32.50 CAN

Your Survival Guide to Client/Server!

Robert Orfali • Dan Harkey • Jeri Edwards

The Essential
Client/Server
Survival Guide
Second Edition

Completely Updated Award-winning Bestseller

Client/Server
Databases
Internet
TP Monitors
Objects

Contents at a Glance

I highly recommend it!

It's as savvy, informative, and entertaining as anything you are likely to read on the subject. Client/server isn't one technology but many—remote SQL, TP, message-oriented groupware, distributed objects, and so on. Like the proverbial blind men feeling the elephant, most of us have a hard time seeing the whole picture. The authors succeed brilliantly in mapping the elephant.

— *Jon Udell, BYTE Magazine*

The scope and depth of topics covered in the Guide, with its straightforward and often humorous delivery, make this book required reading for anyone who deals with computers in today's corporate environment.

— *Bob Gallagher, PC Week*

Absolutely the finest book on client/server on the market today.

— *Richard Finkelstein*
President of Performance Computing

Charmingly accessible.

— *Dr. Jim Gray*
Author of Transaction Processing

Available at Bookstores Everywhere
For more information visit **http://www.wiley.com/compbooks**
ISBN: 0471-15325-7, 676 pages, 1996, $32.95 US / $46.50 CAN

WILEY